Flint Fights Back

Urban and Industrial Environments

Series editor: Robert Gottlieb, Henry R. Luce
Professor of Urban and Environmental Policy, Occidental College

For a complete list of books published in this series, please see the back of the book.

Flint Fights Back

Environmental Justice and Democracy in the Flint Water Crisis

Benjamin J. Pauli

The MIT Press
Cambridge, Massachusetts
London, England

This book was set in Stone Serif by Westchester Publishing Services. Printed and bound in the United States of America.

Library of Congress Cataloging-in-Publication Data

Names: Pauli, Benjamin J., author.
Title: Flint fights back : environmental justice and democracy in the Flint
    water crisis / Benjamin J. Pauli.
Description: Cambridge, MA : The MIT Press, 2019. | Series: Urban and
    industrial environments | Includes bibliographical references and index.
Identifiers: LCCN 2018037773 | ISBN 9780262039857 (hardcover : alk. paper) |
    ISBN 9780262536868 (pbk. : alk. paper)
Subjects: LCSH: Environmental justice—Michigan—Flint. | Political
    participation—Michigan—Flint. | Water quality management—
    Michigan—Flint. | Water quality—Michigan—Flint River. |
    Drinking water—Lead content—Michigan—Flint. | Flint (Mich.)—
    Environmental conditions. | Flint (Mich.)—Social conditions.
Classification: LCC GE235.M53 P38 2019 | DDC 363.6/10977437—dc23
    LC record available at https://lccn.loc.gov/2018037773

10 9 8 7 6 5 4 3 2 1

"FROM
BOTTLED WATER,
TO PIPES,
TO
RECONSTRUCTION"
POISONED
DEMOCRACY
POISONED
WATER
JUSTICE4FLINT

To Julian,
Flynn,
the children of Flint,
and
everyone touched by the crisis.

Contents

Preface and Acknowledgments

We're just not the type of people that's used to being walked on.
—Claire McClinton, "A Democracy Problem"

Long before its water crisis turned it into an international symbol of environmental injustice, Flint, Michigan, was a battered and bruised city. Once a proud General Motors company town whose residents enjoyed the highest standard of living in the United States, by the turn of the twenty-first century, Flint had lost tens of thousands of jobs and half of its population to deindustrialization and white flight. Its rate of violent crime consistently placed it at or near the top of the list of the most dangerous cities in the country. A higher proportion of its houses stood vacant than in any other American city.[1] More than 40 percent of its residents lived below the poverty line. Its underperforming public schools struggled to retain students, an astonishing 68 percent of whom left the district between 2006 and 2015.[2] And with an ever-shrinking tax base, it teetered perpetually on the brink of fiscal crisis, barely able to sustain basic city services.

When I moved with my wife and three-year-old son to Flint in the summer of 2015, I was well aware of the wounds the city had suffered and the uncertainty that lay in its future. But I saw another side to Flint as well. There were the thriving cultural institutions, propped up by the philanthropy of foundations started by former GM executives—an art museum, a performing arts center, a planetarium, a symphony orchestra. There was the reviving downtown, boasting a growing array of food, music, and entertainment offerings as well as one of the best farmers' markets in the state. There were the young families moving into my neighborhood—indeed, onto my street—who lived in Flint not by necessity but by choice, and who had every reason to invest in the city's future. Although I gradually evolved a more nuanced perspective on these features of the city, coming to realize that they inspired mixed or even hostile feelings in residents who felt left out of Flint's development, they certainly helped make it possible to imagine calling Flint home.

What's more, Flint was a city with *character*. While many other Rust Belt cities have experienced similar rises and falls, Flint is not interchangeable with any of them: its place in American history is distinctive. Flint was the home of the sit-down strike of 1936 to 1937, which compelled GM to recognize the United Automobile Workers and helped to launch the organized labor movement in the United States.[3] For forty-four days and nights, thousands of auto workers holed up in three of GM's Flint factories in protest of arduous and dangerous working conditions, bringing production to a halt and forcing the company into negotiations.[4] In one famous episode, Chevrolet Avenue—the street I drive down to get to my office—became a battleground, as workers occupying the Fisher Body 2 plant hurled metal hinges and milk bottles from the rooftop at city policemen attempting to drive them from the building.

Flint was forward-looking on race and civil rights, too. It was one of the first major American cities to have a black mayor: World War II veteran and former Buick employee Floyd McCree. Elected by the City Commission in 1966, McCree temporarily resigned in protest the following year when the mostly white commissioners refused to support a proposed ordinance banning racial discrimination in housing. Other black officials also threatened to resign, and the city's black church community led a months-long mobilization in support of the law that included sleep-ins on the lawn of City Hall.[5] After the commission was pressured into passing a revised version of the bill, the John Birch Society and Ku Klux Klan led an effort to overturn it by popular referendum. The defeat of that effort by the narrow margin of thirty votes was historic: it was the first time in the country's history that an open housing ordinance was affirmed by a vote of the people.[6]

Flint was also the site of two of the more notable environmental justice struggles of the 1990s. In the first instance, a small group of residents fought the construction of an incinerator, the Genesee Power Station, that threatened to contaminate the air around a predominantly black neighborhood with lead particles generated by the burning of painted wood. Although the effort was unsuccessful—the facility was built and continues to operate to this day—it was groundbreaking in its use of federal civil rights law to argue that the siting of the station constituted an unlawful act of racial discrimination. A similar complaint filed by the same group in 1998 against a permit for a steel recycling mill on the same side of town (the so-called Select Steel plant) is widely credited with exposing the thinness of the Environmental Protection Agency's commitment to environmental justice.[7]

For all its hard knocks, then, Flint was not the kind of city where people rolled over or gave up. It was progressive, pugnacious, and—as would be remarked again and again during the water crisis—resilient. It had a fighting spirit.

When I arrived in Flint I was only dimly aware that some of its residents were in the middle of yet another fight, one that would rival anything in the city's past. I'd heard that there had been some issues with the city's drinking water and been warned to expect fluctuations in the water's taste as the utility fine-tuned its treatment methods. But I was given no reason to believe that the water was a safety hazard. Within my social circle, as an assistant professor at a private university and a resident of a predominantly white and (by relative standards) affluent neighborhood, no one seemed particularly alarmed. When I turned on the bathtub faucet one evening to fill the bath for my son and brown, grainy water gushed out, I wrote it off as an anomaly, having been told that periodic fire hydrant flushing could dislodge sediment and cause temporary discoloration. The resident voices pleading that the water was not safe were, from my perspective at the time, faint, drowned out by the reassurances of neighbors and government authorities who said the water was fine and presumably knew what they were talking about.

Over the next few months, those voices were amplified and vindicated in dramatic fashion. In July, EPA drinking water expert Miguel del Toral leaked an internal memo he had written to his superiors outlining his suspicion that Flint's water supply was experiencing system-wide lead contamination. In August and September, a collaborative water sampling effort by Flint activists and Virginia Tech engineers confirmed that there were high levels of lead at the tap in homes across the city. Toward the end of September, a team of researchers led by Dr. Mona Hanna-Attisha of Flint's Hurley Hospital showed through a statistical analysis of blood lead levels that the lead in the water was finding its way into the bodies of the city's children, putting them at risk of a host of developmental deficits. Residents rushed to get their water and their children's blood tested. Politicians declared states of emergency at the city, county, state, and federal levels. The national news media began to pay attention to what was happening in Flint. By early 2016, the "Flint water crisis" had become the subject of widespread public outrage and, in the heat of presidential primary season, a political *cause célèbre*.[8]

For Flint residents like myself, however, the water crisis was first and foremost a deeply personal affair. Our water test results came back at 6 parts per billion (ppb) lead and 70 ppb copper—both below the EPA's action levels of 15 ppb and 1,300 ppb, respectively, but hardly reassuring with a young child in the home. I found myself asking questions I had never fully confronted before: Did the fact that our levels were below federal thresholds mean our water was "safe"? Should the levels that trigger administrative action be the same ones that spur me as a parent to take steps to protect my family? Why had no one ever encouraged me to ponder that distinction or to be proactive about testing my water? It was disconcerting to think that neurotoxic heavy metals were entering my son's body in *any* quantity, and disillusioning to learn that regulatory agencies recognized and tolerated it. Furthermore, how much could one grab sample actually tell us about the quality of our water day by day?

Hoping to avoid bottled water, I purchased a lead-certified filter (in the days before they were widely available for free), only to conclude after two infuriating weeks of repeated trips to the hardware store and many torrents of profanity that it could not be made to fit my kitchen faucet. The whole faucet had to be replaced: an expenditure of time, effort, and resources that many Flint residents confronted by the same problem could ill afford. Then there was my son's blood test. Our family physician informed me that his level of blood lead was normal—"normal" defined as around two micrograms of lead per deciliter of blood (2 µg/dL). The catch was that we had delayed getting the test done until two months after switching to filtered water, a lag caused by our doctor's initial counsel that such a test was not necessary. Because lead leaves the bloodstream in roughly a month's time to roost in the bones, we will never know if, during our use of unfiltered tap water in the months prior, our son was lead poisoned. This is not just our predicament, but that of many, many other Flint parents for whom a "normal" test result did little to assuage their feelings of guilt and anxiety.

Personally, I felt guilty for another reason, too. As someone with a history of activism and an interest in political dissent and social movements, I was ashamed at having written off the voices in the wilderness that had helped to expose the water crisis for what it was. I started paying close attention to the water activists, an easier task now that their activities were getting more coverage. I began to realize that the explosion of the lead issue into a national scandal owed much more to a groundswell of popular agitation than I had previously appreciated—in fact, to something that could legitimately be termed a water *movement*. In January 2016, as Flint activists shifted their focus from convincing the world of the harm being done by the water to fighting for accountability, remediation, and reparations, I decided I could no longer watch from the sidelines. Doing my best to silence the voice in my head reminding me of my already-existing research project and my many responsibilities as a newly minted assistant professor, I threw myself into the water struggle, attending every community meeting, rally, and march I could, collaborating with the water activists on a variety of actions, events, and initiatives, mobilizing students and faculty around door-to-door water canvassing, and—knowing I would have to publish *something* on the crisis to justify the expenditure of time and effort to my institution—conducting interviews whenever possible along the way. When, in April 2016, I was invited to join a multiuniversity, interdisciplinary team conducting a major new study of Flint's water quality, I agreed, spending much of the next two years grappling with how to communicate the science of the water to the public and build bridges between residents, activists, local officials, and the scientific community.

For many reasons, I am glad I silenced that cautionary voice. By joining up with both the water activists and the scientists on the front lines in Flint, I not only had an opportunity to contribute—in admittedly modest ways—to the fight for water justice and the production of scientific knowledge about the water, I gained what I believe to be a unique vantage point on the crisis, conducive to capturing its complex and multifaceted character. I was an activist but also a researcher; a comrade in struggle but also a newcomer to the community and the movement; a resident but also a member of a privileged demographic, whose perspective did not always align—for better or worse—with that of other residents and activists. Although I did not get involved in the crisis response with the intention of writing a book, it didn't take long to realize that I would have more than enough material for one.

It goes without saying that there is no Archimedean point that would allow one to capture the essence or totality of the water crisis (or if there is, I haven't found it). There are already multiple accounts of what happened in Flint, from different perspectives, and, undoubtedly, there are more to come.[9] I can only hope to offer one particular refraction, borne of extensive participant observation, hundreds of semistructured and informal conversations with the people involved, and a scholarly effort to relate the crisis and the community's response to it to broader conversations about environmental justice and democracy. I present it here as *Flint Fights Back*.

It would be impossible to tally all the debts I incurred in the course of writing this book. Nevertheless, I had no trouble deciding where to start in expressing my thanks. To my colleague and friend Laura Sullivan, Professor of Mechanical Engineering at Kettering University and tireless water warrior, I wish to convey my deepest gratitude. I am similarly grateful for the support of another leader in the struggle for justice in Flint, Dr. Lawrence Reynolds—a true moral exemplar and a fearless fighter for the well-being of Flint residents.

I also wish to thank a number of Kettering colleagues who, directly or indirectly, contributed to the success of this project: particularly, Laura Mebert, Karen Wilkinson, Laura Miller-Purrenhage, Michael Callahan, Jim Cohen, Veronica Moorman, and Eric Bumbalough. Thanks also to Pardeep Toor, Jack Stock, Don Rockwell, and especially Robert McMahan and Laura Vosejpka. Outside my own institution, I was fortunate to have the support of other Flint-based academic friends—among them, Jason Kosnoski, Jacob Lederman, Rick Sadler, and Jan Worth-Nelson, to whom I am grateful for many neighborly kindnesses and useful introductions. I was also pleased that this project allowed me to connect with Kyle Powys White, David Pellow, Wendy Jepson, and Paul Mohai, from whom I took insights and heartening words of encouragement. From within the Rutgers family, I must give special thanks to Mark Bray and Joseph Dwyer for much-needed support as I was trying to get the project off the ground, and to Lincoln Addison, Christina Doonan, and Benjie Peters for their enduring friendship. Thank you also to Andy Murphy, Steve Bronner, and Michael Forman for helping me think through my publishing options, and to Temma Kaplan for her methodological reflections. Thanks to Kristy King, David Watkins, and the political theory workshoppers at the University of Michigan for feedback on draft chapters. Finally, thank you to David Meyer for helping to steer me toward the right publisher, and to the eight reviewers who provided valuable feedback on my book proposal.

This project brought me into conversation with a number of other academics, writers, and filmmakers doing work on Flint and water issues in southeastern Michigan. I owe a big thank you, first and foremost, to Andrew Highsmith for his generosity as a scholar and person. I am thankful as well for exchanges with Janice Beecher, Jevgeniy Bluwstein, Sherrema Bower, Jennifer Carrera, Anna Clark, Nadia Gaber, Stephen Gasteyer, Michael Mascarenhas, Mindy Myers, Ashley Nickels, Curtis Pomilia, Rebecca Rutt, Elena Sobrino, Jeanne Woods, and Cheng Zhang. Thanks also to Jason Stanley, to Liz Miller for sending me a copy of her excellent documentary *The Water Front*, and to Eve Mitchell for helping me to make connections within the Detroit activist scene.

Important parts of this book are informed by my work with the Flint Area Community Health and Environment Partnership (FACHEP). Thank you to Shawn McElmurry for bringing me onto the team and for his mostly unknown and unsung but truly inspiring efforts on behalf of Flint residents. While I cannot thank everyone on our large team here, in addition to Shawn I wish to single out Nancy Love, Susan Masten, Mark Zervos, Audrey Zarb, Jessica Robbins, and Tam Perry for their support. In a special category is Quincy Murphy: not only a FACHEP colleague but also a devoted community activist, a partner on projects in Dewey Park, and a good friend.

My involvement in water issues in Flint resulted in multiple spin-off collaborations related to environmental justice that helped, in turn, to shape my thinking about my research. For their assistance in these collaborations, I would like to thank Alan Walts, Michael Burns, and Michael Wenstrom of the EPA's College/Underserved Community Partnership Program, Vincent Slocum of Habitat for Humanity, City of Flint Chief Public Health Advisor Pamela Pugh, Sarah Wilkins of the American Geophysical Union, Maryum Rasool of the Sylvester Broome Empowerment Village, and Mona Munroe-Younis of the Environmental Transformation Movement of Flint. I also came to see another community initiative I was involved in—an effort (successful, I'm happy to say) to found a Montessori program within the Flint Community Schools—as falling within the orbit of my environmental justice work in the community. In that connection, I wish to thank Elizabeth Jordan, in particular, for her assiduous labors and Kathryn Dohrmann for her help in enumerating the advantages of Montessori education for children affected by lead poisoning.

xvi

xvi   Preface and Acknowledgments

While I was working on this book, I developed and taught a course at Kettering titled, simply, "The Flint Water Crisis." The experience was enormously helpful in forcing me to gather, organize, and communicate my thoughts about the crisis, not least because of the excellent contributions of Kettering students. I thank them for their intelligent questions, their passion for the subject matter, and their original research into various aspects of the crisis, which was often highly illuminating. I thank them also for demonstrating their concern for the residents of Flint by coming out for water canvassing and, in some cases, rallies, protests, and City Council meetings. I am also grateful to the students who invited me to speak about the water crisis to the Kettering chapter of the National Society of Black Engineers, the Green Engineering Organization and on WKUF-LP 94.3 FM.

My thinking on the theme of research justice was honed through valuable exchanges with Max Liboiron, Randy Stoecker, and especially Yanna Lambrinidou, who I cannot thank enough for her moral support, keen insights, and passionate commitment to justice in Flint and beyond. In talking with Yanna and with Paul Schwartz of the Campaign for Lead Free Water, I came to appreciate just how critical an understanding of the 2001 to 2004 Washington, D.C., water crisis is to an understanding of Flint. While D.C. does appear in what follows, I was not able to do anything like full justice to the struggle there. Suffice to say (though it does *not* suffice, and I hope more will be written on the subject), Flint was not the first example of residents and activists leading the fight against lead-in-water contamination.

I conducted around seventy semistructured interviews for the sake of this book, but had there been more hours in the day, I would gladly have conducted many more. Given my own limitations as a single interviewer, I benefited greatly from interviews conducted by others—including those featured on GMO-Free News, the Tom Sumner Program, Hashtag Flint, 1470 WFNT, the Morning Gazette Radio Show, and a variety of other local radio programs. I also referred regularly to coverage of the crisis by *The Flint Journal* and *MLive*, Michigan Radio, the *Detroit Free Press*, *The Detroit News*, *Bridge Magazine*, *East Village Magazine*, The Young Turks, and Truth Against the Machine. There were many times I would have been lost without the videos made available by Paul Herring through Spectacle TV. Also, the Virginia Tech team's Flintwaterstudy.org was at times a useful source of information.

In reflecting on my debts to members of the activist community, I wondered whether I should try to name everyone I interviewed, worked with, or received assistance from during the two-and-a-half years it took me to research and write this book. I eventually concluded that any attempt to provide a comprehensive list would be doomed to failure, and I worried that the people I inevitably forgot to mention would feel slighted. I was also concerned to respect the privacy of people who did not sit down for an official interview and might not have wanted to be named. Rather than striving for completeness, then, I will limit my "thank yous" to a few people who went out of their way to offer me material they thought would be useful to my work: Paul Jordan, Florlisa Fowler, Nayyirah Shariff, Sue Whalen, and Bob and Melodee Mabbit (for their wonderful present of a neatly bound stack of back issues of *Broadside*). I also can't resist offering a special thank you to Claire McClinton for her support during some of the rockiest patches on this journey.

This is, perhaps, as good a place as any to offer an apology I feel compelled to make. Not nearly all of the "water warriors" who left their individual marks on the water crisis get named or (directly) credited in this book. No doubt, some of them will feel they should have been characters in the story. I can only plead that *everyone* is, in some sense, a part of this story, even when not mentioned by name. I have put a great deal of effort into carefully considering the variety of perspectives on the crisis within the community and, to the best of my ability, all of the diverse contributions residents and activists made to the crisis response. Unfortunately, I have had to leave out many worthy people and noble acts, for simple reasons of space and composition. I can only hope that those not named explicitly see something of themselves in the book.

This book would not have been possible without a publisher taking a chance on it, and for that (and for their guidance throughout the writing and revision process), I am grateful to Beth Clevenger of the MIT Press, and Bob Gottlieb, editor of the Urban and Industrial Environments series and an inspiration for his scholarship on water and environmentalism. I also received critical assistance from Max Smith, who helped me compile the references for the book, and Jake May, who helped with image permissions.

I am more indebted to my family than I can adequately express. Thank you to my parents (both sets) for their support, and particularly to my mom Elizabeth for help sorting through the lawsuits spawned by the crisis, for introducing me to the operation of local government, and for her careful reading of the manuscript. Thank you to the practitioners at the Dong Shan Institute of Buddhism and the Society of Ksitigarbha Studies—some of the best listeners and most thoughtful people I have ever met, who have never failed to provide valuable guidance when I explain my work to them. Thank you to Mike Galligan for reading parts of the book and offering feedback. Thank you to Pat and Bill Jones for making us feel so welcome in Michigan (and rest in peace, Grandpa Bill). Thank you to my father-in-law, Michael Kao, for all his help with childcare and housework while this book was being written, in what, sadly, turned out to be the last years of his life. Thank you to my older son, Julian, for all the times he shot hoops by himself while he waited for Dad to get to a "stopping point." Thank you to my younger son, Flynn, for his reminder that life goes on, and is renewed, even in the wake of tragedy. Thank you, finally, to my wife Vivian Kao—for her saintly patience with me as I got sucked further and further into this project, for her invaluable help as an editor and interlocutor, for her commitment to Flint, and for her love and support in everything I do.

List of Figures and Tables

Timeline

Water	Democracy
1893: First Flint Water Works opens, drawing water from Flint River.	
1965: Flint commits to a thirty-five-year contract with the Detroit Department of Water Supply, later renamed the Detroit Water and Sewerage Department (DWSD).	
1967: Flint begins receiving water from DWSD, drawn first from the Detroit River and then, after 1974, from Lake Huron. Flint sells water wholesale to the rest of Genesee County—first directly to surrounding townships, then from 1973 onward through the Genesee County Drain Commission.	
	1988: Public Act (PA) 101 takes effect, allowing the State of Michigan to declare financial emergencies in municipalities and assign control of local finances to emergency financial managers (EFMs). The City of Hamtramck is the first to be assigned an EFM under the new law.
	1990: PA 72 takes effect, expanding PA 101's stipulations to school districts.
2000: Flint's contract with DWSD expires, first of a series of one-year extensions signed.	
	2002–2004: Flint under state-appointed EFM Edward Kurtz.

(continued)

(*continued*)

Water	Democracy
Aug. 2003: Four waterless days during a massive power outage raise questions about the reliability of the Detroit water system.	
	2009: Detroit Public Schools placed under emergency financial management.
2010: City of Flint, City of Lapeer, and Genesee, Sanilac, and Lapeer Counties form the Karegnondi Water Authority (KWA) to explore the possibility of constructing a new Lake Huron pipeline.	2010: Cities of Benton Harbor and Pontiac placed under emergency financial management.
	Mar. 16, 2011: PA 4 takes effect, expanding the powers of EFMs (now referred to as "emergency managers," or EMs).
	Sep. 30, 2011: Governor Rick Snyder appoints an eight-member Financial Review Team to evaluate whether a financial emergency exists in Flint.
	Oct. 2011: Occupy Flint sets up encampment at King Street and 2nd Avenue.
	Nov. 7, 2011: Flint Financial Review Team concludes that a financial emergency exists and recommends the appointment of an EM.
	Nov. 10, 2011: Mayor Dayne Walling reelected. State of Michigan announces that Flint will be appointed an EM.
	Dec. 1, 2011: EM Michael Brown takes office.
	Feb. 29, 2012: Stand Up For Democracy coalition turns in 226,637 signatures to put PA 4 referendum on November ballot.
	Jun. 2012: Last remnants of Occupy Flint encampment dismantled.
	Aug. 8, 2012: PA 4 suspended after certification of referendum. State enforces PA 72 in the meantime. Ed Kurtz appointed EFM in Flint under PA 72.
	Nov. 6, 2012: Michigan voters repeal PA 4.
	Dec. 26, 2012: PA 436 signed into law, restoring most of the powers granted by PA 4.

Water	Democracy
	Mar. 14, 2013: Detroit placed under emergency management.
Mar. 25, 2013: Flint City Council votes to support city joining KWA pipeline, under assumption that Flint will remain a customer of DWSD until pipeline is completed.	
	Mar. 28, 2013: PA 436 takes effect.
Apr. 16, 2013: Flint EM Ed Kurtz signs agreement with KWA and informs state treasurer of city's intent to join pipeline.	
Apr. 17, 2013: DWSD sends letter to EM Kurtz announcing termination of water contract in one year's time.	
Jun. 26, 2013: EM Kurtz adopts resolution to prepare Flint Water Treatment Plant to treat Flint River water.	
	Jul. 8, 2013: Michael Brown begins second term as EM.
	Jul. 18, 2013: Led by EM Kevyn Orr, Detroit files for bankruptcy—the largest municipal bankruptcy in US history.
	Sep. 11, 2013: EM Michael Brown resigns and is replaced by Darnell Earley.
Apr. 25, 2014: City of Flint switches water supply to Flint River.	
Spring–Fall 2014: Massive wave of water shutoffs in Detroit attracts international attention.	
	Jul. 1, 2014: EM Earley gives Mayor Dayne Walling control of Departments of Planning and Development, Public Works.
Aug.–Sep. 2014: Three separate boil advisories issued after coliform bacteria detected in water on Flint's west side.	
Aug. 21, 2014: Flint Democracy Defense League opens emergency water relief site at Mission of Hope.	

(continued)

(*continued*)

Water	Democracy
Oct. 10, 2014: Great Lakes Water Authority (GLWA) forms, establishing a regional water partnership to manage Detroit-owned water infrastructure outside the city of Detroit.	
Oct. 13, 2014: General Motors announces it will no longer use Flint River water at its engine plant, citing corrosion of engine parts.	
	Nov. 4, 2014: Flint voters approve proposal to begin a city charter review process.
	Dec. 10, 2014: Detroit emerges from bankruptcy; EM Kevyn Orr resigns.
Jan. 2, 2015: Notice sent to residents informing them that Flint is in violation of the Safe Drinking Water Act due to high levels of total trihalomethanes.	
Jan. 12, 2015: DWSD Director Sue McCormick offers to resume selling water to Flint on an emergency basis.	Jan. 13, 2015: Jerry Ambrose appointed EM in Flint.
Jan. 2015: First community meetings on water quality sponsored by city officials.	
Feb. 14, 2015: Flint water activist groups unite for Valentine's Day march.	
	Feb. 23, 2015: Natasha Henderson begins position as Flint city administrator on a five-year contract.
Feb. 17, 2015: City of Flint announces formation of technical advisory committee and citizens' advisory committee on water issues.	
Mar. 23, 2015: Flint City Council votes 7 to 1 to "do all things necessary"[1] to reconnect to Detroit water.	
	Apr. 2015: EM Jerry Ambrose declares Flint's financial emergency over and steps down. State of Michigan appoints Receivership Transition Advisory Board to review decisions by local officials.
	May 19, 2015: First meeting of Flint Charter Review Commission.

Water	Democracy
Jun. 5, 2015: Coalition for Clean Water files lawsuit alleging that the city "recklessly endangered"[2] the health and safety of residents by switching to the Flint River and demanding a return to Detroit water.	
Jul. 3–10, 2015: Detroit-to-Flint Water Justice Journey.	
Jul. 9, 2015: ACLU reporter Curt Guyette reports on leaked memo by EPA employee Miguel del Toral about lead contamination at the home of LeeAnne Walters and other Flint residents and the city's lack of corrosion control.	
Jul. 9, 2015: Mayor Dayne Walling drinks tap water on the local news to reassure residents of its safety.	
Aug. 2015: Activists begin water sampling effort in collaboration with Virginia Tech engineers.	Aug. 4, 2015: Incumbent Dayne Walling and challenger Karen Weaver place first and second, respectively, in mayoral primaries.
Aug. 17, 2015: Circuit Court judge issues injunction halting water shutoffs and ordering the City of Flint to lower water and sewer rates by 35 percent.	
Sep. 2015: Virginia Tech team announces findings from activist-led sampling effort, warns residents that Flint has a serious lead-in-water problem.	
Sep. 24, 2015: In a press conference at Hurley hospital, Dr. Mona Hanna-Attisha announces findings of study showing doubling of blood lead levels in young children since switch to Flint River.	
Oct. 1, 2015: Genesee County Health Department declares public health emergency in Flint.	
Oct. 2, 2015: State announces Flint water action plan, including money for filters, water testing, and better corrosion control.	
Oct. 8, 2015: Governor Snyder announces $12 million plan to switch Flint's water supply back to Detroit water system.	

(continued)

(continued)

Water	Democracy
	Nov. 3, 2015: Karen Weaver elected mayor of Flint.

Nov. 2015: City of Flint begins mailing water shutoff notices to 1,800 delinquent households.

Dec. 14, 2015: Mayor Karen Weaver declares state of emergency and calls for Genesee Board of Commissioners to approve declaration.

Jan. 1, 2016: GLWA begins operations under CEO Sue McCormick.

Jan. 4, 2016: Genesee County Board of Commissioners approves Mayor Weaver's emergency declaration, opening up possibility of more state and federal assistance.

Jan. 5, 2016: Governor Snyder declares a state emergency, requests federal assistance.

Jan. 12, 2016: Governor Snyder activates National Guard to assist with water and filter distribution in Flint.

Jan. 15, 2016: Michigan Attorney General Bill Schuette launches criminal investigation into the Flint water crisis.

Jan. 16, 2016: Governor Snyder and officials from the Michigan Department of Health and Human Services (MDHHS) announce that a major outbreak of Legionnaires' disease has been ongoing since June 2014, with eighty-seven cases reported and ten (later increased to twelve) deaths, possibly linked to the switch to the Flint River.

Jan. 16, 2016: President Obama declares a federal state of emergency authorizing the Federal Emergency Management Agency (FEMA) to coordinate relief efforts in Flint and making $5 million in federal aid available for ninety days. Obama rejects Governor Snyder's request for a major disaster declaration and $96 million in aid because the water crisis is a manmade disaster.

Water	Democracy
	Jan. 22, 2016: Power to hire and fire city department directors restored to Mayor Weaver.
Jan. 29, 2016: Scott Smith of Water Defense begins sampling in city and sounds alarm about contaminants other than lead that may make bathing and showering unsafe.	
Feb. 3, 2016: House Oversight and Government Reform Committee holds first hearing on Flint water crisis.	
	Feb. 12, 2016: City Administrator Natasha Henderson relieved of her responsibilities by Mayor Weaver.
Feb. 26, 2016: Michigan Legislature passes bill allocating $30 million to cover 65 percent of Flint residents' water bills going back to Apr. 30, 2014.	
Mar. 4, 2016: Fast Start program begins replacement of lead service lines.	
	Mar. 6, 2016: Democratic presidential debate held in Flint.
Mar. 15 and 17, 2016: House Oversight and Government Reform Committee holds second and third hearings on Flint water crisis.	
Mar. 21, 2016: Governor-appointed Flint Water Task Force issues its final report, concluding that the crisis is a case of environmental injustice and that primary responsibility rests with the state.	
Apr. 20, 2016: First criminal charges brought by AG Schuette, against Michael Prysby and Stephen Busch of the Michigan Department of Environmental Quality (MDEQ) and Michael Glasgow of the Flint Water Treatment Plant.	
May 4, 2016: President Obama visits Flint, reassures residents that filtered water is safe to drink.	
	May 26, 2016: Flint City Council's powers restored on a provisional basis.

(continued)

(continued)

Water	Democracy

Jun. 8, 2016: Michigan Legislature passes supplemental spending bill with $114.3 million in immediate aid for Flint, including $25 million for replacement of lead service lines and another $12.8 million for water bill credits.

Jun. 22, 2016: Civil charges announced against private contractors Veolia and Lockwood, Andrews, and Newnam, Inc.

Jul. 19, 2016: Donald Trump wins Republican nomination.

Jul. 26, 2016: Hillary Clinton wins Democratic nomination, Mayor Weaver delivers pro-Clinton speech at Democratic National Convention.

Jul. 29, 2016: Criminal charges announced against six employees of MDEQ and MDHHS.

Aug. 14, 2016: Federal declaration of emergency ends.

Sep. 2016: Flint Area Community Health and Environment Partnership launches new study of *Legionella* contamination in water system.

Oct. 19, 2016: Joint Committee on the Flint Water Public Health Emergency releases final report.

Nov. 8, 2016: Donald Trump elected President of the United States, promises renewed federal emphasis on infrastructure.

Nov. 10, 2016: Federal judge issues preliminary injunction sought by the Concerned Pastors for Social Action, the Natural Resources Defense Council, the Michigan ACLU, and Flint resident Melissa Mays, ordering State of Michigan to deliver bottled water door to door.

Dec. 20, 2016: Criminal charges announced against EMs Darnell Earley and Jerry Ambrose and two city employees.

Feb. 2017: City of Flint officials threaten new round of water shutoffs.

Water	Democracy

Feb. 17, 2017: Michigan Civil Rights Commission releases final report on Flint water crisis, finding that structural racism played a role in causing the crisis.

Feb. 24, 2017: Petition language filed for recall of Mayor Weaver.

Mar. 1, 2017: State of Michigan ends 65 percent reimbursement of Flint water bills.

Mar. 28, 2017: State of Michigan settles civil lawsuit brought by Concerned Pastors, et al. Settlement requires state to pay the City of Flint $87 million to identify and replace at least eighteen thousand unsafe service lines by 2020 and places conditions on the closing of state-funded water resource sites, but excuses state from door-to-door water delivery.

Apr. 2017: City of Flint sends warning letters threatening to place liens on over eight thousand homes with delin-quent water accounts.

Apr. 18, 2017: Mayor Weaver announces recommendation that Flint remain with GLWA as its long-term water supplier, rather than switching as planned to the KWA pipeline.

Apr. 20, 2017: Six activists arrested at town hall on water source decision.

May 17, 2017: Flint City Council passes resolution calling for one-year morato-rium on water liens. A month later, reso-lution is overturned by the Receivership Transition Advisory Board (RTAB).

Jun. 14, 2017: Five officials including MDHHS Director Nick Lyon and EM Darnell Earley charged with involun-tary manslaughter for failure to address threat of Legionnaires' Disease. Crimi-nal charges also announced against Chief Medical Executive Eden Wells.

Jun. 26, 2017: Flint City Council votes to support short-term extension of contract with GLWA but postpones decision on long-term contract.

(continued)

(*continued*)

Water	Democracy
Jun. 28, 2017: MDEQ files complaint in US District Court alleging that council's refusal to back long-term GLWA contract violates March settlement agreement, EPA emergency order, and the Safe Drinking Water Act. In August, federal judge orders state and city into mediation.	
	Aug. 8, 2017: Flint voters decisively approve revised city charter, including changes meant to stop misuse of water and sewer funds.
Aug. 11, 2017: State begins to close water resource sites, citing improved lead levels. Four sites remain open indefinitely.	
	Oct. 2, 2017: US Supreme Court declines to rule on EM law's constitutionality.
	Nov. 7, 2017: Mayor Weaver survives recall election; new pro-Weaver city council elected.
Nov. 21, 2017: City Council votes to approve thirty-year contract with GLWA, with amendments.	
	Nov. 29, 2017: Petition filed with Inter-American Commission on Human Rights requesting investigation into violation of the right to democracy in Flint.
	Dec. 1, 2017: Lawsuit filed alleging PA 436 is racially discriminatory, violates Equal Protection Clause.
	Jan. 10, 2018: RTAB votes to return day-to-day financial decision making to City of Flint.
Jan. 12, 2018: MDEQ announces that last eighteen months of sampling data show Flint's water quality is restored.	
	Apr. 4, 2018: Governor Snyder officially ends state receivership in Flint.
Apr. 6, 2018: State of Michigan announces end of free bottled water.	

Water	Democracy
Apr. 12, 2018: Judge approves $4.1 million settlement in suit brought by ACLU and Education Law Center, committing State of Michigan to screening of Flint children for lead-related health deficits.	
Apr. 23, 2018: Flint resident LeeAnne Walters wins Goldman Environmental Prize.	
Apr. 26, 2018: Virginia Tech team receives $1.9 million EPA grant to conduct nationwide study of lead in drinking water.	
May 10, 2018: Nestlé agrees to donate 1.6 million bottles of water to Flint residents through Labor Day. The company later extends donations through the rest of the year.	
May 10, 2018: FlintComplaints letter sent to variety of scientific and engineering organizations asking for investigation into behavior of Dr. Marc Edwards of Virginia Tech.	
May 17, 2018: Doctors at Hurley hospital argue that Flint children were "lead-exposed" rather than "lead-poisoned," touching off debate over terminology and severity of the water crisis.	
	Jun. 23, 2018: Highland Park school district released from state receivership, marking the first time since the year 2000 that no local government in Michigan is under state control.
Jul. 9, 2018: Marc Edwards files $3 million defamation suit against three water activists from Flint and Washington, D.C.	
Jul. 19, 2018: Academics from universities in the United States and abroad sign letter in support of signatories to FlintComplaints letter.	
Aug. 20, 2018: MDHHS Director Nick Lyon bound over to trial on four counts, including involuntary manslaughter and misconduct in office.	

Introduction

On April 25, 2014, a group of prominent Flint politicians and administrators, along with representatives of state government and local media, gathered at the city's water treatment plant on the northeast side of town to commemorate the switch of Flint's municipal water source. For over forty years, residents of Flint had been drinking Lake Huron water treated by the Detroit Water and Sewerage Department (DWSD) and distributed through a Detroit-owned network of pipes servicing much of southeast Michigan. While "Detroit" water (to use local shorthand) was by all accounts a stable, high-quality supply, Flint was purchasing it at a premium. Over the previous five years, DWSD had raised wholesale water rates over 200 percent, and with the City of Flint's retail markup factored in residents were paying water bills more than two-and-a-half times the national average.[1] To stabilize runaway rates and give the city at least partial ownership of the system that delivered its water, in March 2013 Flint's elected officials declared their support for a plan to construct a new, regionally controlled Lake Huron pipeline under the aegis of the Karegnondi Water Authority (KWA).[2] The next month, DWSD expressed its displeasure with the decision by issuing a termination-of-service notice, effective in a year's time. With the completion of the new pipeline slated for 2016, Flint was faced with the need to secure an interim water supply.

When it was announced that water diverted from the Flint River and treated at the city's own treatment plant would provide the necessary stopgap, many residents were incredulous, sure that it must be a "joke."[3] Not only had the river served as a dumping ground for decades' worth of industrial pollutants, it was popularly known as a repository for shopping carts, old cars, and the occasional corpse. Despite the instinctive aversion that the river elicited in many residents, however, by the summer of 2013 plans

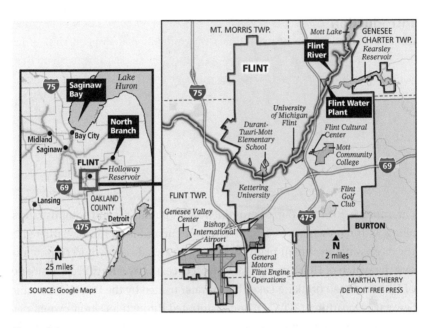

Figure 0.1
The Flint River. Drawing its headwaters from tributaries in the center of Michigan's "thumb," the Flint River travels in an elongated "U" shape, curving southward and bisecting the city of Flint through the heart of downtown before bending north toward its terminus in the Saginaw River and, ultimately, Saginaw Bay. It is no exaggeration to say that without the Flint River there would be no Flint. Early fur trappers and other settlers were drawn to the area because of its convenient concentration of fords (the "Grand Traverse") that allowed for easy crossing, and they named the fledgling city after the flinty rocks borne by the river. Over the years, the banks of the river proved an attractive locale for sawmills, carriage factories, and the automobile plants that would make Flint famous. © Detroit Free Press /ZUMA Press.

were underway to get the Flint Water Treatment Plant into full working order in anticipation of the switch.[4]

Proponents of the switch argued that using the river was not as counterintuitive as it seemed. From 1917 to 1967, after all, the river had served as the primary source of Flint's drinking water, and even after the city entered into its long-term relationship with Detroit it served as Flint's state-mandated backup source. Furthermore, the main considerations that led Flint to opt for Detroit water in the first place had more to do with capacity than quality. Although the river had easily accommodated the city's needs through the first half of the twentieth century, by the end of the 1950s industrial expansion and residential growth had increased demand beyond what the river could comfortably sustain. Now, after decades of economic disinvestment had stripped Flint of its thirsty factories and half of its population, it was more plausible to argue that its water requirements could be met by the river.

Turning to the river during Flint's time of need, then, could be billed by advocates as a reinstatement of past practice rather than a radical innovation. This was not lost on those present at the switchover ceremony. From a podium in the foyer of the water treatment plant, flanked by basins of treated river water making its last stop before flowing out to residents, Flint Mayor Dayne Walling called the switch "a historic moment for the city of Flint to return to its roots and use our own river as our drinking water supply."[5] Although the use of the river would be temporary, it would have the effect—or so Walling and others claimed—of empowering Flint to take long-term charge of its water. Under the pending arrangement with the KWA, Flint would receive raw lake water rather than the pre-treated water it was used to, and would be solely responsible for treatment. Practicing on Flint River water would give the city an opportunity to bring its water treatment plant up to speed and fine-tune its treatment methods before assuming this responsibility. The cost savings Flint would realize by keeping its water source close to home and avoiding Detroit's increasing rates would help finance the necessary capital improvements at the plant.

Of course, these rationales counted for little if the people of Flint could not be convinced to drink the water. In the lead-up to the switch, authorities at the state and local levels sought to assuage popular fears by repeatedly reassuring residents that the treated river water met all federal guidelines and was comparable to Detroit water in quality. Representatives of the Michigan Department of Environmental Quality (MDEQ) told residents that they "shouldn't notice any difference"[6] beyond an increase in the "hardness"[7] of the water that might make it more difficult to produce a lather while showering and bathing. City officials painted a similarly heartening picture. During the inauguration of the new water supply, Mayor Walling acknowledged that there had been "a lot of questions from our customers," but insisted that "the water quality speaks for itself."[8] Addressing the public in the days after the switch, City Spokesperson Jason Lorenz reinforced the message that the water was "of great quality."[9] These were the first in what would become a long line of assurances over the next year and a half that the water was not only safe but eminently drinkable.

On several key occasions, such claims would be driven home by high-profile authorities performatively consuming the water on camera. The first such instance formed the climactic moment of the switchover ceremony. After being accorded the honor of pressing the button that shut off the feed from Detroit—prompting cheers and applause from those assembled—Mayor Walling proposed a celebratory toast. With the exclamation "Here's to Flint!," he and the other participants raised glasses full of freshly treated river water and, with no apparent hesitation, drank them down. Viewers watching the evening news that day witnessed an event designed to suggest confidence and consensus, pitched as a triumphant moment in the city's history.

What would not become clear until much later was that even some of those who took part in the photo-op harbored gnawing doubts about the city's readiness to assume the role of treating river water. One was Mike Glasgow, the treatment plant's laboratory and water quality supervisor, who a mere eight days before had protested in an email to the MDEQ that "if water is distributed from this plant in the next couple weeks, it will be against my direction,"[10] cautioning that more training and staff would be necessary before the city was properly equipped for the task. Glasgow's warning was even more prescient than he could have known at the time. Over the next year and a half, he and his colleagues would find themselves on the front lines of a struggle against a variety of contaminants in Flint's water supply. In August and September 2014, they discovered total coliform bacteria in water on the city's west side, indicating a risk of *E. coli* contamination and hinting at dangerous weak spots in the city's water infrastructure. Attempts to eliminate pathogens in the water system with extra chlorine generated hazardous levels of trihalomethanes—carcinogenic byproducts of interactions between chlorine and organic matter referred to popularly as TTHMs—and brought the city into violation of the Safe Drinking Water Act. The worst was yet to come, however. In summer 2015, activists revealed that the city had a serious problem with lead in its water, a consequence of the MDEQ's failure to mandate the corrosion control needed to prevent the river water from damaging lead-bearing plumbing. Some deemed the population-wide exposure that resulted the worst environmental disaster in the United States since Hurricane Katrina.[11]

As the media began placing the people and events surrounding the water crisis under the microscope in the fall of 2015, it became clear that there was plenty of blame to go around. MDEQ employees not only misadvised local utility workers about water treatment but conspired with them to obscure the city's lead problem. Employees at the Michigan Department of Health and Human Services made misleading claims about blood lead levels in an effort to dampen growing alarm. US Environmental Protection Agency (EPA) officials failed to act with urgency when indications of lead contamination began to appear. Local politicians treated residents' concerns about the water dismissively and reiterated that the water was safe when there was reason to believe otherwise. Private contractors hired to assess the viability of the river water as a municipal supply, upgrade the water treatment plant, and recommend solutions to water quality problems failed to prevent the crisis and did little to end it.[12] All of these individuals and entities own some of the responsibility for what happened.

But it is equally true that they all acted within a context shaped by other, arguably more important, actors. Many of the key decisions made about Flint's water during the period in question were made not by utility workers or regulators, not by local politicians or contractors, but by Flint's state-appointed emergency managers (EMs). In fact, since December 2011, when the State of Michigan took over the city's government in order to rescue it (said state officials) from financial collapse, unelected EMs had been making unilateral decisions about virtually the full spectrum of city affairs. In total, four EMs with mandates to cut costs and increase the efficiency of public services governed Flint between 2011 and 2015. All four added their fingerprints to the string of decisions that led up to and exacerbated the water crisis. It was EM Michael Brown who set Flint on a path to join the KWA pipeline project a year before the City Council's vote on the matter. It was EM Ed Kurtz who made the *de facto* decision to use the Flint River as a temporary water supply while the pipeline was completed. It was EM Darnell Earley, the first to shout "Hear, hear!" in response to the mayor's toast at the water treatment plant, who called the river "the best choice for the city of Flint going forward" and oversaw the implementation of the switch.[13] It was EM Jerry Ambrose who ignored the City Council's symbolic vote to return to Detroit water in March 2015, calling it "incomprehensible."[14] Residents would continue to drink Flint River water for another seven months.

Except for those who didn't: those who shunned it from the beginning, or were repulsed by changes in its color, taste, or smell, or suspected it of making them sick, or who were warned off it by friends and neighbors or by early reports of bacterial contamination and TTHMs. Not all of these residents joined what I will refer to in this book as the water "movement" in Flint—the loose collection of people and groups that vocally protested the condition of the water, demanded that the city cease using the river, helped reveal the existence of systemic contamination, and fought to ensure that residents got what they were owed after the crisis was officially recognized.[15] But those who did join the movement came to realize that fixing their city's water crisis—and preventing similar crises in the future—would require more than just better treatment methods and new pipes. It would require confronting a deeper crisis of democracy.

At first glance, the Flint water crisis has all the hallmarks of a classic environmental justice scenario: A population vulnerable for reasons of race and class. Contamination through human activity of a natural resource essential to life. Residents with little or no background in activism catalyzed into action by their personal experiences with the contamination. Mendacity and feet dragging by "experts" and officials in response to demands for remediation. A popular effort to uncover threats obscured or overlooked by these same experts and officials. All of these aspects of the crisis will receive attention in what follows.

What first stood out to me about the struggle for environmental justice in Flint, however, was what made it distinctive: everyone, it seemed, was talking not just about water, but about democracy. Students of the environmental justice tradition may protest that democracy has long been a central concern of environmental justice activists. I concede the point, and will return to it in chapter 1. But still, there was something unique about the salience of the theme in Flint. Democracy was constantly on the lips of even those who were new to activism, who felt compelled to join the water movement not for ideological reasons but out of burning concern for their own well-being and that of their families. Activists saw the denial of democracy—as personified in Flint's EMs—as the most fundamental cause of the crisis and a major reason for its extent and severity. Likewise, they saw the restoration of democracy as an objective that was complementary to, or even a precondition of, a full recovery from the crisis. At times I caught glimpses, also, of a more radical democratic vision, one that sought to deepen democracy by building off the popular energies liberated by the crisis, the grassroots associations formed in response to it, and the new political consciousness sparked by it. Given my academic background in the study of political thought and social movements, what I encountered in Flint was an unusually intriguing confluence of ideas and action.

In the remainder of this introduction, I will explain the methodological reasons for positioning this book at the intersection of environmental justice and democracy. As will become clear, my emphasis on these concepts is part of my attempt to capture empirically the activists' distinctive perspective on the water crisis in language that was meaningful and evocative to the people on the ground in Flint. I hope to demonstrate that this perspective—aside from being inherently worthy of documentation as part of our collective memory of the crisis—offers a valuable analytical asset to scholars who wish to understand the crisis better. I also use the central concepts of the book as portals into the scholarly literature, through which I pull in other useful concepts further afield from the everyday language of activism, and offer up lessons from Flint I believe to be of more general significance.

Methodology

The core elements of this book are derived from ethnographic immersion in the response to the water crisis in Flint, particularly the activities of water activists and of scientists studying the city's water quality and embroiled in controversies involving activists. I personally became a resident of Flint in June 2015, when the city was still drawing its water from the Flint River, and I am one of many residents whose young child was exposed to the water, but my lived experience of the crisis is not what I am calling the "ethnography" at the heart of this book. My main objective is to understand the crisis from the perspective of the water activists who were especially involved in the response to it. My own residence in Flint of course enriched my understanding of what life was like on the ground in the city from mid-2015 on, and it factored into my positionality as an activist-scholar in important ways. Simply living in Flint was not, however, nearly enough to provide my ethnographic material: I had to make a special effort to enter into the activist community, gradually building relationships and trust and evolving from a fly on the wall into a full-fledged participant observer.[16]

I am not, I must admit, an experienced ethnographer, but I knew enough about ethnography—and, by the time of my initial foray into water activism in January 2016, enough about Flint—to know that this process would be gradual and delicate. For one thing, I was a latecomer, getting involved at a time when the crisis was attracting significant national attention, thereby opening myself up to suspicions of opportunism or at least the "Johnny-come-lately" epithet sometimes applied to people and groups who weren't in the fight from the "beginning" (however defined). Furthermore, I appeared on the activist scene as a white middle-class man at a time when activists were taking advantage of the national spotlight to elevate the stories of poor people of color—especially women, who they argued had suffered special harms from the water and whose agency as leaders of the water movement they made a point of celebrating. While I thought of myself (somewhat arrogantly, I suppose) as someone with special skills and resources to contribute to the movement, the activists were far more interested in the symbolic capital offered by residents with the right kind of look, background, and story. It was all I could do early on to demonstrate that I, too, could be useful, and it was frustrating (though illuminating) when some of my early offers of assistance were met with indifference.

Another complication was that my institutional position at Kettering University was at least as much a liability as an asset. The activists' feelings about Kettering ranged from mixed to openly hostile. Some accused the school (the largest private landowner in the city) of perpetrating an ongoing "land grab" around the fringes of campus, gulping up dilapidated properties for its own purposes, including the formerly public Atwood Stadium (given to Kettering in exchange for repair work by EM Mike Brown in 2013). More generally, I found that activists saw Kettering as being mostly unconcerned with residents beyond its immediate neighbors and complicit in plans by local elites to turn the city into a "college town." Many believed that the school had downplayed the severity of the water crisis for fear of losing enrollment.[17] Thus, even as I worked in a variety of ways to build bridges between the university, activists, and Flint residents, my credibility hinged on showing that I was not "controlled" (an accusation leveled at me by an activist convinced at one point that I was part of a "CYA" effort) and that I had some critical distance from my own institution.[18]

To overcome suspicions about my character and intentions, I very consciously avoided giving any impression that I had a personal or official agenda or was more entitled to speak authoritatively about the crisis on account of my credentials, training, or position. I drew inspiration from what the sociologist Alice Goffman calls "social shrinkage"—a technique aimed at minimizing the impact of one's difference within an unfamiliar social setting.[19] One can justify such minimization methodologically as being conducive to purer observations, but in my case it grew out of the realization that it was the necessary starting point on what would be a longer journey toward acceptance and participation. In truth, I didn't have to be very proactive about "shrinking" myself. I sat through numerous conversations about politics at activist meetings where no one thought to ask the PhD political scientist for his opinion. One activist described the activist culture in Flint to me as "anti-intellectual."[20] At the very least, what I encountered repeatedly was an indifference to credentials that reflected the deeply egalitarian sensibility typical of Flint activism. It was a sensibility I found inspiring on a moral level, but sometimes problematic on an organizing level for its tendency to undervalue academic knowledge and the strategic advantages of status, access, and power. Whereas water activists in Detroit have forged productive relationships with local academics, leading to impressive collaborative work on water shutoffs, foreclosures, and emergency management,[21] nothing comparable exists in Flint, and Flint activists gave no indication that they felt this to be a limitation.

Perhaps it was a twinge of vanity that made me expect a slightly more enthusiastic welcome into the activist ranks, but the reality was that I was already starting to doubt the value of my own supposed expertise in the face of the water crisis's confounding complexity. In some ways, this doubt was a continuation of an earlier humbling experience. In the fall of 2015, a few months after moving to Flint, I joined the Flint Charter Review Advisory Committee, a body of residents that met regularly with elected charter commissioners to contribute to the first review and revision of the city's governing document since the 1970s. At first, I was encouraged by my ability to draw upon my political theory background for guidance. Following the second meeting of the group, I helped rewrite the charter preamble to incorporate more explicit rights language—including, for the first time in the city's history, a declaration of Flint residents' right to water. As the meetings progressed, however, and as the conversations began to delve into the minutiae of city government and the history of Flint politics, I felt awash in local knowledge and, very often, like the dumbest person in the room. When the time came to take a position on such key questions as what form of government the city ought to have, I found myself grasping at straws. It was an awakening, for me, to the irreducible intricacies of place, and it led me to the conclusion that my prior training would be of little use in Flint without an extended period of listening and learning.

This attitude of epistemic humility is, in my view, fundamental to the ethnographic enterprise. Writing of her arrival in Bhopal, India, in the years following the catastrophic gas leak there, the anthropologist Kim Fortun describes her sense of entering a "whirlwind," a "maelstrom" that made it difficult to treat Bhopal as "a bounded unit of analysis."[22] I felt much the same way about the water crisis, like I had to ride the breeze for some time, let the complexity of the situation wash over me, before it was possible to start analytically dissecting what was going on, or even to formulate clear research questions. Part of the difficulty was that by early 2016 the crisis was being held up by commentators as exemplary in so many different ways—notably:

- As a wakeup call about the persistence of lead in the urban environment, and especially the threat of lead in water
- As an illustration of the dilapidation and underfunding of America's infrastructure (and, later, as a virtually unprecedented effort to replace infrastructure at the local level)
- As a revelation of the inadequacy of environmental regulatory frameworks, particularly the federal Lead and Copper Rule, and an indictment of the bureaucratic cultures that work against effective regulatory intervention
- As a dramatization of nationwide controversies about the treatment of poor people of color
- As a landmark environmental justice struggle demonstrating the power of grassroots activists to make change
- As a "gold standard" of "citizen science" illustrating the potential of resident-driven scientific research to aid marginalized communities
- As an example of the dangers of aggressive state intervention into local affairs and the suspension of local democracy

It was clear to me that any treatment of the crisis that did justice to the "whirl" and avoided reductionism would have to touch upon all of these aspects of the crisis's significance. But it was equally clear that I would have to train my focus on the theme or themes that would best allow me to elaborate the perspective on the crisis I was intent upon capturing. The main question that came to guide my research was simple: how did the activists understand the crisis, and how did that understanding affect the way they responded to it?

When I met them, Flint activists were already steering a course through the storm with the kind of performative confidence already familiar to me from encounters with other activist cultures. I decided the most promising approach was to step into the stream of grassroots activism and follow it where it led. In January 2016, I began attending community meetings, rallies, protests, and marches organized by the Flint Democracy Defense League, Flint Rising, and the groups comprising the Two Years (later, Three Years, and then Four Years) Too Long Coalition (also known as the Flint H2O Justice Coalition). At first, I was largely a passive spectator, but gradually I took on a more active role in the development of strategy, the promulgation of public statements, and the organization of events and actions. I also took part in door-to-door canvassing and community organizer trainings arranged by Flint Rising.

The geography of activism shaped the contours of my field site, which was not coterminous with city limits but centered on particular spaces like St. Michael's and Woodside churches (where activists had regular meetings), the front lawn of City Hall (the site of innumerable rallies and a staging ground for marches), and council chambers, and which occasionally extended outside the city, too.[23] Like the activists, I also made a point of attending official meetings about water: town halls, panels, hearings, and the so-called Community Partners meetings at City Hall, which brought together representatives of agencies and groups on the governmental and nonprofit side of the crisis response. Because of my close working relationship with my colleague at Kettering University, Laura Sullivan—an appointee to the state's official crisis response committee, the city's Technical Advisory Committee, and the KWA board—I also enjoyed vicarious access to many closed-door meetings and behind-the-scenes interactions between top officials. In addition to physical spaces of various kinds, I immersed myself to the point of saturation in water-related Facebook and Twitter chatter, which was often just as, if not more, consequential than offline interactions between activists.[24] When I could not be physically present at meetings and events, I benefited enormously from live streams by activists through Facebook Live, the video-streaming feature debuted by the social media site in April 2016.

Allying myself with the activists as closely as I did gave my research the character of what Jeffrey S. Juris has called "militant ethnography" (although "militant" seems a trifle grandiose as a description of any of the activism I actually engaged in). Juris describes militant ethnography as "a politically engaged and collaborative form of participant observation carried out from within rather than outside grassroots movements" that "seeks to overcome the divide between research and practice." The militant ethnographer is not merely a "circumstantial activist" (or, I would add, an "advocate"). Rather, she "has to build long-term relationships of mutual commitment and trust, become entangled with complex relations of power, and live the emotions associated with direct action organizing and activist networking." Juris argues, as would I, that "such politically engaged ethnographic practice not only allows researchers to remain active political subjects, it also generates better interpretations and analyses."[25]

Of course, no ethnography would be worthy of the name without preserving a certain degree of insider-outsider tension, and some scholars may worry that adopting a militant orientation, in Juris's sense of the term, eliminates this tension. What I experienced was quite the opposite. In practice, working in such close proximity to the activists generated tensions that would not otherwise have existed—tensions which, while sometimes unpleasant, were extremely productive of insights.

The activist perspective on the water crisis was not, however, the only one I had the opportunity to enter into, nor were the activists the only people involved to whom I felt a certain allegiance. Joining the Flint Area Community Health and Environment Partnership (FACHEP) in April 2016 added another layer to my direct involvement in the crisis response. An interdisciplinary collaboration between researchers from, among other institutions, Wayne State University, the University of Michigan, Michigan State University, and the Henry Ford Health System, the FACHEP team congealed around several grants awarded in early 2016 by the National Institutes of Health, the National Science Foundation, and the State of Michigan to fund research into Flint's water quality and the point-of-use filters the state had begun distributing to residents. My primary role was to oversee community engagement around the most substantial of the team's projects, a $3.35 million study of the prevalence of *Legionella* bacteria in Flint's water supply. In this capacity, I worked in collaboration with Laura Sullivan to promulgate sampling results and safety-related recommendations through social networks, facilitate direct communication between residents and members of the team, and build trust in the team's work among the activists. To compensate for short staffing, I occasionally performed tasks outside my official job description as well, including scheduling water sampling appointments, building sampling kits, and accompanying sampling teams from house to house to administer a public health survey. I also endeavored to play a diplomatic role when relations soured between the different teams studying Flint's water and the activists allied with them, a story related in chapter 7. As I explain in that chapter, my involvement with FACHEP complicated my ethnographic work in a number of ways: it gave me the aura of someone with inside information and opened doors to certain spaces the activists could not enter directly, but it was also—at least early on—another source of suspicion about my motives and true allegiances.

As a supplement to participant observation, I conducted around seventy semi-structured interviews with people involved in various aspects of the water crisis response.[26] About thirty-five of these were with people I would describe as "activists"—mainly Flint-based activists, but also several who were associated with statewide or national organizations, or with activism in other cities. I also interviewed a number of people who might be better described as activist "allies"—advocates from the worlds of public health, journalism, and public interest law. I talked with elected representatives from city and state government, employees of the EPA, and numerous people involved in the production of scientific knowledge about the water, including some of my own FACHEP colleagues and members of the Virginia Tech team. In only a handful of cases did I fail to connect with a solicited interviewee, usually because I never got a response to my invitation.

One advantage of combining interviews with extended ethnography is that I did not have to rely overly upon the "snowball" method of identifying interviewees, which can introduce bias into a research project by hewing too closely to preestablished social networks. By sinking more deeply into my field of study than the average interviewer, I was able to identify for myself who the main actors were and interview more selectively and efficiently. Furthermore, because many of the people I interviewed I had already gotten to know personally or had even worked with, I was able to craft detailed, tailor-made questions to complement my generic interview template. Sometimes putting on an "interviewer" cap with friends and acquaintances was awkward, for it cast me conspicuously in the role of the researcher rather than that of comrade. Also, I found it difficult to talk neutrally with certain activists and officials as I became tangled up in some of the divisions within the activist and scientific community. But on the whole, I believe my personal involvement in the same issues consuming my interviewees allowed for much subtler and more candid conversations than would otherwise have been possible. Interviews proved to be critical not only for mapping in more detail various perspectives on the crisis, but also (supplemented by news coverage[27] and archived social media content) reconstructing what went on from 2011 to 2015 before my personal involvement.[28]

Themes of the Book

It was through a combination of close observation in group settings and probing questions in one-on-one settings, then, that I arrived at the themes that animate this book.[29] Firstly, and perhaps unsurprisingly, the activists understood themselves to be fighting for "justice." Justice is, of course, a capacious concept; its utility, from an activist standpoint, is in part its ability to accommodate a wide range of demands. For Flint activists, "water justice" encompassed everything from securing safe, affordable water, to replacing damaged infrastructure, to declaring water a human right, to community revitalization.[30] The broader idea of "environmental justice," too, was very much in the air. Whether or not activists employed the term explicitly from the start, they came to see their struggle as part of a longer tradition of everyday people battling pollution and official obstruction, and the connections they forged within the environmental justice community were some of the most significant to come out of the crisis. The concept only became more salient when multiple investigative bodies determined that the crisis was an example of environmental injustice, and when the city organized an environmental justice summit in 2017 at which a number of water activists were honored.

What made the activists' discourse around justice distinctive, however, is what I have already alluded to: their conviction that the injustice of the water crisis was the product of a prior crisis of "democracy." Democracy is, arguably, at least as capacious a concept as justice, and also tends to be used at the popular level without adjectival qualifiers. Nevertheless, it is possible to differentiate analytically between distinct conceptions of democracy implicit in activist thought. When activists argued that the usurpation of local democracy in Flint caused the crisis, they had something like "representative" democracy in mind: what was lost when emergency management was imposed by the state was the right of residents' elected representatives at the local level to have any say over decisions about Flint's water (among other things). As a consequence, when residents began to raise issues about water rates and water quality they found that the mechanisms of redress associated with representative democracy—chiefly, electoral turnover and petitioning of elected officials—were, if not entirely unavailable, mostly ineffective. For this reason, the restoration of representative democracy was intertwined in activists' minds with the restoration of their water.

The story activists told about their *response* to the crisis, however, invoked more radical democratic ideas. It was a story about ordinary people who operated—by necessity—outside the channels of representative democracy, people who distrusted the water forums sponsored by officials and opted for a more contentious political response situated in the "streets." The activists preferred to create alternative deliberative spaces of their own, "free" spaces where they could make their own assumptions about what was politically possible, where decision making was direct, where previously apolitical people could learn to exercise political agency. They also sought to democratize the epistemological realm, fighting to establish the legitimacy of popular knowledge and for a vision of "citizen science" that insisted on residents setting the scientific agenda within their own community. Some of the activists consciously sought to build off of these popular energies to advance a more participatory democratic ideal by channeling activism into long-term community capacity building.

It is no accident that I describe the activists' account of the crisis as a story, for if there was any concept coequal to justice and democracy in their thinking it was the concept of "narrative." As they saw it, establishing that the water crisis was caused by a denial of democracy required dispelling the "false narrative" promulgated by state agencies and the Snyder administration, which downplayed state culpability and hinted that Flint was to blame for its own problems. It also required establishing the preferability of the activists' "political narrative" (as I will call it) of the crisis's origins to other possible narratives of the crisis that were not "false" per se, but whose emphases (as shown in chapter 2) were not wholly congruous with activist objectives.

Activists also targeted "false" narratives of the response to the crisis, narratives they felt obscured the collective action of ordinary residents in favor of a media-friendly saga of heroism focused inordinately on the interventions of expert allies. The feeling that their story of popular self-liberation was being hijacked—in some cases, by the experts themselves—generated a kind of dialectical backlash, pushing the activists in an even more populist direction. Their rhetoric sometimes implied that they didn't need *anyone*, that they were entirely capable of fighting their own fight. This message resonated in Flint more than it might have elsewhere, given that Flintstones (as locals sometimes call themselves) were already inclined to mythologize popular resistance, with the 1936 to 1937 sit-down strike—in which a small contingent of hardscrabble workers beat GM against all odds—serving as their Genesis. I got the sense that some activists wanted the water movement in Flint to be remembered as a similar beacon of resistance, comprising another homegrown chapter in the universal history of the fight for justice and democracy.

In some ways, this book is in the service of that ambition. As both a contribution to the movement and a work of scholarship, however, the book consciously resists romanticizing grassroots activism—a trap I believe I have been able to avoid precisely because I grew close enough to the activists to know them as full-bodied people and to observe some of the movement's internal controversies and limitations firsthand. In a few instances, activists expressed to me the hope that my work would expose the shortcomings of other activists and activist organizations, or at least offer a more balanced account of Flint's water activism than the celebratory depictions that emerged after the crisis became a national story. While I in no way wish to exacerbate tensions and divisions within the grassroots, the book would be incomplete if I did not give voice to these dissenting perspectives. I also, in chapter 8, offer my own assessment of the ways in which activists' staunch insistence on self-determination created, at times, a problematic gap between rhetoric and reality. For reasons I have already mentioned, exercising this interpretive power is a delicate matter in Flint, but I do so in the hope that it will contribute to what Julie Sze and Jonathan London describe as "a more critical and reflective mode of community organizing,"[31] in ways that prove constructive at the local level as well as instructive on a scholarly level.

The Significance of Flint

It is notoriously difficult to extract insights of general scholarly interest from research as locally rooted as that which went into this book. When I first conceived of the project, it was as a descriptive case study of an unusually significant event in the nation's history, written from an engaged vantage point and without the intention of advancing any particular theoretical framework. I took inspiration from Henry Kraus's classic firsthand account of the sit-down strike *The Many and the Few,* as well as from the many notable case studies of environmental disasters and the popular responses they have provoked, beginning with Kai Erikson's *Everything in Its Path* and including some of the books in this series.[32] A richly descriptive case study distinguishes itself, in part, precisely by resisting generalization, incorporating idiosyncrasies and deviations that complicate whatever core themes may be present.[33] These should build up like pebbles in the shoe, reminding the reader of the artificiality and incompleteness of even the most robust conceptual framework. Given that much of the water crisis's complexity was missed by the media entirely, or erased as waning news coverage wore representations down to their bare outlines, painting a fuller picture of what went on in Flint is, I maintain, an important contribution of this book.

There are political reasons, as well, to be cautious about generalization, for the basis of many of the activists' demands was the singularity of the water crisis. Moving Flint to the front of the queue for state and federal assistance, they believed, depended on the crisis being seen as unique, and often their leading antagonists were those who argued that what was going on in Flint was happening in other cities, too. The predicament of the militant ethnographer, then, is that framing the crisis in generalizable terms for scholarly purposes risks coming off as politically counterproductive, or at least politically tone-deaf. In his account of interactions with Oxford activists, David Harvey usefully articulates this dilemma as a tension between the "tangible solidarities" embedded in community life and the scholar's search for more "abstract" conceptions that have "universal purchase." From a community's perspective, Harvey points out, the shift to the latter "conceptual world ... can threaten that sense of value and common purpose that grounds the militant particularism achieved in particular places."[34] Attempts to convey the significance of particular struggles in the language of scholarly abstractions may be seen by community members as diluting those struggles or implying that they are important only as instantiations of more general phenomena.[35]

On the other hand, there was political utility in the idea that the water crisis contained lessons for the world beyond Flint. The national conversation the crisis generated around lead contamination, moribund infrastructures, and spotty regulations created a platform for activists to take their story around the country. And ultimately, no matter how focused that story was on the exceptional nature of Flint's plight, it did have a larger moral, a message about the integral relationship of justice and democracy. Earlier, I suggested that these concepts could be used as portals to scholarly literatures and discourses that stand to be illuminated by the crisis even as they help to illuminate it. Here, I attempt to make good on this claim in ways that set up later discussions in the book.

Environmental Justice and Its Critics

There is, of course, an extensive literature on environmental justice and good reason to situate the Flint water crisis within it.[36] It is worth noting, however, that environmental justice frameworks have been criticized by scholars on a number of grounds. One common complaint, voiced by urban political ecologists and others influenced by the Marxist tradition, is that these frameworks are theoretically shallow, centered on moralistic condemnations of environmental inequities that rely uncritically on liberal notions of "justice" and "rights." This kind of normative language, some have argued, has proven to be highly co-optable into the postpolitical "consensus" of neoliberalism, with favorite activist ideas like the "human right to water" operationalized by elites in ways compatible with privatization and other neoliberal agendas.[37] What those who rely on such concepts often miss, contend Eric Swyngedouw and Nikolas Heynen, is that the processes by which nature is "metabolized" for human use under capitalism not only tolerate, but actually depend upon disparities of various kinds. Consequently, it is naïve to call for the elimination of environmental inequities without working for more fundamental economic and political change.[38]

The alleged naïveté of environmental justice activists is reflected in their tendency to get absorbed in what Swyngedouw and Maria Kaika call "the allocation dynamics of environmental externalities," like battles over the siting of polluting facilities.[39] When such activists call for structural reforms at all, their demands are often limited to thinly procedural changes that would do little more than give communities modestly more influence over the distribution of environmental goods and harms. A more radical orientation, suggest Swyngedouw and Kaika, would keep the focus on the deeper dynamics of capitalist urbanization, the "decision-making processes that organize socio-ecological transformation and choreograph the management of the commons."[40]

In a similar, albeit more sympathetic, vein, David Pellow argues that environmental justice frames are often empirically simplistic, reducing the complex social interactions that generate environmental injustices to dichotomous "perpetrator-victim" narratives.[41] When seen in the proper historical perspective, Pellow argues, environmental injustices are products of competition for resources by diverse (and unequal) stakeholders who usually have no intention of wronging others. Implying that environmental harms are straightforwardly foisted upon innocent communities by evildoers not only filters out a good deal of social complexity, it overlooks the ways in which members of affected communities may themselves be complicit in injustice.

If my main priorities in this book were theoretical sophistication and empirical comprehensiveness, I would have approached the subject of water activism in Flint differently. I would likely have proceeded from the outside in, beginning either with an analytic framework derived from a prior scholarly agenda (and only tangentially concerned with the ideas of the activists themselves), or with a wide angle that immediately put the activists' admittedly partial view of reality into perspective. Instead, I have written the book from the inside out, concerning myself first and foremost with capturing ethnographically the perspective of Flint activists, and using their conceptual language as a springboard to construct a thematized account of the crisis and glean scholarly insights of broader relevance.[42] On a conceptual level, I am most interested in exploring not the polished diamonds of the professional theorist but the roughhewn coal of the layperson—a little jagged, often, but generative of fire and motion. In short, I am interested in ideas that *move* people, and for this reason I have found myself drawing from those strains of social movement theory that emphasize cultural spurs to action: identities, frames, and narratives that shape how people think about what needs to be done and how they go about doing it. Considerations of "resources" and "opportunities" are important, too, as part of the context in which collective action transpires or fails to transpire,[43] but ultimately my concern in this book is with the relationship between ideas and action.

I do not deny that the often black-and-white conceptual world of activism, shaped as it is by utilitarian and rhetorical considerations, may sometimes obscure more than it reveals. Certainly, the activists' way of framing the water crisis, like any other attempt to construct a politically serviceable account of a complex social reality, included embellishments and blind spots. The case of Flint water activism, however, offers a compelling example of how rich and productive the view from the grassroots can be. It is no exaggeration to say that Flint activists are, in some sense, coauthors of this book, for it is their analytic of the crisis that animates it. Their perspectives are not so much empirical data points I gather together and look *at* from a more enlightened vantage point as they are lenses I have learned much from looking *through*. As I consolidate and burnish these perspectives into a particular narrative of the crisis in the first few chapters of the book, I invite the reader to adopt a similar vantage point. In the process, I contest the tendency to see activist ideas as superficial by showing how the emphasis on democracy in Flint encouraged deeper thinking about the origins and implications of environmental injustice.

Another concern scholars have raised about environmental justice frameworks is that they lack breadth as well as depth, being "narrowly focused" on "specific geographic locales."[44] For David Harvey, the challenge for environmental justice activists is to "transcend particularisms" by using local issues to expose and confront more systemic injustices.[45] One of the transcendent lessons of the Flint water crisis, however, is precisely the importance of the *local*, a lesson that will manifest itself in a variety of ways in the chapters that follow. Most important for our purposes here is the activists' association of democracy with what they sometimes called "local control."[46] They believed that the interests of the city of Flint were separate from (and arguably superior to) those of the state of Michigan, and that decisions made about matters of local concern should flow out of local knowledge and politics rather than being handed over to expert administrators beholden to outside agendas. The principle of local control implied not only that people had a right to political autonomy but that they were best off when they looked after themselves. In Flint activist Claire McClinton's words, "If we control our water, it's not gonna get poisoned."[47]

Water Governance and Infrastructure

The relationship McClinton and other activists posited between local democracy and the integrity of water raises larger questions of water governance. It is a truism within the environmental justice movement that water "thrives" under some structures of governance and not others,[48] with democratic processes productive of better outcomes. Even within mainstream water management, there has been a shift in recent years away from state-based, technocratic "command-and-control" approaches to more inclusive governance structures that provide for the participation of local "stakeholders."[49] Clearly, subsuming decisions about water under unilateral EM structures is contrary to this general trend, and in this sense the Flint water crisis lends support to the idea that democratic governance is preferable to the alternative. As we will see, however, even under emergency management Flint residents had opportunities to participate in deliberations about their water, under the pretense that these deliberations would actually influence official decision making. The limitations of these deliberative forums (detailed in chapter 6) lend credence to skeptics who maintain that public participation can easily become a mere formality, or even a technique for sublimating disruptive political energies into deliberative consensus building.[50] With these skeptics, I maintain that the existence of deliberative forums does not negate the importance of contentious popular mobilizations that eschew deliberative frameworks.[51] Furthermore, as various examples in this book demonstrate, opening up channels of public participation by no means guarantees that water issues will cease to be seen as fundamentally technical in nature and thus best adjudicated by experts.[52] Flint activists understood that the more the technical side of the water question was emphasized, the less their opinions would matter, regardless of how many opportunities they had to express them. This made it all the more imperative that they advance a "political" narrative to counteract what I will call the "technical" narrative of the crisis.

It must also be remembered that the prospects of democratizing water governance are integrally related to the physical arrangement of infrastructures, which may foreclose or constrain certain political possibilities. From the late 1960s onward, the fact that Flint's water pipes were tied into the Detroit system meant that every drink residents took depended on decisions made outside the city and pipes that extended far beyond it—an awkward arrangement for a city that prided itself on self-determination. Flint was far from alone in this predicament, for much of southeast Michigan was similarly reliant upon Detroit's vast regional water network. For the wealthy white suburbs of Detroit, the solution was the Great Lakes Water Authority (founded in 2014), a regional governance structure that shifted predominant influence over the water system outside of the city. For Flint, the solution proposed by some elites was to withdraw from the politics of water in southeast Michigan entirely and enter into another regional arrangement—the KWA—over which the city would have more control. Flint activists, however, regarded regionalization of any kind as ominous. Not only was regional governance insufficiently empowering at the local level,[53] removing infrastructures from municipal control was a stepping stone, they feared, to what they considered the worst of all worlds: privatization. The ultimate question, though—never answered (at least not to my satisfaction)—was what the *alternative* was, what water democracy *would* look like if using the water source closest at hand (i.e., the Flint River) was not an option. That unanswered question haunts this book in ways that highlight some of the thorniest conundrums of modern-day water management.

The fact that Flint's water pipes are not only conduits for precious resources, but also vehicles for political aspirations reflects the fact that infrastructure is far more than the sum of its material parts: it is infused with political, social, and cultural meaning.[54] To be sure, infrastructure is not always marked with such rich significance, for it often sinks—when functioning smoothly—into the social unconscious, out of mind if not entirely out of sight.[55] Usually it is when infrastructures break down that they suddenly become visible, their inner workings exposed to people who once paid them little mind. Stephen Graham has suggested that these moments are pregnant with opportunities for critical social analysis, offering the chance to "excavate the usually hidden politics of flow and connection, of mobility and immobility, within contemporary societies."[56] What is more significant from the perspective adopted in this book is the de-reifying effect of infrastructural disruption on those who come to see a usually hidden part of their environment as an imperfect product of human agency. Crucially, what Flint residents gained from this experience was not only new knowledge of water systems, but also knowledge of what is not known—and in some cases cannot be known—about them: knowledge of the gaps in our recordkeeping on the pipes under our feet and of the unruliness and unpredictability of those pipes as components of a "large technical system" that strives for but never achieves closure.[57] In contrast to the commonsensical view of infrastructure as the sturdy skeleton upon which our life in common hangs, it was precisely infrastructure's *lack* of stability that became a key assumption of Flint activists, a point of emphasis whenever anyone presumed to make authoritative pronouncements about the water system's recovery. For this reason, whenever residents were enlisted by officials to alter their water usage (usually by increasing water consumption) to help stabilize the system, the choice to participate took on a political as well as a personal character.

As this example implies, infrastructure is not just part of the context in which political agency plays out: agency is also exercised *on* and *through* infrastructure.[58] This generally takes place at the extremities of infrastructural networks, where "mediating technologies" allow users some control over how systems operate.[59] In Flint, the most significant mediating technologies were the "point-of-use" filters distributed by the State of Michigan, which residents were encouraged to use as short-term solutions to lead contamination. Normalizing filter use within an everyday context—or at least showing that filters had been provided to all residents of the city—became the state's main strategy for ending its provision of free bottled water. While some have touted the democratic potential of household-level filtration technologies, Flint activists viewed filters not as technologies of empowerment but as projections of the state's power and interests. They feared that embracing the filters meant dampening calls for infrastructure replacement, distracting from structural issues with the water system, modifying everyday behavior in unwanted ways, and exposing residents to bacterial contamination that the filters could not eliminate or even exacerbated. To win public acceptance for the filters, the state strategically produced ignorance about them, neglecting to educate residents about their limitations and discouraging academic research into their efficacy. Refusing the filters—and, as a corollary, demanding that the state continue to provide free bottled water—became an archetypal expression of political resistance in Flint.

Knowledge, "Citizen Science," and Expertise

The battle over filters was, like so many of the crisis's other subplots, in part a battle over knowledge. Should the filters provided by the state just be accepted graciously and operated unthinkingly or did residents have the right to problematize them, to make them objects of inquiry, to expect that concerns about their functioning would be properly investigated? Who was entitled to speak with authority about the filters, to appeal to scientific evidence either to encourage or discourage popular trust in them? Did residents have the right to know everything they wanted to know about the filters, or were officials and experts warranted in withholding information that might cause anxiety and alarm? We can rephrase these questions in more general terms as: *Who decides what deserves to be known?*, *Who gets to speak authoritatively about what is known?*, and *Who decides who gets to know what is known?* To view these kinds of questions as purely epistemological would be a mistake. In Flint, as elsewhere, such questions were matters of power and justice as well as matters of knowledge, and the answers rendered to them were full of political implications.

To these questions we must add a fourth: *who produces the knowledge that is known?* The Flint water crisis appeared at a moment of surging interest in "citizen science," a term used to capture various forms of lay involvement in the production of scientific knowledge.[60] In fact, it could not have been a more formative time for the citizen science community, with the recently founded Citizen Science Association holding its inaugural conference in February 2015 and leading practitioners working to develop consensus around the theoretical and practical contours of the field. As the partnership between water activists and the Virginia Tech team led by environmental engineer Marc Edwards began to attract national attention, citizen science boosters seized upon it as a "gold standard"[61] for the genre that fused the idea of citizens acting as data-gathering helpers to trained scientists with the prioritization of community-driven needs and objectives. In an agenda-setting edited volume, Caren Cooper and Bruce Lewenstein held up the collaboration as a paradigmatic example of what they called "democratized and contributory" citizen science.[62]

The irony was that by the time accounts like Cooper and Lewenstein's began to appear in 2016, the relationship between Edwards and the activists was well on its way to degenerating completely. By the time I finished the fieldwork for this book in summer 2018, it was hard to find an activist with a good word to say about him. Both sides had their explanations for the breakup. The activists often claimed that Edwards had "sold out," changing his tune about the safety of the water once he started working with the State of Michigan and accepting money from the very agencies he had come to town criticizing. For his part, Edwards—who, like the activists, fancied himself a storyteller[63]—began to narrate the story of Virginia Tech's intervention as a "dream" turned into a nightmare by "a few reporters, academics, actors, activists, and pseudoscientists [who] came to Flint, exploiting the tragedy to promote their own agendas and creating yet another human tragedy in the process."[64] It was these serpents slithering into the garden, he implied, that caused the activists to turn against him, sundering the conduct of good science in Flint (as exemplified by Virginia Tech's work) from local water activism. Forced to choose a side, Edwards chose "science," casting himself as a martyr to the cause who would speak scientific truths and defend the scientific method to the end, no matter how unpopular it made him.

One problem with this paradise-lost narrative is its erasure of fundamental disjunctures of outlook between the activists and Edwards that existed from the inception of their collaborative sampling effort in 2015.[65] The activists did not, for example, share Edwards's views on the nature or the origins of the water crisis, nor his conviction in the superiority of scientific ways of knowing or interest in reestablishing public trust in the scientific establishment. Eventually, they discovered (much to their chagrin) that they also did not share his measures of recovery from the crisis. But by then it was too late: Edwards had become the go-to authority on all things Flint water, the state's favorite expert as well as the media's. The activists paid a price, then, for the narrowly focused relationship of convenience they struck up with Virginia Tech in 2015: long after they hoped Edwards would disappear, he continued to act as an advisor to the state and to influence perceptions of the crisis in ways that ran directly counter to their objectives, using his website and speaking appearances to ridicule and attack his critics and the ever-growing list of people he accused of doing fake or shoddy science in Flint and/or exploiting the crisis for their own gain.

Contained in the saga of Edwards and the activists—related mainly in chapter 7 but set up in earlier chapters—are a variety of cautionary lessons about the relationship between citizen science and democracy and the role that citizen science can play in obtaining justice for marginalized communities. Advocates of citizen science who underscore its qualities of popular empowerment have stressed the need for laypeople to have influence over every step in the scientific process, an arrangement sometimes called "extreme citizen science." This principle was never implemented in Flint, where activists took the lead in data gathering but were at the mercy of Edwards and his team when it came time to interpret and communicate the data. This power differential did not present itself as much of a problem at first, when the activists saw Edwards as speaking on their behalf about the science. But as he strayed off message, the activists realized that *Edwards* saw it the other way around: he was not speaking for *them*, but rather speaking for the *science* (at least purportedly), and would do so however he saw fit, whether they wanted him to or not. The distinction was crucial, for it meant that ultimately Edwards's sense of entitlement to speak about Flint's water stemmed not from democratic delegation by the activists as part of a common struggle but from his own independent status as a scientific expert.

These different ways of thinking about the basis of a scientist's discursive authority (not to mention the ultimate objectives of scientific inquiry) illustrate the difference between approaching citizen science from the scientific end, as Edwards did, and approaching it from the social movement end, as I do in this book. Explaining the logic of "social movement-based citizen science," Gwen Ottinger points out that "activist groups design studies not only to improve knowledge but to foster collective action and political change,"[66] and that there are sometimes "tradeoffs between scientific legitimacy and political efficacy."[67] In such cases, one would hardly expect activists to prioritize scientific legitimacy for its own sake. When activism "mobilizes" science, writes Marta Conde, scientific knowledge is valued principally as a "political tool" that activists can use to "express and exercise power."[68] When the science on offer fails to perform that function, activists often seek to redirect attention to other ways of knowing (a subject of chapters 5 and 8) or to competing forms of scientific knowledge produced by counter-experts.

None of this should lead us to conclude that activists are inevitably less scientific than experts. Certainly, Flint activists felt strongly that some of their own claims were more scientifically defensible than those made by Edwards. Philosophers of science like Sandra Harding have argued that politically motivated science can actually "produce less partial and distorted results of research than those supposedly guided by the goal of value-neutrality."[69] One reason is that science borne of political struggle fosters what Harding calls "strong objectivity" by turning our attention to the credibility of knowledge producers themselves and alerting us to the ways in which power and perspective shape truth claims.[70] But we should be careful about measuring the scientific worth of activist-driven knowledge production by its conformity to traditional scientific standards (like "objectivity") or the extent to which activists behave like "scientists." It may be that under conditions of high risk and uncertainty the assumptions and methods of "normal" science are inadequate, that in these circumstances nonscientific ways of knowing have value equal to or greater than their scientific counterparts, and that unorthodox approaches are called for (or at least a plurality of scientific voices).[71] There is no straightforward answer to what constitutes "good" science in a context as complex and indeterminate as that created by the water crisis, and whenever Edwards made black-and-white distinctions between good scientists and bad scientists, real scientists and fake scientists, it provoked backlash by the activists, who could see that there was more to the story.

Environmental justice activists who appeal to the "technical rationality" of experts for support often experience, in David Pellow's words, "a complex mix of loss and triumph, empowerment and disempowerment."[72] While the collaboration with Virginia Tech had an empowering effect early on, contributing to the water movement's signature victory (getting Flint off the river), its long-term effects on the community were dubious, as the controversy around Edwards shattered personal relationships, prevented collaboration (scientific and otherwise), and ultimately left activists even more vulnerable to the state. At the same time, the Edwards experience made the activists more determined than ever to prove that the fight for justice and democracy in Flint was not about the exertions of hero figures but, rather, the collective action of ordinary residents. The water crisis became an opportunity to show the world just how capable Flint residents were: they could know for themselves, speak for themselves, and act for themselves, with their own organizations taking the lead as the main agents of justice in Flint. They could prove to the world that their political voices should never have been taken away in the first place. In the last chapter of the book, chapter 8, I trace these attitudes, along with some of their prickly contradictions, through the activism and community organizing efforts that postdated the return to Detroit water in October 2015.

Chapter Summary

To summarize: in chapters 1 through 3, I distinguish the political narrative of the water crisis from other possible narratives and show how the activists' emphasis on democracy allowed them to overcome some of the limitations of standard environmental justice frameworks and fostered deeper political thinking about the causes of the crisis. In chapter 4, I trace the origins of the activists' ideas about democracy back into the struggle against emergency management, where activists first made the connection between democracy and water. In chapter 5, I examine the development of political agency among residents newly mobilized by personal water troubles and the convergence of those residents with pro-democracy activists, resulting in the particularly uncompromising form of activism discussed in chapter 6. Chapter 7 details controversies over science and expertise, while chapter 8 finds the activists trying to channel water activism into sustainable "people power," weaving the most democratic impulses within the water movement into a more radical political vision for the future of Flint.

1 Flint First: The Injustice of the Flint Water Crisis

In a ballroom at the University of Michigan-Flint, a short walk away from the Flint River, Dr. Mona Hanna-Attisha sat facing a panel of state legislators. It was March 29, 2016, six months after her announcement that lead leaching from water pipes was finding its way into the bloodstreams of Flint's children.[1] State officials had disputed the claim at first, calling Hanna-Attisha's research "unfortunate" and suggesting that it was politically motivated.[2] Within a matter of days, however, their resistance broke as the state's own epidemiologists replicated her findings. From that point forward, the contamination of Flint's water would forever be known to the world as the "Flint water crisis."

It had taken Hanna-Attisha two weeks of intensive research to deliver what was received as smoking-gun evidence of a public health emergency in Flint. But her intervention—as she acknowledged during the September 2015 press conference at which she released her findings—had been a long time coming. Many in the medical community had been slow to accept that the water in Flint posed a threat to human health. By contrast, she pointed out, Flint's "grassroots organizers" had been fighting to keep the city's water problems "in the public view" for months.[3] These activists were the first to describe the situation as a "crisis" and the first to argue that system-wide contamination was causing demonstrable harm to residents— and they had been amassing the evidence since 2014. Again and again, they were ignored, dismissed, and derided by politicians, administrators, and so-called experts. In confirming the activists' longstanding claim that Flint's water was unsafe, Hanna-Attisha's data led directly to the realization of their demand that the city disconnect from the Flint River. Now, as she testified before one of the three state bodies tasked with investigating the crisis, many of those activists sat attentively in the audience behind her.

Hanna-Attisha noted that during the year and a half that Flint drew its drinking water from the river, the number of children age zero to five testing positive for elevated blood lead levels rose from 2.1 percent to 4 percent. But she cautioned the committee against concluding that this figure captured the full extent of the damage done. In fact, it was almost certainly a significant underestimate. Because lead leaves the blood and enters the bones within a month's time, blood tests were of limited value in capturing past exposure. A "normal" result (2 µg/dL or below), then, could not be taken as a sign that no harm had occurred. Everyone in Flint had to be "assumed as being potentially exposed," irrespective of what tests showed about their blood lead levels.[4] Furthermore, Hanna-Attisha explained, her analysis depended on data derived from routine, Medicaid-mandated lead screening at the ages of one and two years. But lead in water poses a special danger to infants reliant upon formula, who are unlikely to be tested during their period of highest exposure.

Hanna-Attisha also stressed that even low levels of lead exposure can cause harm. Warning that there is "no safe level of lead," she pointed in particular to lead's effects on cognition and behavior. Lead exposure in childhood, she said, is known to result in lower IQs, attention deficits, hyperactivity, and impulse control disorders. Infants in Flint who consumed tainted water through formula were at the most "developmentally vulnerable" age, and because lead "crosses in utero," they may have been exposed before even being born. Furthermore, the epigenetic effects of lead exposure can alter DNA in ways that make impairments inheritable across two generations, meaning that the community would see "decades-long consequences" from the exposure.

It would never be possible to say with certainty that any one deficit in any one child was directly caused by lead. But because lead exposure in Flint was population wide, the working assumption had to be that all Flint children needed, and deserved, the maximum possible attention and care: as Hanna-Attisha put it, "There is no way to predict which child is going to have which problem and that is why we need to do everything for all children." Wraparound support—nutritious food, health care, education— she argued, should be made available not just to the six thousand-plus Flint children under the age of six but to *every* Flint child. In addition, because lead is harmful to people of all ages, the same support should be extended to every Flint adult, and to anyone who regularly spent time in Flint during the years of 2014 and 2015. In total, upward of 150,000 people, by her estimation, were entitled to all "the necessary interventions to mitigate the impact of this disaster"—in addition, of course, to the replacement of lead infrastructure to prevent further exposure.

No doubt aware of the high esteem in which Hanna-Attisha was held by those in the room, the committee treated her with respect and, for the most part, deference. During the question-and-answer session, however, State Representative Ed Canfield, a Republican from Michigan's 84th District and a physician himself, pushed back against her assessment of the extent of the harm done to Flint children. With the insistence that he was attempting not to "diminish" the crisis but rather to give worried parents "a better understanding" of its severity, Canfield sought to introduce some historical perspective. He pointed out that as recently as 1998, over 44 percent of Michigan children had blood lead levels above the cutoff now used to diagnose lead poisoning (5 μg/dL). In 2015, Flint's second year on the river, which encompassed both the peak of the lead contamination and a surge in voluntary blood lead tests, 3.3 percent of the city's children had been confirmed to have elevated blood lead levels.

Furthermore, Canfield continued, even in the present this figure could be compared favorably against rates of lead poisoning in many other parts of Michigan. Citing 2012 data, he pointed to Branch County, where 10.1 percent of children had elevated blood lead levels, to Jackson County, where the number was 8 percent, to Kent County, where it was 6.2 percent, and to Huron County, where it was 5.4 percent. Even if one conceded Hanna-Attisha's point about the underdiagnosis of infant lead poisoning, Canfield implied, surely the harms caused by Flint's lead problem were not substantially worse than, or even as severe as, those found elsewhere. Why, then, should Flint be given special consideration? Invoking his responsibility as a state representative to consider the needs of all Michigan citizens, Canfield argued that "this is a statewide problem and we have to help everybody in the state."

Canfield's argument was no mere academic exercise. The State of Michigan was being asked to provide Flint with an "unprecedented" amount of resources (in Governor Rick Snyder's estimation) to remediate the effects of the crisis.[5] By March 2016, three supplemental appropriations bills had already been approved by the state legislature, amounting to $67.4 million—money for reconnecting Flint to the Detroit water system, for bottled water and filter distribution, for health care and education, for lead service line replacement. Another $126.7 million of state aid for Flint was under consideration.[6] Looking even further ahead to the 2016–2017 fiscal year, tens of millions, perhaps hundreds of millions, more would be needed for infrastructure and the wraparound care championed by Hanna-Attisha. If, as some residents demanded, *all* of the city's pipes were to be replaced, rather than just the lead service lines thought to be the main source of the lead problem, the bill could come to $1.5 billion for infrastructure alone. Given the available data on lead exposure, were the residents of Flint, much less all of the 150,000 people invoked by Hanna-Attisha, really entitled to the "so much" that she was calling for? More so, anyway, than fellow Michiganders who had similar, if not more serious, needs of their own?[7]

As Canfield pursued this line of reasoning, the atmosphere in the room grew palpably tense. People shifted uncomfortably in their seats. The activists in attendance, never shy about speaking out when they disagreed with something, were unusually quiet. Finally, in the middle of Canfield's disquisition, Hanna-Attisha broke in impatiently. The difference in Flint's case, she asserted, was that Flint had been *"poisoned by policy."*[8]

With these words, the audience erupted in a cathartic, prolonged cheer. As a flustered Canfield continued to plead the case of other lead-plagued cities, activists shouted *"Flint!* Flint first!"

Hanna-Attisha's riposte to Canfield—that Flint had not just been poisoned, but poisoned by *policy*—offers an instructive articulation of the view of the water crisis I will elaborate in the first part of this book: what made the crisis distinctive, what made it especially egregious, was not just *how badly* residents were harmed, but *how* they were harmed. The enthusiastic response her words elicited from the crowd attests to the popularity of this interpretation of the crisis in Flint itself. In fact, the argument was not, really, Hanna-Attisha's at all, though she made a point of elevating it in her public appearances: it was the argument the activists had been making about the crisis all along.

This is not to say that Flint activists were prepared to concede Canfield's point about the quantity of harm inflicted by the water. Using the same logic as Hanna-Attisha, they argued that the damage caused by lead was far worse than what was reflected in official lead poisoning statistics. They also pointed to health symptoms that went beyond anything that could be chalked up to the effects of lead alone, suggesting the presence of other contaminants in the water that were wreaking havoc on residents' bodies. Adding up all of the various harms popularly attributed to the water led many in Flint to the conclusion that they were victims of an injustice of historic proportions.

But as the exchange between Hanna-Attisha and Canfield illustrates, the argument that Flint had suffered an unfair share of harm relative to other communities (i.e., suffered a *distributive* injustice) was not always enough. The problem was not only that some harms could be downplayed by putting them into historical or comparative perspective. There was also the larger problem of demonstrating that causal links between contamination and health ailments existed at all. Those unsympathetic to worst-case-scenario analyses could always argue that there was an essential difference between potential harms and confirmed ones, or that existing data were not robust or reliable enough to support the full gamut of claims made about the water's effects. What advocates for Flint needed was a way of talking about harm qualitatively as well as quantitatively, in terms of origins as well as outcomes. Framing the crisis as a product of policy brought attention not just to *what* happened but to *how* it happened, to the context in which critical decisions about Flint's water supply, water treatment, and water infrastructure were made, and, ultimately, to the question of democracy.

Dilemmas of Distributive Justice

The discovery of lead in water and blood turned the Flint water crisis into a national news story in the fall of 2015. Flint became the centerpiece of a reinvigorated national discussion about aging infrastructure and served as a wake-up call about the lingering presence of lead in the urban environment. According to an oft-used metaphor, Flint was the canary in the national coal mine, a foreboding of crises to come if water systems were not upgraded and regulatory standards tightened. Many Flint residents took pride in the role the city played in raising this kind of awareness and potentially preventing future crises. "Because of Flint," Pastor Alfred Harris of Saints of God Church told me, "municipalities all over the country and the world began to take a look at their water and their infrastructure." For Harris, it was a sign of the Apostle Paul's assurance that "all things work together for good."[9]

But along with this pride came the burgeoning realization that Flint's lead woes were far from unique. Although the percentage of lead-poisoned children in Flint was higher than the nationwide average (estimated by the Centers for Disease Control and Prevention [CDC] to be 2.5 percent), it was considerably lower than percentages found in thousands of other cities and neighborhoods across the country. As a flurry of articles began to appear comparing Flint to other municipalities, its blood lead levels became the

standard by which other cities measured the severity of their own lead problems. Reuters, which carried out the most extensive analysis, concluded not
only that Flint was "no aberration" but that it "doesn't even rank among
the most dangerous lead hotspots in America." Looking at blood test results
in census tracts and zip codes in twenty-one states, Reuters found nearly
three thousand areas with lead poisoning rates "at least double" those in
Flint during the peak of the water crisis. More than eleven hundred of these
had rates "at least four times higher." In Flint's most affected ward, Ward
5, the percentage of children age 0 to 5 with elevated blood lead levels got
as high as 16 percent—one of the points made by Dr. Hanna-Attisha as a
rejoinder to Rep. Canfield. But in some parts of the country—in forty-nine
census tracts in Pennsylvania alone, for example—upward of 40 percent of
children have similarly high levels.[10]

Some also compared Flint favorably to what was arguably its closest parallel in the recent history of water contamination events: the Washington,
D.C., lead-in-water crisis of the early 2000s. In D.C., a well-intentioned
change in the city's water treatment process from chlorine disinfectant to
chloramine turned out to have a corrosive effect on lead pipes, causing
lead levels to spike starting around spring 2001. Virginia Tech professor
Marc Edwards, whose intimate involvement in the D.C. crisis presaged his
intervention in Flint, estimated that the resulting harms to human health
were twenty to thirty times worse than those suffered by Flint residents.
As the local water utility, the Environmental Protection Agency (EPA), and
the CDC resisted acknowledging the problem and taking action, D.C. residents were, he said, exposed to "astronomical" levels of lead for 3.5 years.[11]
Hundreds of young children between the ages of one and six were lead
poisoned, and lead exposure may have contributed to as many as two thousand miscarriages and two hundred fetal deaths.[12]

Despite the severity of the D.C. crisis, the facts took much longer to come
to light there than in Flint, a process stalled by obfuscation on the part of
government agencies but also by debates over whether lead in water was
much of a health threat at all.[13] In the meantime, the harms were ambiguous
enough that in April 2004, the *Washington Times* could deride the "ongoing
hysteria" about lead in the water, calling it "much ado about nothing."[14]
In Flint, similar sentiments denying outright the existence of a crisis were
expressed, in a few notable instances, even after the basic facts about lead
exposure were known. Conservative political analyst and part-time Flint

resident Bill Ballenger argued in January 2016 that the crisis was "nowhere near as bad" as the media was making it out to be, going so far as to question whether the whole thing wasn't some kind of politically motivated "hoax."[15] Later that year, Michigan Department of Environmental Quality (MDEQ) Chief Deputy Director Jim Sygo remarked that the crisis had been "over-played" and was "more created than anything else," citing comparable lead problems as nearby as Grand Rapids and Kalamazoo. Like Ballenger, he sug-gested that there were "ulterior motives at play," and accused Dr. Lawrence Reynolds, a well-known advocate for residents on the Governor's Flint Water Task Force and Flint Water Interagency Coordinating Committee, of a calcu-lated ploy to brand the situation an ongoing "crisis" so as to secure resources for the city.[16]

Ballenger and Sygo were roundly condemned for their comments,[17] but they had spoken at least a partial truth: the people fighting for Flint *were* invested in creating and maintaining a sense of crisis around the water situ-ation. The struggle for clean water began, after all, as a struggle to convince officials as well as the general public that a crisis existed at all.[18] Early evi-dence of water quality problems brought forward by residents was dismissed as anecdotal, falsified, or irrelevant to considerations of public health. Con-firmed problems at particular homes were brushed off as anomalies. Flint's water activists knew that getting Flint off the river meant making the case that the water posed serious, pressing, and systemic threats to residents. They began speaking of a water "crisis" when the local media would only put the term in scare quotes, and many months before confirmation of system-wide lead contamination.[19]

The battle over terminology did not end there. After the existence of a "cri-sis" was generally acknowledged, a debate emerged over whether that descrip-tor would trigger the necessary state and federal assistance. During the mayoral race of 2015, incumbent Dayne Walling and challenger Karen Weaver, who had won the support of many activists as a fellow "water warrior," clashed over whether the city should declare an "emergency" in the hopes of prompt-ing similar declarations at the state and federal levels. Upon winning the election, Weaver fulfilled her campaign promise to make such a declaration, triggering the hoped-for chain reaction and prompting the deployment of the National Guard and $5 million in emergency federal funds.

Activists were not satisfied with the "emergency" declaration, however. They had taken to describing the situation as a "disaster," a term embodying their demand that Flint be declared a federal disaster area, thereby opening up the possibility of more federal assistance. In this matter they were, atypically, on the same side as Governor Snyder, who petitioned the Obama administration for a disaster declaration in January 2016.[20] In Snyder's case, the request was almost certainly a matter of political optics, made in the knowledge that Stafford Act stipulations limit federal disaster aid to "natural" disasters. The activists, however, took the demand quite seriously, insisting that some sort of exception could be made,[21] and over the next two years they persisted in using the term "disaster" as a means of keeping this demand alive.

The declaration, however, never came, and even the federal "emergency" expired in August 14, 2016. As officials, citing dropping lead levels, began to claim that Flint water was as safe as water anywhere else in the country, the debate over whether the city was in "crisis" at all resurfaced. Activists feared a declaration of mission accomplished would mean that Flint would fade from the national spotlight, that the State of Michigan would discontinue emergency water relief, that the damaged pipes would remain in the ground, and that residents with lingering concerns would find themselves marginalized all over again. What began as a struggle to create a sense of crisis evolved, then, into a struggle to ensure that the crisis was not pronounced over prematurely.

To suggest that there was strategy behind the semantic interventions made by activists is not to imply that they were made in bad faith. I found no evidence that the people insisting that Flint was experiencing a "crisis," "emergency," or "disaster" did not genuinely believe it to be true. Granted, their assessments did not always rest on a robust comparative perspective: some were content with the knowledge that Flint's problems were bad enough, in an absolute sense, to require immediate and decisive action, and viewed comparisons to other cities as a "distraction."[22] But the idea that the harm done to Flint was unusually or even uniquely bad repeatedly cropped up as a justification for giving the city special priority in the distribution of state and federal resources. Some of the activists took to describing what was going on in Flint as "the largest public health disaster in the history of this country."[23]

Claiming that Flint had it worse than other cities brought the water crisis under the umbrella of distributive justice.[24] Within an environmental justice framework, distributive justice refers to the distribution of benefit and harm that people derive from their environments, under the assumption that no one is inherently entitled to more benefit, or less harm, than others. A distributive *in*justice exists either when one group benefits disproportionately from environmental goods or when there is "inequity in the distribution of environmental risks," and/or confirmed harms.[25] Diagnosing a distributive injustice in this latter sense is dependent on being able to quantify in some measure the risks faced and harms incurred. This quantification is especially critical when it is used to determine the amount of resources needed to rectify an injustice.[26]

Quantification of harm cannot take place in the abstract, for harms do not exist in a vacuum; they are visited upon flesh-and-blood people likely to be impacted in different ways, and to different degrees, by the same harm depending upon their circumstances. A child in good health, with a strong social support network and many opportunities, will be less impacted by lead poisoning than a child inhaling polluted air, attending an underfunded school, and focused on day-to-day survival rather than self-realization. A holistic view of the life chances of Flint children suggests that any lead-induced deficit they experience will, on average, be more consequential than a similar deficit in a city like Grand Rapids or Kalamazoo. Residents had an intuitive sense of this: I observed much distress over the thought that an entire generation of children already fighting the odds would be set back *further*, even if only by a notch.

Any application of the principle of distributive justice, then, must be cognizant of the relativity of harm, factoring in the context in which harms occur, the characteristics of the people to whom they occur, and the cumulative impact of multiple harms. But, of course, one must also show that the harms exist in the first place. The difficulty posed by environmental contamination is that concrete linkages between exposure and public health outcomes can be hard to trace.[27] Often it is difficult to establish even a simple correlation between increases in exposure to contaminants and increases in symptoms, due to a lack of the data necessary to make firm before-and-after comparisons. Hard evidence of causal relationships can be even more elusive. The resulting ambiguity sets the stage for disputes among experts about the extent of the harm, as well as conflicts between experts and laypeople. When quantifiable scientific evidence of harm is underwhelming, it often clashes with the public's sense that much greater harms *must* have occurred.

Sometimes uncertainty can actually be a boon to those who wish to argue that an environmental crisis is worse than officially acknowledged. As detailed earlier, uncertainty around lead exposure was the basis of Mona

Hanna-Attisha's exhortation to err on the side of caution by offering maximal assistance to everyone conceivably exposed. It also allowed residents to attribute a wide array of health and behavioral problems to lead, the power of their stories often overshadowing caveats about medical plausibility. Despite admonitions from doctors (including Hanna-Attisha) that the effects of lead poisoning are typically "invisible," or visible only over the long term, many parents in Flint believed they could already detect changes in their children: increased aggressiveness, impulsiveness, fatigue, forgetfulness. Reports started to appear of an epidemic of misbehavior in the schools, with some teachers saying they had never seen anything like it in all their years in the classroom. Speaking of her own family, Flint mother Tammy Loren captured a common sentiment, echoed in much of the media coverage of the crisis: "They're not the same kids."[28]

The same uncertainty that underpinned expansive attributions of harm could also, however, lend itself to far narrower interpretations of the damage done by the water that clung more tightly to strict probabilities and hard data. One number kicked around by skeptics like Rep. Canfield was "43," the number of residents (twenty-three of them young children) found to have lead poisoning during the surge of testing from October to December 2015—less than 2 percent of those tested.[29] It was a gross underestimate of past exposure to be sure, but still a vanishingly small figure when considered against Hanna-Attisha's plea on behalf of 150,000. Two years after Canfield and Hanna-Attisha's exchange, a paper published in the *Journal of Pediatrics* went even further, claiming that there was no statistically significant increase in blood lead levels in Flint in 2014 to 2015 at all, and that whatever lead exposure took place had never risen to "the level of an environmental emergency."[30] In response, Hanna-Attisha doubled down on her claim that the baby-formula factor meant that all existing data on blood lead levels massively underestimated exposure.[31] As the debate over the severity of the harm done by lead ramped up, spilling into the pages of the *New York Times*,[32] Flint activists grew increasingly concerned that an effort was underway to erase the crisis entirely. Appearing at a board of managers meeting at Hurley Medical Center in May 2018, they denounced a proposal by local doctors to describe Flint children as lead-*exposed* rather than lead-*poisoned*, calling it "preposterous."[33]

If activists were concerned to ensure that the effects of lead were not minimized, however, they were even more concerned to make another point:

there was much more to be worried about in Flint than lead alone. In fact, it is no exaggeration to say that for the activists, as for many other members of the community, the Flint water crisis *was never a lead-in-water crisis*—at least not *only* that, not nearly. The "crisis" was the sum total of everything that residents had suffered since the switch to the river in 2014, and were likely to suffer in the future as a result of compromised health and degraded infrastructure. It included, of course, whatever harms lead was responsible for and the costs associated with removing lead from the water system. But it included much more, too: a plethora of physical ailments residents blamed on other contaminants, the profound psychological burden caused by the crisis, and damage to personal property and to parts of the water system not directly associated with lead. Whenever the tendency to frame the water crisis as a lead crisis obscured its other consequences, or inspired declarations that the crisis was over, it became, as we will see, a target of the activists.

If looking at the crisis in its totality offered a richer portrait of harm, however, it did not necessarily eliminate ambiguity around the causes and quantities of particular harms. Surrounding each aspect of the crisis mentioned above was a similar tug-of-war between worst- and best-case interpretations of what the water had wrought. When residents were alerted to the presence of high levels of carcinogenic chlorine byproducts (total trihalomethanes) in the water in January 2015, for example, it became common to blame them for a host of skin and lung problems, as well as miscarriages and cancers of various kinds. But officials countered by pointing out that levels had only been above the federal maximum of 80 parts per billion (ppb) for about six months (the highest reading coming in at 99 ppb) and that for most people exposure to the chemicals was only risky if it took place over many years. Similarly, the popular belief that Flint was in the grip of an epidemic of rashes and other skin problems—even after the reconnection to Detroit water—was challenged by a CDC study that could not confirm that rashes were more prevalent in Flint than elsewhere (at least by 2016) or establish with any certainty that what rashes did exist were caused by the water.[34]

It was harder for officials to brush aside the news that broke in January 2016: during the eighteen months when Flint was on the river, Flint and Genesee County had experienced one of the worst outbreaks of Legionnaires' Disease (a severe form of pneumonia caused by the waterborne bacterium *Legionella pneumophila*) in U.S. history, resulting in at least twelve deaths. The failure to alert the public to the outbreak when it was still ongoing became the basis of involuntary manslaughter charges filed against several state officials. But here, too, there was plenty to argue about. The state maintained that the cause of the outbreak was not the water source switch but rather a maintenance lapse at McLaren Hospital, one of Flint's two major healthcare facilities. A retrospective analysis led by Sammy Zahran and Shawn McElmurry, however, suggested otherwise, demonstrating that 80 percent of Legionnaires' cases in 2014 to 2015 could be explained by the switch and revealing a strong correlation between contraction of the disease and low household chlorine residuals.[35] In response, the state dismissed the conclusions, accusing the research (despite having funded it) of having "numerous flaws."[36]

Even if one accepted that the source switch was the cause of the outbreak (the activists' feeling on the subject was something like "*duh*"), there was still a debate to be had over how many people were sickened and killed. Legionnaires' is a notoriously underdiagnosed disease, often mistaken within clinical settings for generic pneumonia, and some research in Flint suggested that the serogroup of legionella most prevalent there was especially liable to be missed in urine antigen tests.[37] It was entirely possible, then, that at least some of the 177 people in the area who died from "pneumonia" between spring 2014 and fall 2015 were in fact Legionnaires' victims.[38] The worst-case interpretation of the data favored by activists (who were suspicious that misdiagnoses were part of a "cover-up"), held that *many* of these people had died from Legionnaires', and that many more who had been diagnosed with pneumonia and survived had probably had the disease too. At the other end of the spectrum, however, the state contested even the two cases chosen as the basis of the involuntary manslaughter charges, arguing that these residents had actually died of other health conditions.[39]

The psychological harms suffered by Flint residents sparked another kind of debate.[40] Although even harder to quantify with any exactness,[41] these harms were everywhere in evidence, and there was little doubt they were severe. Residents faced feelings of guilt for having unwittingly exposed their loved ones to injury, and anxiety for their children's futures. They faced feelings of uncertainty and constant vulnerability, never sure what would emerge from their taps and uneasy within their own homes. They faced the loneliness of avoidance by friends and family wary of visiting. They faced feelings of anger, grief, depression, despair. They faced the fatigue of having to trek daily to water distribution sites and open their doors repeatedly to aid workers and researchers. Then there was the catastrophic breakdown in trust—trust in political and scientific authorities, trust between members of the community, trust in the future. There was the humiliation of having paid for one's own poisoning. There were the children who learned to think of themselves as irreversibly damaged, less capable than their peers. There was the triggering of historical traumas within the African American community in particular, as residents found in their present-day travails echoes of past abuses like the Tuskegee Experiment, pogroms, and Jim Crow. There was the general feeling that the people of Flint didn't matter.[42]

Although these effects of the crisis were not in dispute, there was some controversy over who was to blame for them. The "kicking and screaming" that was necessary to get officials to take action, wrote Kevin Drum of *Mother Jones*, led to vast overstatements of the physical trauma residents, and especially children, had experienced. The claim that "irreversible brain damage" had been "inflicted on every single child in Flint" (to quote filmmaker Michael Moore) was "panicking children into thinking they've been turned into idiots."[43] Marc Edwards, similarly, lamented that turning the crisis into a political battleground had made Flint children into victims twice over, casting them as the tragic figures in a "victim narrative" premised on the assumption that "their lives will be less fulfilling, less productive."[44] He also suggested repeatedly that the activists themselves were stoking fear, uncertainty, and mistrust in Flint by promulgating scientifically dubious claims about contaminants in the water beyond lead and unfairly impugning the motives of the scientific authorities and political officials who were trying to help (a subject taken up at greater length in chapter 7).

Moving beyond bodies and minds, the damage done by the water to Flint's infrastructure was perhaps the most tangible of all, but even here there was room for disagreement. Edwards estimated that during the city's eighteen months on Flint River water, its pipes—many already overdue for replacement—aged the equivalent of at least ten years.[45] No one argued with that assessment, but gauging its implications meant deciding what all needed to come out of the ground. If the pipes could be "healed," as Edwards maintained, there was little reason to spend tens of millions of dollars to replace them, at least not urgently. On the other hand, if the activists were right to demand, as they sometimes did, that the whole water system be replaced, the bill could run as high as $4 billion—the estimated cost of excavating and replacing every pipe in the city plus rebuilding aboveground.[46]

Then there was the matter of damage inside homes. As one would expect, the corrosive water took a toll on interior plumbing, fixtures, and appliances like hot water heaters and washing machines—damage estimated at $310 million.[47] But how was an individual homeowner to prove that any particular component of their household infrastructure was destroyed by the water? Did my ten-year-old hot water heater burst in 2016 because of corrosion caused by eighteen months of river water, or would it have happened anyway? There was even doubt about the effects of the water crisis on overall home values, which everyone expected would plummet below even their abysmally low starting point. Residents frequently asserted that, because of the crisis, their homes were worth little to nothing, and at least one analysis found that "Zip Codes in Flint witnessed a 24 percent reduction in the number of homes sold, a 13 percent reduction in inventories (or homes listed for sale), and a 14 percent reduction in the average price of transacted homes" following the city's declaration of emergency.[48] Confusingly, however, it was reported on multiple occasions that values actually went up rather than down during the crisis years.[49]

Even if one consistently adopts a best-case perspective, sizing up the totality of harm attributable to Flint's contaminated water can be a bewildering task, and it is hard not to conclude, with the activists, that from April 2014 onward Flint residents underwent an ordeal unlike anything most Americans have ever experienced. For all of the reasons mentioned, however, rooting activist demands in distributive claims was not always sufficient. Skeptics could argue that the water was not, in fact, the source of most of the ills attributed to it, that some harms (particularly psychological ones) were the fault of the activists themselves, and that Flint's bid for priority in the distribution of scarce resources was unpersuasive given the existence of equivalent needs, or worse, in other cities. The naysayers surfaced only occasionally in public discourse and were usually drowned out by the overarching consensus that Flint was a national embarrassment that called for quick and decisive remedial action. But the general feeling among activists was that behind the scenes, particularly at the state level, the belief that the crisis was overblown was very much an influence on the thinking of officials.

This is why it was so critical that when pressed as to why Flint should come "first," Flint's water warriors always had an answer in reserve, an answer that could trump any attempt to play up the ambiguities and uncertainties of the crisis and play down its harms. The reason why the Flint water crisis was different from other crises, why it was especially heinous, why it deserved to be a state and national priority, was that Flint was not just poisoned, but poisoned by *policy*. It was poisoned because residents were stripped of their self-determination and rendered vulnerable to the criminal neglect of the state. Looking beyond the outcomes of the crisis to its origins led to the conclusion that the distributive injustices inflicted—however one cared to rank them with respect to their severity—were the products of prior injustices related to the denial of democracy.

Justice and Democracy: Beyond Distribution

Flint activists knew that without establishing clear lines of responsibility for the water crisis, no amount of demonstrable harm would result in the help the city needed. They knew, in other words, that their calls for justice had to have a "retributive" aspect, pointing not just to wrongs but to wrongdoers who could be held accountable for rectifying those wrongs. At the most general level, the activists demanded that those responsible "fix" what they "broke," but also, on occasion, that they be arrested and imprisoned. In some cases this was phrased as a blanket demand that "people should go to jail for what's happened"[50] or even that "they should all go to jail."[51] In others, it was phrased as a focused demand that singled out specific actors, particularly Governor Snyder.[52]

Just as activists' claims about harms caused by contamination were locked in a dialectic with official proclamations about the safety of the water, their attributions of blame for the crisis were made within a context shaped by officials' attempts to deny or minimize their own culpability. In the early days of the crisis especially, there was much passing of the buck back and forth between officials at various levels of government. By the beginning of 2016, the State of Michigan had officially accepted primary responsibility and Snyder had personally apologized for the crisis. But as explored in the next chapter, his insistence on framing the crisis as the result of a technical blunder caused by a few "career bureaucrats" had the effect of narrowing the scope of the state's responsibility as much as possible.[53]

When Michigan Attorney General Bill Schuette launched a criminal investigation into the crisis on January 15, it initially appeared that his focus would be equally narrow.[54] He first brought charges against some of the very "bureaucrats" referenced by Snyder—relatively low-level employees at the MDEQ and Michigan Department of Health and Human Services, as well as some of their collaborators at the city level. The charges were serious enough—they included misconduct in office, tampering with evidence, and conspiracy—and few denied that they were well deserved. But Schuette's choice of targets could also be seen as sacrificial scapegoating intended to draw attention away from the real power players. In an interview on MSNBC, activist Melissa Mays praised the charges but expressed her hope that Flint's emergency managers and Snyder would be next, because "at the end of the day, they're the ones that made the decisions."[55]

Few actually believed that Schuette would make the leap from prosecuting bureaucrats to prosecuting high-profile political appointees of the Governor, much less the Governor himself. But Mays's wish was at least partially fulfilled when, in December 2016, Schuette announced felony charges against two of Flint's four emergency managers, Darnell Earley and Jerry Ambrose. The charges focused on their involvement in financial finagling that set the City of Flint on a course to join the Karegnondi water pipeline project and created pressure to use the Flint River as a cost-saving water source in the interim (a story told in Chapter 3). But in the charges some saw glimmers of a broader critique of the emergency manager system as a whole: Schuette chastised Earley and Ambrose for having "put balance sheets ahead of Flint residents," taking what appeared to be a shot at the philosophy of fiscal austerity at the heart of the emergency manager law. Flint Mayor Karen Weaver depicted the charges as a welcome repudiation of the system that had "taken the voice of the people and taken our democracy,"[56] and Congressman Dan Kildee called them "an indictment not only of [the emergency managers'] decisions, but an indictment against the administration's failed emergency manager law that contributed to this crisis."[57] Statements like these implied that the crimes allegedly committed by Earley and Ambrose were not just misdeeds by bad actors, but products of the political context created by emergency management. This claim—the claim that emergency management, by eliminating democracy, enabled or even encouraged decision makers to act abusively and recklessly—was central to what I will later call the "political" narrative of the crisis.

There is a long history of tracing the roots of environmental injustices back to questions of popular influence over and involvement in decision-making processes. Although much of the focus of the early environmental justice movement was on distributive injustices—particularly the disparate health burdens borne by poor, majority-minority communities living near polluting facilities[58]—concerns about popular exclusion from decision making were also prominent. They reflected the belief, in Iris Marion Young's words, that democratic decision-making procedures are both "an element and condition of" social justice more broadly.[59] As an "element" of justice, democracy entered into some of the Principles of Environmental Justice developed at the First National People of Color Environmental Leadership Conference in 1991, including the right of all peoples to "political, economic, cultural, and environmental self-determination" and the right to "participate as equal partners at every level of decision making."[60] Since then, the emphasis on "procedural" justice (or conceptual cousins like "participatory" justice) within the environmental justice literature has only grown stronger.[61]

One major reason for this turn toward procedural justice is precisely the fact that distributive justice frameworks are often plagued by ambiguities that limit their power when applied to environmental contamination events. As we have seen, efforts to quantify exposure to contamination can be hamstrung by inadequate data and efforts to quantify harm can bog down in complex questions of causation, making it difficult or impossible to demonstrate disparate impacts. Furthermore, when outcomes are shaped by a diverse set of actors operating more or less independently, as well as by underlying sociological factors like race and poverty, it can be hard to pin down who, exactly, is to blame for them. For these reasons, legal claims dependent on proving disparate distributional impacts have had difficulty getting much traction within the American legal system, which usually demands hard evidence of cause and effect, and, in cases of alleged discrimination, identifiable culprits acting out of ill intent.[62]

The benefits of being able to appeal to procedural justice when evidence of distributive injustice is insufficient is perhaps nowhere better illustrated than in the second-most important environmental justice story ever to come out of Flint: the case of the Genesee Power Station. In the early 1990s, the predecessor of the MDEQ, the Michigan Department of Natural Resources (MDNR), received a permit application for a wood-burning incinerator, to be sited in Genesee Township just over the border from Flint. Whereas Genesee Township itself was overwhelmingly white, the closest neighborhood to the proposed site was predominantly African American and already surrounded by several other polluting facilities. The community's biggest concern about the incinerator was that it would contaminate the air with lead as it burned wood coated in lead-based paint from demolished homes—in an area, moreover, where blood lead levels were above average to begin with.[63]

In response to the proposal, a group led by Father Phil Schmitter and Sister Joanne Chiaverini of Flint's St. Francis Prayer Center took the innovative step of filing a Title VI claim with the EPA alleging that the siting of the plant constituted environmental racism and violated residents' civil rights. The first part of their claim focused on the distributive injustice of the plant siting, given its proximity to an already-vulnerable and disadvantaged population and the likelihood that it would cause disproportionate harm. The second part of their claim, however, focused on the process by which the permit had been approved. Permit hearings had been poorly publicized and held as far away as Lansing, causing logistical headaches for residents of limited means who wanted to attend them. At one key hearing, residents were given insufficient time to review proposed changes to the permit before the public comment period, and when the meeting ran long, several white speakers were allowed to give their testimony out of order to accommodate schedule conflicts while black speakers were not accorded the same courtesy. When the MDNR finally got around to holding a more accessible meeting near the incinerator site, it employed uniformed and armed officers to watch over the proceedings—a decision, the complaint alleged, that contradicted the department's usual practice and was tinged with racial bias. And although the crowd was by all accounts civil, officials ended the meeting abruptly in the middle of testimony by an African American resident.

The activists responsible for the discrimination claim would have to wait two-and-a-half decades for a decision by the EPA, a delay that was widely seen as a sign of the agency's shameful disregard of civil rights. In fact, the EPA had not entirely ignored the complaint, making a concerted effort to evaluate the activists' claims of disparate impact. But given the incinerator's proximity to other toxic facilities, among other confounding variables, it had found the matter to be too complex to settle conclusively. It was unwilling, in other words, to say that the siting of the incinerator—which ultimately went forward despite community opposition—constituted a distributive injustice.

What the EPA did find, in an unexpected and virtually unprecedented ruling announced in January 2017, was that racial discrimination had occurred during the permitting process. African Americans, it concluded, had been "treated differently and less favorably than Whites."[64] The agency concurred with the activists' criticisms of the public hearings, but found that the problem was not just with a few poorly run meetings. Rather, on a structural level, the MDNR lacked the "procedural safeguards" required by nondiscrimination regulations,[65] as well as a defined plan for public participation.[66]

The ruling also suggested that when the MDNR became the MDEQ, it passed on these procedural shortcomings. In 2014, just before the water crisis rose to public attention, the EPA finally began to apply informal pressure to the MDEQ to address these longstanding issues. After its efforts were largely rebuffed, and after the department's oversights in Flint became a national scandal, the agency issued its long-awaited ruling, implying that the MDEQ's decades-long failure to take procedural justice seriously had contributed to the water crisis. In fact, as pointed out by the authors of the ruling, the crisis had spawned a new civil rights complaint that harkened back to the Genesee Power Station affair, raising "similar issues regarding public participation."[67] In response, the EPA promised to redouble its efforts to evaluate MDEQ's "procedures for public notification and involvement."[68]

In addition to inspiring heightened scrutiny of decision-making processes at the MDEQ, the water crisis also helped to revive a related effort to establish a statewide environmental justice plan that would create new inlets for popular influence at the state level.[69] An earlier effort in 2008 and 2009 to produce such a plan, which derailed after opposition from business and industry, included a proposal for an Interdepartmental Working Group at the state that would receive petitions about environmental matters directly from aggrieved residents and investigate the concerns they raised. According to environmental law expert Sara Gosman—one of the drafters of the plan—had the state implemented this recommendation the water crisis would have been "much less likely." The petition process, she maintains, "would have allowed Flint residents to elevate their concerns" and increased their chances of being taken seriously by state departments like the MDEQ.[70]

As illustrated by the above examples, one reason for invoking the principle of procedural justice is to bring attention to flaws in already-existing decision-making processes—a lack of nondiscrimination protections, for example, or a concrete participation plan, or a petition process. The EPA ruling in January 2017 and the formation of a new state-sponsored Environmental Justice Work Group the next month helped to spark discussion about how these kinds of flaws could be addressed in light of the water crisis, focusing on mechanisms for enhancing public influence over state government.[71]

From the perspective of Flint activists, however, concerns about flimsy procedural safeguards within state departments were trivial next to the real matter at hand: the state's complete suspension of democracy in Flint and the deeply unpopular decisions about water (and a great many other things) it enabled. The problem was not, then, just with surface-level "procedures" and the distributional inequities they produced, but with the structurally disempowered position the city found itself in and the political-economic philosophy that had shaped it. The activists' emphasis on democracy, in other words, took them beyond the kinds of concerns that environmental justice activists are sometimes accused of getting hung up on, fostering a wider-ranging analysis of the origins of the crisis. Because the political architecture that activists blamed for Flint's poisoned water was a creation of Governor Snyder and other state politicians, this analysis added extra weight to the claim that the state should put Flint "first." But just as important, it meant the fight for justice in Flint could not stop at reparations, or criminal convictions, or modest reforms to state permitting processes. The fight would not be over until democracy was a reality: not just in the negative sense of freedom from emergency management, but in the positive sense of a community of people empowered to take charge of their water, their infrastructure, their health, their city, and their future.

2 How Did It Happen? Two Tales of the Origins of the Crisis

As the eyes of the nation began to turn toward Flint in the fall of 2015, expressions of outrage were accompanied by a logical enough question: *how*, in the United States of America, in the twenty-first century, had it come to pass that citizens were being poisoned by their own tap water? The query provoked a proliferation of water crisis timelines over the ensuing months, as journalists endeavored to offer their readers some context, tracing the crisis back to its origins and giving it a narrative arc. In the vernacular of journalism, sculpting a chronology of the crisis was part of a broader obligation to get to the "truth" of what happened. Assembling "as complete a picture of the Flint water disaster as can reasonably be provided," wrote *Bridge Magazine*'s "Truth Squad" in introducing its own timeline, would enable readers to sort "fact from fiction and spin from credible analysis." A "complete" picture of the water crisis would offer not just the truth, but the *whole* truth, capturing the "full weight, detail, and step-by-step context" of the crisis "all in one place and in one narrative."[1]

The idea that there was a "whole truth" of the Flint water crisis waiting to be uncovered through determined fact-finding was a common—and perhaps predictable—component of journalistic accounts of the crisis. Epistemologically, it suggested the possibility of a neutral, omniscient vantage point from which every component of the crisis could be surveyed comprehensively and objectively. It also, however, played a powerful rhetorical role in demands for political accountability. The progressive media group Progress Michigan, for example, appealed to Flint residents' right to know the "whole truth" when it sent a Freedom of Information Act request to Governor Snyder in January 2016 demanding that he release his emails from 2013 forward.[2] In a similar vein, at the first Congressional hearing on the water crisis the next month, Representative Elijah Cummings thundered at the Michigan Department of Environmental Quality (MDEQ) interim head Keith Creagh that he wanted "the truth, the whole truth, and nothing but the truth," accusing Creagh of helping Snyder to dodge blame for the crisis. When Snyder initially declined to offer his own Congressional testimony, Representative Dan Kildee called the decision "deeply disappointing," insisting that Snyder make himself available for questioning "so that the whole truth can be found."[3]

One possible way of depicting the struggle over the "truth" of the water crisis would be to frame it as a quest by crusading truth seekers—journalists after the "facts," residents, activists, and their allies in search of "answers"—to wrest it from mendacious elites or expose truths overlooked by others. There is certainly something to be said for this characterization. There *were*, after all, numerous instances of obfuscation and spin on the part of officials, several of whom found themselves facing felony charges for what was widely reported as a "cover-up."[4] There were also critical moments when activists, with the support of members of the medical and scientific communities, fundamentally altered the discourse around the water by bringing new information to light and fighting back against those who sought to discredit it.

But, ultimately, any simplistic dichotomy that pits agents of truth against purveyors of falsehood breaks down. Although the concept of "whole" and impartial truth was espoused as a journalistic ideal and used to ground certain demands for political accountability, in reality those who sought to contest official narratives of the crisis answered back not with an exhaustive compendium of "facts," but with *counter*-narratives. The reason the world came to know of the water crisis, maintained Flint activist Nayyirah Shariff, was that the "grassroots resistance" had countered proclamations about the safety of the water with a narrative of its "own."[5] When Shariff used the term "narrative" in this sense, she did so more broadly than I do here. To capture Shariff's meaning, I prefer to speak of a "discourse" around the water, within which officials framed Flint's water quality as a nonissue (at least prior to October 2015 and again after lead levels returned to "normal") and activists framed it as a public health crisis (or, more commonly, "disaster"). However, within that discursive struggle, the *narrative* of the water crisis—understood more narrowly as an account of how it unfolded—was a central point of contention. Shariff often spoke of the importance of promoting a grassroots "narrative" of the crisis in this narrower sense as well, one that reinforced activist demands by assigning blame to the proper people and policies and that featured residents and activists as the main protagonists.

The relevant point here, though, is that counternarratives are narratives, too. Although fighting to get them accepted may involve bringing suppressed "truths" out into the open, it is not the same thing as impartially pursuing the "whole" truth. Narratives are, by necessity—by definition, in fact—selective, notwithstanding *Bridge Magazine*'s pretentions to an all-encompassing narrative of the crisis.[6] Of course, there are important differences between narrators who strive to be inclusive and honest and those who are deliberately partial and duplicitous. And the narratives narrators relate may be more or less "true" when measured against external criteria of truth—we do, after all, dismiss some narratives as "false." But even narratives that are, by relative standards, "true" are constructed through omissions as well as inclusions, through arrangement and emphasis, through decisions about where the story begins and where it ends. The shape narratives take is influenced, furthermore, not only by the objectives of the narrator, but also by the narrator's perception of the expectations and aptitudes of her audience. And even the most scrupulous narrators are limited by imperfect information and unconscious biases. For all of these reasons, any narrative of the water crisis is an act of interpretation rather than neutral reportage, even when narrators strive to speak of what "really happened."[7]

Naturally, if our objective is to construct an accurate account of what happened in Flint, weighing the relative veracity of different narratives of the crisis matters. When one approaches narratives from the vantage point of social and political struggle, however, asking how true they are is often less meaningful than asking how *useful* they are to specific actors. And the utility of a particular narrative is sometimes inversely related to its accuracy and objectivity. This is clear enough when we consider official narratives spun to deflect responsibility and manage popular perceptions. But counterhegemonic narratives, too, incorporate strategic elisions and calculated points of emphasis. We would be foolish to expect those engaged in a struggle for their lives and livelihoods to make impartiality an absolute value.

This does not mean we should expect to find activists embracing outright deceit. What is more common is the idea that "we" who struggle have "our" truth—a truth rooted in our experiences, a truth that may serve as an antidote to the falsehoods perpetrated by others, but a truth with a small "t," tacitly tailored to our needs and objectives. By extension, the tale activists tell of how things came to be as they are, and why action is imperative, is not an attempt to relay the "whole" story but, rather, to construct a representation of social reality that justifies and buttresses a particular struggle.[8]

The fight for clean water in Flint began as a fight over perceptions of social reality—with officials, on one hand, proclaiming that there was no cause for alarm, and activists, on the other, insisting that the city was in the midst of a "crisis."[9] Once the existence of a crisis was generally acknowledged, the narrative of how it happened became a critical site of struggle. In chapter 1, I argued that directing attention to the "how" of the crisis was a useful way of getting around the ambiguities of a distributive justice framework and raising questions of procedure, participation, and democracy. In this chapter, I argue that answering the "how" question the "right" (or at least most useful) way was an essential means of creating a discursive framework in which the claims and demands made by activists took on meaning and power—not least because a robust account of how the crisis happened implied answers to subsidiary questions like *when* the crisis began, *who* was chiefly responsible, and *what* should be done to solve it and prevent future crises.

Advocating for the narrative favored by Flint's water activists—what I will call the "political" narrative of the crisis—would not have been a struggle without its coming up against competing narratives that offered different answers to the same questions. In what follows, I focus on two in particular. The first is what I will call the "technical" narrative. Briefly, the technical narrative framed the crisis narrowly as a product of faulty water treatment caused by technical incompetence. It placed the start of the crisis at the first infusion of improperly treated water into Flint's pipes, identified those directly overseeing the water system as the principal culprits, and proposed short-term solutions to the crisis focused on adjustments to water treatment processes. For longer-term solutions, the narrative recommended repair or replacement of damaged infrastructure and more consistent enforcement and/or tightening of water regulations. The second narrative, which I will call the "historical" narrative, was considerably broader in scope. It pushed the origins of the crisis back into Flint's early history, attributing the contemporary vulnerability of the city to a wide range of racial, economic, and political dynamics operating over many decades, and arguing that the response to the crisis had to address these deeper structural factors.

To say that these narratives are in "competition" with the political narrative of the crisis risks giving the wrong impression, because I do not mean to suggest that they are logically incompatible with it. In fact, in many ways all three narratives are symbiotic, and separating them out is, to some extent, artificial. Furthermore, preferring one need not mean dismissing the others. It is entirely possible to stress the political causes of the crisis while acknowledging the technical and historical aspects of the crisis.

But the logical compatibility of different narratives is, like their truth value, not always what matters most in practice. In practice, placing emphasis on one or another account of the crisis's origins had important consequences. The narrative one chose to foreground committed one to either an expansive or a narrow view of the scope of the crisis and the proper response to it. It created a backdrop for the indictment or exoneration of specific individuals whose actions or inactions arguably contributed to the crisis. And it established the parameters within which one could claim either that the crisis was approaching an end or that more work remained to be done.[10]

The Technical Narrative of the Crisis

One can find a consensual core of technical details in almost every account of the water crisis. All are agreed that the water drawn from the Flint River between April 2014 and October 2015 and treated at the Flint Water Treatment Plant was more corrosive than the Lake Huron water Flint was used to receiving, corrosive enough to destroy the protective mineral crust, or "passivation layer," that normally prevents water from coming into direct contact with the pipes that carry it. This allowed the water to begin eroding the pipes themselves, producing the dramatic oranges and browns of iron corrosion, opening up pinhole leaks in galvanized pipes, and releasing lead in both soluble and particulate form from the city's thousands of lead service lines, as well as from lead solder and brass fixtures.[11] The disruption of the system also broke up the "biofilm" that forms on the inner surface of pipes, liberating the bacteria that grow there. Combined with the smorgasbord of iron, which serves as food for microbes, the potential for contaminants to enter the system through holes, and difficulties maintaining consistent chlorine residuals throughout the city, this created an environment in which bacterial growth was difficult to keep under control.[12]

These basic facts are, for all intents and purposes, beyond dispute. What I am calling the "technical" narrative of the crisis, however, begins much more controversially. It begins with the claim that Flint River water, for all the damage it did to the city's infrastructure, could have been rendered harmless with the right kind of treatment. This claim clashed, of course, with the commonsensical view residents had of the river as broken beyond repair. Initially even some experts had doubts. When researchers from Virginia Tech first traveled to Flint in August 2015, they took samples of the river and questioned whether its corrosivity could ever have been adequately neutralized.[13] The conclusion they ultimately reached, however, was that there was nothing in the river water "that proper treatment couldn't render potable."[14] Other water experts agreed.[15] According to the technical narrative, then, the crisis had its origins not in a water *source* problem but in a water *treatment* problem.

What, then, went wrong at the Flint Water Treatment Plant? The answer, in its pithiest form, is that rather than counteracting the natural corrosivity of the water, the treatment process employed while Flint was on the river actually exacerbated it. Delving into the details, however, reveals a rather more complicated story, one that is hard to piece together because of spotty data on day-to-day operations at the plant. In the most authoritative account yet assembled, Susan Masten, Simon Davies, and Shawn McElmurry reveal that ferric chloride added to help settle out organic contaminants increased the water's already high level of chloride by 28 percent to 100 percent. Other aspects of the treatment process, they show, had the effect of lowering the pH of the water and making it more acidic, another factor in its overall corrosivity.

In his own assessment of the water distributed by the treatment plant in 2014 and 2015, Virginia Tech's Marc Edwards concluded that "any competent person should have seen this water will eat up iron and eat up lead."[16] The picture that emerges from Masten, Davies, and McElmurry's account, however, is one in which the requisite skills, experience, and preparation were in short supply at the plant. Utility operators used to receiving stable, treated lake water were all of the sudden asked to oversee the treatment of water that was not only more corrosive, but also highly variable and unpredictable. Lacking a clear treatment plan, they were forced to resort to *ad hoc* improvisation. Masten and her coauthors found that there were no "treatability studies on which to determine chemical dosages until late August

2015," and that "plant personnel were left to attempt to address the plethora of complex water quality issues and complaints by trial and error. Significant changes were made to chemical dosages, and the reasons for these changes were often not apparent."[17] Thanks in part to this inconsistency, the switch to the river introduced chaos into the water system.

Despite the higher degree of complexity involved in treating river water, however, the technical narrative holds that the change in water source would have been deemed a "success" (as Marc Edwards put it[18]) if some simple changes had been made to the treatment process. Above all, what was missing was what water engineers call "optimized" corrosion control. The water that Flint had received previously came pretreated by the Detroit Water and Sewerage Department with orthophosphates, which bind to metal and coat pipes as they travel through the water system, reinforcing the passivation layer. An adequate dose of these chemicals should, in theory, shield pipes from any ill effect from corrosive source water. However, the water sent out to Flint residents from the treatment plant had no orthophosphates or any other corrosion inhibitor.[19]

Why the MDEQ, which was advising the plant on its treatment process, did not mandate the use of corrosion control is a question that has never been answered satisfactorily. As the MDEQ saw it, after a system switched to new source water, the federal Lead and Copper Rule (LCR) allowed for two six-month periods of monitoring before determining that a corrosion inhibitor was necessary. This monitoring was, at least in the short term, the extent of the MDEQ's plan to comply with the LCR. Later, after the MDEQ came under fire for its role in the crisis, it protested that the addition of lime to the water—part of the water softening process—amounted to a kind of corrosion control. Marc Edwards, however, scoffed at this explanation and proceeded to show through an analysis of pH that the water had in fact grown increasingly corrosive as lime was added.[20]

As puzzling as it was to many experts, the MDEQ's failure to ensure that proper corrosion control was in place was often framed as a "mistake" caused by genuine misinterpretation of the LCR—a mistake from which a series of "unintended consequences" followed.[21] Edwards concluded that the whole affair "started relatively innocently."[22] Where wrongdoing began to creep into the actions of MDEQ employees (and the city employees taking their direction) was in their water monitoring practices, which exploited loopholes in the LCR that allowed for sampling procedures known to underrepresent the prevalence of lead. One such procedure was "preflushing"—a method of clearing accumulated particulate lead from water lines the night before taking a grab sample. The MDEQ also distributed small-neck sampling bottles that residents were prone to fill cautiously, with a weak stream of water unlikely to dislodge particulates from their service line and premise plumbing.

These practices followed the letter of the LCR but violated its spirit. Other practices flouted it more directly. During a critical round of LCR-mandated sampling in summer 2015, in the midst of growing popular fears about lead contamination, MDEQ and city employees failed to seek out (as required) high-risk homes known to have lead service lines, relying instead upon a convenience sample in which more than half of the homes had copper lines.[23] Even more brazen was the conscious exclusion of two high-lead samples that would have put the city's ninetieth percentile for lead over the Environmental Protection Agency's (EPA) "action level" of 15 parts per billion (ppb).[24] The MDEQ maintained that there was good reason to disqualify the samples because of idiosyncrasies within the homes tested. Part of its rationale for dropping the data points, however, seems to have been a desire to avoid taking cumbersome remedial action, including notifying residents of the results, as would have been mandatory had the city exceeded the 15 ppb action level.[25] Decisions like this were indications, Susan Masten suggested to me, that the incentive for the MDEQ and other such agencies to remain in "compliance" with the law—by any means necessary—was stronger than their commitment to public health.[26]

In instances where MDEQ and City of Flint employees manipulated data and delayed bringing public attention to potential health threats, their actions were sufficiently out of step with state and federal law that they resulted in felony charges for tampering with evidence and misconduct in office. As Marc Edwards stressed, however, much of their behavior was perfectly ordinary, part of an epidemic of cheating on federally mandated lead testing made possible by lack of specificity within the LCR.[27] It so happened that the Flint crisis materialized when the EPA was already in the process of revising the LCR, and the law's failures in Flint inspired much discussion about how it could be strengthened.[28] As part of his effort to demonstrate leadership during the crisis, Governor Snyder inserted himself into the debate, calling the existing version of the LCR "dumb and dangerous" and pledging to institute a stricter action level of 10 ppb at the state level.[29]

Aside from highlighting the ways in which problems caused by faulty water treatment were compounded by lax monitoring and regulation, advocates of the technical narrative like Edwards pointed to "chronic underinvestment in infrastructure" as another contributing factor to the crisis.[30] That underinvestment was evident, firstly, at the Flint Water Treatment Plant itself, a facility opened in 1954 and used only lightly during the nearly fifty years that Flint purchased treated water from the Detroit Water and Sewerage Department. As the city prepared the plant to operate full time in late 2013 and early 2014, it spent a paltry $4 million on upgrades—far short of recommendations made by private contractors hired to evaluate the plant's needs.[31] The city also hired some new personnel, but not nearly enough to compensate for budget-slashing layoffs in previous years. On the eve of the switch, the plant had twenty-six employees—down from around forty a decade earlier when it was a backup facility—with only four employees on duty at any given time and no fully licensed F1 operator on site.[32]

After the corrosive water left Flint's underequipped and understaffed water treatment plant, it traveled through pipes that were well past their prime. Most of Flint's water infrastructure was built in the early twentieth century, when its population grew exponentially along with its booming auto industry, and its water mains were over eighty years old on average when the switch was made.[33] Even before the switch, the city was plagued by water main breaks, and the problem only got worse during the Flint River period (there were 296 breaks in 2014 alone). Every day, millions of gallons of water were lost.[34] From the mains, the water entered service lines about which little was known due to poor record keeping, but which often dated back to the era when lead was widely used. Like dozens of other cities around the country, Flint once had an ordinance on the books, passed in 1897, that required homes and business to connect to the water grid through lead service lines.[35] Although some of these lines were replaced over the years, tens of thousands remained. Furthermore, the material often used as an alternative to lead, galvanized iron, proved in some ways to be an even bigger liability during the crisis: not only did it corrode much faster, corrosion caused its surface area to grow and sorb passing dissolved lead, a complicating factor in the recovery effort.[36]

Just as the crisis exposed weak spots in water quality regulations and monitoring that inspired reevaluations of federal law, the pitiable condition of Flint's water system offered an opportunity to talk about infrastructure

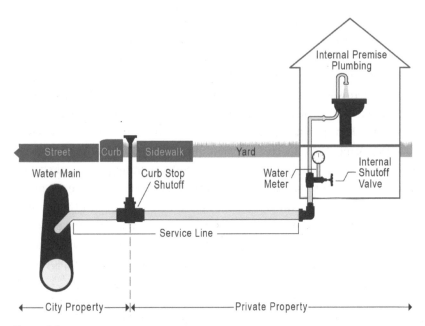

Figure 2.1
Water infrastructure from main to tap. Audrey Zarb.

on a national scale. As many commentators pointed out, Flint's aging and oversized pipe network was in many ways emblematic of a national infrastructure crisis. Marc Edwards warned that the United States was destroying the "very fabric of … civilization" by cutting corners on its infrastructure.[37] The data on national infrastructure needs supported this grim assessment: in successive "report cards" in 2013 and 2017, the American Society of Civil Engineers gave the nation's drinking water infrastructure a "D" and estimated that it needed at least $1 trillion worth of investment over the next twenty-five years.[38] By some estimates, over a quarter of that total would be required just to replace the nation's estimated 6.1 million lead service lines.[39] And only a fraction of the cost could be covered through municipal water bills without raising rates significantly, even in cities like Flint where rates were already far above the national average. To get around the problem of steep rates, advocacy groups closely involved in Flint like the Natural Resources Defense Council and Food and Water Watch called for the reinvigoration of federal financing for infrastructure projects.[40]

The technical narrative's theme of crumbling infrastructure in need of investment, like its theme of defective federal regulations, proved amenable to the Snyder administration, which made infrastructure initiatives an official part of its response to the water crisis. In January 2016, Snyder announced the formation of a "commission on twenty-first-century infrastructure," which ultimately found that the state would need to spend around $4 billion simply to address existing infrastructural needs.[41] A related initiative was inspired by the complications caused by Flint's incomplete data on its pipes, which came to light when engineers trying to track down the city's lead service lines in fall 2015 found that its records on pipe composition were stored on tens of thousands of index cards and physical maps. University of Michigan–Flint professor Marty Kaufman and a team of students put in a Herculean effort to digitize the information over the next few months, but having a digital database did not change the fact that much of the data was flat wrong (when Kaufman looked up my house on his map, for example, it wrongly indicated a galvanized rather than a copper and lead service line). Even after University of Michigan–Ann Arbor professors Eric Schwartz and Jacob Abernethy began applying a sophisticated statistical model to pinpoint the likely location of lead lines, the crews digging them up still found pipes made of other materials 22 percent of the time.[42] With these challenges in mind, Snyder began to push a plan to create an accurate and comprehensive digital map of the state's infrastructure.[43]

Although the technical narrative spawned broader discussions about lax regulations and antiquated infrastructure, these themes were in some sense tangential to its account of how the water crisis actually came about. As flawed as the LCR was, it was not flawed enough to explain the MDEQ's strange interpretation of it. As old as Flint's pipes were, they were not so old that they would have crumbled in the presence of properly treated water. In the final analysis, the crux of the technical narrative was a singular decision: the decision not to use optimized corrosion control during the water treatment process. The crisis would never have happened, in other words, if a select few people in charge of water treatment had simply done their jobs.[44] From an accountability standpoint, the implication was clear: those in search of the origins of the crisis needed look no further than the MDEQ. In its final report, the Governor's Flint Water Advisory Task Force was blunt: "MDEQ caused this crisis to happen."[45]

The Snyder administration did not have to stretch much to make this conclusion politically and ideologically serviceable. The idea that "career bureaucrats" were chiefly liable for causing and perpetuating the crisis kept the focus on relatively low-level state employees without direct political ties to the administration.[46] It also offered an opportunity to impugn the culture of bureaucracy, which Snyder argued had produced (so-called) public servants who were "ineffective, inefficient, and unaccountable." Snyder's bureaucracy-gone-wrong account of the crisis was also useful because it could be used to spread blame beyond the state level to the EPA, whose callous and out-of-touch employees, said Snyder, "allowed this disaster to continue unnecessarily."[47]

Technical explanations for the crisis also encouraged a focus on technical solutions within the recovery effort. If the crisis was primarily a consequence of botched water treatment, the most urgent need was to fix the treatment process. Marc Edwards became the most prominent advocate of the idea that the immediate health risks Flint residents faced from the water could be mitigated through the introduction of corrosion control, combined with the deployment of point-of-use faucet filters. Although by October 2015 Flint was no longer using river water, orthophosphates, he said, were still necessary to "heal" damaged pipes by reestablishing a passivation layer and preventing further leaching of lead. Activists, however, worried that "healing" the pipes would help the state shirk responsibility for taking them out of the ground, and that selling residents on filtered water would detract from their demand for safe *un*filtered water.

The technical narrative of the crisis lent itself, then, to a narrow, water treatment–centric explanation for the crisis's origins that came to be associated in activists' minds with an equally narrow response to its effects. If missteps around corrosion control and regulatory failures were at fault, the state could get away with sacrificing some of its low-ranking bureaucrats to popular demands for accountability and placing the rest of the blame on the EPA. And because the pipes could be "healed" through orthophosphate treatment (a notion that became the object of much scorn and ridicule on the ground in Flint), the state could argue that replacing them gradually—or even not at all—would not compromise public health. Even if an emphasis on the technical implications of the crisis did not lead inevitably to such conclusions, its compatibility with a constrained and apolitical approach to remediation made it more than a little suspect in the eyes of activists.

The Historical Narrative of the Crisis

At the opposite end of the spectrum from the technical narrative in breadth is what I will call the "historical" narrative of the water crisis. The fortuitous appearance of historian Andrew Highsmith's *Demolition Means Progress: Flint, Michigan and the Fate of the American Metropolis* in July 2015, right on the cusp of the revelations about lead, provided anyone seeking a historical backdrop for Flint's present-day water woes with a towering point of reference. Based on a seven-hundred-page dissertation written while at the University of Michigan—a dissertation that some residents, convinced of its explanatory power, had trekked through before the appearance of the book version—*Demolition Means Progress* was the most comprehensive scholarly history of Flint ever published. It became the obvious touchstone for conversations about the prehistory of the crisis.

In interviews,[48] a scholarly article, and an op-ed in the *Los Angeles Times*, Highsmith encouraged those who would understand the crisis to put it into historical context, arguing that "Flint's toxic water crisis was fifty years in the making."[49] He explicitly juxtaposed this claim to what I have called the technical narrative—the idea that the crisis could be boiled down to "the simple failure to use proper anticorrosive agents" and subsequent "government mismanagement." The crisis, he insisted, was "also the product of a variety of larger structural problems that are much more difficult to untangle and remedy."[50]

One advantage a historical perspective offered, Highsmith argued, was a deeper understanding of the infrastructural challenges afflicting the city. The problem with Flint's water system was not just that it was composed of toxic materials and poorly maintained, but that it was designed for a different kind of city than the one Flint had become. As already mentioned, most of Flint's pipes were laid during its period of rapid growth in the early twentieth century, as General Motors (GM)—which evolved out of the Durant-Dort Carriage Company on the north bank of the Flint River—grew into the largest automobile company in the world and attracted job seekers from all over the country. Workers originally lived in shantytowns in the immediate vicinity of the city's car factories, an embarrassing eyesore and potential source of unrest GM sought to alleviate by constructing residential neighborhoods. To accommodate these new housing developments, Flint's water infrastructure crept gradually outward from the water treatment plant on the northeast side of town.

Up through the 1950s, the city laid its pipes on the assumption that it would continue to grow, well past what in retrospect was its peak population of around two hundred thousand people. As the population plateaued and then began to shrink over the next several decades, the pipes stayed in place, and the city was left with an oversized infrastructure it could not afford to maintain. Underuse of the system by residents now far too small in number to need its full capacity created dead spots of stagnant water throughout the city, making all the challenges of water treatment and distribution even thornier.

The expansion of infrastructure was also a key driver of suburbanization, which transformed the geographic, racial, and economic character of the city. In the early twentieth century, suburban development was limited by the absence of amenities like paved roads and water and sewer lines, which made the suburbs ineligible for federal mortgage insurance. To address this problem, suburban developers convinced residents to agree to the higher taxes necessary to fund infrastructure projects. The city of Flint itself also helped facilitate the growth of infrastructure beyond its borders. In the 1940s and 1950s, in search of more space and cheaper land, GM began building factories outside the city, successfully lobbying city officials to extend city infrastructure to service them. This policy reflected an economic philosophy Highsmith calls "metropolitan capitalism" that "rejected distinctions between the city and its suburbs" and held that "growth anywhere in a metropolitan region was a boon to everyone in that region."[51] What made this kind of development distinctive in Flint's case, however, was the hope that Flint and its suburbs would eventually be incorporated into one overarching tax- and resource-sharing metropolitan government—a supermunicipality that planners deemed the "New Flint."[52]

Suburban developers and residents had different ideas. Through the middle decades of the twentieth century, they became increasingly convinced that the economic growth of suburban areas was best served by preserving their political independence. Suburbanites also began to develop distinctive cultural identities that were in some ways explicitly antiurban, reinforcing their desire to keep their political affairs separate from Flint's. Because of Michigan's generous home rule provisions—which allow for easy incorporation and even charter townships with some of the self-governance privileges of villages and cities—it was possible for suburbs to protect themselves from the absorption prescribed by the New Flint plan. As they grew from primitive encampments into politically autonomous cities and townships, they formed a hard ring around the "old" Flint that constrained the latter's ability to expand geographically and annex development outside its borders. By the early 1960s, the dream of metropolitan consolidation was dead, forcing Flint to resort to small-scale strip annexation to expand its tax base.

The dynamics driving suburbanization came from inside as well as outside the city, as the breakdown of Flint's rigid pattern of racial segregation sparked white flight to the overwhelmingly Caucasian, and increasingly affluent, surrounding areas. When African Americans first began arriving in Flint in large numbers in the 1940s, they were funneled into the city's two black neighborhoods—Floral Park, just southeast of downtown, and St. John's, on the fringe of GM's Buick City complex. Until the US Supreme Court's *Shelley v. Kraemer* decision of 1948, the racial homogeneity of other neighborhoods in the city was assured through racially restrictive housing covenants forbidding home sales to anyone but members of the Caucasian race. Even after these covenants were ruled unconstitutional, racist real estate practices and popular pressures made it difficult for black families to move into traditionally white areas. The city's groundbreaking open housing ordinance of 1967 was a victory for racial justice, but it only accelerated the exodus of Flint's white residents. Altogether, Highsmith writes, "between 1950 and 2010, the number of whites living in Flint dropped precipitously, from 149,100 to 38,328, while the city's African American population increased from 13,906 to 57,939."[53]

Some whites were inherently uncomfortable with racial integration. Others feared the decline in property values associated with it—fears stoked by blockbusting real estate agents who sought to profit off whites looking to sell their homes after blacks started moving into the neighborhood. Whatever their reasons for leaving, white residents took with them a substantial part of Flint's tax base, creating stresses on the city's ability to provide basic services and maintain its infrastructure. These stresses only further intensified as GM began to withdraw its manufacturing operations from the city in the 1980s and 1990s, eliminating tens of thousands of jobs and raising Flint's unemployment rate to one of the highest in the nation.[54] Among the city's increasingly desperate, and ultimately futile, attempts to convince

GM to stay was a highway project that obliterated the historically black Floral Park neighborhood in order to build the I-475/I-69 freeway interchange. During the same period, GM also successfully challenged the city's property tax appraisals, resulting in a $34 million rebate and a tax cut of 30 percent that further depleted the city's coffers.[55]

Meanwhile, the center of the city began to hollow out as businesses fled downtown for more hospitable suburban locations. Rates of poverty and crime skyrocketed, discouraging new economic investment. Hundreds of city employees were laid off and city services like trash collection, police, and fire were scaled back. With help from Michael Moore's unflattering 1989 documentary *Roger & Me*, Flint also became the poster child for misguided attempts at urban renewal: most notably, the infamous Autoworld, a short-lived Six Flags theme park at the center of the city's quixotic campaign to reinvent itself as a tourist destination. Thanks to Moore's film, the highest-grossing documentary in history up to that point, Flint developed a reputation for being cartoonishly inept in addition to dilapidated and dangerous—a city with a rich past but hard to take seriously in the present, and best avoided for safety's sake. When an EPA employee sent an internal email at a critical juncture in the water crisis suggesting to colleagues that Flint was not "the community we want to go out on a limb for," it is hard to believe these stigmas did not enter into her assessment.[56]

Pulling all of these various threads together—industrialization and deindustrialization, suburbanization, segregation, the decline of government services, ill-fated urban renewal—into a schematic of the prehistory of the water crisis yields a complex causal chain that extends all the way back to the early twentieth century and implicates a wide range of actors. As a scholarly aid to tracing the historical processes by which environmental inequalities and injustices are produced,[57] such a wide-ranging account of the crisis's origins is invaluable. It also offered a potential resource to the activists who championed the political narrative of the crisis described in the next chapter. The political narrative rested upon the argument that aside from being an affront to democracy, emergency management was a failure on its own terms, incapable of solving managerially problems that were in essence structural and cumulative. Deficits could be eliminated temporarily through the reduction of operating costs, but without addressing the structural inequalities underpinning them—inequalities of race, class, and geography built up over time—they would inevitably reappear, and cities like Flint would be

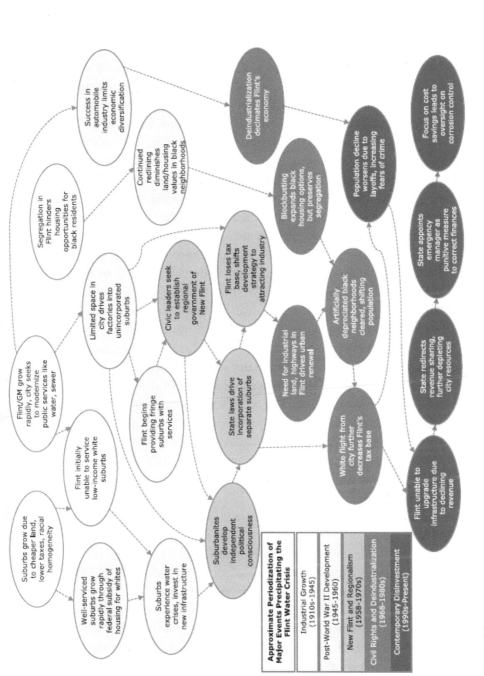

Figure 2.2

The causal chain of the Flint water crisis (from Sadler and Highsmith, "Rethinking Tiebout").

perennially tempted to make reckless decisions that subordinated public health to cost considerations. Ultimately, the only way to prevent another water crisis, Highsmith argued, was to solve the *urban* crisis from the roots up. And, contrary to the philosophy of austerity enacted by emergency managers, he maintained, "You can't cut your way out of urban crisis."[58]

From a political perspective as well as a scholarly one, then, the historical narrative had its advantages. But it also had limitations. The political accountability the activists were after depended on being able to pinpoint specific actors, actions, and policies as direct or proximate causes of the crisis. While putting the crisis into historical perspective was not inherently incompatible with this objective, sometimes taking a bird's-eye view had the effect of diffusing responsibility and distracting from more immediate political objectives.

The clearest example emerged from the proceedings of the Michigan Civil Rights Commission (MCRC), a state body charged with investigating acts of discrimination, which held three hearings on the water crisis in 2016. After state-sponsored investigations into the crisis by two other bodies failed to convince activists that the state was taking the crisis seriously, the MCRC was seen by some as the city's "last hope" of redress from a state agency,[59] and many of Flint's water warriors turned out to offer their testimony during public comment periods at each of the three hearings. Because the commission's stated objective was to investigate possible civil rights violations associated with the crisis, some activists hoped it would recommend that legal action be taken against specific guilty parties.

When the MCRC released its final report in February 2017, however, the report's effect was anticlimactic at best. The commission announced that it had been unable to uncover evidence of justiciable discriminatory intent behind any of the most immediate decisions that caused or perpetuated the water crisis. Consequently, it focused its discussion of civil rights on Flint's past, turning the bulk of the report into a history lesson on the roots of "structural and institutional discrimination and racism" in the city.[60] Arguing that the causes of the crisis were "much broader" and "more complex" than could be captured through narratives of water source changes and engineering decisions,[61] the report summarized the history of the various forms of discrimination chronicled in Highsmith's work, concluding that "past racism played an important role in creating the conditions that allowed the water contamination crisis to occur." To the disappointment of activists, however, as well as some of the experts invited by the commission to testify, the report had little to say about the responsibility of anyone directly involved. When the commission did address the state's response to the crisis, it gave it high marks: though "imperfect," the response had demonstrated the state's "goodwill and moral acceptance of responsibility" as well as its "resolve" to make things right.[62]

Some of the commission's recommendations suggested that it had had difficulty deriving concrete and timely prescriptions from its broad historical analysis. Several called simply for better "listening,"[63] deeper "understanding,"[64] and more "acknowledge[ment]" of the role of race in "our history."[65] Where the recommendations got more specific, they used Highsmith's work as the basis for demands that ran directly counter to what activists were calling for. Impressed by Highsmith's account of the interweaving of Flint's fate with that of its metropolitan neighbors, the report suggested creating and implementing "a form of regional government (or at least regional cooperation)"[66]—a suggestion that grated on the ears of activists suspicious that the state was scheming to abolish Flint as a political entity and absorb it into the county. (On numerous occasions, I heard activists say that the water crisis would be used as an excuse to do just that.) Furthermore, when the commissioners got around to considering the role of emergency management in the crisis, they disappointed activists again by calling for the replacement or restructuring of the emergency manager (EM) law rather than its repeal, while floating the idea of actually *expanding* the power of EMs by giving them regional authority—another suggestion borne of the regional emphasis of Highsmith's work but greeted with incredulity by members of the community.[67]

Toward a Political Narrative of the Crisis

In some respects both the technical and the historical narratives offered ammunition to Flint activists. Even the narrowest version of the technical narrative placed the lion's share of the blame for the crisis on actors at the state level, feeding into activists' demand that the state "fix" what it "broke." On occasion, activists also took up the idea that the crisis was a product of people not doing their "jobs," implying that it could have been prevented if decision makers had followed laws already on the books and lived up to their professional obligations. When the Coalition for Clean Water—an alliance focused on ending the city's use of the river, whose story is told in chapter 6—released a series of demands in the summer of 2015, it ended with an ultimatum directed at the MDEQ: "DO YOUR JOB THE WAY THE EPA INTENDS FOR YOU TO DO IT."[68]

But the technical narrative could also be used to depoliticize the crisis, steering attention away from political actors and political policies. Marc Edwards, for example, said he could empathize with residents' opposition to emergency management (calling the EM law "un-American"), but maintained that decisions about corrosion control were made from "a science and engineering perspective," by civil servants with specialized skills, not by EMs or any other political figure.[69] Former EM Darnell Earley, in written Congressional testimony, concurred, arguing that "this was not a leadership issue—this is purely a water treatment issue."[70] Similarly, Snyder's description of the crisis as a "massive error of bureaucracy" centered responsibility on technocrats charged with ensuring the smooth operation of government and directed attention away from the political context he was instrumental in creating.[71] From this perspective, preventing future crises was principally a matter of replacing a few personnel, tightening up some regulations, and, perhaps, making a general commitment to reinvest in infrastructure. The technical narrative required some admission of guilt on the part of the state—Snyder made a point of saying he was "sorry" and would "fix it"[72]—but it also allowed the state to limit accountability to a handful of bad actors and avoid addressing the structural political and economic issues raised by activists.

The historical narrative, too, was useful to activists in some ways but not others. It could be used to show that the bulk of Flint's infrastructural and financial woes were caused not by poor management but by deep-seated structural dynamics stretching back decades. It supported the idea that the injustice of the water crisis was amplified by the cumulative effect of a long history of past injustices. As evidenced by the disappointment that followed the MCRC report, however, the historical narrative could also be employed in ways that were at odds with the message, strategy, and objectives of the water movement—diffusing responsibility across time rather than concentrating it in contemporary political actors, and contradicting the demands of the moment with poorly timed, if well-meaning, proposals aimed at addressing longstanding structural inequality.

The activists' preferred narrative of the crisis was more expansive than the technical narrative but more focused than the historical narrative. It homed in on the political context within which key decisions were made about Flint's water. It held that the ultimate problem was not with low-level bureaucrats who didn't do their jobs, but with powerful political appointees who *did*. It framed the crisis as evidence of the terrible consequences of the usurpation of representative government, and the struggle for clean water as part of a larger struggle for democracy. And it situated the beginning of the crisis not in April 2014 or in the mists of history, but in 2011, when emergency management came to Flint.

3 Poisoned by Policy: The Political Narrative of the Crisis

Democracy is what makes Flint work. The dismantling of Democracy in Flint is poisonous.

—Flint Democracy Defense League, "The State of Flint under Emergency Management"

On the afternoon of Election Day, November 8, 2011, with voters still filing in to the polls, Flint Mayor Dayne Walling received a phone call from State Treasurer Andy Dillon. Walling was already well on his way to winning a decisive victory in his reelection bid against challenger Darryl Buchanan, and he was gearing up to deliver a victory speech later that evening at the White Horse Tavern, a popular local haunt. But Dillon bore unwelcome news: a state review panel had decided that Flint was in the midst of a financial emergency. Under the provisions of Michigan's Public Act (PA) 4, signed into law by Governor Snyder in March of that year, Flint would receive a state-appointed emergency manager (EM) who would assume both the executive and legislative functions of city government. At 5 p.m., still three hours before the polls closed, the story broke, and Flint voters learned that the person they were in the process of electing would be, institutionally speaking, powerless.

With the announcement, Flint became the first Michigan city to enter state receivership under the new law. It joined the Detroit Public Schools and the cities of Pontiac and Benton Harbor, which had already been taken over by the state under PA 4's predecessor, PA 72. PA 72, passed in 1990 during the administration of Democratic Governor James Blanchard, had provided for the appointment of emergency financial managers (EFMs) to units of local government like cities, counties, and school districts the State of Michigan deemed to be in financial distress and nearing bankruptcy.[1] The law empowered EFMs to make fiscal reforms aimed at eliminating deficits and returning local governments to solvency. When the state turned control of Flint's finances over to EFM Ed Kurtz in 2002, for example, the city was facing a $30 million deficit. Kurtz slashed the pay and eliminated the medical benefits of city officials and employees and pressured unions to negotiate cuts or face layoffs. He temporarily closed the city's recreation centers and the ombudsman's office. He forced the city Retirement Board, under the threat of layoffs and removal of board members, to reduce what the city paid into its retirement system. He raised water rates. By 2004, Flint was back in the black, and Kurtz stepped down.[2]

As significant as Kurtz's actions were, his powers as an EFM were relatively limited compared to those enumerated by PA 4. Under PA 4, whose official title was the "Local Government and School District Fiscal Accountability Act," emergency *financial* managers came to be called, simply, "emergency managers." The dropping of the adjective hinted at the fact that EMs had control over far more than just finances. PA 4 enabled EMs to strip locally elected officials of all their powers, alter or abolish union contracts unilaterally, and even disincorporate units of local government altogether.

PA 4's advocates insisted that the state would appoint EMs only as a last resort. The early warning system embedded in the law, they said, was designed to detect burgeoning fiscal crises so they could be remedied before an emergency situation arose.[3] PA 4 increased the number of "triggers" that would prompt a preliminary state review of local finances and included provisions for "consent agreements" enhancing the powers of local officials, potentially enabling them to take more decisive remedial action in the event of financial difficulty and avoid further state intervention.[4] If local efforts to avert emergency were unsuccessful, however, the law allowed the state to take more sweeping action than had been possible under PA 72. The alternative to the law, warned its advocates, was to put the fates of insolvent cities in the hands of federal bankruptcy judges—an outcome that was not only disempowering, but that would also imperil the pensions of retirees and ruin local credit ratings.

Arguments for PA 4 often invoked the concept of "fiscal responsibility."[5] Proponents liked to point out that occasional financial challenges were not uncommon at the local level but that most local governments were able to pull through them with a little belt tightening. More often than not, then, when financial trouble grew intractable it was because of careless mis-management of taxpayer dollars by local officials too incompetent, spine-less, or corrupt to change their behavior even when disaster loomed. State Representative Al Pscholka, one of PA 4's sponsors, touted the ability of EMs to put such officials in the "timeout chair."[6] Although EMs could not remove elected officials from office outright (at least not without approval from the Governor), they could cut or eliminate their salaries, prevent them from holding meetings, and require them to take courses in municipal gov-ernment. Pscholka assumed that state-appointed EMs would be more able[7] and willing than local elected officials to make the tough choices necessary to end a financial emergency. Because they were not beholden to special interests at the local level and could operate without fear of electoral reprisal, EMs enjoyed the freedom to make decisions that would destroy the political careers of duly-elected officials. They could also act expeditiously, without the inconvenience of citizen oversight or consensus building.

The pro-emergency management position depicted EMs as swooping in to salvage basic services rendered unsustainable by the ineptitude of local officials, thereby preempting much unnecessary suffering on the part of residents. This characterization made emergency management out to be in the best interests of ordinary people living under failed local regimes, people who deserved better than what they were getting from their paid public servants. However, critics of PA 4 disputed the claim that the law was designed to put the interests of residents first. Flint activist Claire McClinton noted that one of the few restrictions the law placed on EMs was to forbid them from missing debt service payments to the holders of city bonds.[8] Her gloss on this proscription was that "bondholders are sacred. They cannot be touched. People are not sacred."[9] McClinton and other activists argued that the prioritization of private over public interests under emergency manage-ment was visible in other ways, too. Rather than trying to salvage strug-gling cities, they maintained, the state's real intention was to pick them clean of their remaining assets, handing city services, facilities, and infra-structure over to private entities under the pretense of taking them off the city's books. By shrinking the public sphere and purging cities of potential sources of revenue just because they had become unprofitable or difficult to keep up in the short term, EMs were not preparing cities like Flint to stand on their own two feet but rather reducing them to unsustainable shells of their former selves.

When the bill that would become PA 4 was making its way through the Michigan State Legislature, there was much speculation about which cities might receive EMs under the law. Having slipped back into insolvency since exiting emergency financial management in 2004, Flint was recognized to be a potential "test case."[10] Aside from underlying structural issues like population loss and economic disinvestment that were already making it difficult for the city to function, the housing crisis and recession of 2007 to 2009 dealt a heavy blow to Flint's revenue stream. The total taxable value of property in the city fell by $500 million, with the median sales price of Flint homes plummeting from $57,000 in 2005 to $15,000 in 2010. Per capita personal income plunged, too, costing the city 39 percent of its income tax revenue between 2006 and 2012. At the nadir of the recession, unemployment got as high as 25 percent. And although Flint's mayors desperately tried to cut back on spending, eliminating over four hundred city jobs between 2008 and 2010, overall expenditures remained stubbornly steady due largely to the fixed legacy costs of retiree pensions and health care.[11]

To make matters worse, cuts by the State of Michigan to statutory revenue sharing—a mechanism for redistributing state sales tax revenue to cities in need—deprived Flint of around $55 million from 2002 to 2014.[12] The cuts were part of a larger effort by the state to balance its budget as it compensated for the economic downturn and reductions in business taxes. Through its Economic Vitality Incentive Program, announced in 2011, the Snyder administration made what revenue sharing remained conditional on the implementation of austerity policies at the local level, incentivizing local governments to operate more "efficiently" by consolidating departments and reducing labor costs.[13] The overall effect of the cuts, however, was to further erode the foundations of municipal financial health and, in University of Michigan-Flint sociologist Jacob Lederman's words, "[open] the door to claims that cities like Flint and Detroit were living beyond their means."[14] When activists characterized Flint's financial crisis as "manufactured,"[15] they meant that the state, not city administration, was really to blame for taking the city from a surplus into a deficit. By abjuring its traditional role of propping up structurally disadvantaged cities through financial assistance, they argued, the state was helping to create the very "crisis" it then purported to solve through emergency management.[16]

Not long after PA 4 took effect, the state started to take a closer look at what was going on in Flint. A state-appointed financial review team conducted a preliminary assessment of Flint's finances in late August to early September 2011 and found the city to be in dire fiscal straits. It was running an estimated deficit of around $25 million. Its pension system was "less than 60 percent funded," with the unfunded portion amounting to $39 million annually and increasing each year—over $860 million in aggregate.[17] Simply to stay afloat, the city was poaching $5.3 million from its water and sewer fund annually to pay for general fund operations. It was borrowing from other specialized funds as well, despite rules prohibiting the practice. This interfund borrowing, the review team found, "was not booked as such in the City's records."[18] If Flint stayed the course, its deficit would not be eliminated until the year 2030, and even that outcome was dependent on incurring another $12 million of debt.

The review team's report portrayed Flint as a city in denial. Local leaders were in the habit of adopting "budgets that knowingly overestimated revenues, knowingly underestimated expenditures, or both," and they were slow to modify these budgets even in the face of obvious shortfalls.[19] Furthermore, the city had repeatedly failed to live up to the deficit elimination plans it submitted to the state treasurer. Attempts to reduce labor costs had led to locked horns with unions, and local officials were understandably wary of making even deeper cuts to police and fire services after layoffs of public safety personnel coincided with a dramatic surge in homicides and arsons. The review team concluded that "no satisfactory plan" existed to resolve the emergency, citing "a lack of political will among a succession of City officials to confront reality and render difficult, but necessary, financial decisions." For this reason, it rejected the option of enhancing the powers of local officials, who could not be trusted to act with the requisite "urgency and vigor."[20] The only plausible way of turning Flint's fortunes around, the team concluded, was through the appointment of an EM.

The decision had its supporters at the local level. The *Flint Journal* opined at one point that Flint needed "the emergency manager's sweeping powers and political immunity to make the drastic changes and tough decisions to secure the future of the community."[21] Unlike in 2002, when the City Council spent three months and over $200,000 fighting the state's appointment of EFM Kurtz, the council voted 7 to 2 against an appeal. Councilmen Josh Freeman, Scott Kincaid, and Dale Weighill, frustrated by the lack of progress on the deficit, had actually lobbied for the review by the state, knowing it might culminate in emergency management.[22] Others, like

Councilwoman Jackie Poplar, concurred that the city needed "help" and promised to look at the EM as a "partner."[23] Newly reelected Mayor Walling went along somewhat more begrudgingly (the determination that he was not a good candidate for expanded powers was something of a slight), but similarly declined to fight the decision or even request a hearing on the review team's findings, calling the appointment of an EM "the Governor's decision to make."[24] Believing that the fastest way to extricate Flint from receivership was to cooperate with the state rather than fight it, Walling adopted a conciliatory disposition toward the city's EMs. Many activists came to view him as a collaborator who was sympathetic to key aspects of the state's agenda in Flint or at the very least was "going along to get along," a perception that would heavily damage his political reputation during the water crisis.[25]

Not everyone was prepared to concede. As described in the next chapter, the imposition of EMs on Flint and several other communities in Michigan under PA 4 inspired staunch resistance from activists and unions, leading to the repeal of the law through referendum in November 2012. A month later, however, state legislators passed a new EM law, PA 436. Unlike its predecessor, PA 436 gave local officials the opportunity to choose from four options in the event of a state-declared financial emergency: a consent agreement, bankruptcy, mediation, or the appointment of an EM.[26] Because the law also stipulated that EMs appointed under older laws were retained under the new law, however, Flint officials were given no such choice. Consequently, when PA 436 took effect in March 2013, it allowed emergency management to continue more or less as before in the city. Bracketing a six-month period between the suspension of PA 4 and PA 436's taking effect (during which

Table 3.1

Flint's EFMs and EMs.

	Emergency (financial) manager	EM law in effect
July 2002–June 2004	Ed Kurtz (EFM)	PA 72
Dec. 2011–Aug. 2012	Michael Brown	PA 4
Aug. 2012–Mar. 2013	Ed Kurtz (EFM)	PA 72
Mar. 2013–July 2013	Ed Kurtz	PA 436
July 2013–Sept. 2013	Michael Brown	PA 436
Sept. 2013–Jan. 2015	Darnell Earley	PA 436
Jan. 2015–Apr. 2015	Jerry Ambrose	PA 436

time PA 72 was revived and Ed Kurtz served, once again, as the city's EFM), Flint remained under emergency management from December 2011 to April 2015. A total of four EMs governed the city during this period (see table 3.1).

The effects of emergency management on Flint were multifaceted, and in the next chapter, I consider a range of actions taken by Flint's EMs and the resistance they inspired on the part of activists.[27] The focus of this chapter is narrower. Here, I wish to trace the logic of the argument that the suspension of representative government at the local level in Flint was principally to blame for the water crisis (i.e., that the city was "poisoned by policy"[28]). This political narrative of the crisis implicated the state in ways that went beyond the missteps of bureaucrats and administrators responsible for water treatment and public health. It found fault in the EM law itself and the politicians who crafted, sponsored, and defended it, all the way up to Governor Snyder. It also raised bigger questions about democracy: questions about the merging of political power and private interests, the implications of austerity for the integrity of the public sphere, the competence of the *demos* to oversee its own affairs at the local level, and the viability of democratic principles during times of "emergency."

Flint activists were not the only ones who espoused the political narrative of the crisis, but they were its primary authors and leading champions. In their signs and slogans, they fused the themes of poisoned democracy and poisoned water and called for the prosecution of Flint's EMs and their overseers in Lansing. Although they were critical of the full range of officials—city, county, state, and federal—who they felt had let the people of Flint down, they rejected Governor Snyder's characterization of the water crisis as a "failure of government at all levels,"[29] pointing out that during the period in question there *was* no meaningful distinction between "levels" of government in Flint. Organizationally, all lines of responsibility led back to the state-appointed EM (see figure 3.1).

Elected officials who enjoyed any authority under emergency management—like Mayor Walling, who was given responsibility for public works shortly after the switch to the Flint River—did so because it was voluntarily delegated by EMs. Administrators technically on the city's payroll were often brought in by EMs, like Director of Public Works Howard Croft, who was responsible for the day-to-day operation of the water system.[30] And lower-level decision makers operated, naturally, within an environment shaped by the higher-order decisions made by EMs. As the Flint Water

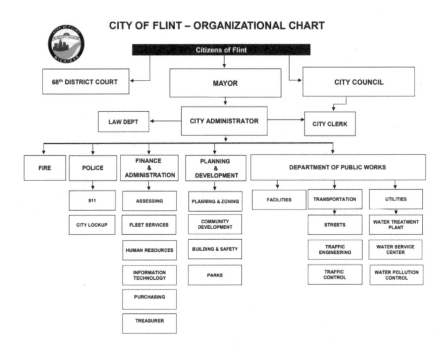

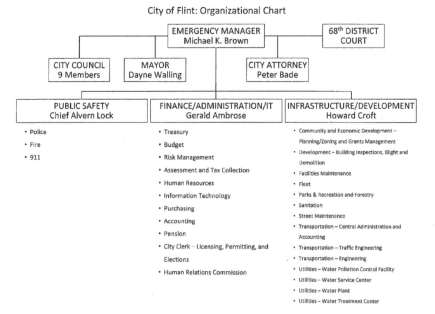

Figure 3.1
Structure of Flint city government as specified in city charter (top) and under emergency management (bottom).
Source: City of Flint.

Advisory Task Force put it, emergency management created the "frame-work" within which decisions about Flint's water—and all other city affairs, for that matter—were made.[31]

In his analysis of the key decisions that precipitated and prolonged the water crisis, Wayne State University law professor and water activist ally Peter Hammer argues that Flint "serves as a morality play illustrating all that is wrong with Emergency Management."[32] In what follows, I borrow Hammer's metaphor in dividing the series of official decisions about Flint's water into three "acts." The first act deals with the decision to end Flint's decades-long water partnership with Detroit and commit to joining a regional pipeline project overseen by the Karegnondi Water Authority (KWA). This decision created the need for an interim water source, and the second act looks at why the Flint River was chosen as that interim source in preference to a short-term contract with the Detroit Water and Sewerage Department (DWSD). The third act examines why it took officials eighteen months to agree to switch the city back to Detroit water despite significant public outcry. In each act of the drama, state actors within the EM system in Flint and Lansing are central players, putting the city on an ever-more settled trajectory toward using the river, overseeing the source change, and insisting upon staying the course once the switch is made. The political narrative casts these actors as its principal villains, depicting the crisis as a story of state abuse and local victimhood.[33]

One might expect the governance structure imposed by emergency man-agement to lend itself to precisely this kind of dichotomous perpetrator-victim narrative: if all roads lead back to the EM organizationally, it should be straightforward to assign responsibility to the state for the decisions that poisoned Flint's water and kept residents drinking it for longer than nec-essary. Careful consideration of the political narrative's main plot points, however, reveals some surprising murkiness around who was responsible for what, including the all-important switch to the Flint River. Counterintui-tively, some of this murkiness stems from the structure of emergency man-agement itself. Although EMs are imposed by the state, for example, there is at least some ambiguity around whether they are properly considered state or local actors.[34] Furthermore, even if one accepts that EMs act on the state's behalf, it does not necessarily mean that the "state"—complex and multifac-eted entity that it is—acts with one unified will. Spreading state power across multiple scales creates new potential for conflict among actors within the state system, as when EMs in Flint disagreed at key moments, seemingly, with officials in Lansing about water-related decisions. Finally, state power is not deployed into a vacuum: although EMs sometimes try to wipe the slate clean before they set to work—eliminating salaries, offices, public meetings, and so on—they are nevertheless forced to coexist with an array of local actors, institutions, and interests that retain some influence. Even under emergency management, there were times when it appeared that locals were influencing or even driving decision making. In some instances, Flint's EMs intentionally comingled their own powers with elements of the local power structure through the selective delegation of authority (e.g., over public works) and offered local elected officials opportunities to express their will. The gray area created by these structural ambiguities was further exacerbated, of course, by the complex tangle of finger-pointing that accompanied attempts by both state and local actors to deflect responsibility during the water crisis.

Activists dealt with these complexities in various ways. They rejected categorically the claim that EMs were in any sense local rather than state actors. They boiled away the apparent differences of opinion among state officials, portraying the full array of state actors from Flint's EMs on up as being in cahoots, working together to advance a consistent agenda shaped by bondholders and other private interests with ties to the Snyder administration. Most important, they argued that the appearance of local complicity in decision making was being deliberately, and duplicitously, cultivated by the state. Whenever it seemed that locals had played a meaningful part in a key decision about water, activists cautioned that the "real story" was "between the lines."[35] Complementing the repressive and direct power exercised by EMs and other state actors within the EM system, they believed, was a kind of creative and surreptitious power, operating through discreet manipulation rather than open command.[36] The idea that the state was, in many ways, deliberately masking its influence in Flint, and that activists had a special responsibility to root out and expose that influence, colored activist strategy and tactics throughout the crisis and crisis recovery effort.

The counterpoint Flint activists posited to the power of the state was what we might call, following legal scholar Richard Schragger, "city power," or what activists themselves sometimes called "local control." Within the context created by emergency management, when activists demanded "democracy" it was understood to mean *local* democracy—defined, at the very least, by the full functioning of representative government at the municipal level and all the benefits of home rule. Although activists knew that local politics, like state politics, was susceptible to domination by private interests, for the most part they strongly associated local control with public things and public purposes. And although they had many complaints about local officials, they nevertheless felt a sense of ownership of city government that was completely lacking in their sentiments about government at higher levels. Consequently, they experienced the state takeover as a personal violation that struck at the heart of their municipal identity as Flintstones, aside from stripping them of a fundamental human right to self-determination.[37]

The focal point of the political narrative, however, was not the intrinsic injustice of denying Flint residents democracy, but the ways in which this denial spawned the injustice of the water crisis. Its moral was that democratic procedures and local control of resources cannot be sacrificed—"emergency" or no emergency—without also sacrificing public health. Lurking in each act of the story, then, is the same counterfactual question: what if Flint's democracy had been in place all along?

Act I: The Karegnondi Water Pipeline

In his 2016 State of the State address, delivered while activists outside Michigan's capitol building called for his resignation and arrest, Governor Snyder dated the origins of the water crisis to an act of the Flint City Council.[38] The crisis began, he asserted, when the council voted 7 to 1 in March 2013 to commit Flint to participating in the KWA pipeline project. This vote, he implied, was the catalyst for the string of events that resulted in the short-term use of the Flint River and all the terrible consequences that followed. Snyder may not have said it outright, but the subtext of his comments was clear: Flint was complicit in its own water crisis, and its complicity began with the KWA decision. None other than PA 4 champion Al Pscholka—who also happened to be Michigan House Appropriations Chairperson—invoked this notion as an excuse to hold up state aid to the city.[39] Activists' first task in combating the "false" narrative of the crisis promulgated by the state, then, was to show that the KWA project had never had genuine local support and that EMs had been instrumental in pushing it forward.

The backstory to Snyder's claim that the KWA decision was locally driven was Flint's decades-old desire for water independence. Since it had first begun receiving water from Detroit in 1967, Flint had been at the mercy of the administrators of the Detroit water utility (known from 1975 on as DWSD).[40] DWSD oversaw a water system that stretched far beyond the boundaries of the city of Detroit into the surrounding counties and ultimately to Flint, but being a division of city government, it had a strong incentive—and indeed was designed institutionally—to run it in a manner that put Detroit's interests first. It favored Detroit-based companies when doling out contracts and only hired workers who lived within city limits (at least until residency requirements were outlawed in 1999). The mayor of Detroit appointed all the members of its Board of Water Commissioners, with four out of seven mandated to be Detroit residents. To demonstrate a commitment to regional cooperation, Detroit's mayors settled on the practice of appointing representatives of Wayne, Oakland, and Macomb Counties to the three remaining positions. But despite being DWSD's largest customer (accounting for about 5 percent of overall water purchases), Flint was not accorded a seat on the board.

Where Flint's lack of influence within DWSD mattered most, arguably, was with respect to the setting of water rates. Given that DWSD charged more depending on the distance and elevation over which its water was transported, Flint's location at the system's northwestern extremity put it at an inherent disadvantage within the department's pricing scheme. And while the counties with representatives on the DWSD board could exert some influence over their rates, there was little Flint could do to resist increases. By paying higher rates than it might have been able to negotiate with more institutional pull, Flint—and by extension Genesee County, which purchased Detroit water through Flint—was effectively subsidizing the cheaper rates paid in other areas serviced by the Detroit system. As long as DWSD's rates stayed relatively low overall, Flint and Genesee County tolerated this structural inequity. But in the 2000s, rates began to climb steeply, with annual increases averaging about 11 percent. Genesee County Drain Commissioner Jeff Wright, who as CEO of the KWA became the leading proponent of the city and county breaking free from Detroit, contended that by setting "unsustainable" rates DWSD was pricing Flint and Genesee County "out of its system."[41]

The deeper problem with DWSD, Wright argued, was that it operated in an "authoritarian manner," with little concern for Flint's and Genesee County's well-being.[42] Aside from the persistent rate issue, it had long resisted building a backup pipeline to service the area in case of emergency, the consequences of which were driven home when a massive power outage in 2003 left residents without water for several days. It was also, Wright claimed, rife with corruption—most glaringly, in the form of contract-rigging, which over the years had led to the criminal convictions of two DWSD directors and Detroit mayor Kwame Kilpatrick. Although the water DWSD provided was of good quality, its mismanagement of the system, Wright maintained, made water provision "very unreliable." The "only reasonable solution," he argued, was for Flint and Genesee County to break up with Detroit and tap into Lake Huron via their own pipeline.[43]

The idea had been around since at least the 1940s, when Flint was still drawing its drinking water from the Flint River and its needs as a growing city were beginning to exceed the river's capacity. After a plan to build a pipeline northward to Saginaw Bay was abandoned as too costly, an alternate plan for a pipeline extending eastward to Port Huron began to take shape, and in the early 1960s, the city began buying up land along the proposed route in preparation. But so did a prominent Flint businessman—in collusion with the city manager—whose intention was to sell the land to the city at a profit. The resulting scandal led to public corruption charges which, although eventually dismissed, destroyed a good deal of support for the project.[44] While this was going on, Detroit was preparing to build a Lake Huron pipeline of its own to reduce the dependence of its water system on the Detroit River. In April 1964, Flint's commissioners voted to abandon the idea of a Flint-owned-and-operated pipeline and enter into a long-term agreement with Detroit.

The contract signed by the two cities in December 1965 committed Flint to the partnership for at least thirty-five years. Beginning in the early 2000s, Flint began to renew the agreement annually. But its newfound freedom from a long-term contractual obligation, combined with growing tensions with Detroit, revived the impetus to build an independent pipeline. Exploratory work by Jeff Wright and other Genesee County officials over the next decade ultimately led to the formation of the KWA in 2010. The vision developed by its board was of a regionally owned and operated water system, a partnership between Flint, the City of Lapeer, and Genesee, Sanilac, and Lapeer Counties. According to Wright, the KWA, unlike the DWSD, was designed to give all members "a fair representative voice."[45] Each stakeholder had one position on the original board, with Flint's seat occupied by Mayor Dayne Walling, a vocal supporter of the project. When the board expanded to fifteen members in 2013, Flint's share comprised four seats, with Walling serving as chairman.

New water for Flint and neighbors

The Karegnondi Water Authority is set to come on-line in June or July, and locals hope it will bring a long-term solution to the region's long-term water issues.

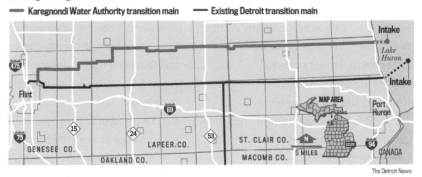

Figure 3.2
The Karegnondi water pipeline. The Detroit News.

Hooking up to the KWA pipeline would also offer Flint the opportunity to make fuller use of one of its most significant assets: its water treatment plant.[46] Detroit water was treated shortly after being withdrawn from Lake Huron, and required little attention upon arriving in Flint. KWA water, by contrast, would arrive raw, and Flint would be solely responsible for treating its portion of it. Between 1998 and 2006 the city had invested $50 million into its plant so that it could treat Flint River water as a backup supply. Although it would need further upgrades to prepare for long-term treatment of raw lake water, Operations Supervisor Brent Wright described it as already "pretty much state of the art."[47]

The prospect of giving Flint more control over the governance and operation of its water system was attractive from the standpoint of the city's self-determination, but supporters also pitched the KWA project as a financial boon. Wright promised that the KWA would establish cost parity throughout the region served by the pipeline, with each community paying "the same rate for its water."[48] He also claimed that this rate would be lower than what Flint paid to DWSD, saving the city $600 million over thirty years, even with a $7-million-per-year bond payment.[49] Wright's thirty-year rate projection made the KWA option out to be a major savings over another long-term contract with Detroit, which DWSD began to solicit from Flint as plans for the KWA pipeline gathered steam in late 2012 to early 2013.[50] Wright accused DWSD of trying to torpedo the project by luring Flint away from it, thereby preserving Detroit's water monopoly in the region. He insisted, however, that the department's machinations were futile: the pipeline would move forward with or without Flint's participation.

This is not to say that Wright was disinterested in Flint's participation—on the contrary, he repeatedly stressed that the KWA was eager to have the city on board as a long-term partner. But he insisted that the choice between DWSD and the KWA was "Flint's decision, and Flint's decision alone to make."[51] The problem was that when the time came to make a firm commitment to financing the new pipeline in early 2013, determining where "Flint" ended and the state began was more complicated than ever. The situation, in brief, was this: in August 2012, PA 4 was suspended, pending a November referendum on the law, and EM Mike Brown was forced to step down. Claiming that PA 72 had gone back into effect, Governor Snyder tapped Ed Kurtz to reprise his role from the early 2000s as EFM, while Brown took the position of city administrator. The City Council sensed an opportunity to reassert its authority, resuming regular meetings, filing a lawsuit to oust Kurtz, and threatening to launch an investigation into the torrent of resolutions (sixty in total) that Brown discharged before leaving office.[52]

Even under the revived PA 72, however, the state still had considerable say over any major decision pertaining to Flint's water. The city's choice of source water clearly had financial implications, bringing it under the jurisdiction of EFM Kurtz, and because it entailed a transaction exceeding $50,000, it also required the approval of State Treasurer Dillon. Dillon only became aware of the KWA project in late 2012, but he quickly came under pressure from the project's backers to make a speedy decision about whether he would support Flint's participation, which would help to determine aspects of the engineering like the number of pumping stations and the diameter of the pipe. To assess the project's cost, he commissioned a study from the private engineering firm Tucker, Young, Jackson, Tull, Inc. (hereafter "Tucker Young"), which determined that the KWA would be at least $100 million more expensive than predicted and recommended that the city stick with DWSD water, perhaps blending in some water from the Flint River.[53] Seizing on Tucker Young's estimates, DWSD began to float long-term contract offers it claimed were substantially cheaper than the KWA.

Jeff Wright excoriated the Tucker Young study, accusing it of wildly overinflating the cost of the KWA pipeline and pointing out that the firm had a clear conflict of interest as one of DWSD's contractors. Dayne Walling dismissed the study's findings as "propaganda" and a "scare tactic" aimed at making a new DWSD contract look more attractive than it really was.[54] Concurring with this position was EFM Kurtz, who since taking office had conducted a thorough study of Flint's water options. Kurtz provided the pro-KWA forces with ammunition when he commissioned a competing study by KWA contractor Rowe Engineering, which purported to rebut Tucker Young and DWSD's assertions.[55] According to Wright, Kurtz had concluded by early 2013 that the KWA was "the best permanent source of potable water for the City of Flint" and "was entirely comfortable" making this recommendation to Treasurer Dillon.[56]

Despite the fact that Kurtz, the state's man in Flint, was leaning toward the KWA, it was widely believed that Tucker Young's critique of the project was what the higher-ups in Lansing wanted to hear. In early 2013 the Snyder administration was, after all, preparing to place Detroit under emergency management using PA 436, a near reincarnation of the repealed PA 4 scheduled to take effect on March 27. Allowing Flint to run off with the KWA, taking a substantial piece of DWSD's revenue with it, would hardly be conducive to improving Detroit's fiscal standing. Wright warned that if Lansing were to have the final say about Flint's water, it would force the city into the thirty-year contract being offered by DWSD. He urged city officials to make their position on KWA known before the state regained full control of Flint under the impending PA 436.[57]

What ensued was one of the most unusual events of the EM years. Although he was under no obligation to do so, EFM Kurtz invited the City Council to vote on whether Flint should commit to the KWA. Technically, of course, the decision was not the council's to make. However, Wright insisted that it was "not an idle exercise," assuring the council that "if it voted 'no,' KWA would not sell water to Flint" (though the pipeline would be built anyway).[58] Under the assumption that Wright was a man of his word, this gave the council genuine power in the event it decided against joining the pipeline, for no one—not Kurtz, not Snyder—could force the KWA to accept Flint as a customer. Wright would later claim that the council vote "was one of the few moments of true democracy Flint had during the EM reign."[59] Happily for him, it produced the outcome that he, Kurtz, and Mayor Walling wanted: the council came down in favor of the KWA, 7 to 1.

In his critique of Wright's account of the KWA decision, Peter Hammer disputes the authenticity of the council's vote that day, calling it a "sham."[60]

In Hammer's telling, what Wright depicted as an exercise of "true democracy" was little more than a symbolic rubber stamp on what was already a "done deal,"[61] with "the city and its residents ... manipulated as means to the predetermined ends of others."[62] Documents released during the water crisis revealed that Flint's first EM, EM Mike Brown, had been working with Wright since at least February 2012 to build the assumption that Flint would be buying KWA water into the authority's planning process, suggesting that there was considerable, perhaps irresistible, momentum behind the KWA partnership by the time the council vote was taken. Hammer alleges that during the council's deliberations, Wright encouraged it to adopt a "myopic focus" on the relatively lower wholesale rates that Flint would pay under the KWA, without full consideration of "the costs of operating Flint's water treatment plant and maintaining the city's water infrastructure system."[63] He also maintains that council members were not given all of the relevant information (including, notably, the Tucker Young report) before casting their votes; Third Ward Councilman Bryant Nolden, who lodged the lone dissenting vote, complained that "we get the information at the last minute and are asked to make decisions."[64] Hammer's theory is that Kurtz offered the council a vote not to genuinely solicit its input but to give the KWA decision a firmer legal standing in the event the EM law was ever successfully challenged in the courts, which some believed could retrospectively invalidate EM resolutions.[65] Public proclamations that the vote was an expression of "democracy," then, masked this private intent to use the council's apparent endorsement of the project as an "insurance policy" against legal challenge.[66]

One final detail of the ostensibly democratic vote made the limits of the council's power apparent. Wright asked the council to agree to purchase eighteen million gallons of water per day (mgd) from the KWA, despite the fact that Flint's average daily water use was several million gallons less than that, with its population continuing to shrink by the year. The council settled on sixteen mgd as a compromise, with the potential for blending in water from the Flint River if needed.[67] Following the vote, however, Kurtz unilaterally signed off on the excess capacity rejected by the council, at an estimated cost of an extra $1 million a year.[68] While the surplus water was arguably unnecessary from Flint's perspective, it would justify a larger-diameter pipeline that would increase the amount of water the KWA could carry to the region—allowing for, in Wright's words, "future expansion."[69] For Hammer, as well as for Flint activists, Kurtz's flagrant disregard for the council's will illustrated the "meaninglessness of the council vote."[70] The Flint Democracy Defense League lamented that the water purchase agreement drafted by the council itself "was utterly ignored by the emergency manager," who proceeded to pass on to the Governor "his own version," created "without any democratic input."[71]

Even with Kurtz advocating for the KWA, however, it was still necessary to get backing from Treasurer Dillon. Faced with competing assessments of the KWA's cost by Tucker Young and Rowe, Dillon turned to an agency he believed could be a neutral arbiter: the Michigan Department of Environmental Quality (MDEQ). Officials at the MDEQ, he said later, were "firm" that the KWA was better[72] and did not seem to have "any agenda" in saying so.[73] With the MDEQ's endorsement of the KWA, Dillon was sold. Negotiations, however, were not quite over yet: at the eleventh hour, Governor Snyder personally intervened, calling a meeting of all the major players in the hopes that Flint and DWSD could strike a deal—an apparent sign that the state actors involved were still not entirely aligned.[74] By the time DWSD extended its *final* final offer in late April, however, Kurtz—knowing he had the backing of Dillon—felt empowered to reject it summarily. Jeff Wright publicly declared that the decision was a "done deal," saying there would be "no looking back."[75]

Now that Dillon's initial hesitation had turned into approval, the treasury began to work with the other state actors involved to make Flint's participation financially possible. Flint's commitment to the project obligated it to cover about one-third of the project's bond debt, amounting to $85 million total. The logistical problem to be confronted was how a city struggling just to break even, and prohibited by state law from issuing bonds except in cases of "fire, flood, or calamity," could take on such an obligation.[76] The matter became pressing toward the end of 2013 and into early 2014, during the tenure of EM Darnell Earley, when the KWA was preparing for a $220 million bond issue that would allow it to begin the next phase of pipeline construction.

At first, Earley had trouble obtaining the treasury's authorization to borrow the money needed to finance Flint's share. KWA's bond attorneys, however, came up with a creative solution that ultimately won the treasury's approval.[77] The idea was to ask the MDEQ for an administrative consent order (ACO), a device typically used by the department to force a local government to fix an environmental violation. An ACO allowed a municipality to issue bonds related to environmental remediation that did not count toward its debt limit. What made this ACO different was that it was, in the bureaucratic lingo of the MDEQ, a "sweetheart" bond, a rare instance in which an ACO was being sought voluntarily.[78]

The official reason given for the ACO was to enable the cleanup of lime sludge, a byproduct of the water treatment process, that was actively leaking into the Flint River from a dumping site upstream of the treatment plant's intake pipe. Jeff Wright claimed that the lime sludge issue was preventing the plant from operating legally, as was necessary under the KWA plan, and that this was the real reason the city needed the ACO.[79] As Hammer points out, however, the language of the ACO was broad enough to facilitate financing of much more than just the lime sludge remediation. It was "drafted with the express intent of being broad enough to permit financing of Flint's participation in KWA pipeline construction," making Flint's use of the treatment plant contingent upon an "improvement project" vague enough to encompass the building of the pipeline.[80]

The dubious ACO proved to be the piece of the water crisis puzzle that opened Flint's EMs up to legal accountability. Arguing that the real motivations for the ACO were strategically hidden, the attorney general's office described it as "a sham transaction designed under false pretenses to obtain money for the KWA" and hit EM Earley and then–Finance Director (later EM) Jerry Ambrose with false pretenses charges.[81] Hammer, however, stresses that the treasury was equally to blame: within the "draconian regime" created by emergency management, it was "the ultimate decision maker."[82]

The EM-requested and treasurer-approved ACO helped put Flint in a position to issue KWA bonds but it did not, of course, guarantee they would be repaid. For obvious reasons, purchasing bonds from a financially shaky city like Flint was a risky prospect from an investment perspective. To ensure that the KWA's $220 million bond issue got a high rating—and thereby a favorable interest rate—Genesee County pledged to secure Flint's portion of the debt,[83] an assurance strong enough to help win the bond issue *The Bond Buyer* magazine's Midwest Region Deal of the Year award. The catch was that, in the event Flint defaulted, the county could siphon off 25 percent of its constitutional revenue-sharing money, force Flint to levy a tax to reimburse the KWA, and seize Flint's water assets. Genesee County Board of Commissioners Chairman Jamie Curtis warned that Flint would "lose everything" if it withdrew from the KWA because of how heavily its debt was secured.[84]

As momentous as the KWA decision was, popular awareness of its implications, and even of the project's very existence, was minimal among Flint residents even after the water crisis revived the debate over Flint's long-term water supply. As late as June 2016, state water crisis liaison Harvey Hollins estimated, based on focus group data, that 80 percent of residents had "no idea what KWA is."[85] But within Flint's activist community, the KWA project had raised red flags as early as 2013, when activists led a campaign (discussed in the next chapter) to put Flint's participation to a public vote. In the context of the water crisis, deep suspicions grew up around the project even among activists who had not contributed to—or even been aware of—that earlier effort. They depicted Drain Commissioner Wright as a shady and untrustworthy character (one nicknamed him, simply, "The Scum Bag") and occasionally speculated that Mayor Walling stood to profit personally from the deal in a manner that mirrored the public corruption scandal of the 1960s. But they also believed that the state had conspired to impose the KWA on the city, even suggesting, in some instances, that Flint was placed under emergency management in order to accomplish that objective.[86]

Activists posited a variety of ways the pipeline would advance the state's agenda. It was no secret that the project was not only about drinking water, but also economic development, an effort to open up the region to the "blue economy" by offering large quantities of fresh raw water well suited for agriculture and industry.[87] Aside from this officially acknowledged economic rationale, however, activists speculated that the water requirements of fracking interests with ties to Governor Snyder were being factored into inflated water quantity requests like the one signed off on by Ed Kurtz. Some even suggested that by (indirectly) contaminating private wells with fracking waste and forcing out-county residents onto its grid, the KWA would expand its customer base.[88]

Activists also suspected the project of being part of the Snyder administration's agenda of privatization. Sometimes they described the KWA pipeline itself as "privatized" despite its not being privately owned or managed; at other times, they said the project "open[ed] the door to privatization," in the belief that the international water giant Veolia (or some other such private interest) was waiting in the wings to buy up the infrastructure.[89] Activists also argued that the KWA was designed to ruin DWSD and lay the foundation for the regionalization of Detroit's water infrastructure, tearing control of southeast Michigan's water away from the majority–African American city and placing it in the hands of the neighboring, predominantly white, counties, which had always resented being subject to Detroit politics and administration.[90] Finally, activists saw the possibility of Flint's forfeiting its assets to the county as a sign that the KWA could be used as a roundabout way of regionalizing the city out of existence, popularly believed to be the state's ultimate vision for Flint.

Convinced the KWA was a "scam," or at the very least a bad deal for the city, activists started turning up at KWA board meetings and speaking out against the project. But the intensity of the emotions on display at these meetings—the denunciations, for example, of Jeff Wright and other members of the board as "murderers" at a particularly contentious meeting I attended in May 2016—is hard to explain without reference to another belief: the belief that it was the KWA plan that triggered the switch to the Flint River.

Act II: The Break with Detroit and Switch to the River

State officials made the same claim about the decision to use the Flint River as an interim source as they did about the KWA: that it was locally driven, with state officials merely following the lead of local officials in executing the switch. Once again, the implication was that the city had brought the crisis upon itself—in this case, even more directly.

In fact, the city *had* at one point seriously considered returning to the river for its drinking water—not just temporarily, but permanently. In the late 2000s, as patience wore thin with DWSD's rate hikes, city officials began to explore "all available options for Flint's long-term water,"[91] including whether using the Flint River would be cheaper than staying with Detroit.[92] Some made an effort to change public perceptions of the river, stressing that it was "quality water" and suggesting that its low credibility with residents was "more of a psychological issue."[93] Engineering reports by Wade Trim in 2009 and Lockwood, Andrews, and Newnam (LAN) in 2011 lent some credence to this position, finding that although the river would be trickier to treat than lake water, it could be brought up to regulatory standards.[94] Long-term, full-time treatment of river water would require more extensive upgrades to the water treatment plant than what the KWA proposal called for, but given local interest in putting the plant to good use, some saw this as a worthy investment.[95]

According to Dayne Walling, the extra "costs and complications" of using the river effectively dropped that possibility to the bottom of the list of Flint's long-term water options by mid-2011.[96] This did not end all consideration of using the river in some capacity, however.[97] As already mentioned, the council voted to blend Flint River water with KWA water as a cost savings in March 2013. The possibility of similar blending with DWSD water had also been widely discussed, although it required convincing DWSD to allow the practice.[98]

But demonstrating the willingness of some local officials to consider using the river is one thing, and demonstrating that they actually decided to do so another. As part of his effort to exonerate himself, ex-EM Darnell Earley portrayed the City Council's vote for the KWA as having included a vote to use the river while the pipeline was built. However, Earley's suggestion that the KWA decision and the Flint River decision were one and the same was, as Dayne Walling put it, "blatantly false." In fact, the council opted to purchase water from the KWA upon completion of the pipeline on the assumption that Flint would remain with DWSD in the meantime. No council vote on the river ever took place.[99]

It was still possible to argue, however, that the KWA vote spawned the switch to the river indirectly. After EM Kurtz finalized the KWA decision in April 2013, DWSD promptly announced that it would be dropping Flint as a customer in a year's time. In a press release, it accused the supporters of the KWA of launching "the greatest water war in Michigan's history" and of having "a 'political' objective that has nothing to do with the delivery—or the price—of water."[100] Losing out to the KWA, Kurtz said later, made DWSD "mad, angry, vindictive."[101] Some believed the department would actually follow through on its threat to cease water delivery even in the event that Flint failed to arrange an alternative interim supply.[102] With the KWA pipeline still an estimated three years from completion and relations with Detroit worse than ever, Flint was supposedly forced into the temporary fix of full-time use of the Flint River.

But the activists were firmly of the opinion that, in Peter Hammer's words, the DWSD termination notice "plays no legitimate role in the story" of the switch to the river.[103] In March 2014, as the threatened shutoff date approached, DWSD Director Sue McCormick wrote to EM Darnell Earley of her willingness to negotiate a new contract. Earley informed her tersely that Flint no longer had need of Detroit water, even in the short term, because it had "actively pursued using the Flint River as a temporary water source."[104] As Earley was turning DWSD down one last time, Genesee County was actively making preparations to remain with the department as a customer until the KWA was ready, ultimately purchasing a nine-mile section of pipeline from Flint for $3.9 million to make this possible. The county's interim arrangement with DWSD provides a glimpse of what might have been had Flint pursued a similar path: for the next few years, it resentfully paid a higher rate for Detroit water (20 percent higher, in fact[105]), but it also enjoyed clean, safe water.

Just *who*, in Earley's words, "actively pursued" interim use of the river between the KWA vote in March 2013 and the source switch in April 2014 is perhaps the most perplexingly opaque question in the entire water crisis saga. The crisis timeline released by the state stated that in June 2013, the *"City of Flint* decide[d] to use the Flint River as a water source" (emphasis added).[106] What, exactly, was meant by the "City of Flint" was not explained. By June, Flint's elected officials wielded even less power than they had a few months earlier, for EFM Kurtz had become EM Kurtz under the now-active PA 436. The documentary record shows Kurtz preparing the city to use the river. On June 26, he signed a resolution authorizing LAN to begin evaluating what upgrades the water treatment plant would need to process river water full time. Retrospectively, the issuing of this resolution was widely depicted—by everyone from Wright,[107] to Walling, to the Flint Water Advisory Task Force[108]—as the moment when the die was cast, when the decision to use the river was made definitively. Bewilderingly, however, Kurtz later denied that he was responsible for the switch. Preparing the water treatment plant to operate was not the same, he insisted, as finalizing the source switch. In summer 2013, he maintained, the city was still in an exploratory stage, with a variety of officials discussing the feasibility of using the river. Asked who made the final decision about the river, Kurtz said he didn't know.[109]

Exploratory or not, Kurtz's actions with respect to the water treatment plant set the tone for a string of cost-conscious decisions later cited as evidence that the use of the river was driven by "economics."[110] The need to prepare the plant to treat KWA water in the long term and Flint River water in the short term put Kurtz in a bind: treating the river water properly would require more of an investment in the plant than would be needed later on to treat lake water. Convinced that the city could ride out any complications arising from using the river given that the arrangement was only temporary, Kurtz gambled on Flint being able to get away with the bare minimum required by the MDEQ. Representatives of LAN later said that when company employees raised concerns about this attitude, recommending a test period to evaluate the corrosivity of the river water, Kurtz declined because the MDEQ did not deem it necessary.[111] While the MDEQ was of course responsible for its own bad advice, Kurtz's bare-minimum mentality made him seemingly quick to accept any recommendation that entailed less cost and hassle with the treatment plant.

Kurtz hoped that the money the city would save while on the river (about $5 million over two years relative to what a temporary deal with DWSD would have cost) would cover whatever new equipment was needed.[112] As Finance Director Ambrose explained, the switch "was made because it ... offered an immediate cost-savings opportunity which translated into the ability to upgrade the Water Treatment Plant without having to seek financing."[113] The MDEQ's position on corrosion control (i.e., that it could be withheld until proven necessary over an extended trial period) was welcome news—not, as some news outlets breathlessly reported in their coverage of the water crisis, because it would save the city a measly $100 per day for the chemicals, but because it would obviate the installation of costly equipment that would be useless after the KWA pipeline came online. Still, estimates of the size of investment the plant needed were disconcertingly high. Recommendations made by Rowe in December 2013 called for around $25 million worth of work.[114] It appears that considerably less was spent prior to the switch—enough to squeak past the MDEQ's regulatory goalpost, but no more (see chapter 2).

The cost-averse logic on display in EM decisions about Flint's water gave rise to the accusation that public health had been sacrificed on the altar of austerity, recklessly entrusted to glorified accountants whose powers were broad but whose expertise was thin or nonexistent on subjects central to residents' well-being.[115] Of course, EMs could always claim that they shouldn't have *had* to be public health experts, that they should have been able to rely on the direction of those who were. A defensive Ed Kurtz argued in November 2016 that his job as EM was "strictly finance" and "did not include ensuring safe drinking water."[116] It was the duty, not of EMs, he said, but of the MDEQ and the Environmental Protection Agency to oversee water quality and prevent lead poisoning—he had simply accepted their advice. Darnell Earley, for his part, protested that during his time as EM he had never received "any information that would even remotely indicate that the use of the Flint River was unsafe in any way."[117] However, the Flint Water Advisory Task Force found that MDEQ employees had "deferred to state emergency manager decisions to proceed" even when they knew that "use of Flint River water would be problematic."[118] It also concluded that the breadth of the powers bestowed by the EM law made EMs responsible even for the nominally "technical" decisions made on their watch.

Given that the EM system was undemocratic by design, it is hardly surprising that deeply unpopular decisions emerged from it, but within the political narrative of the water crisis, the *pièce de résistance* was the switch to the Flint River. The choice of the almost universally maligned river for Flint's water supply was the ultimate example of the ability of EMs to disregard public opinion and act in ways unthinkable to elected officials.[119] One could debate whether letting popular inclinations prevail would have kept Flint off the river for the right reasons—the capabilities of modern water treatment methods, for example, may have weighed less heavily in the balance than ingrained prejudices about the river being a who-knows-what toxic stew. However, it is harder to argue with the activists' central contention: if the people of Flint—or at least their representatives—had been the ones deciding on the city's water future, there would never have been an opportunity to bungle the treatment of the river water, for the river, in all likelihood, would never have been a character in the story at all.

Act III: Prolonging the Crisis

When activists began to pool their energies and demand a return to Detroit water in early 2015, they sometimes implied that reconnecting would be as easy as flipping a switch or, more accurately, pressing a button. The defining image of the original source change, after all, was of Dayne Walling doing just that to shut off the feed from Detroit. Sensing an opportunity to reinsert itself into the conversation about Flint's water source, DWSD began to encourage the impression that getting Detroit water flowing again was straightforward and could be done more or less immediately, a notion that began to spread through the activist community via Councilman Eric Mays, a key ally of the water activists.[120] On January 12, DWSD Director Sue McCormick wrote a letter to Flint officials indicating that Detroit was "ready, willing, and able" to resume selling water to Flint. On January 26, she testified to the Flint City Council that DWSD was willing to reopen the pipeline for "emergency services" and that doing so was "not contingent" on conversations about a long-term contract.[121]

But EMs Darnell Earley (in office September 2013 to January 2015) and Jerry Ambrose (January to April 2015) both insisted that switching back to Detroit water would not be so easy.[122] For one thing, Earley had, as said earlier, sold to the county the nine miles of pipe Flint once used to connect to the Detroit system under the assumption that the city would never again need it (a decision activists "begged" him not to make[123]). For another, the ACO that Earley and Ambrose helped to finagle for KWA financing purposes in early 2014 required that Flint use the river as its interim drinking water source.[124]

These constraints stemmed from decisions made before the possibility of an urgent return to Detroit water was seriously considered. But Ambrose erected three additional barriers to such a return in the spring of 2015, several months after systemic problems with water quality appeared. Firstly, as he prepared to return Flint to partial local control, he obtained a loan from the state's Local Emergency Financial Assistance Loan Board to cover the nearly $8 million deficit still on the books. The loan included the stipulation that the city could not return to Detroit water without the approval of the state treasurer.[125] Secondly, before stepping down he signed an order that prohibited city officials from overturning any EM decisions for a year. Even though no single EM was willing to take responsibility for the switch to the river, that decision was presumably covered by the order. Finally, Ambrose broadened the powers of City Administrator and Earley-appointee Natasha Henderson to give her substantial influence over city affairs.[126] As support for a return to Detroit began to build among Flint's elected officials, Henderson actively resisted the proposition because tying the city's pipes back into the Detroit system would complicate the eventual transition to the KWA.[127]

Aside from the matter of structural impediments to switching back to Detroit, Flint's EMs argued that it would be cost prohibitive. Ambrose warned that Flint would pay $12 million more per year on an interim DWSD deal and that rates would have to rise by 30 percent or more to compensate.[128] Earley and Ambrose clung staunchly to this logic even as members of the administration in Lansing began to voice doubts. After GM got special permission to leave Flint's water system in October 2014 in an effort to stop corrosion of its engine parts, Valerie Brader, deputy legal counsel and senior policy advisor to Governor Snyder, questioned whether using the river still made financial sense and advised a return to DWSD, calling the water situation in Flint "an urgent matter to fix."[129] In February 2015, after the state provided its employees working in Flint with bottled water to enable them to avoid the tap, Chief of Staff Dennis Muchmore wrote in an internal email that it would "look pretty stupid hiding behind some financial statement" if the water posed a true threat to public health.[130] Earley and Ambrose, however, were "unequivocal" in their insistence that switching off the river would be "difficult and expensive" and that the quality problems were not serious enough to merit it.[131]

In the same email that found him questioning the optics of pleading finances to residents while arranging for state employees to get safe water, Muchmore argued that since the state was "in charge" in Flint, it could "hardly ignore the people of Flint."[132] The structure of emergency management, however, allowed Flint's EMs to steer a deeply unpopular course through the city's water troubles. In March 2015, the City Council joined a growing chorus of activists in calling on Ambrose to discontinue use of the river. On March 23, it voted 7 to 1 to do "all things necessary" to return to Detroit water. Ambrose called the vote "incomprehensible" and disregarded it.[133] It was yet another sign that while EMs occasionally solicited the council's endorsement of decisions, and while the council could lodge symbolic protests of various kinds, under emergency management it was unable to generate any institutional friction when opposed to EM dictates.

Emergency management also dampened the impression that popular discontent about the water might otherwise have made on decision makers. Because the EM system was designed precisely to force through unpopular policies, it took for granted a moderate amount of grumbling on the part of residents. Its combination of unchecked power and single-minded focus on finances fostered a governing style that was both arrogant and willfully disinterested in the range of considerations (beyond technical and financial ones) that enter into popular preferences and demands. And because it intentionally insulated EMs from popular accountability, it deprived residents of institutional mechanisms of redress.[134]

Some officials later protested that every time problems had been confirmed with the water, they had been addressed: discoloration with a concerted flushing campaign, bacterial contamination with increased chlorination, total trihalomethanes with the installation of new carbon filters at the treatment plant, lead contamination with reconnection to the Detroit system, orthophosphates, and pipe removal. From a popular perspective, however, every one of these responses was either inadequate or too slow in coming. The state's initial strategy, hypothesizes Peter Hammer, was to "run out the clock" on environmental enforcement until the KWA pipeline was ready, hopeful that some minor tweaks would prevent the problems with the water from reaching a critical mass.[135] But for residents and activists, the switch back to Detroit could not come soon enough. And when it did come, it came only after months of butting up against a political edifice expressly designed to shut them out.

Epilogue

Political theorists have long fretted about the fate of democracy during periods of so-called emergency. They have singled out the ability to declare an emergency and use it to justify suspensions of laws and rights as one of the most important powers wielded by the state—even as the quintessential expression of state sovereignty.[136] They have noted that under the exceptional circumstances defined and delineated (however vaguely) by the state itself, state power tends to grow stronger and more centralized, and democratic deliberation tends to take a backseat to unitary expressions of will by political leaders. Citizens are told that it is necessary to cease temporarily the mechanisms of democratic decision making and eliminate inconvenient checks and balances.

PAs 4 and 436 went further in that direction than most state takeover laws, enabling the State of Michigan to impose EMs without local consent, push local charters and officials completely aside, and exercise near-absolute control over every aspect of local government. Legal scholar Michelle Wilde Anderson has described the effects of these laws, aptly, as "democratic dissolution."[137] As we have seen, however, Flint's EMs did not operate within political conditions entirely of their own making or completely smother all local initiative. The entanglement of their will with local actors and institutions sometimes served to blur—at least on the surface—the distinction between state and local responsibility for political outcomes like the KWA decision and the switch to the Flint River. Nevertheless, Flint activists argued that regardless of whatever complicity EMs were able to elicit from local elites, it was the state—not the people of Flint or their elected representatives—that supplied the main political motive force during the period when the critical decisions were made about the city's water. Telling the tale of the origins of the crisis was not just a matter of holding up transparent state abuses for the world to see, but of rooting out and exposing subtler ones—part of the activists' larger project of unveiling the undemocratic exercise of state power when it cloaked itself in the appearance of popular consent.

Distilling the essence of all that led to the water source switch and the subsequent reluctance to reverse it, the political narrative can be summarized succinctly: disregard for democracy in Flint led to disregard for public health. Shortsighted and narrow-minded efforts to end one "emergency" created another—an example of what Anderson calls the "severe collateral damage" of democratic dissolution.[138] Suspending democracy at the local level, even if only temporarily, can have lasting effects on the health of the body politic, too, undermining political legitimacy and participation by alienating citizens from their most intimate political environment. Certainly, in Flint, the feeling that traditional forms of political engagement were pointless as long as the city was in state receivership was strong, and it eroded trust in the political system in ways that were every bit as poisonous as the water.

But as political theorist Bonnie Honig has argued, there are "opportunities, invitations, and solicitations to democratic orientation, action, and renewal even in the context of emergency."[139] The abolition of democracy at the institutional level need not preclude the preservation, or even the stimulation, of democratic energies elsewhere. In Flint, this phenomenon was evident in a variety of ways: in the fight against the EM law and EM decrees, the formation of new groups within civil society, the development of new forms of political agency, and the use of the water crisis/emergency/ disaster as an opportunity to advance more radical democratic visions. That is the story of the rest of this book.

4   The Pro-Democracy Struggle in Michigan and the Prehistory of the Water Movement in Flint

This water crisis is because we have a democracy crisis in Michigan.
—Nayyirah Shariff, quoted in *Democracy Now!*, "On World Water Day"

Michigan Public Act (PA) 4 took effect in March 2011—the eve, ironically, of a democratic uprising of international proportions. The self-immolation of Tunisian fruit vendor Mohamed Bouazizi in late 2010 touched off a cascade of political rebellions that swept through the Arab world and beyond the next spring and summer. From Western Africa to the Arabian Peninsula, a generation of young Libyans, Egyptians, Iranians, and others used the language of democracy to contest the abuses of authoritarian regimes and give expression to political aspirations. Later that year, a throng of activists gathered in the heart of Manhattan's financial district to encamp in Zuccotti Park and broadcast the demands of the "99 percent." Speaking for the millions of Americans left behind by the government's response to the economic recession, they condemned the growing influence of corporate elites over the American political system and called for higher taxes on the wealthy and stricter economic regulation. Occupy Wall Street, too, had a catalytic effect, inspiring a chain reaction of similar occupations throughout the United States and the world. While the issues addressed by Occupy activists varied from country to country, the movement's shared objective, according to one prominent protest sign, was "real global democracy now."

In the meantime, in Michigan's next-door-neighbor Wisconsin, progressives and organized labor launched their first sally against the wave of far-right Republican politicians elected by Rust Belt voters during the 2010 midterm elections. As the Wisconsin legislature considered a so-called budget repair bill being pushed by Tea Party darling Scott Walker, targeting the wages, benefits, and collective bargaining rights of public-sector employees, protesters began to flood the lawn of the state capitol. Over the next several months, they staged some of the largest rallies in the state's history, buoyed by an influx of supporters from all over the country. For two weeks in February, protestors physically occupied the capitol building, forming a makeshift community that anticipated the Occupy movement's commandeering of public space. Although the anti-union bill eventually passed, the opposition continued, phasing into efforts to recall Governor Walker and various state senators that stretched into the summer of 2012.

Each of these struggles was shaped by local priorities and local vernaculars of resistance. But the near-ubiquitous theme of "democracy" suggested parallels between them. Activists fought to institute democracy where it had never before existed, or defend democracy against threats posed by plutocratic elites, or make what was *called* democracy more "real." Some activists played up the similarities, sensing some sort of Zeitgeist that bridged the various uprisings, and expressions of solidarity and mutual aid crisscrossed back and forth between them. Zuccotti Park drew comparisons to Egypt's Tahrir Square and prominent Egyptian activists visited to share their wisdom with their American counterparts. Protestors in Wisconsin, too, were the beneficiaries of help from afar: Flint activist Nayyirah Shariff remembers when, outside of the Madison Capitol building, pizzas began to arrive, purchased in a gesture of camaraderie by sympathizers in Egypt and other parts of the Middle East.[1]

Michigan saw its own pro-democracy movement emerge around the same time. As in Wisconsin, it began as a backlash against a radical Republican agenda set into motion after 2010's midterm electoral coup. Newly-minted Governor Rick Snyder may not have had the Tea Party credentials of Scott Walker, but his administration quickly set to work enacting policies that shifted the state sharply to the right: corporate tax breaks, restrictions on collective bargaining, and school privatization, among others. If there was one piece of this agenda that crystallized and focused the opposition like Walker's anti-union bill had in Wisconsin, it was the legislation that would become PA 4. Despite not bringing the subject up during the campaign, Snyder announced in his January 2011 State of the State address that his administration would seek to revise Michigan's existing emergency manager law so as to establish greater "clarity" about "the powers of the financial managers."[2] Although Snyder hinted that the changes would involve "strengthened provisions," few were prepared for just how much strengthening he had in mind.

As Snyder's intentions became clearer, what inspired the most concern at first was the possibility that the new law would be used against organized labor, as yet another weapon—and a powerful one at that—in a broader war on collective bargaining. Granting state appointees the ability to render null and void existing union contracts with police officers, fire fighters, 911 operators, teachers, and other public employees would amount to a state veto over the bargaining process at the local level. As the emergency manager (EM) bill began to take shape in the state legislature, Michigan's major unions sprang into action. In February and March, they sponsored rallies at the capitol that drew thousands of protestors, prompting the *Lansing State Journal* to write that "Wisconsin fever" had "officially hit Michigan."[3] Apparently, the Snyder administration agreed: in a fact sheet about the proposed upgrades to the EM system, it warned that the protestors were "trying to use this issue to provoke the kind of fighting seen in Wisconsin."[4]

There was more at stake in opposing the law than collective bargaining, however. As activists would come to frame it, the battle in Michigan was not just between organized labor and union-busting politicians in the pockets of the corporate elite, but between "democracy" and "dictatorship." Given the near-absolute power EMs enjoyed over local government, this was no mere hyperbole. PA 4's advocates, after all, were so unabashed in their disregard for local democracy that they described the statute unapologetically as a kind of "financial martial law."[5] Opponents of the law called it "un-American," "fascist," "tyrannical," and "autocratic." Its dramatically disproportionate impact on African Americans—at one point about half of Michigan's African American population lived under an EM—drew comparisons to historical forms of racial disenfranchisement like slavery and Jim Crow.[6] Activists also saw in the law shades of the authoritarian regimes under challenge by fellow activists in other countries. The Reverend David Bullock, a pastor in Highland Park, Michigan, who emerged as one of the law's most outspoken critics, vowed to "show the world that democracy is at stake in Michigan just as it is in Libya or Egypt."[7]

Those who turned out for rallies at the capitol in early 2011 held out some hope, however farfetched, of impeding the EM bill's progress through the legislative process, or at least amending the bill. But with Republicans in control of the state House and Senate (not to mention almost all other important state offices), there was little that protesting and lobbying could do to delay, much less prevent, the inevitable. Asked if the demonstrations at the capitol were having any effect, State Senator Phil Pavlov responded that legislators "had to talk a little bit louder," but because Republicans were "pretty lock stepped" on the issue, demonstrating wouldn't "sway any votes either way."[8] With only one lone House Republican dissenting, the state legislature passed PA 4 along otherwise strict party lines. Snyder signed it into law on March 16 and it took effect immediately.

Effectively shut out of state government, opponents of the law had little choice but to pursue other avenues of resistance. In Wisconsin, activists were beginning to talk about recalling Governor Walker and his allies in the legislature, but they were stalled, for the time being, by a state law limiting recalls to officials who had served at least a year in office. Unhindered by such a restriction, Michigan activists began to employ the tactic almost immediately. Through the spring and summer, they initiated recall efforts against twelve state representatives who had won narrow victories in 2010. Most of these efforts petered out—eleven of the twelve failed to get recall language onto the ballot for lack of signatures. But in District 51, just to the south of Flint, Flint activists helped to oust arch-conservative Paul Scott in the first successful recall of a Michigan state legislator since 1983.

Contemporaneously with these district-level efforts, a group calling itself the Committee to Recall Rick Snyder initiated a campaign to remove the governor from office. In late April its petition language was approved, and it began an ambitious push to collect 1.1 million signatures in ninety days. Much to the chagrin of the recall's backers, the Michigan Democratic Party and most of the state's major unions declined to offer their support, and the campaign ran up against the limits of its leaders' meager organizing experience. It fell well short of the signatures needed to put the recall on the ballot.[9]

Wisconsin activists commenced their own attempt at a gubernatorial recall in late 2011. Over the ensuing months, they gathered over a million signatures despite only needing half that many, setting the state on course for a special election. Energized by this development, Michigan activists decided to try again to get rid of Snyder. The Committee to Recall Rick Snyder reorganized as the Super PAC Michigan Rising and began a new petition drive in May 2012. This time around, the group had experience, a clear strategy, and better fundraising prospects. But even with a more fine-tuned operation, signature gathering proved to be slow going. When

Walker handily won Wisconsin's special election in June, it deflated the hopes of Michigan activists looking for a success to imitate. Discouraged by their prospects, they ended the campaign. In December of that year, Snyder signed legislation erecting new barriers to getting a recall onto the ballot. Not until the Flint water crisis heavily damaged his reputation would he be subjected to another recall challenge.

In between the failed recalls of Governor Snyder, the pro-democracy movement in Michigan got a fresh injection of energy from the reverberations of Occupy Wall Street. In early October 2011, Occupy events and encampments started to spring up around the state in places like Grand Rapids, Muskegon, Ann Arbor, and Kalamazoo. In Lansing, Occupy activists convened their General Assembly on the steps of the Capitol. In Detroit, they camped out for a month in Grand Circus Park, holding protests outside nearby banks and carrying out direct actions. In Flint, they set up on private property on the north side of downtown and endured through the winter as other camps around the country voluntarily disbanded or were driven from their territory by police. By the spring, Occupy Flint was the only camp still standing in Michigan. Its longevity was significant not only because it was a testament to the hardiness of Flint activists, but also because it provided a local base of support for the activities of the pro-democracy movement through the spring of 2012.

In January 2012, on Martin Luther King Jr. Day, about a thousand activists from around the state turned out for an "Occupy for Democracy" march that took the spirit of the Occupy movement straight to Governor Snyder. After gathering in Ann Arbor, they proceeded to march a mile and a half to the entrance of Snyder's gated community in Superior Township.[10] Although the marchers "occupied" the area only temporarily—long enough to make speeches and deliver a letter of complaint to one of Snyder's representatives— they attracted considerable attention for their controversial decision to bring the struggle against emergency management to a residential neighborhood. With some of Snyder's more curious neighbors looking on from the other side of the fence, Reverend Bullock proclaimed to the crowd that if democracy was good enough for Egypt, it was good enough for Michigan.

While large-scale protests helped to bring statewide attention to PA 4 and recall efforts challenged it indirectly by seeking to punish the Governor and Republican legislators for enacting it, three more direct routes of contesting the law and its application emerged that gave further definition to the pro-democracy movement. The first was an effort in 2011 and 2012 to repeal PA 4 through referendum. The second was a legal challenge to the constitutionality of the law, beginning in 2011 and continuing in different forms into 2018. The third consisted of diverse forms of local resistance to particular EMs and EM decrees within cities under emergency management. Through their contributions to all three forms of pro-democracy activism, a small but devoted contingent of Flint activists helped make Flint into one of the hotspots of anti-EM resistance.

The understanding of democracy that would later animate the water movement in Flint was heavily indebted to the ideas of the pro-democracy movement. Pro-democracy activists like the members of Stand Up for Democracy and the Flint Democracy Defense League believed democracy to be under assault by private interests that were using the cover of "emergency" to enact unpopular neoliberal policies by authoritarian means. This notion percolated through activist circles nationwide thanks partly to the popularity of Naomi Klein's 2011 book *The Shock Doctrine* and the idea of "disaster capitalism,"[11] but in Michigan it seemed especially relevant, for nowhere—in the United States, at least—was the abrogation of democracy more literal or glaring. PA 4's affront to fundamental democratic values was so egregious, activists believed, that it could be used to catalyze popular resistance across lines of class, race, and geography. Mixed in with their populist clarion call to rise to the defense of representative democracy, however, was a less obvious but more radical current associated with the Occupy movement: a resolve to think beyond traditional democratic institutions, to seize the moment to deepen rather than merely defend democracy. The exigent circumstances created by the state takeover and the deterioration of Flint's water were not always conducive to the concerted pursuit of this ambition, but the water crisis, especially, generated popular energies and political opportunities that some activists tried to channel in such a direction (see chapter 8).

Flint activists came to see the assault on democracy theorized by Klein as intersecting with a global assault on water that was also especially salient in Michigan. Among the private interests who stood to benefit from emergency management, they believed, were those looking to privatize public water systems. By contrast, the people suffering worst under EMs in cities like Detroit and Flint were those struggling with rising water rates and water shutoffs. The more that water issues came to disrupt everyday life, the more they became a basis for the kind of broad-based organizing the activists aspired to, as well as a starting point for awakening residents to the larger issues of privatization and democracy connected with them. As efforts to contest the EM law directly ran into obstacles, pro-democracy activists in Flint, taking inspiration from compatriots in Detroit, shifted their struggle onto this new terrain. No one could have anticipated that the crisis of water affordability and accessibility that first drew their attention would soon be supplanted by a crisis of water quality. But thanks to the effusion of political activity called forth by the attack on local democracy in Flint and beyond, when that crisis hit the activists had already laid the groundwork for a political analysis of it and a popular response to it. If, then, the Flint water crisis really began with the passage of PA 4 in 2011, as these activists believed, so too did the Flint water movement.

Repealing PA 4

Recall of elected officials was not the only mechanism of direct democracy Michigan activists turned to in the absence of influence over the legislative process. As the passage of an augmented EM law began to look like an inevitability in early 2011, they started to discuss the possibility of repealing the law through referendum. In March, the Traverse City–based group Reject Emergency Managers began drumming up interest in a repeal effort over social media. Spokesperson Betsy Coffia described the strategy as "a very small version" of the spur to action provided by social media during the Arab Spring.[12] Shortly thereafter, Reject Emergency Managers teamed up with the Detroit-based urban policy think tank Michigan Forward, which took the lead in bringing together a coalition of groups throughout the state willing to lend their support to the repeal. The result was the Stand Up for Democracy (SUD) coalition.

Although organized labor decided to keep its distance, for the most part, from the recall efforts that began to appear around the same time, it threw its support behind the repeal. The first group to step up was Council 25 of the American Federation of State, County, and Municipal Employees (AFSCME), which became SUD's chief financial benefactor, kicking in $185,000 over the next year and a half. Support also came from the Michigan Education Association and the United Auto Workers. Because labor in general was "diametrically opposed" to the law, SUD spokesperson Greg Bowens remembers, even relatively conservative unions endorsed the repeal effort.[13]

Legal support came from groups like the Advancement Project, the Sugar Law Center, and the ACLU. Groups like the Michigan NAACP, the Michigan Welfare Rights Organization, and the Rainbow Push Coalition helped mobilize volunteers to collect petition signatures. And Flint activists who would later take leading roles in the water movement contributed in significant ways. Claire McClinton, a former GM electrical engineer, union organizer, and matriarch of sorts within the Flint activist scene (known affectionately as "Mama Claire," a nickname she disliked), and Nayyirah Shariff, a ubiquitous activist and trained community organizer, served as community action team leaders. Bishop Bernadel Jefferson, another GM retiree whose fight against emergency management began in 2003 with a campaign to reopen community centers closed by emergency financial manager (EFM) Ed Kurtz, represented AFSCME and served as SUD's Genesee County chair. As pastor of Flint's Faith Deliverance Center, a member of the Concerned Pastors for Social Action, and former president of the Greater Flint Council of Churches, Jefferson also offered the coalition an important anchor within the faith community.[14]

The referendum's path to the ballot was not as steep as the one that twice thwarted efforts to recall Governor Snyder, requiring a considerably more manageable tally of 161,304 signatures. Another advantage the repeal effort had over the recall effort was that it could be framed as nonpartisan. Organizers knew their success depended upon making the case for repeal not only to the predominantly liberal residents of large, majority-minority, economically depressed cities already under emergency management (or next in line for it), but to conservatives living in parts of the state that were predominantly rural, white, and, by relative standards, affluent. SUD settled on two principal arguments it expected to resonate with the latter demographic. The first of these was an argument from self-interest: while postindustrial cities like Flint, Benton Harbor, and Pontiac may have been the first to be saddled with emergency management, PA 4 made every city, village, county, and school district in the state vulnerable to unwanted takeover. After all, the lingering effects of the Great Recession, combined with deep cuts to state revenue sharing, were being felt not just in Michigan's most troubled cities, but all over the state. The ACLU of Michigan warned that "over one hundred local governments are potentially in a state of 'fiscal watch' and forty school districts or charter schools are in deficit while another 150 are in danger of going into deficit."[15] Reports started to appear of majority-white cities like Northville, Suttons Bay, and Taylor being threatened with emergency management.[16] And municipalities and school districts that were currently solvent could, conceivably, fall on hard financial times at some point in the future. The takeaway, as SUD activists put it, was that emergency management was "coming to a town near you."

Their other argument was more ideological, framing PA 4 as a recipe for a particularly nefarious form of big government at odds with conservative principles. The emergency manager system, activists contended, was an implicit attack on the idea of self-determination, premised on the belief that unelected, "expert" bureaucrats were better at governing people than people were at governing themselves. Even Michiganders sympathetic to Governor Snyder's overall agenda had reason to see PA 4 as an overreach—as anti-American, even. While the Tea Party movement spoke of being "Taxed Enough Already," proponents of the repeal often used a slogan that was, ironically, a more direct reference to colonial resistance against British tyranny: "No Taxation without Representation."[17]

Through 2011 and into 2012, SUD brought these arguments to venues around the state as it worked toward its signature goal. Bishop Jefferson described the repeal as a "genuine grassroots effort," with organizers braving the rain, snow, and sleet to collect signatures, setting up tables at every possible event regardless of what or where it was.[18] By February, SUD had more than enough signatures to qualify the referendum for the November ballot. On February 29, 2012, busloads of activists from Detroit, Flint, and other Michigan cities converged on Lansing for a celebratory rally. The activists ended by marching to the Secretary of State's office to hand-deliver the petitions.

Two months later, the repeal ran into an unanticipated roadblock when the Board of State Canvassers, splitting 2 to 2 along party lines, declined to certify the petitions. The decision followed a challenge brought by the conservative group Citizens for Fiscal Responsibility arguing that the heading printed on the petitions failed to conform to stipulations in state law about font size. The issue was not, to be sure, one of readability—to the layperson's eye, the text was close enough to the required fourteen-point size that the differences were microscopic. Expert witnesses including a graphic design professor from Michigan State University and one of the state's premier printers confirmed that the font was correctly proportioned, but their testimony was disregarded by the Republican members of the board.[19]

For advocates of the repeal, it was hard not to see the challenge and the board's ruling on it as anything other than cynical attempts to deny the people of Michigan an opportunity to have their say about PA 4. The decision not only threw the future of the repeal effort into doubt, it also ensured that the law—which would be suspended upon certification of the referendum—would remain in effect for as long as it took to litigate the matter in the courts. Flint activist Bob Mabbitt remembered the "Fontgate" episode to me as a moment when the members of the Flint SUD contingent gained new insight into the extent to which the system was rigged against them.[20] Nayyirah Shariff described it as a "wake-up call."[21]

SUD lawyers immediately launched a legal challenge to the ruling, but it took months to close the case. Finally, on August 3, the Michigan Supreme Court ruled in a 4 to 3 decision that the font issue was too trivial to keep the referendum off the ballot. The voters would have their say after all—and in the meantime, PA 4 would go dormant.

The suspension of PA 4 did not, however, mean the suspension of emergency management altogether, despite arguments to that effect by SUD. Instead, Attorney General Bill Schuette concluded that in PA 4's absence, its predecessor, PA 72, had gone back into effect, allowing the state to convert EMs into EFMs for the time being. The decision was not just a disappointment in the moment, but a foreboding of things to come. It was clear that even if voters repealed PA 4, the state would simply fall back on PA 72 as a stopgap, keeping its appointees in place while it crafted a replacement law.

Still, Michigan voters would at least have an opportunity in November to make their feelings on PA 4 known. When polled about the proposed repeal in early 2012, respondents leaned toward upholding the law. As election day approached, however, new polls showed that the tide had turned. Support for the repeal was, as expected, much stronger in Michigan's larger cities than it was in the suburbs, and stronger with Democrats than Republicans. Overall, however, the polls suggested that the repeal's advocates had made considerable headway with a wide range of Michiganders from all over the state. The results on November 6 confirmed as much: voters rejected PA 4 resoundingly, with majorities in almost all of Michigan's eighty-one counties voting against it. Some regarded the outcome as a "miracle."[22]

One effect of SUD's repeal campaign was to open up a discursive space for a conversation about what a viable alternative to emergency management might look like. For its part, SUD offered an eight-point plan centered on municipal finance reforms meant to prevent cities from ending up in desperate fiscal situations to begin with. The plan proposed, among other things, restoring state revenue sharing and reforming the municipal bond system to place cities in a stronger position relative to creditors. It also insisted upon preserving local involvement in decision making even in "emergency" situations, suggesting that councils comprised of state and local officials could be established to solve financial problems collaboratively rather than placing sweeping powers in the hands of individual appointees. After the repeal, SUD activists had an opportunity to make their case directly to Chief of Staff Dennis Muchmore and other members of Governor Snyder's cabinet. As impressive as the repeal itself was, however, the coalition was not in a position to exert much influence: Republicans still had a firm majority in both houses of the state legislature, meaning there was little to stop them from pushing through a virtual duplicate of the law. This is, in fact, exactly what happened when, on December 26, Snyder signed PA 436.

The governor claimed that the new law demonstrated that the administration had "clearly heard, recognized, and respected the will of the voters" by incorporating new provisions for "local control."[23] Unlike PA 4, PA 436 allowed local officials the choice of four different options upon a state declaration of financial emergency: a consent agreement, mediation, an EM, or Chapter 9 bankruptcy (although, crucially, the state retained veto power over the choice). PA 436 also gave local officials the ability to suggest alternatives to specific proposals made by EMs as long as they yielded similar cost savings, as well as the power to remove an EM after a year in office by a two-thirds majority vote.

Snyder may have believed these to be substantive changes, but SUD saw the new law—hastily passed during a lame-duck session and reviving the broad powers that made PA 4 controversial—as an expression of the administration's contempt for the popular will. It released an analysis of the many similarities between PA 436 and PA 4 and questioned just how much the law had actually changed. As Greg Bowens put it at the time, "We think that the Governor's view of what the will of the voters is is quite different from what the actual voters did."[24] Republican legislators seemed to concede this implicitly when they took steps to shield the new law from another referendum, attaching an appropriation to it and thereby rendering it immune from repeal under Michigan law.[25] SUD vowed to continue fighting, but there would be no redux of the statewide petition drive that had been the reason for the coalition's existence. Resistance would have to proceed through other channels.

The Constitutional Challenge

Running parallel to the repeal effort through 2011 and 2012 was a complementary legal challenge to the constitutionality of PA 4, filed by the Sugar Law Center for Economic and Social Justice and other legal partners on behalf of twenty-eight Michigan residents from around the state.[26] The decision to mount a legal challenge to PA 4 was far from automatic—the general attitude within the legal community in early 2011, John Philo of Sugar Law recalled to me, was that not much could be done through the courts to contest the law. But with the repeal petition drive underway, he and his colleagues decided that the value of a lawsuit transcended its likelihood of success. A lawsuit was not only another means of raising awareness about PA 4, it was a means of bringing otherwise obscure details about the origins and intent of the law to light through the discovery process. Philo hoped this would provide fodder for those making the case for repeal and keep the issue alive as the repeal effort proceeded. Beyond that, he and others were convinced that the law was "undemocratic and wrong and can't be legal."[27]

The lawsuit was filed in state court on June 22, 2011, with the expectation that it would eventually find its way to the Michigan Supreme Court.[28] Flint resident, teacher, and former school board member Paul Jordan agreed to sign on as one of the plaintiffs. As part of a coordinated rollout of the suit around the state, he held a press conference outside Flint City Hall at which he announced the filing and denounced PA 4 as "a cynical attempt to grab power in Michigan's most vulnerable cities and schools."[29] In the months that followed, Jordan became one of the most prominent critics of PA 4 in Flint, working to spread the word about the law through op-eds, panel appearances, and public protests, and acting as a link between the legal challenge and other forms of resistance by local activists.

The lawsuit named Governor Snyder and State Treasurer Andy Dillon as defendants and took aim at the facial language of PA 4, alleging that the law violated the Michigan Constitution in several different ways. First, the plaintiffs claimed, it violated provisions establishing municipal home rule by empowering EMs to repeal local ordinances and disregard local charters and contracts. Second, by depriving elected officials of their ability to govern, the law violated citizens' right to vote and petition. Third, it abolished the separation of powers, enabling appointees of the executive branch to establish new legislation unilaterally. Finally, it allowed the state to impose unfunded mandates on local governments, forcing local taxpayers to cover the cost of EM (and EM staff) salaries.[30]

After surviving what John Philo called an "unbelievably unheard of" attempt by the Snyder administration to quash the lawsuit quickly by skipping the discovery phase and moving it directly to the majority-Republican State Supreme Court, it was rendered moot by the repeal of PA 4.[31] The legal wing of the pro-democracy movement took on renewed importance, however, after the passage of PA 436. The same group of attorneys who had challenged the constitutionality of PA 4 decided to file a new lawsuit against PA 436—this time in federal court, in the belief that federal judges would be more likely to understand the underlying issues of democracy at stake.[32] The suit charged that PA 436, in usurping republican government, interfering with voting rights (and thereby freedom of speech), and discriminating against African Americans and the poor, violated the US Constitution's Due Process Clause, Guarantee Clause, Equal Protection Clause, and First and Thirteenth Amendments, as well as the federal Voting Rights Act. This time, the attorneys drew their plaintiffs exclusively from cities that had been directly impacted by emergency management. In Flint, Bishop Jefferson from SUD and City Council President Scott Kincaid joined Paul Jordan on the lawsuit.

In November 2014, the suit suffered a major setback when a district court judge dismissed eight out of its nine charges. The judge found, firstly, that the Fourteenth Amendment does not include the right to elect local officials and that at the local level there is no right to republican government under the Guarantee Clause. With respect to claims of discrimination against the poor, the judge found that there was a "rational basis" for differential treatment of municipalities based on finances, and that this did not amount to discrimination under the Equal Protection Clause. Furthermore, because the imposition of an EM did not involve the outright firing of local officials, and because local elections proceeded as usual under emergency management, PA 436 did not violate the Voting Rights Act. Nor did the law infringe on First Amendment protections for freedom of speech. And Thirteenth Amendment protections against slavery did not apply because, even under emergency management, residents still had "every device in the political arsenal" available to them.[33]

The one charge left standing was the charge that PA 436 violated the US Constitution's Equal Protection Clause on the basis of race. But pursuing this charge in isolation was risky. An equal protection argument would have to meet a heavy burden of proof, showing that PA 436 was not only discriminatory in implementation, but also discriminatory in intent.[34] This required a "much deeper dive" during the discovery period, said John Philo, which the state was determined to fight doggedly every step of the way.[35]

The attorneys opted to save the equal protection charge for a later date and pursue an appeal of the whole suit, focusing their accusations of discrimination on wealth rather than race. The case proceeded into the Sixth Circuit Court of Appeals, where, in September 2016, it was finally dismissed. In a unanimous decision, the judges wrote that PA 436 was "rationally related" to the "legitimate legislative purpose" of improving the financial situation of distressed localities. They echoed the earlier district court determinations that the law did not violate citizens' freedom of expression,[36] or constitutional protections against slavery, or the Voting Rights Act, pointing out that citizens "are still provided a vote" and that the local officials they elect remain in office. Also, the law was "facially entirely neutral with respect to race" and had been "passed by state-elected bodies for which African Americans have a constitutionally protected equal right to vote."[37] The court also rejected the claim that selectively applying the law based on the financial situation of local governments was tantamount to wealth discrimination, ruling that the solvency of government and the wealth of residents were separate matters.

Having shot down these eight charges for the second time, the court concluded that the "vast" powers possessed by EMs were appropriately tailored to the equally vast challenges faced by local governments in fiscal distress. One of the attorneys for the plaintiffs, Herb Sanders, lambasted the decision, saying that the court "took a fascist view toward the democratic rights of the citizens."[38]

The Sixth Circuit decision finding PA 436 constitutional left Sanders, Philo, and the rest of the legal team with few options.[39] But at the very least, Philo maintains, the legal challenge helped to "flip" the "public perception" of the EM law.[40] Consequently, even before the Flint water crisis dealt the EM system its worst-ever black eye, EMs were growing warier of exercising the full range of their powers.[41] Ironically, then, the legal battles against PA 4 and PA 436 may have had their most important effects outside a legal context. By diminishing the standing of emergency management in the court of public opinion, they arguably helped to generate *de facto* constraints on the exercise of state power—a precedent replicated in dramatic fashion during the water crisis.

Local Resistance to Emergency Management

The day Herb Sanders and his colleagues delivered oral arguments to the Sixth Circuit in August 2016, several buses full of activists from Flint, Detroit, and elsewhere made the journey to Cincinnati to be present for the hearing. Addressing the activists on the steps of the courthouse after a discouraging appearance before the skeptical and impatient circuit judges, Sanders told them that "there's only so much we can do as attorneys. This issue is going to be determined not in the courtroom, but in the streets."[42]

The sentiment met with vocal approval from the onlookers, many of whom had, in fact, been fighting emergency management in the "streets" since 2011. At times, they had taken the fight directly to the state politicians responsible for the EM law. An early opportunity to do so came in May 2011, when Governor Snyder and PA 4 sponsor Al Pscholka were slated to march in the Grand Floral Parade at the annual Benton Harbor Blossomtime Festival. Benton Harbor had entered state receivership under PA 72, but in April now-EM Joe Harris had used the expanded powers available to him under PA 4 to neutralize the local government. Citing mismanagement of funds and infighting among elected officials, he kicked the latter out of their offices and prohibited them from doing anything without his express permission except calling a meeting to order, approving meeting minutes, and adjourning a meeting.[43] It was a vivid illustration of what an EM could do that an EFM could not, and for critics of PA 4, Harris's actions became emblematic of the law's anti-democratic implications. Progressive blogger Chris Savage called Snyder and Pscholka's scheduled parade appearance "an audacious display of arrogance and chutzpah." It smacked, he wrote, "of a conqueror reviewing the lands recently vanquished."[44] After getting wind that protests were in the works, Pscholka pulled out, scolding "professional agitators" for trying to turn a "wholesome community event" into a "political sideshow."[45] Snyder, however, went ahead with the parade. As he made his way along the route, protestors hounded him relentlessly, chanting, waving signs, and turning their backs on him at strategic moments. For a number of Flint activists, it was their first experience protesting the new EM law. Claire McClinton remembers being heartened by the fact that union members were joined by members of the "community," suggesting that a "broader social movement" was taking shape around what people correctly recognized as a "community-wide" issue.[46]

Pro-democracy activists saw Benton Harbor as an instructive example of what kind of city the Snyder administration would choose for emergency management. Its population was overwhelmingly African American. Its poverty rate was one of the highest in the state. Its economy was in shambles from lost manufacturing. Its local government was in poor financial condition, as evidenced by dwindling cash reserves, an underfunded pension system, and faltering municipal services.[47] Just as important, however, the city had something to offer: a Lake Michigan shoreline ripe for development, and a corporate partner (some would say master) in the Whirlpool Corporation, headquartered in Benton Harbor since 1911, that was eager to help bankroll that development. The main thing preventing the recuperation of the city's economy, argued Al Pscholka, was the "play government" at City Hall.[48] A "stable" political environment, he said, would create a more favorable climate for investment, from which the city would reap desperately needed revenue.

But activists suspected the state would use emergency management in Benton Harbor to advance development projects that left poor residents behind while transforming the city into a lakeside playground for the wealthy. Their suspicions centered on the $500 million Harbor Shores development, comprised of a Jack Nicklaus–designed golf course and associated luxury housing. It wasn't just that the payoff the average resident would see from this development was indirect at best—it was that building it had required taking a sizable bite out of a public park, Jean Klock Park, part of which was leased out for the construction of three holes with scenic lake views. This development scheme was already in an advanced stage by the time PA 4 expanded EM Harris's powers, but activists liked to point to ways in which he was using those powers to push it forward.[49] The larger takeaway, from the activists' perspective, was this: the most attractive cities for state takeover were those where private developers saw opportunity, cities where the state could use financial distress as a pretext to advance private interests.

For all the above reasons, the debut of the EM law's strengthened provisions in Benton Harbor had symbolic resonance that reverberated through activist circles around the state. But Benton Harbor was exemplary in another way, too: when emergency management came to town, local activists rose to the occasion and fought for their city. Sometimes they fought side by side with allies in high-profile actions like the aforementioned

Blossomtime protest and the later "occupation" of the Senior PGA Championship at the much-maligned golf course in May 2012.[50] But most of their resistance was more quotidian. Led by the firebrand Reverend Edward Pinkney, they maintained a relentlessly contrarian presence, continuously scrutinizing, publicizing, denouncing, and resisting the actions of EM Harris and the local power elite. For Flint activists like Claire McClinton, a long-time supporter of Pinkney (who became the pro-democracy movement's signature prisoner after being convicted of election fraud, a conviction later overturned),[51] the tenacity with which Benton Harbor activists resisted the takeover of their city was an inspiring retort to the creeping "culture of fascism" and "atmosphere of dictatorship" that develops, she said, when people start getting used to being overruled.[52]

When PA 4 claimed Flint in December 2011, Flint activists had a similar chance to prove themselves. They were already involved in state-level challenges to PA 4 through recall, repeal, and legal action. Now it was imperative to open up a local front of resistance, too—all the more so because local officials in both branches of city government had apparently rolled over, or even laid out the welcome mat, for EM Mike Brown. *Someone*, the activists felt, had to show that democracy would not die in Flint without a fight.[53]

Anti-EM initiative in Flint came from several different directions. There were outspoken members of the church community like Pastor Reginald Flynn, arrested during a provocative "one-man" protest of EM Brown's budget inside City Hall. In his "A Letter from the Flint City Jail," he denounced the "climate of political suppression, economic exploitation, and racial domination" created by the "implementation of Public Act 4."[54] There were legal challenges by local attorneys Greg and Alec Gibbs to Brown's attempts to restructure retiree health care, leading to two precedent-setting victories that won the attention of other cities under emergency management and the respect of local activists (who held regular meetings in the Gibbs's conference room for a time).[55] There was the Flint and Genesee County SUD group, consisting of seven to ten people focused primarily on the repeal but who had more time to devote to local issues after the end of signature gathering in February 2012. And there was a new group formed out of Occupy Flint in January 2012 that called itself the Emergency Manager Work Group. The group lent its support to the repeal effort but also acted as a study group aimed at better understanding the EM law and the actions being taken by

Flint's own EMs. On Fridays, the City of Flint would upload the text of the EM's latest resolutions and executive orders, and the group would meet to pore over them. Sometimes group members would read them aloud in public settings in order to publicize them.[56]

The activists placed particular stress on bringing the inner workings of emergency management into the light because of their feeling that, in Flint, PA 4 was manifesting itself as an insidious "bastardization" (Nayyirah Shariff's term) of the democratic process rather than a bald-faced, hostile takeover. Some of the steps taken by Flint's EMs seemed designed to create the impression of business as usual. In other cities and districts under emergency management, there was no doubt that EMs ran the show—in Pontiac, for example, City Council meetings were canceled altogether, and in Detroit, school board members met as the Detroit School Board in Exile to protest their marginalization. In Flint, by contrast, the council (after a brief hiatus) was allowed to meet once a month, and Mayor Walling was delegated a measure of responsibility. These local officials, Shariff told me, were "not honest," pretending to have power they did not actually possess or that what little power they did have couldn't be revoked at a moment's notice on a whim. Furthermore, the appointment of Flint native and former Interim Mayor Mike Brown as the city's first EM gave the impression that residents were merely being placed into paternalistic hands of an old friend, or at least a familiar and palatable figure, a benevolent dictator. Activists saw it as their task to expose the fact that the people of Flint were no longer living under a democracy, to get them to see Brown as "the face of fascism."[57] When, during the early months of his tenure, Brown made a point of holding a series of public meetings to discuss his agenda, activists followed him from venue to venue, heckling him and forcing him to defend the legitimacy of his regime.[58]

For the most part, however, the residents who came out to these meetings were concerned not about abstract questions of democracy, but about how Brown proposed to deal with issues like violence, vandalism, the closure of senior centers, and new fees on city services—tangible issues that predated emergency management. Much of the activists' strategizing revolved around finding ways to make the implications of emergency management itself equally concrete. Residents, they believed, had to be able to *see* EMs reshaping their city and diminishing their quality of life before they would begin to appreciate the size of the threat the EM law posed. The controversy in

Benton Harbor over Jean Klock Park provided an important lesson: when treasured public assets were at risk, people paid attention. Given that the privatization of such assets was an integral part of the EM "playbook,"[59] the activists warned that a fire sale was on the horizon in Flint. Working with local playwright Andrew Morton, they staged a political theater event and demonstration on the lawn of City Hall conceived as a "mad hatter tea party."[60] Participants donned costumes and acted out the roles of Governor Snyder, EM Brown, Representative Pscholka, and the conservative Mackinac Center, a longtime advocate of a stronger EM law—all engaged in a poker game in which they gambled away public assets listed on "Garage Sale" signs.[61]

The activists' warning proved prophetic. In June, Brown put the city's garbage trucks up on the auction block. In August, he sold Genesee Towers—Flint's tallest building and part of its downtown skyline since the 1960s—for one dollar to the Uptown Reinvestment Corporation, which proceeded to demolish it and create an urban plaza. Activists staged a protest against the decision at the starting line of the annual Crim race in downtown Flint (they had toyed with the idea of physically blocking the runners) and hung a banner from the building prior to the demolition pointing out that "nobody asked US."[62] On the same day as the Genesee Towers resolution, Brown gave the Food Bank of Eastern Michigan permission to lease part of a public park next door so it could expand its parking lot.[63] A group of residents and activists circulated a petition to stop the transaction, protesting that the community had its own plans for the park.[64] Brown also gave Atwood Stadium, a city-owned venue for high school football games and other events that had fallen into disuse and disrepair, to Kettering University, its humble "FLINT" lettering at midfield eventually replaced by a Kettering bulldog logo. Even the Santa Claus and reindeer that traditionally graced the roof of City Hall during the holiday season were put up for sale. In response, activist Melodee Mabbitt organized a successful campaign to buy the decorations, carting them around the city on a "democracy tour" and promising to return them to City Hall if democracy was ever restored.[65] For Mabbitt, the effort was only partially tongue in cheek: standing up for "beloved" parts of Flint's public sphere, she told me, was a noncontroversial way of dramatizing the effects of emergency management.[66]

After the dissolution of Occupy Flint and Stand Up for Democracy, a core group of activists who had gotten to know each other through the fight against PA 4 concluded that Flint needed a designated pro-democracy group focused primarily on local issues. Over the course of several months of formative discussions in 2013, the Flint Democracy Defense League (FDDL) was born. The group's founding document articulated its "vision of democracy":

> Democracy is your right to meaningfully participate in the decisions that affect your life, including the planning and governance of the cities where you live and work. Democracy is not for sale. Wealth does not determine your eligibility to participate in democracy. You always have a voice. You always have a vote. Dictators are never allowed to take those rights from you.[67]

Despite its juxtaposition of democracy to dictatorship (i.e., emergency management), the statement was crafted to reflect higher ambitions than merely the restoration of representative democracy in Flint. Putting an end to emergency management was the immediate priority, but the FDDL envisioned itself as a group that could serve a broader democratic purpose in the city. In the same document, the group clarified that "FDDL doesn't just 'defend democracy.' We *exercise* democratic rights, *educate* others about their democratic rights, and strive to *expand* democratic rights within schools, workplaces, and beyond."

For the FDDL, every objectionable EM action was an opportunity to initiate a deeper conversation about democracy. When EM Darnell Earley put new constraints on public comment at open meetings, for example, FDDL members turned out to City Hall with their mouths taped shut to protest what they described as an assault on the civil liberties fundamental to a democratic society. When EMs sold off public assets, FDDL argued that emergency management was facilitating a kind of "vulture capitalism" that turned democracy into a "rigged, lucrative game for oligarchs."[68] The issue that rose to the top of the group's priorities during mid-2013 to late 2014, however, was water. It fit the bill perfectly: it was an issue of direct and dire significance to residents, an issue that EM decisions (about matters like water infrastructure, rates, and supply) were shaping in lasting ways, and an issue that allowed for broader discussions of subjects like human rights,[69] privatization, and self-determination. Well before there was an officially recognized Flint water crisis, in other words, the themes of water and democracy were beginning to draw together in Flint.

Figure 4.1
Members of the FDDL protest changes by EM Darnell Earley to public comment rules. *MLive, Flint Journal.*

Water and Democracy

"One of the things that's going to bring Michigan back," EM Mike Brown told Flint residents at the first of his public meetings in 2012, "is water."[70] The Karegnondi Water Authority (KWA) pipeline, he suggested, would be one piece of that renaissance. More important, for Flint, it was the answer to the city's decades-old desire to control its own water system.

Brown's endorsement was hardly a mark in the KWA's favor from the activists' perspective, of course. But it was not until 2013, following the City Council's affirmative vote on the project, that they began closely scrutinizing the claims made by Brown and the pipeline's other supporters. Activists were sure they could smell a rat, that there was more to the project than met the eye and that some sort of corruption was at play. The main issue they highlighted at the time, however, was the possibility that taxpayer money would be spent to finance the pipeline's construction. Genesee County Drain Commissioner Jeff Wright dismissed the concern as patently unfounded, but that did not stop the activists from insisting that residents have a direct say about the city's participation in the project. In October, a group calling itself the Water Pipeline Question Committee, including the members of the FDDL, launched a petition drive to get the issue onto the November ballot and inject at least a "sliver of democracy" (as Nayyirah Shariff put it) into the decision about Flint's long-term water source.[71] A demonstrably annoyed Wright warned that the vote could slow down the project and force the city into another thirty-year deal with the Detroit Water and Sewerage Department (DWSD).[72] According to some activists I spoke to, he paid people to hang around the petition sites and try to convince potential signers that the activists were telling lies about the project.[73]

Faced with the daunting task of collecting eight thousand signatures in forty-five days, the activists fell well short of their goal, killing the referendum. Wright argued that the "lack of support for the petition drive shows clearly that the vast majority of the citizens of Flint are behind this project."[74] The activists, of course, virulently disagreed with this interpretation; Claire McClinton insisted to me that "there was no popular appetite for the KWA."[75] But it was clear, at least, that the kinds of concerns activists were raising about the future of Flint's water supply and water infrastructure had not yet captured the imagination of the average Flint resident.

What *was* a pressing matter in the minds of residents was the cost of water. In 2011, Mayor Walling raised water and sewer rates twice—first, in January, by 47 percent, and then, in September, by another 35 percent.[76] The next spring, EM Brown raised them 25 percent, bringing the average water bill of a Flint resident to over $100 a month.[77] The threat of having one's water shut off entirely loomed over anyone behind on payments.[78]

Desperate for relief, residents inundated nonprofit agencies with requests for help with water bills. They explored digging wells and disconnecting entirely from the municipal system. Some turned to what city officials called "water theft" (a term derided by activists, especially after the city spent precious resources on two special investigators hired to crack down on the practice), utilizing various more-or-less creative methods of accessing municipal water without paying for it.[79] In recognition of the affordability problem, in December 2012 EM Ed Kurtz created an "indigent water fund," a pool of donated money that could be used to help struggling ratepayers on an as-needed basis. But he also continued to make water even more expensive, raising the water service deposit paid by new renters by three-and-a-half times the next March.[80]

With the switch to the Flint River cementing the break with Detroit in April 2014, many hoped and expected that the city would lower rates, but instead they continued to climb, rising another 6.5 percent in 2014. Even on the river, a water bill in Flint was $35 higher per month than in the next most expensive municipality in Genesee County and almost three times higher than in the cheapest.[81] The city *was* saving money by using the river, of course, but officials insisted that it was better funneled into long-term infrastructural improvements than into short-term respite for cost-weary residents.[82]

The city making headlines for its water troubles in 2014, however, was not Flint but Detroit, another city under emergency management, and another city, like Benton Harbor, to which Flint activists had strong connections through pro-democracy channels.[83] In the spring and summer of 2014, EM Kevyn Orr signed off on a massive wave of water shutoffs targeting tens of thousands of residences. Activists suspected that the spate of shutoffs was a prelude to the privatization of Detroit's water system: if DWSD could unburden itself of the "bad debt" of unpaid bills, it would make the department more attractive to potential investors. Furthermore, shutoffs, along with water liens (unpaid water bills transferred onto property taxes) would push unwanted residents out of the city as their houses were condemned or taken over, clearing the ground for future development. The situation in Detroit was shaping up to be another example, from the activists' perspective, of EMs balancing a city's budget on the backs of its most disadvantaged residents while proffering public assets at bargain-basement prices to private buyers, cleansing the city of its undesirables in the process and handing it over to the rich and powerful.

If the spate of shutoffs had one silver lining, it was that its timing—shutoffs peaked in June to July 2014—proved to be fortuitous. From July 17 to 21, Netroots Nation, the nation's largest annual conference for progressive political activists, was held at the Cobo Center in downtown Detroit. It featured panels with activists from Flint and Detroit who had been fighting for water and democracy in the "trenches," including a keynote panel on resistance to the shutoffs. The nurses' union National Nurses United, which had warned that the shutoffs were creating a public health crisis, called a march through downtown Detroit on July 18 that was joined by many of the conference attendees, including the actor Mark Ruffalo, whose organization Water Defense would later play a significant role in the response to the Flint water crisis. On the same day, police arrested a group of activists for physically blocking the passage of trucks on their way to shut off water. The principled militancy of the "Homrich 9," as they came to be called (after the demolition company contracted by DWSD to carry out the shut-offs), helped to create a spirit of civil disobedience within Michigan's network of water and democracy activists that clearly made an impression on the Flint activists I knew.

The Netroots Nation conference helped to launch the water crisis in Detroit into the national and international spotlight. Maureen Taylor of the Michigan Welfare Rights Organization called its impact "magnificent"— people from around the world had "heard," "learned," and "understood," and were "changed."[84] On the heels of the conference, an international convoy sponsored by the Council of Canadians delivered a large shipment of water to the city. In October, there was another surge of international press when UN Special Rapporteurs Catarina de Albuquerque and Leilani Farha came to Detroit to investigate the impact of the shutoffs. They collected testimony throughout the city, visiting homes without water, speaking directly with affected residents, and concluding that the shutoffs constituted a violation of basic human rights.

They also invited residents to speak about the struggles they were facing with water at a town hall on October 19. One of those who testified was Claire McClinton, who stressed the parallels between what was happening in Detroit and what was happening in Flint. In Flint, too, she pointed out, residents faced prohibitively high water rates and were being kicked off the water grid. As examples of the latter, she referred to the Ambassador East mobile home community, where residents had been living without water for over a year and a half, and to shutoff notices just issued to an apartment complex and a homeless drop-in shelter where people went to take showers and wash clothes.

By the time McClinton brought Flint's water troubles to the attention of the UN in October 2014, Flint activists had already been working for several months to bring the water wars raging in Detroit to Flint. In June, July, and August, City Councilman Wantwaz Davis called several protests and a march against high water rates, which members of the FDDL used to recruit residents to their weekly meetings. The FDDL also presented itself as a resource to residents who were having trouble accessing water, offering to investigate cases like the ones McClinton highlighted for the UN. Taking inspiration from the Detroit Water Brigade, which had formed rapid response teams and water distribution sites in June as shutoffs began to escalate in Detroit, on August 21 the FDDL organized an emergency water relief site at Mission of Hope, a shelter in Flint's north end. In an eerie anticipation of what would, in a year's time, become a daily ritual for residents throughout the city, the group invited anyone in need to pick up cases of donated water between 10 a.m. and 2 p.m., Monday through Friday.

The FDDL realized that popular discontent over water rates and shutoffs, much like discontent over the selling off of public assets, could be a potent source of opposition to emergency management. Like their counterparts in Detroit, Flint activists consistently stressed the role played by EMs in shaping policy around water. At the third of Councilman Davis's protests, in August 2014, Claire McClinton told the crowd assembled outside City Hall that "in order for us to win our right to water, we got to fight the emergency manager."[85] People were being forced to live without water, she said, because of "corporate greed and fascism." Nayyirah Shariff spoke of the need to get rid of the EM, Governor Snyder, and "anyone who is a puppet for the corporate regime to privatize water."[86] Fellow pro-democracy activist and councilman Eric Mays—whose own water had been off for seven months—told the marchers that addressing the problem of water rates would require them to "attack the emergency manager."[87] Under emergency management, he pointed out, any vote by the City Council to lower rates would be purely symbolic because the EM could simply raise them again. The only real way for the city to retake control of its rates, he argued, was to remove the EM from office.[88]

That this interweaving of the struggle for affordable water and the struggle against emergency management was catching on was evident in the slogan featured on a ubiquitous protest sign that day: *"Down with water rates, up with democracy!"* But already, there were indications that the affordability and accessibility of water would not be the only issue that turned pro-democracy activists into water activists in Flint. Another, humbler, handwritten sign at the same rally raised a portentous question: *"Why does the water have an odor and unusual color? Is it safe to drink?"*

5   The Rise of the Water Warriors: Transforming Personal Troubles into Political Action

At the end of the day, we are not just victims, we're fighters.
—Melissa Mays, interview with author, February 17, 2016

In July 2014, three months after the switch to the Flint River, Melissa Mays began to notice changes in her water. It would turn yellow sporadically, sending her three sons charging through the house "running and screaming" to relay the news to their mother.[1] Filling up the family's porcelain bathtub revealed a more consistent bluish tinge. The water also began to smell peculiar: depending on the day, it would reek of rotten eggs, dirt, or bleach.

Mays remembers thinking these developments were "weird," but her initial impulse was to brush them off. The city, she recalled, had warned residents at the time of the switch that river water was different from lake water, and that the water would take time to "level out." Although Mays later came to see official explanations like these as "excuses," at the time they seemed like logical and well-intentioned efforts on the part of knowledgeable authorities to inform and reassure residents. She assumed the government agencies entrusted with public health had done their due diligence and would alert the public if there was any cause for concern.[2]

What began as mild uneasiness about the water's fluctuations developed into real alarm, however, when Mays and her family were beset by a mysterious series of ailments. Upon contact with the water, she told me, their skin would break out in rashes—"bumpy and lumpy" rashes that felt like a "chemical burn" and were unresponsive to eczema cream. The water seemed to be affecting the family's hair, too. Mays watched her sons' naturally "silky" hair become "rough and wiry."[3] Her own hair started falling out in the shower.

Even the family cat's fur, she said, would slough off whenever someone would pet it.

In September, Mays instructed her family to stop drinking the water. But this was not the end of their exposure (they continued to use the water for cooking and showering) or the end of their perplexing health issues. The boys started complaining of muscle and bone pain: eleven-year-old Cole told his mom that his bones "burn from the inside out." Soon thereafter, Mays said, she started suffering from similar pains herself. When Cole fell off his bicycle and thrust his hand out to absorb the impact, his wrist buckled in two places, leading his doctor to surmise that his bones were unusually brittle. Mays's oldest son, seventeen-year-old Caleb, began to develop holes in the smooth sides of his teeth, a sign that rather than decaying in the usual fashion they were crumbling from the inside out. Furthermore, all three boys became lethargic, "tired all the time." Their sluggishness was mental as well as physical, manifesting itself in "brain fogs" that led to difficulties at school.[4] Twelve-year-old Christian, a consistently straight-"A" student, got his first "C," and Caleb and Cole, who were forgetting skills already learned and finding it hard to remember new information, had to be assigned tutors.

Unbeknownst to Mays at the time, her family's ordeal was not unique. Across town, LeeAnne Walters and her family, too, began breaking out in rashes in the summer of 2014. Three-year-old Gavin would emerge from the bath with a visible water line, below which he was so red and scaly that when Walters tried to apply moisturizing ointment, "he would scream and cry about how bad his skin burned."[5] Walters had to start giving him Benadryl before bath time as a preemptive measure.[6]

At first, the doctors said Gavin's rashes were contact dermatitis caused by an allergy of some kind. Then their diagnosis shifted to eczema and they instructed Walters to apply cortisone to the affected area. When the rest of the family began to develop rashes of their own, however, the diagnosis changed yet again: this time Walters was told that everyone had scabies. The treatment was another prescription cream, a pesticide meant to kill the tiny mites thought to be the source of the problem.

In the meantime, further evidence emerged that the water, not mites, was the real culprit. At a party celebrating eighteen-year-old Kaylie's high school graduation, a group of invited guests broke out in the same telltale rash after swimming in the family pool.[7] With this incident fresh in her mind, Walters balked when doctors returned a third diagnosis of scabies the next time she took Gavin in, insisting on further testing by a dermatologist outside city limits. A skin sample showed no evidence of any organism that would have accounted for the rashes.

Like the Mays family, the Walters family also experienced hair problems. Walters recounts rushing up the stairs in response to Kaylie's screams to find her "standing in the shower, staring at a clump of long brown hair that had fallen from her head."[8] Kaylie was not the only one: the other members of the family were losing hair, too. At one point, Walters lost all of her eyelashes.

Problems with skin and hair were bad enough, but once again they were merely preludes to more serious conditions. In November, fourteen-year-old J. D. began to experience "terrible pains, dizziness, nausea." He had "a hard time walking up steps" and grew so ill that he missed an entire month of school between Thanksgiving and Christmas. At one point during the barrage of inconclusive tests that followed, doctors speculated that he had some form of cancer.[9]

Just as J. D. was getting over his symptoms, the water in the Walters household turned brown. Walters's initial reaction was disbelief: all water coming into the house was passing through the whole house filter she and her husband had installed when they purchased and renovated the home in 2011. Even after swapping out filter cartridges, though, the water continued to arrive at the kitchen sink the same disconcerting rusty shade. Deterioration of pipes within the house could be ruled out, given that they were only a few years old. There could only be one conclusion: the water coming in from the city was so contaminated that even a filter was no match for it. In December 2014, the family began to use bottled water.

While the whole Walters family had suffered in one way or another up to that point, Gavin, who was already immunocompromised and who tested positive for elevated blood lead, was ultimately impacted worst of all. Despite Walters's efforts to prevent his coming into contact with the water, his health continued to deteriorate. He developed anemia and speech issues, having difficulty pronouncing words he had already mastered. Most alarming of all, he stopped growing. As his fraternal twin Garrett continued to gain height and weight, Gavin plateaued. Two years after the switch to the river, more than two inches and almost thirty pounds separated them.

Before their lives were turned upside down by contaminated water, neither Melissa Mays nor LeeAnne Walters considered herself a political activist, or even politically inclined—Mays had been to one political march in her

life, Walters had dabbled in advocacy around stillbirth awareness. But out of
the conjuncture of foul water, poor health, and the responsibility they felt as
mothers to protect their families, they would develop into two of Flint's most
prominent "water warriors." In the process, they would come to understand
their personal experiences of contamination as products of larger socio-
political dynamics that converged to cause the crisis, and their determination
to protect themselves and their families would evolve into a broader commitment to the people of Flint and a newfound sense of political agency.

Many of Flint's water warriors followed a similar path to political action,
driven not by prior political commitments but by the personal impact of contaminated water.[10] For these residents, the first manifestations of the water
crisis were often tangible harms to bodies, minds, and property: a stubborn
rash, a child afraid to take a bath, a water heater corroded before its time and
in need of replacement. These kinds of harms comprised the human face of
the crisis, and they generated much of the emotion, energy, and resolve that
fueled the burgeoning water movement in Flint. For personal troubles to be
translated into collective political action, however, residents had to develop
the belief that there were political remedies to their problems. They had to
learn to direct their anger toward specific people, institutions, and policies.
And they had to see their own struggles as intertwined with those of their
neighbors and demanding of a common solution.

Residents also had to develop a belief in themselves as political actors,
people who were capable of understanding what was going on with the
water, judging what needed to be done, and mobilizing to do it. The treatment they received at the hands of officials was not, *prima facie*, conducive
to fostering such self-confidence: with eye rolls and snide remarks, officials
implied that residents were overreacting to changes in the water, jump-
ing to conclusions about the causality of health symptoms, and unable (or
unwilling) to assess the situation rationally. But far from causing residents
like Mays and Walters to doubt themselves and withdraw back into the
private realm, the experience of being dismissed caused them to grow even
more certain of their views and assertive in voicing them. It also got them
thinking about politics: the problem in Flint was not just that government
failed in its protective function—*"they" didn't keep us safe*—but that it failed
in its representative function—*"they" didn't listen to us and act on our concerns.* In light of these failures, residents vowed to take charge of their *own*

health, carry out their *own* research on the water, and force unresponsive decision makers to act.

Into this formative moment stepped the politically seasoned activists of the Flint Democracy Defense League. They introduced into the discourse of the water movement concepts and demands drawn from the pro-democracy movement, infusing immediate concerns about water quality with a farther-reaching political consciousness and strategic agenda. Thanks in large part to their influence, rusty water in the bathtub and blotches on the skin came to symbolize more than just a water crisis: they were the stigmata of democracy denied. Even newly politicized residents came to embrace the idea that the crisis would not be over, nor justice for Flint realized, until democracy was restored.

What I will call the water "movement" in Flint consisted, then, of the potent fusion of activists who came to water through democracy and residents-turned-activists who came to democracy through water. I tell the story of the collective action that fusion spawned in the next three chapters. Here, I examine its roots in residents' everyday experiences of contamination and ill health, in the disrespect they suffered in their interactions with political officials, and in their developing sense of being united in the same predicament—and the same struggle.

The Phenomenology of the Water Crisis

To state the obvious: there was no one, universal experience of the water crisis. For some residents, the crisis began with perceptible changes in the quality of their water. For others, it began with the emergence of health symptoms they attributed to the water. For those without obvious water quality or health problems, it began with warnings from neighbors, friends, and family to avoid the water, or with news coverage of water issues, or with official notices about invisible contaminants in the water. Some residents realized there was something wrong right away, others drank the water for almost two years before they were alerted to the existence of a serious problem.

The crisis also caused varying degrees of hardship. For the minority of residents whose water showed no signs of contamination, who trusted filters to remove invisible threats, and who had no adverse reactions to bathing or showering, life under the crisis could proceed largely as before. For others, the crisis had a devastating effect on their psychological and physical well-being and created considerable financial and logistical burdens.

Despite these variations, it is possible to sketch out a rough "phenomenology" of the water crisis, a set of generalizations about how the crisis appeared on the scene of everyday life, how it affected bodies and minds, and how people coped with it.[11] Within this outline of residents' experience of contamination are clues about why they responded to it the way they did, seeds of the particular species of political agency that blossomed in Flint. In the intellectual journey inaugurated by these experiences, one can also trace the development of a "political etiology" of suffering that traced the causes of specific harms back to the state's structural violence and neglect and warmed residents to the idea that the dissolution of democratic institutions was at the root of their troubles.[12]

For many residents, the first glimmers of a water quality problem appeared in the form of discernable changes in the taste, smell, and color of the water. Residents complained of the water tasting like chlorine and smelling like "bleach," or, alternately, like a "swamp," "raw sewage," "rotten eggs," or "fish."[13] It was rarer, at least at first, to experience discoloration, because it took time for the corrosive river water to destroy the protective passivation layer and leach metal from the pipes. By late 2014 and early 2015, however, as the water began to eat into cast iron mains and service lines made of galvanized steel, some residents saw their water turn shades of yellow, brown, and red—sporadically in most cases, but consistently in some. Sometimes the water contained visible sediment or was unusually cloudy, milky white. Sometimes clothes would emerge from the washing machine with stains from the water itself.

Before widespread water testing became the norm in Flint, empirical changes to the water offered the most concrete available evidence of contamination. Residents were quick to equate such impurities with danger. Some switched to other sources of water as soon as they sensed their tap water had taken a turn for the worse. The phenomenon was widespread enough by mid-June 2014—less than two months after the city began using the river—that Mayor Walling went on record opining that people were "wasting their precious money buying bottled water."[14] In the period before any official acknowledgment of a problem, however, even residents whose water didn't seem right from time to time were, like Melissa Mays, likely to dismiss hiccups in water quality as anomalies, trusting that the people paid to protect them wouldn't allow a hazardous substance into their homes.

Residents who developed health problems concurrently with observable changes in their water had more reason to believe something was seriously awry. The same was true of residents who saw symptoms emerge more or less immediately after direct contact with water, as in cases where showering, bathing, and even hand washing produced ill effects ranging from dry skin and rashes to burning eyes and hair loss. Residents also blamed the inhalation of steam for a variety of respiratory problems.

Those whose water was clear, palatable, and easy on the skin and lungs were slower to conclude that it was a threat to them. Activists derisively related to me stories of residents glibly reporting that *their* water was just fine and that all the fuss seemed overblown. Once news started to break about invisible contaminants, however, even "normal"-looking water began to take on an ominous appearance. First came the boil water advisories of late summer 2014 after the discovery of total coliform bacteria. Even outside the select parts of the city deemed to be at risk, these seem to have inspired avoidance of the water.[15] More alarming still was the news in October that chloride in the water was corroding engine parts at GM. It was not until later that thoughts of corroded parts led to thoughts of corroded pipes—instead, residents imagined that what was eating away at engines must be eating away at their bodies.

By the end of 2014, skepticism of the water was running high, but officials still had not admitted to any public health threat implicating the population as a whole: the total coliform problem, they said, was limited in scope and soon under control, and the chloride was not, counterintuitively, abrasive to human flesh the way it was to metal. This changed with the city's acknowledgement in January 2015 that residents all over Flint had been exposed to high levels of total trihalomethanes (TTHMs), known carcinogens associated with liver, kidney, and neural disorders. The caveat that exposure to TTHMs had to take place over many years to be a concern to residents in good health did little to dampen the impact of the news. The "good health" qualification served mainly to conjure up thoughts of the many residents who fell into higher-risk categories, like the elderly, the immunocompromised, and pregnant women, and the aura of unfamiliarity around TTHMs fostered wide-ranging speculation about the unexplained ailments for which they might be responsible.

Arguably, however, the main significance of the TTHM notice was the damage it did to trust. When the flyer began to arrive in mailboxes in early January, residents learned that the city had been aware of the TTHM problem for months before it informed the public (a delay technically allowed by the Safe Drinking Water Act). The sense of betrayal residents felt not only factored into their wariness of the water coming out of their taps—which from that point forward bore the invisible mark of broken trust—it altered the way they received all subsequent official communications about water. Thereafter, many residents operated on the assumption that officials were not being forthcoming, especially when the latter's message was that the water was safe.

Trust in the medical community began to erode around the same time. As popular hypotheses of causal links between exposure to the water and ill health began to proliferate, residents began to seek confirmation of them from medical professionals. Physicians found themselves caught off-guard: unsure of what "TTHMs" even were, they were ill prepared to render assessments of their likely health impact, and as for symptoms like rashes and other skin problems, it was difficult or impossible within a clinical setting to link them definitively to the water. Miffed by the noncommittal, cautious responses they received to their inquiries, some residents concluded that Flint-area physicians were complicit in a broader conspiracy to deny that the water was causing harm. Those who had the means sometimes, like Lee-Anne Walters, went off in search of second opinions outside Flint or even outside Michigan.

For residents who chose to shun the water in whole or in part—a trend that picked up steam with the TTHM notice and accelerated greatly after the discovery of systemic lead contamination—once-routine activities involving water, like cooking, brushing teeth, washing dishes, and preparing the baby's bottle became sources of anxiety and inconvenience. Many residents ultimately chose to use bottled water as much as feasible, phasing it into their lives selectively at first (when they had to pay for it out of pocket), and more comprehensively from January 2016 forward, when it became widely available for free at point of distribution sites (PODs) in each of the city's nine wards. New routines evolved around the acquisition of bottled water, as visiting the PODs became a regular trek. The chore was not only dreary but often difficult: a strain on time, resources (even a trip to pick up free water required bus fare or gas money), and the body, especially as less physically able residents struggled to hoist the heavy cases out of the car, up the stairs, and to their final destination. The stockpiling of water—a practice driven in part by fears of losing the PODs—became so common that the American Institute of Architects issued a warning that stacking cases of water too high could cause the floor to collapse.

Once free bottled water became abundant, residents began to substitute it for every conceivable activity involving water: they used it to prepare their food, wet their toothbrushes, rinse their dishes. They gave it to their pets. In some cases, they used it for bathing and showering, and even for filling kiddie pools in the summer. In representations of the crisis to the outside world, the ubiquity of bottled water and the extra hardship it imposed on residents became the most vivid illustration of the crisis's transformation of everyday life. Posing for a CNN profile with the 151 bottles of water she and her family used each day, resident-turned-activist Gina Luster invited outsiders to imagine using bottled water, day in and day out, for everything but flushing the toilet.[16]

Even with free water available at the PODs, however, using bottled water for *everything* was difficult to sustain. For washing, many residents opted to use shower filters instead, or simply took showers that were colder (because TTHMs and bacteria could be inhaled through steam), shorter, and altogether less pleasant. Some preferred to shower outside the city at friends' or relatives' houses. For cleaning children, baby wipes were popular, and hand sanitizer often stood in as an alternative to soap and water.

The intimate character of the harms caused by contaminated water, combined with these disruptions of everyday life (particularly the life of the home), may help to explain the prominence of women and mothers, especially, in the fight for clean water in Flint.[17] Their contributions were so important, especially early on, that sometimes the movement as a whole was described as a movement of mothers—"No one would be doing anything now," remarked Melissa Mays at one point, "if it wasn't for a bunch of moms getting mad."[18] Noting that women are often overrepresented in environmental justice struggles,[19] scholars have proposed a variety of reasons why this may be the case. Some have suggested that women have distinctive "ways of knowing" more attuned to phenomena that are concrete, immediate, and associated with personal relationships, making them especially sensitive to changes in their environment, as well as in their bodies and the bodies of those around them.[20] Whether or not one accepts this epistemological premise, it remains true sociologically that women are disproportionately tasked with the oversight of the household and the care of children and are therefore often on the front lines when the signs and symptoms of environmental contamination first appear.[21] As Bishop Bernadel Jefferson put it to me, "When the child has broke out who gonna see it first? *Mama.* When you combin' the baby's hair and the hair comin' out, who gonna see it first? *Mama.*"[22]

For the same reason, women often have to shoulder a larger proportion of the daily burdens created by contamination events. Most of the female activists I spoke to heartily endorsed the idea that women and mothers had been especially impacted by the crisis and that this was an influence on their activism. Bishop Jefferson asked me rhetorically, "Why did the women step up? Who cooks food? Who takes care of the children? Who gets them off to school? ... And so, when you talk about water, who do it affect first?"[23] Mother-turned-activist Maegan Wilson expressed similar sentiments:

> Women have to ... prepare the meals and women have to ... cart the water a lot of times and women have to go get the water and make sure that they have the water ... and then the women have to take care of the kids, take them to the doctor's appointments, find out if they have lead problems or psychological problems or even mental health problems at this point because they can't understand why this would happen to them and will anybody ever really care. That's a lot of the women's worries, and they deal with a lot of the behavior issues and things like that. ... [Men just] do their thing, they go work, they come home, but they don't realize all the stuff that the woman has to go through, like ... the water didn't get the clothes as clean this week or ... what if they smell now, or whatever, and so it's extra work.[24]

Mothers also spoke to me of having to rearrange their daily routines so they could visit the city's water distribution sites before work, and of the inconvenience and awkwardness of having to drive their children to relatives' homes in the suburbs for bathing and showering purposes. Summing up the cumulative effect of these everyday burdens, Flint mother and activist Laura Gillespie MacIntyre put it pithily: mothers' activism springs from "life."[25]

The disruption of "life," of the routines and spaces (like the home) that structure everyday experience, acted as a springboard to activism for residents who came into the water crisis without prior political commitments. As hard as life already was for many in Flint, the crisis created a pervasive sense of a loss of normalcy, a sense that everyday existence had become riskier and less certain in addition to being more difficult.[26] Residents no longer viewed their homes as places of safety and respite, they no longer associated water with cleanliness and health, they no longer assumed that authorities were trustworthy or were keeping them safe. They could no longer tend to basic necessities by raising a lever or turning a knob. While there was no one experience of the crisis, a sort of archetype emerged—invoked frequently by activists—of what it was like to live in Flint from April 2014 forward: constant fear of what could emerge from the tap, the nursing of water-related injuries, and the rearranging of one's whole life around bottled water.

The Construction of Victimhood

The first step in converting the experience of injury into a proactive mindset in previously apolitical individuals is often the development of a sense of victimhood. Victimhood is often contrasted with "agency," with victims depicted as helpless, cowering figures who are acted upon rather than acting themselves. But it is a mistake to think of victimhood as simply debilitating, leading to withdrawal and passivity. For one thing, to be a victim implies the existence of a victimizer who is responsible for the harm one has suffered and who can potentially be confronted.[27] Flint residents' belief that the water crisis was an unambiguously "manmade" (rather than "natural") disaster tended to foster a fighting rather than a fatalistic mentality, fueled by righteous anger in search of specific targets.

Furthermore, in cases of environmental contamination where ambiguities exist around the severity and causes of harm, defining the boundary between victim and nonvictim is often itself a struggle. Flint residents frequently complained that officials were operating with too narrow a definition of victimhood, overly focused on the newborn to six-year-old demographic at the expense of adults and seniors. Determining who counted as a victim was not just a matter of semantics, for it directly implicated the recognition and resources residents stood to receive from the state, especially with the emergence of class-action lawsuits, which the State of Michigan fought all the way up to the US Supreme Court. In tangible ways, ordinary residents as well as activists found themselves locked in a battle over their status as victims that laid a foundation for political consciousness and political action.[28]

The particular construction of victimhood that would come to underpin the water movement in Flint held that residents were both "victims" *and* "fighters," with the implication that these identities were not only reconcilable, but in some sense symbiotic. Residents often drew attention to their victimhood, and the victimhood of their children, as a tactical means of stoking outrage and inspiring action, especially through the graphic display of their victimized bodies (some activists, for example, were known for waving bags full of lost hair at rallies). Such displays came to express—and indeed were instrumental in constructing—what Phil Brown and his colleagues call a "collective illness identity."[29] In Flint, this identity was not built around a particular illness *per se* (as in, say, the AIDS community) so much as the assortment of harms that residents traced back to the common cause of exposure to the water.

Noting the role that shared identities play in fostering collective action, Brown et al. argue that a collective illness identity can serve as "a unifying and mobilizing force."[30] For such an identity to be unifying, however, it has to be constructed in an inclusive way. This does not necessarily rule out subcategories of victimhood—as already noted, the idea that women and mothers had suffered in special ways was popular among the Flint residents and activists I knew. But some distinctions between victims can be difficult to draw without generating controversy and division.

Perhaps the most instructive example from Flint was the claim—made repeatedly by commentators in academia, the press, and beyond—that the crisis was an instance of "environmental racism."[31] It was often remarked that what happened in Flint would not have happened, or at least would have been quickly acknowledged and remediated, in a majority-white city. The crisis became part of an ongoing national debate about racial injustice spawned by incidents of violence against African Americans in places like Ferguson, Missouri, and Baltimore, Maryland,[32] and one commentator even suggested that, in the absence of the Black Lives Matter movement, the crisis would not have been a national story.[33]

As intuitive as it was for outsiders looking in to depict the water crisis as a racial affair, what I encountered on the ground in Flint were far more complicated and mixed feelings about the racialization of residents' victimhood. Certainly there were residents, especially within the city's African American community, who saw the crisis through the lens of Flint's long history of racial discrimination and disadvantage. Some believed the crisis would displace residents in predominantly black parts of the city, thereby advancing the city's recently adopted master plan, seen by many as an effort to reinvent Flint as a "college town" geared toward affluent whites (on more than one occasion, I heard it described as the *"master's"* plan). One black activist told me that "they" wanted "all African Americans up out of Flint,"[34] implying that the crisis was a means to this end. The common lament that officials viewed residents as "guinea pigs" also had a racial tinge to it, as evidenced in comparisons of the switch to the Flint River and subsequent tinkering with the water treatment process to the infamous Tuskegee syphilis experiment. There were also signs that fears of outright extermination by white conspirators—fears with deep roots in black history[35]—were very much alive. Some of the people I spoke to believed that the parts of the city with the worst lead contamination were those with the highest percentage of black residents, suggesting deliberate targeting of the black population.

A notable difference between these invocations of race and those made by outsiders was their implication, sometimes made explicit, that Flint residents were the victims of conscious racial animus and that the water crisis itself was orchestrated for racist reasons. The gap between this perspective and more mainstream understandings of environmental racism—a concept often invoked to capture patterns of racial disadvantage that are not intentional in origin—became especially clear upon the release of the final report of the Michigan Civil Rights Commission (MCRC) on the crisis, which (as discussed in chapter 2) treated racism as a historical, structural phenomenon whose influence on decision making in the present was "implicit" at most.[36] Those who believed that more insidious forms of racism were being missed had reason to feel vindicated when, a few months later, an activist journalist recorded a Genesee County Land Bank official saying the crisis was caused by "niggers not paying their bills."[37] The remark became justification for reading dog-whistle racism into official comments that seemed to undervalue the lives of residents, like the earlier-mentioned quip by an Environmental Protection Agency employee that Flint was not "the community we want to go out on a limb for."[38]

Although some of these sentiments inevitably found their way into the water movement, where the theme of environmental racism surfaced from time to time, what struck me was how many activists resisted, or even flatly rejected, the idea that race had anything to do with the crisis's impact or its origins. One example was the common remark that lead "does not discriminate," meant to emphasize that everyone who had come into contact with the water, whatever their race, had been harmed. At the first public meeting of the MCRC in Flint, when residents were invited to speak to whether they felt racially discriminated against, activist Tony Palladeno told the commission that "this is not a black and white thing because this is killing all of us."[39] Although he was in the minority at that particular meeting, it was a sentiment I encountered repeatedly, in a variety of contexts.[40] The way LeeAnne Walters put it to me was that "there's nothing racist about lead." In early 2016, she refused an award from filmmaker Michael Moore because he had described the crisis as a "racial killing"—she had no use for his "racism stuff," she said.[41] It was perhaps understandable that white activists like Palladeno and Walters would resist racial framings of the crisis that threatened to diminish their victimhood or at least treated the harms they suffered as collateral damage. But I encountered similar sentiments coming from many black activists, too. In E. Yvonne Lewis's words, "The disaster is framed as a poor, black, African American issue, but everyone of every race has been affected."[42]

Just as they rejected the idea that people of color were especially harmed by the water, many activists resisted the claim that the crisis was a product of racism. Of the possible demographic explanations for the crisis, a sizable majority of the activists I spoke with preferred to emphasize class rather than race. Typical was Gina Luster's comment that, although race may have been a factor, the crisis was "more about class than anything."[43] Claire McClinton, who balked whenever she was asked to speak on the racial dimensions of the crisis, thought it a "travesty" that the MCRC had placed so much stress on race instead of looking more concertedly at class.[44] Melissa Mays concurred when I asked her if a term like "environmental classism" would be more accurate than environmental racism to describe the crisis. She told me that the crisis was "all based on class" and that its effects on the black population were "byproducts" of class-based injustices.[45] A common belief was that poor white people and black people were in more or less the same category as far as oppression was concerned, and that there was little point in differentiating them—in Abel Delgado's words, "If you're a poor white person, you might as well be black."[46] One of the reasons Flint was able to organize successfully around the water issue, Desiree Duell told me, was because of the large number of poor whites in the city, with class providing a bedrock of commonality between white and black activists.[47]

I also found that language that appeared racially charged—talk of being "experimented" on, of being disposable, of being victimized by the "master's" plan, of being the targets of extermination, and so forth—was often stretched to encompass poor whites as well as blacks, and in the process purged of any specifically racial content. Activists often spoke of "genocide," for example, as a class-based rather than a race-based phenomenon. Gina Luster suggested that the crisis was part of a plot to "cleanse" the city of its lower-class residents.[48] Wantwaz Davis, an African American activist and councilman who made headlines in early 2015 after calling the water contamination "an obvious genocide" against residents,[49] warned that the water problems would have the effect of running "low/moderate income people" out of the city.[50] Like Luster, he suggested that this was the plan all along.[51] The notion that genocide could proceed along class lines allowed white activists, too, to take up the term enthusiastically and use it freely, without worrying about its traditionally racial connotations.

The way activists talked about race was not only an expression of their convictions about the nature of the crisis but a matter of *strategy*, informed by the imperatives of organizing a city that despite being mostly African American was split fairly evenly between black and white. At first, Claire McClinton remembered, water activism in Flint was mostly a "black" thing, focused on concerns about affordability and led largely by members of the black church community and black elected officials. When the deterioration of Flint's water quality mobilized a new contingent of affronted white residents more worried about contamination than cost, it became necessary to foster cooperation across the racial divide. As McClinton put it, Flint was so segregated along racial lines, with people "living in different worlds"— each of which had a "skewed" perception of the other—that it was "a challenge to unite the two communities."[52]

Activists' usual assumption was that cross-racial solidarity was best served by downplaying the significance of race. Occasionally, I heard activists claim that the powers-that-be were trying to use race to turn the grassroots against itself; one black activist called the MCRC's foregrounding of race in its final report a "trick" by the state to divide the movement.[53] The idea that the water struggle was an opportunity to put aside racial differences and model racial unity was reflected in the widely circulated motto "No religion, no color, no violence," and a popular Facebook image showing two intertwined hands, one black, one white. The universal qualities of water itself came to stand for a kind of elemental human solidarity that paid little heed to racial categories. As Pastor Al Harris of the Concerned Pastors for Social Action told *Belt Magazine*:

> I think the beautiful thing is that we found out we're really not separated. If it really was an issue to bring the people together, this was it. Everybody needs water. Black, white, rich, poor, educated, uneducated. Everybody needs and deserves safe, clean water and so that caused people to come in from all different spheres, all different levels of government. We all had this one common goal to bring us together, so that's the good part of it. I wish we didn't have this situation, but everybody understood we've got to work together.[54]

In Harris's formulation, common dependence on water unites people of every description—notably, across class as well as racial divides. The idea that residents' "human right" to water had been violated, that they had been victimized in their capacity as human beings—full stop—was certainly a pervasive sentiment in Flint. Part of its utility to activists was that it could be used to situate the movement in Flint within a wider world of activist discourse and praxis, making the city the latest front in a global struggle for water and eliciting solidarity and support from water activists elsewhere. The point was driven home at a September 2017 water summit in Flint headlined by renowned international water activist Maude Barlow, who emphasized that she and the many people from "outside the community" who had made the journey were there "to offer solidarity in our struggle for water justice here in Flint and around the world."[55]

As important as affirmations of common humanity are in tying together the struggles of geographically disparate people, however, they offer thin gruel to activists whose objective is to forge a robust sense of shared identity at the local level. What proved to be most effective in uniting residents across racial, and even class, lines in Flint was building off of the mixture of victimization and pride that residents felt in being *from Flint*. The water movement's most prominent slogan, "Flint Lives Matter," obviously invited comparisons to Black Lives Matter, but its transcendence of racial categories was not accidental: it embodied the feeling that the city as a whole had been victimized, that all residents were in danger of being written off or abandoned, and that therefore everyone within city limits was, in some sense, in the same boat. This municipal identity formed the container that was gradually filled out by residents' sense of having experienced the same harms from the water.

The experience of emergency management greatly contributed to the salience of this municipal identity and to the belief that the city itself, in its corporate capacity, was a victim, too. Listening to the way that activists would talk about Flint, I got the sense that they saw it almost as an organism barely clinging to life, dismembered by the sale of its assets, emaciated through cutbacks into a fleshless skeleton (or "shell"), and now its innards rotted by corrosive water. I repeatedly encountered the belief that the city was "under attack" (as activists sometimes chanted, "What do we do when our city is under attack? Stand up, fight back!"), its very existence as a political entity threatened by the power of EMs to extinguish it. Although I did encounter fears that municipal dissolution would put blacks at a special disadvantage by turning them into political minorities within mostly white Genesee County, the specter of disincorporation lent itself to the feeling that everyone who called Flint home was at risk of having that home not only taken over, but taken away. Fighting for one's own life, then, had everything to do with fighting for the life of the city.

Epistemic Injustice and Recognition

The evolution of residents into activists was a function not only of the personal impact of contamination and the indignation they felt at being victimized, but also of the response they got from officials upon coming forward with their concerns. Residents found their claims about the water and their own bodies dismissed as hyperbolic, uninformed, paranoiac. They repeatedly had their common-sense intuitions about the danger they were in explained away by an "expert" in the authoritative register of scientific elocution. More than one person described this phenomenon to me as "gaslighting"[56]: an attempt to convince residents that their worries were fanciful, merely the products of their imagination.

Following the philosopher Miranda Fricker, we might describe such reactions as instances of "epistemic injustice," defined as "a wrong done to someone specifically in their capacity as a knower." The dimension of epistemic injustice relevant here is what she calls "testimonial injustice," which "occurs when prejudice causes a hearer to give a deflated level of credibility to a speaker's word."[57] The credibility, or epistemic trustworthiness, we impute to a speaker is, Fricker argues, built on our perception of the speaker's competence and sincerity. The question of competence frequently arises when members of the general public attempt to understand and respond to environmental contamination events. The issue of Flint's water quality involved highly technical matters of chemistry, microbiology, and infrastructure with which most residents had little prior experience. Grasping the complexities would have been daunting for members of any community, but, in Flint, residents faced the added hurdle of low educational levels: only 11 percent of the population over age twenty-five had a bachelor's degree, compared with a statewide average of 27 percent.[58] For anyone inclined to be skeptical of lay knowledge, these factors worked against the idea that residents could form meaningful judgments about the water or make valid recommendations about how to solve the quality problems.

The competence of residents was seen as suspect not only because they were assumed to lack technical knowledge, however, but because they supposedly didn't know *how* to think. Without a broader perspective on what they were experiencing, they were at risk of reading far too much significance into anecdotal experiences, placing too much stock in their knee-jerk reactions to sensory data (like brown water), and arriving at unshakable convictions and sweeping generalizations without adequate evidence. Regardless of how much truth there may or may not have been in these characterizations, they inflicted the epistemic harm of impugning, not only residents' knowledge, but their very *ability* to know. This helps to explain why the refrain that residents were not "stupid" and deserved *a priori* respect when putting forward claims about the water was woven into activist discourse.

If the occasional suggestion that residents were fooling themselves cut deep, even more insulting was the accusation that they were consciously trying to fool others. In an infamous encounter at a January 2015 public meeting, LeeAnne Walters held up two bottles of brown water in front of emergency manager Jerry Ambrose to illustrate what was coming out of her tap. Ambrose's response was to ask if she really expected him to believe the samples were from her house. The grimace this provoked from Walters, captured in a widely circulated photograph that became one of the enduring images of the water crisis, embodied the sting residents felt at the implication that they were deliberately misrepresenting their struggles with the water. To preempt the kind of skepticism voiced by Ambrose, residents began collecting videos of discolored water coming straight out of their faucets and sharing them over social media.

Figure 5.1
LeeAnne Walters presents her tap water to EM Jerry Ambrose. © Detroit Free Press
/ZUMA Press.

Epistemic injustice, in Fricker's formulation, is an outgrowth of prejudice,
understood as a prejudgment of a speaker's reliability premised on assumptions about his or her social identity. Identity prejudice, according to Fricker,
"distorts the hearer's perception of the speaker," filtering perceptions of what is
spoken through the lens of who the speaker is—or is perceived to be.[59] In
this sense, epistemic injustice is related to what theorists of social justice call
"recognition."[60] Political recognition hinges on a general social perception
of individuals and groups as having a legitimate perspective on social reality, as well as legitimate needs that should be factored into political decision
making. Theories of recognition pay particularly close attention to the way
in which prejudices around ascriptive characteristics and social categories—
like race and gender—can result in people and groups being written off,
ignored, or rendered "voiceless" or "invisible."

Activists were keenly aware that their race and gender affected whether
their knowledge was recognized as legitimate. In the early stages of the water

struggle, when they were being treated like alarmists and liars and were desperate to gain some sort of foothold of credibility, whiteness served as an epistemic resource. A number of activists told me that racial considerations influenced who was put out front to represent the movement and that it was not coincidental that the leading activist voices—among the political newcomers, anyway—were, like Melissa Mays and LeeAnne Walters, white. At the very least, the greater prominence of white activists in the media was tolerated as a strategic necessity (though not without a certain amount of resentment) because "America needed a particular face" if it was to take the crisis seriously.[61] The discomfort both Mays and Walters felt when others highlighted their race as if it carried special epistemic privilege undoubtedly fed into their desire to avoid the subject altogether.

But any epistemic advantage that activists like Mays and Walters enjoyed on account of their whiteness was, to some extent, counteracted by assumptions about the epistemic limitations of women and mothers. Stereotypes about the subjective, experiential, and relational character of women's "ways of knowing" can undermine women's credibility in contexts, like environmental contamination events, where the (purported) objectivity, detachment, and universality of scientific knowledge is accorded special authority. Added to these stereotypes, often, are others about women's supposed susceptibility to affect, thought to have a distorting effect on their perception and judgments, especially when imperiled children are involved. Mays, for example, remembers being called a "crazy mom," as if suffering from a special kind of hysteria fed by mother love.[62] Less pejorative was the term "Mama Grizzly" (Walters told me she was "100 percent comfortable" being described this way[63]), which at least celebrated the protective ferocity of that love. The epistemological connotations of describing mothers as enraged animals, however, were not as flattering, suggestive of unapologetic partiality and blind devotion.

In many ways, the core of the struggle for clean water during the first eight months of the water movement was a struggle by residents to be taken seriously as knowers—by officials, by the media, even by fellow residents. The city and state said the water was safe; a growing chorus of residents said it wasn't. The relative respect with which these competing perspectives were treated was not just a matter of their truth value, it was a matter of power and justice. And in a city whose residents had already had their competence and judgment called into question by the imposition of emergency management, it was necessarily a matter of political recognition as well.

From Troubles to Issues to Collective Action

A critical turning point in the genesis of a social movement is when individuals begin to see their personal "troubles" as outgrowths of a broader "issue" that cannot be adequately addressed without collective action.[64] Within weeks of the switch to the Flint River, water troubles began popping up throughout the city, but because they did so within the private space of the home, residents first needed a way of determining that they were not isolated, singular events. Before there were any physical meetings about the water, Facebook served as an essential medium for residents not previously acquainted, in disparate parts of the city, to discover that they were living through the same thing. The Flint River Water Support Group page began accumulating testimony as early as May 2014, but it was principally the Flint Water Class Action (FWCA) group, created by business student and mother Florlisa Fowler in September, that activists would later look to as one of the kernels of the water movement.

The FWCA page served as a clearinghouse for tales of water and health woes and a vehicle for a kind of collective investigation of the city's water quality problems. It became a repository for a growing pile of visual evidence that Flint's water problems were systemic: when one resident would post a photograph of cloudy or discolored water, or a nasty rash that appeared in the shower, several more photographs of the same thing from other residents would pour in. When residents who had connected online started mingling in person at the first rallies and town halls about water quality in January 2015, they got further confirmation that their troubles with the water were shared by people all over Flint. Melissa Mays remembers the revelatory effect this realization had on her: "Different parts of the city, different ages, different backgrounds—we were all having the same problems."[65]

Fowler attempted to steer the discussion on the FWCA page toward something like "popular epidemiology," a term used to describe grassroots efforts to assess the distribution of disease and its contributing factors.[66] She asked people posting with complaints to identify the parts of the city they lived in so that a possible geographical pattern could be discerned, leading to much speculation about which neighborhoods were most affected. As this investigation proceeded, the group began to spawn other forms of collective action as well. Fowler began to encourage members to contact political representatives, media outlets, and environmental justice advocates like

Erin Brockovich. Members began to talk of legal action, of in-person meetings, of protests.

And along the way, the pro-democracy activists became part of the conversation. They were already working to convince residents that the steep price of water and the threat of shutoffs were products of the assault on democracy in their city and their state. Now they began to convince residents that the decline of their water quality and the deterioration of their health had the same origin.[67] As Melissa Mays put it to me, activists like Claire McClinton, Nayyirah Shariff, and Bishop Bernadel Jefferson helped her and other residents to understand that "every single thing that's going to happen to us and has happened to us is politically backed and motivated."[68] That realization not only imparted a political hue to what residents were experiencing, it refined, elevated, and channeled the popular energies that were bubbling up: the fear and the anger, the indignation and the insult—and most importantly, the determination to band together and fight until justice was done.

6 Demanding the Impossible: Deliberation and Activism in the Battle over the River

If you got real democracy, why you gotta go to the street?
—Claire McClinton, interview with author

At a Flint City Council meeting on January 26, 2015, Gertrude "Tru" Saunders rose to speak during public comment. A grandmother and lifelong Flint resident who was still getting used to being called an "activist," Saunders had unilaterally launched a daily protest regimen outside City Hall. For the next two months, she would brave the bitter cold of an unusually severe Michigan winter, holding homemade signs and warning passers-by against using the water.

Addressing her fellow residents, Saunders said that the water was not only "harming us," but "killing our babies." Those in a position to help "hear us," she lamented, "but they don't care. They don't care." Calling for a picket every day of the week, she urged residents "to chain yourself to the water company, whatever it take to say 'hell no, we ain't takin' this no more.'" Direct action, she suggested, was all the more necessary because of the ever-looming presence of the emergency manager (EM). Under the circumstances, she warned, the council "can't do nothing for us. They can't help us. It's time for us to help us." Turning from the podium to face the audience, she said: "*We* have to help us. *We* have to do this."[1]

Contained in Saunders's brief speech before the council is an encapsulation of the reasoning that led newly mobilized Flint residents away from traditional avenues of political redress and into the realm of activism. It went something like this: the imminent threat posed by the water made urgent action imperative, but pushing for change through the usual channels of representative democracy was pointless as long as the city was under state control. Taking one's concerns directly to the EMs (as LeeAnne Walters did when she presented her tainted water to Jerry Ambrose) was also a dead end, for the EMs were determined to ride out the water quality problems until the Karegnondi Water Authority (KWA) pipeline came online and did not care what it meant for residents in the interim. With local democracy eviscerated and Flint's state-appointed sovereigns indifferent to residents' cries, activists would have to take the fight for clean water into the "street."[2]

The end of emergency management in April 2015 did not fundamentally alter the situation, for, as Flint's pro-democracy activists insisted at every opportunity, the state still had its thumb firmly on the city. The City Council's powers remained suspended. EM-appointed City Administrator Natasha Henderson exercised enhanced powers that would otherwise have belonged to the mayor, thanks to a resolution by outgoing EM Ambrose. And a governor-appointed Receivership Transition Advisory Board retained veto power over any decision by local officials it deemed fiscally irresponsible. The members of the Flint Democracy Defense League (FDDL) continued to describe the city as being under "dictatorship." This political assessment of Flint's predicament colored activists' view of the official response to the water crisis from top to bottom.

For as common as it was to hear that officials had done "nothing" to address the water issue, they *did* respond: they made numerous tweaks to the treatment and distribution process, installed $1.6 million worth of granulated carbon filters at the water treatment plant, and spent $40,000 on a private assessment of the water system. They also sent out repeated notices about the water, sponsored town hall meetings and informational sessions, and established two water advisory committees ostensibly aimed at creating channels of communication between residents, technical experts, and decision makers. But what they *didn't* do—at least not without a drawn-out fight—what they insisted was not possible and therefore not even worth discussing, was return the city to Detroit water, the central demand of the water movement through the summer of 2015. And all along their message was consistent: however it looked, however it smelled, however it tasted, the water was *safe*.

In light of that suspiciously counterintuitive message, and of officials' flat refusal to abandon the river, and of the general feeling that residents were caught up in an authoritarian and duplicitous political system that did not have their best interests at heart, the officially sponsored water forums that began in January 2015 provoked profound skepticism and disdain.

Residents and officials brought to these fleeting instances of face-to-face interaction fundamentally different assessments of the gravity of the situation and what could be done to rectify it. What one side framed as unreasonable and impossible the other framed as commonsensical and purely a matter of political will. Because both sides rejected the very terms of the discourse the other tried to set, it was exceedingly difficult to make any progress through dialogue. Just as crippling were mutual suspicions that the other side didn't really *want* to have a meaningful discussion to begin with. Officials saw activists as melodramatic and unnecessarily confrontational, more interested in causing a scene than in collaborative problem solving. Activists, for their part, saw officials as conceited and uncaring, their efforts at public outreach phony and manipulative.

Clashing styles of communication had something to do with these assessments, to be sure. For Flint activists, however, the more fundamental problem was the underlying pretense that it was even possible to engage in meaningful democratic deliberation when the city was under state control. The philosophy of emergency management was, as they saw it, inherently anti-deliberative in addition to being undemocratic, premised as it was on unilateral, technocratic decision making that actively disregarded public opinion.[3] Residents had already been given the message, via the state takeover, that they lacked the knowledge, competence, and will to properly manage their own affairs: would officials suddenly now start trusting them to formulate independent judgments about as "technical" a matter as water contamination? And in light of the vast power differential created by the EM system, would it even matter what those judgments were? By all appearances, officially sponsored water meetings lacked the two most essential qualities of deliberative forums: they were neither *authentic* nor *consequential*.[4] They put activists in a fighting rather than a talking mood.

Although the first major battle the water movement fought had a narrow objective—getting the city off the river—it brought activists up against the broader epistemological and political framework that officials employed to understand and decide water issues in Flint. When activists found themselves unable to operate adequately within that framework, as they often did, they chose to operate outside it. They created their own spaces of deliberation, where "lay ways of knowing" were taken more seriously,[5] and they used a variety of tactics designed to pressure officials into action rather than persuade them to do the right thing.[6]

The feeling of being at odds with the whole system responsible for causing and perpetuating the crisis fostered a political subjectivity that embraced what was defined by that system as illegitimate, unreasonable, and impossible.[7] At the heart of the water movement was the spirit represented by Tru Saunders: the grandmother-turned-activist who left the warmth of council chambers to protest in the cold, to demand what political realists said was not going to happen, in a language barely intelligible to the technocrats governing her city. But if this was the movement's spirit, its flesh was somewhat more grounded in political "reality." In practice, activists did, at times, talk to officials they thought might listen. They forged alliances with people whose strategy of social change was to work within the halls of power as well as outside them. They sought to influence the 2015 mayoral race even as they disparaged the way local politics had been corrupted by emergency management. And they began to learn the language of the powerful, the language of science, so that they could command the respect of those insufficiently impressed by their experiential knowledge. They even produced new scientific knowledge that they believed—correctly, it turned out—would finally pierce the fog of official obfuscation and wrest a remedy to their plight from within the system itself.

The spirit and the flesh, as we know, do not always coexist harmoniously. To the extent that activists worked within the system, they became enmeshed in epistemologies, in technical languages, in institutions and relationships that complicated later efforts to parlay the battle over the river into a farther-reaching struggle for justice and democracy. But through October of 2015, when the impossible became reality, the pieces of the movement held together remarkably well, and the activists, driven by a potent combination of pathos and politics, authored one of the most triumphant chapters in Flint's proud history of popular struggle.

The Dead End of Deliberation

By January 2015, workers at the water treatment plant had been wrangling with Flint River water for eight months, trying to improve chlorine residuals, fiddling with pH, and working to reduce total trihalomethane (TTHM) levels. During the same period of time, state officials fretted about the outbreak of Legionnaires' disease in the summer of 2014 (speculating that it might have been caused by the water source switch) and expressed concern about news of total coliform contamination in parts of Flint's water system. They even debated whether it might not be better for Flint to switch back to Detroit water until the KWA pipeline was ready, or at least until the kinks in the water treatment process were worked out.[8] But all of this was unknown to Flint residents, who were assured all the while that the water was safe.

The first official indication of a systemic problem was the January TTHM notice (the Legionnaires' news would not break for another year). Officials now faced the unenviable task of explaining to residents why it had taken so long to alert them to the presence of a carcinogenic contaminant in their water. Technically, the timing of the notice was consistent with the letter of the law, but residents interpreted its issuance many months after the emergence of a problem as an egregious lack of transparency on the city's part. All of the statements about the water being safe during the preceding eight months now looked like bald-faced lies. It was more than enough to stoke conspiracy theories: as then-Mayor Dayne Walling put it to me, the TTHM notice "became the proof for the community that the EM, and the state and the Governor, were trying to destroy the city," confirming what many people had "felt … all along."[9]

The feelings of broken trust and betrayal prompted by the notice colored the way residents received all subsequent communications about the water. More often than not, the manner in which officials tried to engage the public only made matters worse. The trend was set by a calamitous town hall meeting at the "Dome"—a circular auditorium attached to City Hall—on January 21. Hoping to overcome its credibility deficit by bringing in outside authorities to speak to the water quality issue, the city assembled a panel of experts from the Michigan Department of Environmental Quality (MDEQ), the Genesee County Drain Commission, the contractor Lockwood, Andrews, and Newnam, and Michigan State University, granting them primacy of place onstage. The hierarchical and controlled atmosphere in the building made some uncomfortable right away. Upon entering, residents were immediately greeted by the sight of city police officers, who maintained a watchful eye over the meeting from the back of the room. Director of Public Works Howard Croft led things off with a warning that anyone deemed disruptive would be removed from the premises.

Croft expected residents to listen rather than speak, telling them the meeting was for "information only" and would focus on what the "experts" on the panel had to communicate.[10] Those with questions would have to submit them in writing to a "public information officer" and wait until the end of the meeting for responses. Residents, however, were determined to have their say one way or another. As the meeting progressed, they became increasingly agitated and demonstrative, waving signs and bottles of brown water in the air and jeering the speakers.

While the panelists avoided sweeping statements about the safety of the water, their takeaway points were designed to dispel the sense of alarm in the room: firstly, TTHMs were commonly found in water systems and did not pose a notable health risk, except perhaps to pregnant women in their first trimester. Secondly, the quality problems that stuck out to residents—problems of taste, smell, and color—had nothing to do with TTHMs, being matters of aesthetics rather than public health, probably caused by the system adjusting to the new source water. Thirdly, the city had been "proactive" and had "responded very quickly" to the TTHM problem, alerting the public and conducting an operational evaluation "well in advance of the state and federal requirements." Fourthly, whatever rockiness the city was experiencing with the quality of its water would be temporary, because the new pipeline would be ready in just over a year's time. Michigan State University microbiologist Joan Rose told the audience that it was "just gonna take time to correct the distribution system" and to "hang in there."

Each successive speaker was interrupted more frequently and raucously by the crowd. In the moment, residents were angered less by the reassurances about TTHMs than by the panelists' seeming dismissal of the empirical evidence of bad water being proffered by members of the audience. When Rose said there wasn't yet "very much evidence" to tie discolored water to health problems like rashes, residents responded indignantly—one crying out, "The evidence is right in front of you!" Whenever there was any hint of a suggestion that the water was safe, or that further testing and study was required before it could be declared *un*safe, activists Tony Palladeno and Gladyes Williamson would hold up bottles and jugs of discolored water and demand to know if it *looked* safe.

There were other exchanges that evening, too, that made it seem like the experts just didn't get it. When they advised residents to seek advice from medical professionals about health concerns, the response they got was "Are *you* gonna pay my doctor bill?" When they counseled patience until the KWA pipeline was finished, residents were scandalized, demanding that the city stop charging for water in the meantime, and firing back with the question,

Figure 6.1
Town hall meeting at the "Dome" on January 21, 2015. Top: © Detroit Free Press /ZUMA Press. Bottom: *MLive, Flint Journal*.

"Do you live in Flint?" Efforts by Councilmen Eric Mays and Wantwaz Davis to calm tempers produced only fleeting effects. As the meeting progressed—or, rather, degenerated—it became clear that not nearly everyone who submitted a written question would receive an answer. People began to storm out of the room. With the proceedings spiraling into disorder, Howard Croft declared the meeting over. Everyone agreed it had been a disaster.

A few weeks later, the city took another tack. On the advice of Veolia, the transnational water contractor it had hired to evaluate its water system, it announced in February that it would create a technical advisory committee (TAC) and a citizens' advisory committee (CAC) to facilitate ongoing communication about the water and bring residents and stakeholders in the community into more intimate contact with officials.[11] The TAC, which included representatives from the city, county, MDEQ, and the Environmental Protection Agency (EPA), as well as Flint's universities and hospitals, would work through the relevant scientific, infrastructural, and public health issues in closed meetings, preparing the city to enter the CAC meetings, which were open to the public, with a fleshed-out and consistent message.

Mayor Walling liked the idea and, with the support of EM Ambrose, worked to make it happen. He saw it as an opportunity to create the kinds of deliberative settings the city had employed from 2012 to 2013 in crafting its first master plan in fifty years, *Imagine Flint*.[12] During that process, the city organized over two hundred public meetings, focus groups, community workshops, and input sessions, in addition to making "DIY" meeting kits available to groups that wanted to host events of their own. It also set up seven advisory groups and reached out to residents for input through social media and text messages. Altogether, upward of five thousand residents from diverse backgrounds participated in some form, suggesting buy-in from a wide range of constituencies, including the activist community. In fact, some of the water activists had served on one or more of the advisory groups. Walling remembered the process as a model of inclusivity, constructive public discourse, and collaborative decision making. That it had taken place while the city was still under emergency management made it all the more significant: it seemed to show that even in the absence of representative democracy, something like participatory deliberation was still possible.

The activists, however (some of whom did not share Walling's fond memories of the master planning process[13]), saw little need for the committees. From their perspective, the solution to Flint's water woes was simple: *push the button* and reopen the feed from Detroit. What was there for a committee to discuss? In an article for the *People's Tribune*, Claire McClinton wrote that the dilly-dallying with committees gave "new meaning" to the phrase "Justice Delayed, Justice Denied."[14] As Councilman Eric Mays put it, "How much advice do you need to know you got bad water and high rates?"[15]

Aside from the matter of their superfluity, there were other concerns about the committees. The fact that they had their genesis in a suggestion by Veolia, the *bête noir* of water activists the world over, did little to inspire confidence. The activists suspected the corporation was up to more than it was letting on. At the very least, officials seemed inclined to accept its recommendations before even hearing residents out. Laura Sullivan, a professor of mechanical engineering at Kettering University and member of the TAC who became a key ally of the activists, remembers the first meeting of the committee as an attempt to "rubber stamp" Veolia's proposed changes to the water system so that they could be presented with more authority to the public at the CAC meeting the next day.[16]

One problem with the premise of a deliberative citizens' committee, then, was that it was supposed to operate in a context where the most important, "technical" questions about the water had already been settled behind closed doors. Another problem became clear when the city's initial invitations went out: some of the main grassroots groups working on water had been snubbed, while establishment groups that had never spoken out about water were granted seats at the table. Although the oversight was quickly remedied, it gave the impression that officials either lacked a commitment to full inclusivity or were, at the very least, seriously out of touch with the shape the popular response to the water issue was taking.

Nevertheless, activists turned out in full force to the committee's first meeting on March 5.[17] Things began civilly enough. Determined to avoid a repeat of the disastrous town hall, the city had hired as emcees two professional facilitators, who started by laying down "norms" of discussion, focused on keeping interactions respectful and comments and questions succinct and in turn. Because the CAC was supposed to be a body that would meet regularly, they assured participants that all of their questions, if not addressed at the first session, would be collected and answered eventually. The packets distributed to committee members at the door included sticky notes for writing questions and posting them to the wall under a variety of water-related categories.

Despite the thought put into the organization of the meeting, it failed, like the town hall, in the most critical respect: residents once again felt like they were being spoken to rather than spoken with, and that they had to break the rules in order to express themselves adequately. Amid pleas by the facilitators for mutual respect and fidelity to the agenda, the meeting began to deteriorate into accusatory shouting by activists and defensive retorts by the officials arrayed at the front of the room. Tony Palladeno, an activist known for passionate, autobiographical monologues that occasionally turned into angry outbursts, was escorted out by the police after repeatedly shouting that the water was "killing" him, holding up a ball of his hair as evidence.[18] In the lobby, he explained to the media the reason for his frustration: "We're havin' the carpet pulled over our eyes. I don't believe anything they're sayin' right now." Other activists tried to steer the conversation toward a possible reconnection to the Detroit system. Jerry Ambrose took the opportunity to blame Detroit's cancellation of service letter for the switch to the river, prompting exclamations of "That's a lie!" and "That's not true!" Interim City Treasurer Al Mooney responded by saying that a return to Detroit would be possible—if money grew on trees: "We don't have a money tree. And you guys would be sorry. ... So that's the answer to that question."[19]

The next CAC meeting, two weeks later, went the way of the first. Once again, the proceedings turned confrontational and the facilitators had difficulty getting through the agenda. Once again, in lieu of giving residents open mic time to speak, attendees were asked to write questions down. Tensions came to a head when residents, frustrated by the mediation of the facilitators, began to stand and chant at Mayor Walling, "*Answer the question! Answer the question!*"[20]

After the disintegration of the second CAC meeting, Walling told the press that he was considering restructuring the format and trying again.[21] But instead, the meetings ceased altogether. The TAC, too, went dormant—it would not meet again until October, when Marc Edwards presented the committee with the Virginia Tech team's lead findings.[22]

Although Walling conceded that the format of the public meetings was flawed, he blamed their failure on "a handful of people with a high level of frustration" who took them over. What began as outspokenness, he told me, became "disorderly conduct" as the meetings veered off course and became unnecessarily hostile. "We would spend hours getting ready for a community advisory meeting with the hopes of having constructive dialogue on two or three things," he lamented, "and then we would go to that meeting and there would be yelling and raised voices." Consequently, there was never "a constructive engagement with the issues." He saw it as a missed opportunity that had the effect of prolonging the crisis:

> I would like to think that if we would have had more constructive public dialogue we would have together figured out that there were more problems than what were recognized at the time. ... I would have gotten a lot more out of it than being part of another protest spectacle. To the extent that I would have learned more or connected more dots sooner then I think we would've done more at the city.[23]

The activists, on the other hand, lost little sleep over the collapse of the CAC. The meetings had only reinforced their belief that officials were not being open and honest about the water, were not really interested in what residents had to say, and were therefore not worth engaging with politely.[24]

Many of the well-known limitations of deliberative democracy are apparent in these seemingly doomed interactions between officials, residents, and activists. As the political theorist Iris Marion Young influentially argued, officially sponsored deliberation tends to operate within an "already given political trajectory" in which political possibilities are implicitly or explicitly constrained before the conversation begins.[25] These constraints determine what kind of positions and arguments are considered to be "reasonable." Her point is well illustrated by the flippant remark about the nonexistent "money tree": the official view was that reconnecting to Detroit was simply not an option, and that the matter needed to be put to rest so that the group could have a real discussion.

Deliberation of this kind also typically calls for constrained ways of interacting. Participants are expected to persuade each other with reasoned argument while remaining open to alternative points of view. They must treat each other with respect, as equals, and use language that others can understand and accept, working toward agreement. This ideal of the deliberative citizen conflicted sharply with the style in which many Flint activists (and other residents, for that matter) felt compelled to express themselves. They came to meetings filled with emotion and urgency, and were irked by the comparatively stoic demeanor of the officials they encountered there. The rigid format of the meetings did not make space for them to vent their anger and frustration, which then tended to erupt in disruptive ways. Residents also came with a different understanding than officials and experts of what constituted "evidence." They expected to prove their case with graphic displays of ugly water, raw skin, and lost hair, and when this evidence did not produce the desired effect, they chalked it up to willful blindness and obstinacy if not calculated conspiracy. Every meeting was arranged so as to imply that residents would have the water situation explained to *them*— *not* be given the chance to explain it to someone else. Knowledge of what was "really" going on was the province of a select few, and it was to be conveyed unidirectionally.[26]

Most of all, the conversations officials tried to initiate about the water required residents to treat with respect people they either believed were the authors of their misfortune or powerless to alleviate it. The "reality of the EM," Walling told me, was "a really big part" of why interactions with activists were so unconstructive. One reason was that the EMs in office from January 2015 onward, Earley and Ambrose, adopted a "very combative" posture on the water issue, to which the community was merely "responding" with similar combativeness. But more fundamentally, "emergency managers poison the democratic process. It's asking an awful lot of the community to show up and suspend the reality of the emergency manager and have a constructive dialogue with myself, Howard Croft, and Natasha Henderson," because "the reality was the emergency manager was making those decisions." The "complication" of emergency management "was just always front and center," and it introduced "static" into the deliberations about the water that could not be overcome.[27]

Beyond Deliberation: The Coalition for Clean Water

As officials made abortive attempts to engage the public about water between January and March of 2015, new currents of activism were materializing, comprised mainly of residents so frustrated with official inaction they felt they had to take matters into their own hands. But it was an already-existing group, the FDDL, that was first on the scene after the TTHM notice went out on January 2. As described in chapter 4, water was by that time already a priority for the FDDL. Like activists in Detroit, the group had chosen to foreground issues of water affordability and accessibility through the summer and fall of 2014, and the decline in water quality after the switch to the river was at first mainly used to reiterate the absurdity of the high rates—residents were now not only paying through the nose, but doing so for an inferior product. As evidence started to pile up that the water was truly toxic, the water quality issue began to take on its own independent importance, and FDDL activists began to strategize around it. In fall 2014, they looked into setting up an escrow account residents could pay into instead of paying bills for water they didn't feel comfortable drinking. They also hatched an idea that sputtered out initially but would be revived later: securing a judge's injunction to force the city back onto Detroit water.

On January 5, a group of about twenty activists led by core FDDL members held a press conference at City Hall to discuss what it called the "Flint

FLINT WATER
STATE OF EMERGENCY
What *WE* Can Do:

GIVE OUR TESTIMONY!
• Our Voices Must Be Heard
– from Lansing to the United Nations!

MAKE OUR DEMANDS,
NO MORE OF THEIR EXCUSES!
• Detroit Water Now! If It's Good Enough for GM,
It's Good Enough for Us!

STRATEGIZE REAL SOLUTIONS
& TAKE ACTION TO IMPLEMENT THEM!
• It Will Take All of Our Ideas & Energy to
Bring Quality, Affordable Water to Flint!

MONDAY, FEBRUARY 2	MONDAY, FEBRUARY 9	MONDAY, FEBRUARY 16	MONDAY, FEBRUARY 23
BETHEL UNITED METHODIST CHURCH	MT. OLIVE MISSIONARY BAPTIST CHURCH	ANTIOCH MISSIONARY BAPTIST CHURCH	WOODSIDE CHURCH
1309 N. Ballenger Highway	424 Kennelworth Street	1401 E. Stewart Street	1509 Court Street
A.M. Session: 9:30am to 11:30am	A.M. Session: 9:30am to 11:30am	A.M. Session: 9:30am to 11:30am	A.M. Session: 9:30am to 11:30am
P.M. Session: 5:30pm to 7:30pm	P.M. Session: 5:30pm to 7:30pm	P.M. Session: 5:30pm to 7:30pm	P.M. Session: 5:30pm to 7:30pm

Figure 6.2
Flyer for February 2015 water meetings hosted by the FDDL.
Source: Flint Democracy Defense League.

water crisis." In language that mingled concerns about contamination and cost, the activists denounced the city's "plummeting water quality, soaring water rates, [and] misappropriating resources toward alleged water theft."[28] They expressed their support for Councilman Eric Mays's efforts to initiate investigative hearings by the City Council into the water. And they announced that the group would be holding a series of four community meetings on water through the month of February.

The stated objective of the "Flint Water State of Emergency" meetings was to create a nonhierarchical "space" in which residents could come together "to develop strategies for collective action."[29] The meetings became, in effect, counterpoints to the town halls and committee meetings devised by officials. As alternatives to those deliberative forums, they had several advantages: they were purer in origin and therefore easier to trust, they treated residents' concerns and testimony as valid *a priori*, they did not attempt to shut down or remove people for outbursts of emotion. And they were not "*information*"-oriented but rather *solution*-oriented, with the assumption being that answers to Flint's water problems would come from residents themselves. In the invitation it sent out through social media, the FDDL declared that "this is the time for us to come together and create action plans for our own liberation."

As the FDDL geared up for its water meetings, activists began to apply what Claire McClinton liked to call "street heat." On January 15, outside City Hall, a group of about twenty protestors waved signs bearing morbid images of skeletons and nuclear waste. Again, the affordability and quality issues were fused. One sign read: "Welcome to Flint / We pay the most for poisoned water / Your experiment failed / Fix it now!" Another accused Flint officials of trying to "kill" residents with "toxic water." Other signs said "Water is life" and "Clean water is a right, not a privilege" and questioned whether it was safe to take a bubble bath.[30]

This rally and the next one, a week later, reflected the *ad hoc* nature of some of the early activism around the water, being spearheaded by a concerned mom not connected to any particular group. By the time the second rally was held on January 21, however, the various rivulets of grassroots water activism were beginning to draw together. Members of Flint Water Class Action, FDDL, and the newly formed Water You Fighting For? all participated, chanting "Don't drink the water!" and "No more poison!" at the cars driving down Saginaw Street.

Over the next month, Water You Fighting For? (WYFF) emerged as the group at the forefront of most of the water rallies and marches, its "Don't Drink the Water" message emblazoned on the distinctive T-shirts that became a uniform of sorts for many of the activists. The group was started by Melissa Mays and LeeAnne Walters after meeting at the disastrous Dome town hall, along with a longtime Flint activist associated with the hacktivist group Anonymous.[31] Mays took inspiration from environmental justice matriarch Lois Gibbs, famous for her role in publicizing the effects of underground chemical waste in Love Canal, New York, in the late 1970s, and founder of the Center for Health, Environment, and Justice (CHEJ), an organization providing mentorship and resources to grassroots community groups working on environmental justice issues. In response to Mays's appeal for help, Gibbs sent her a CHEJ handbook with guidance for starting an organization. Initially, the mission of WYFF was focused on consciousness raising about the water, its website serving as a digital bulletin board for water-related information and a resource for other residents. The group, however, quickly came to embrace other forms of activism as well.

Although there were water quality rallies as early as January, in the people's history of the water struggle activists often dated the annunciation of the water movement's arrival to a march through downtown Flint on Valentine's Day. A collaboration between several grassroots groups, the march turned out over fifty people despite frigid temperatures hovering around ten degrees. The activists remembered their trudge through the snow from City Hall down Saginaw Street, over the Flint River and back again, as a feat of determination that symbolized their seriousness and commitment.[32]

Over the next few months, the grassroots groups that had begun to collaborate on rallies and marches would cement their partnership by forming the Coalition for Clean Water. The idea for the coalition originated with the Concerned Pastors for Social Action (CPSA), an influential network of local religious leaders, mostly from black churches, whose history of social activism went back to the civil rights struggles of the 1960s. The CPSA prided itself on its efforts to combat institutional racism and bring attention to the needs of the underserved, using its influence over a large segment of the population—upward of fifty congregations—to command respect from political candidates and elected officials.

The Concerned Pastors had political connections not only at the city level, but also at the state level. Not long after they began hearing from

Figure 6.3
Valentine's Day march. *MLive, Flint Journal.*

members of their congregations about problems with water quality, they initiated talks with officials in Lansing about the possibility of getting off the river—talks that took on new significance after the TTHM notice. On February 4, in a meeting with Governor Snyder's Chief of Staff Dennis Muchmore and Director of the Office of Urban Initiatives Harvey Hollins, the pastors called for "immediate reconnection to the Detroit water system," arguing that "lake water is 100 percent better than river water."[33] After two months without any movement, they held a press conference calling out the state for its inaction and threatening a lawsuit.[34]

As dialogue with the state turned to deadlock, the pastors decided there would be value in more coordinated pressure from below. They enlisted Bishop Bernadel Jefferson, a member of both CPSA and the FDDL, to help pull the city's grassroots groups together into a coalition.[35] Chaired by Reverend Allen Overton of CPSA, the coalition included the FDDL, FWCA, WYFF, CAUTION (Bishop Jefferson's group), and Woodside Church, a social justice–oriented congregation deeply involved in water issues. Tru Saunders and Councilman Eric Mays signed on as individuals. The coalition's main focus became the strategy explored the previous fall by the FDDL and threatened by the pastors in their April press conference: a legal injunction forcing the city back onto Detroit water.

In the activists' minds, the case for compelling a return to Detroit was cut and dry, supported by a mountain of evidence of the water's toxicity. But legally speaking, it stood on shaky ground: the quality problems that jumped out at residents were, according to experts, merely "aesthetic"—no one had proved any connection between the water and health symptoms—and the city's latest round of sampling showed that TTHM levels had fallen to well below maximum allowable levels. In fact, no site tested by the city had been over the EPA limit of 80 parts per billion (ppb) for TTHM since the beginning of the year, and once the city completed installation of new carbon filters at the water treatment plant, levels were supposed to drop even lower. As far as officials were concerned, they were following through on their promises to solve the water problem, and it seemed more likely than ever that it would be possible to make the river water work for the time being. Incurring the costs associated with switching back to Detroit—estimated at some $12 million just for the reconnection, plus another $1 million for water—would, they argued, be unnecessary and shortsighted.

Activists countered that declaring the TTHM situation under control was premature, warning that levels could rise again during the warmer months of the year, that the water treatment plant was still not up to par, and that more testing was necessary. As long as there was any threat whatsoever from TTHMs—which by the city's own admission could be harmful to some segments of the population—the state and the city, they argued, had a responsibility to offer residents a safe alternative. Laura Sullivan, who joined the coalition as a representative of Woodside Church, summed up the logic for me: "If you're going to use this source water and some people are at risk, then you have to provide bottled water to them or change the source water." This, she said, was the "hook."[36]

On June 5, the coalition filed a civil injunction against the City of Flint and City Administrator Natasha Henderson, alleging that the city "recklessly endangered" residents by switching to the river and calling for a return to Detroit water "on an immediate and an emergency basis."[37] It would take more than three months for the suit to reach a conclusion as it was bounced from county to federal court and back.[38] In the meantime, the activists found other ways to keep the water struggle in the headlines. In July, they helped organize the Detroit to Flint Water Justice Journey, a seven-day, seventy-mile series of marches that wound through cities affected by emergency management and struggling with problems of water quality, cost, and privatization: Detroit, Pontiac, Highland Park, and finally Flint, culminating in a march from Woodside Church to City Hall for a rally organized by the coalition. With the assistance of the advocacy group Food and Water Watch, the coalition also launched a petition drive to demonstrate the strength of public demand for reconnection to the Detroit system. On August 31, Melissa Mays and Reverend Overton along with a dozen other activists hand-delivered an imposing stack of paper with 26,856 petition signatures collected from people all over the country to Mayor Walling at his office.[39]

By this time, activists had opened up another front in the war they were fighting to get Flint off the river—the one that would finally break things open. It began with a fateful shipment that arrived two weeks prior to the delivery of the petitions—three hundred water testing kits, sent by a team of engineers at Virginia Tech—and with the growing feeling that the contaminant that would finally force the hand of officials was not *E. coli*, or chloride, or TTHMs, but lead.

Figure 6.4
(Top) Coalition for Clean Water files suit seeking return to Detroit water.
(Bottom) Delivery of petitions to Mayor Dayne Walling. *MLive, Flint Journal.*

Lead in the Water

There had been rumblings of lead in the water as far back as February. That
was the month a water sample taken at LeeAnne Walters's house came back
at 104 ppb, prompting a frantic call from Mike Glasgow at the water treatment plant telling her not to drink her water. Glasgow eventually determined that the house had an unusually long lead service line, which the city
offered to replace at no cost. There was a catch, however: Walters would have
to sign a form indemnifying the city against all liability for any injury caused

by the lead. Presented with an opportunity to remove the immediate danger to her family, Walters was torn: should she take the deal and let the city off the hook? After talking it over with other activists, she decided not to sign.

She also began to look for help from someone outside of city and state government. After reaching out to the EPA, she connected with Miguel del Toral, regulations manager for the Ground Water and Drinking Water Branch of the EPA's Region 5. Del Toral, in turn, enlisted the assistance of Marc Edwards, who began conducting independent tests on Walters's water. His results showed lead levels that were off the charts: one sample came back at an astonishing 13,200 ppb of lead, more than twice the amount necessary for the water to qualify as toxic waste by EPA standards. Edwards said he was "shocked" by the results, musing that he had never in his "twenty-five-year career seen such outrageously high levels going into another home in the United States."[40]

As bad as the condition of the water in the Walters household was, the bigger story was what Walters uncovered when, in a search for answers, she began digging into operational reports from the water treatment plant: the city was not using corrosion control. When she informed del Toral of this discovery, his initial reaction was disbelief. He reached out to the MDEQ for clarification, sure that there must be some mistake, and was told that the city had a "corrosion control program" in place. The semantic subtlety of the phrase did not jump out at del Toral until later: a corrosion control *program* was not the same thing as *corrosion control*.[41]

Walters's sky-high lead levels and the revelation about the MDEQ's unorthodox approach to corrosion control caused del Toral to suspect more widespread problems with lead in Flint's water system. In July, he detailed his concerns in a memorandum circulated internally at the EPA. He also, however, sent the document to Walters herself, knowing it would become public and fearing, correctly, that it would not be acted upon promptly by his own agency. For this act, he came to be known as the main "whistle-blower" of the water crisis.

Walters promptly forwarded the memo to Curt Guyette, an investigative journalist well known to the activists who had been hired by the Michigan ACLU to cover the effects of the state's EM law. In a series of articles and documentary films produced with his collaborator Kate Levy, Guyette broke the story of Walters's plight and shed light on the larger issues of water quality in

Flint.[42] EPA officials reacted to Guyette's reporting by trying to discredit del Toral and minimize his findings. When Dayne Walling learned of the memo and reached out to EPA Region 5 Director Susan Hedman with concerns, she apologized for the alarm caused by the leak and assured him that the findings were only preliminary and undergoing review. MDEQ spokesperson Brad Wurfel characterized del Toral as a "rogue employee" and said that "anyone who is concerned about lead in the drinking water in Flint can relax."[43]

Realizing that the presence of lead in the water would greatly bolster their case for returning to the Detroit system, and fearing that the city's next round of sampling data would mask the problem,[44] members of the coalition began to encourage people to get their water tested and report the results back to the activists. Melissa Mays picked up sampling kits from the water treatment plant and distributed them to residents, taking them to festivals, churches, and meetings. As lead results came in, she incorporated them into a map of Flint on the WYFF website that showed the distribution of a variety of water issues across the city. The goal was to illustrate that the lead problem, like other problems, was not confined to Walters's house or to any one area. Although the sample size was limited, the numbers, Laura Sullivan recalls, were "pretty high," suggestive of a hitherto underappreciated threat.[45]

With these new numbers on their side, the coalition decided to try again to pique concern in Lansing. In a meeting with Dennis Muchmore and Harvey Hollins on July 22, the activists had the opportunity to present their data, with Mays displaying a blown-up version of the WYFF map. Just as significant, however, was their presentation of Laura Sullivan, introduced for maximum dramatic effect as *Dr.* Sullivan, who Reverend Overton asked to "tell them what lead does to people."[46] Muchmore looked on with concern as Sullivan did her best (mechanical engineer that she was) to explain what lead does to the human body. The meeting ended with Muchmore promising to look into the lead issue and get back to them. For a moment, it seemed like an injunction might not be necessary: civil conversation, enhanced by Sullivan's credentials, was finally getting somewhere.

At the follow-up meeting on August 4, however, Muchmore had assembled a group of MDEQ employees who greeted the activists, Sullivan recalls, with "smug" expressions. He said he had good news to relate: the MDEQ had looked at the available data and determined that the ninetieth percentile for lead was below the EPA action level. Sullivan didn't think it

Figure 6.5
Water You Fighting For map (detail).
Source: Water You Fighting For?

was possible. How could the state's numbers and the activists' numbers be so far off? She made the point that "there may be a problem when the entity that collects the samples and the entity that analyzes the samples are both benefitting when the samples are good." But she was too "afraid" and "inhibited" to say more. The looks on the state officials' faces gave her the impression that she and the activists were "fools" and had "no place in the room."[47] Emails sent between Muchmore and Hollins the following day offer some insight into their take on the meeting. Their disdain for those they label "activists," who they imply came in with the wrong demeanor and irrelevant political concerns, is apparent:

Muchmore: I didn't think that meeting was as useful as others. If people won't accept the factual information, I'm not sure there is much we can do about it. ... We can't do too many more of these. The three activists in the room just want to be right; they don't want answers. No matter what we say they'll always want something else to be the answer.[48]

Hollins: I agree. It's hard to get to yes or satisfaction with certain types of community advocates because no matter what you do, they will always grind an ax on something. ... I think one more meeting with the pastors and maybe the professor from Kettering (who I think is reasonable) to put closure on the outstanding questions is warranted. The other women who were there to argue for the sake of arguing should not be apart [sic] of that meeting. Regarding more state money to Flint or democracy discussions on the question of emergency management isn't something that I have too much of an appetite for.[49]

Once again, activists had come forward with what they felt to be compelling evidence of system-wide problems that more than justified switching off the river, and once again, officials had responded by overruling their data and shutting down their concerns. It had a deflating effect, at first: LeeAnne Walters, for one, began to slide into a "rabbit hole" of depression, calling Marc Edwards in a "hysterical" state of mind and looking for direction.[50] That direction came from an idea first proposed to Edwards by Curt Guyette: what if the activists worked with Virginia Tech to collect a larger sample, one that officials could not simply brush off as statistically insignificant? Edwards said at least seventy-five samples would be necessary. Guyette offered to pay for one hundred tests,[51] and began contacting activists to stir up interest in the sampling campaign.[52]

From Walters's perspective, it was a last-ditch effort, but one she threw herself into with gusto. After receiving sampling kits and instructions in the mail, she and the other members of the coalition organized a rigorous sampling protocol. They began by recruiting participants, mainly through pre-established personal networks, making a conscious effort to ensure robust participation in all parts of the city. They also instituted strict procedural guidelines for quality control, convinced that the results would never be believed unless everything was "perfect."[53] When residents came to pick up their kits at Saints of God Church, the activists had them watch an explanatory video explaining how to collect the samples. When it was time to pack samples for transport to Virginia Tech, the activists asked residents to initial the sealed boxes to ensure there was no appearance of their being tampered with. They also devised a system of documentation, keeping track of everyone who picked up a kit and carefully recording the information in an Excel spreadsheet.

Instead of the seventy-five-sample minimum mandated by Edwards, in less than a month's time the activists collected 269 usable samples—a 90 percent success rate. Moreover, they succeeded in distributing the samples across a wide geographical area, with strong representation of every ward in the city. The contrast to the city's most recent sampling effort could not have been starker: the utility had struggled to break even the one-hundred-sample threshold, and the samples had been heavily concentrated in a few convenient areas. Members of the Virginia Tech Flint Water Study team (as they began to call themselves) marveled at the activists' success: graduate student Siddartha Roy said that "they did the job better than most scientists."[54] The team's analysis showed that 10 percent of sampled homes in Flint had lead levels of 27 ppb or higher, indicating that the city, as announced in a blaring headline on the recently launched Flintwaterstudy. org, had a "VERY SERIOUS LEAD IN WATER PROBLEM."[55]

The findings could not have been timelier. On September 14, Circuit Court Judge Archie Hayman threw out the coalition's lawsuit, killing the injunction. The very next day, coalition members, along with Marc Edwards, Siddartha Roy, and Curt Guyette, held a press conference at City Hall. Speaking to the cameras, Melissa Mays said it was "a huge, huge, day for the water fight in Flint," calling the sampling data a "strong punch." Edwards explained that the same problem that was turning people's water brown— high corrosivity—was also "causing excessive lead to go into people's water." Guyette asserted that the "reason everybody is here today is because the emergency managers appointed by Governor Rick Snyder, in an effort to save the city money, made the decision to switch from clean Detroit ... water to the Flint River." Reverend Overton called yet again for the city to return to Detroit water "immediately." Other members of the coalition then took turns articulating new demands: Nayyirah Shariff demanded that the MDEQ distribute filters to every household in Flint, Laura Sullivan demanded that the city replace "all lead-containing service lines" at no cost to residents, Melissa Mays demanded that the EPA step in and "take over Flint's

Figure 6.6
Press conference with activists and Flint Water Study team announcing sampling results. *MLive, Flint Journal.*

treatment decisions and the MDEQ's testing and oversight," and LeeAnne Walters demanded that there be an "audit" of MDEQ's sampling and a crackdown on its exploitation of loopholes in the Lead and Copper Rule.[56]

State officials could not dismiss Virginia Tech's results as easily as they did the first batch of lead data activists presented to them. Nevertheless, the MDEQ claimed to be "perplexed" by the findings and by the team's warning to residents not to drink the water without filtering it or flushing their pipes first. "While the state appreciates academic participation in this discussion," said spokesperson Brad Wurfel, "offering broad, dire public health advice based on some quick testing could be seen as fanning political flames irresponsibly."[57]

It took a reverberation from the Washington, D.C., lead-in-water crisis of the early 2000s to finally break the state's resistance. It came from water expert Elin Betanzo, who had worked for the EPA in D.C. during that time and remembered how critically important it was to show that lead in water was getting into the bloodstreams of children. After learning of the lead data being analyzed by Virginia Tech, she encouraged her old friend Mona Hanna-Attisha to look into whether there was a correlation between Virginia Tech's lead results and blood lead levels. Hanna-Attisha's analysis (see chapter 1) showed, on average, a doubling of elevated blood lead levels in children ages 0 to 6 as well as the hypothesized correlation with lead levels in different parts of the city. The state made one final effort to push back, with Michigan Department of Health and Human Services (MDHHS) officials presenting a chart that attributed the increase in blood lead to seasonal variation (a chart that would later lead to felony charges). Upon closer examination of the data, however, both the MDHHS and the MDEQ conceded their mistake: lead was a danger in Flint after all. It had taken eighteen months of resident complaints and nine months of focused activism around water quality, but for local, state, and federal officials, the "Flint water crisis" had finally begun.

Realizing the Impossible

After Hanna-Attisha publically released her data, Mayor Walling indicated at a press conference that all options were now on the table, including reconnection to the Detroit system. But he warned that the final decision about Flint's water source was the governor's to make.[58] Three days later, the coalition held a press conference of its own at which it threatened large-scale protests in Flint and Lansing if the switch was not made immediately.[59] Shortly thereafter, it filed a petition with the EPA asking the agency to take control of the situation.[60]

But still the state seemed determined to avoid the source change. On October 2 at Kettering University, the day after the Genesee County Health Department declared a public health emergency in Flint, state officials announced a "Flint water action plan" that included $1 million for point-of-use filters, water testing at schools and homes, blood lead testing, and corrosion control—but no return to Detroit water. Outside, activists held a protest featuring Nayyirah Shariff and Melodee Mabbitt in yellow hazmat suits. When they heard that the state was not yet prepared to change Flint's water source, they were furious. Reacting to the news, Reverend Al Harris of the Concerned Pastors said residents were "back to square one."[61]

In fact, the activists were on the cusp of getting what they had been fighting for. On October 8, after nine months of insisting that reverting to Detroit water was "not going to happen,"[62] the city and state announced that they had struck a deal to make it possible.[63] Melissa Mays described the decision as "a little unreal."[64] Dayne Walling was even more stunned: he hadn't thought there was that kind of money "sitting out there" for a reconnection. "And then, in light of the lead crisis, *bam*—there it is."[65]

It would be hard to overestimate the profundity of the validation the activists felt after the reversal. It was not just that their framing of the water situation (i.e., that it was a public health crisis) had gone mainstream, or that officials had capitulated and adopted the activists' position on what needed to be done. It was that their whole approach to creating social change had been affirmed. They had refused to accept officials' definition of what was reasonable, or the ceiling officials set on what was possible, or the standards of "evidence" officials used to form their judgments about the water. They had shown, at times, at least a minimal willingness to enter into conversation with officials about the water; but even in these instances, they thumbed their noses at the proprieties expected of them and clung firmly to their demands rather than showing any signs of compromise. They had preferred disruption, protest, and petition to the tightly controlled deliberative settings crafted by the city—settings they saw as not only unwelcoming, but inauthentic. And when the data on water quality produced by the city and state in summer 2015 conflicted with the activists' message and objectives, they had gone out and generated data of their own that confirmed the water's dangers.

The reinforcement the activists got from their victory only made them less inclined to limit their demands to what was considered "reasonable." As soon as the matter of the reconnection was settled, their attention shifted to another controversy: whether the city should declare a state of emergency in order to encourage similar declarations at the state and federal levels, or even lobby for a stronger federal "disaster" declaration. In a series of mayoral debates (for in addition to all the other excitement, it was the middle of election season), incumbent Walling came out against the idea, arguing that the county's declaration of emergency was enough to get Flint what resources it could rightly expect, and pointing out that the crisis, being manmade, did not fit federal criteria for disaster status.[66]

Unsurprisingly, the activists chose to align themselves with a candidate who, like them, did not share Walling's sense of political possibility. Despite the fact that Flint had not yet wriggled entirely free from the state's grip, the activists—long frustrated by Walling's civility toward the EMs, general "Boy Scout" demeanor, and proactive complicity in creating a "false narrative" around the water—sensed that the election of a fighter to the mayor's office during this moment of opportunity would have real consequences. They found their candidate in Karen Weaver, a Ph.D. clinical psychologist relatively new to the political arena but strongly supported by the Concerned Pastors and the Flint NAACP—two pillars of the city's African American community. Weaver had earned herself the label of "water warrior" by coming out to activist rallies and shown that she, too, was willing to demand what others said was impossible. During her campaign, she promised what Walling would not: a return to Detroit water (before it became a reality), a city-level declaration of emergency, and a fight for federal disaster status.

In fact, Weaver's own candidacy was a longshot: a bid to become the first African American woman mayor in the city's history by unseating a polished, pedigreed, white (always a factor within Flint's highly racialized political culture), male incumbent. Once again, however, expectations were confounded. With decisive support from the pastors and the activists, Weaver scored an upset victory on November 3 with a sizable twelve-point margin.[67] On December 14, as promised, she filed an emergency declaration.[68] After initially waffling, the county signed off on it on January 4, opening up the possibility of more state and federal assistance. The very next day, Governor Snyder declared an emergency at the state level and requested federal help. Although the activists never got their desired "disaster" declaration, on January 16 President Obama declared a federal state of emergency in Flint. Reeling from his defeat and watching from the sidelines now, Walling remembers being amazed by how quickly it all happened.[69]

The sequence of events from October 2015, when the city switched off the river, through early January of the next year only further emboldened the activists and reinforced the lessons they had taken away from the water source fight. When I first encountered them personally, at a rally and march on January 8, they were brimming with confidence and full of demands: full replacement of the pipes, social services for those harmed by the water, federal disaster relief (Stafford Act be damned), and the arrest of Governor Snyder. By that point, the rest of the country—the world, even—was behind them, with solidarity and support from the broader activist community converging on Flint from all sides.

As a newcomer, I was impressed by the apparent unity, strength, and purpose of the water activists. It was a somewhat distorted impression, influenced by the headiness of the moment, and by my own distance (at that point) from the movement's internal controversies. There was an aura around the activists, however, that I found alluring on both a personal and scholarly level. Over the next two and a half years, I witnessed firsthand their fight for justice in Flint, and their efforts to turn crisis into opportunity by channeling the popular uprising sparked by poisoned water into a longer-term political agenda.

I came to realize, however, that the storybook quality of the battle over the river—good enough for a *Lifetime* movie[70]—belied some of the tensions latent in the alliances struck up along the way. These tensions were exacerbated by the media's elevation of some of the central players into "hero" figures, including people from outside the community whose perspectives on the nature of the crisis and status of the recovery effort proved to be sharply opposed, in some fundamental ways, to those of activists.[71] As enamored as many activists were with the storybook version of events, looking back on 2015 nostalgically as a time of unity and power, they soon came to realize that advancing their struggle for justice and making good on the democratic potential of the movement would require a reckoning with some of the "heroes" of that chapter of their story. That reckoning began with another battle over the reality of the crisis itself.

7 The Water Is (Not) Safe: Expertise, Citizen Science, and the Science Wars

The water movement in Flint was multifaceted, a unity-in-diversity of long-time activist and political neophyte, preacher and protestor, councilman and professor, but its message was simple: *the water is not safe*. The demand attached to that message was equally simple: *get us off the river* now.

The medium used to transmit the message varied depending on the audience. Sometimes activists embodied it—literally—in vivid displays of corporal harm. Sometimes they expressed it in the form of personal testimony. Increasingly they pieced it together—on social media, on makeshift maps—into mosaics of accumulating experiences from all over the city. And gradually, they translated it into the language of science, first through the exploratory research of enterprising individuals, later through the systematic collection of sampling data.

Not everyone believed this act of translation was worthwhile. Some activists were convinced there was little point in turning to "research" (a term sometimes employed sneeringly) for "proof" that the water was bad. The water movement's basic premise, after all, was that the water was *self-evidently* bad, and that the reason officials were stalling was not for want of proof but out of indifference or malice. It was futile, then, to speak scientific truth to power: officials did not care what the truth was, as shown by their disregard for the wealth of experiential evidence of contamination and harm residents had been bringing forward since spring 2014. The only way to fight their mendacity and delay, from this perspective, was through militant activism in the streets.

The activists who did turn to science did not dispute that the badness of the water was unmistakable, or that officials were disinterested and dishonest, or that militant action was necessary. Indeed, what attracted them to science was precisely that it could be used as a weapon (a "punch," as

Melissa Mays put it[1]) in the service of popular struggle—not to convince people who were beyond convincing, but to compel action from people who were resisting doing the right and obvious thing. For activists to be scientifically literate, and even, in some sense, practitioners of science, altered the balance of power, allowing them to push back more forcefully whenever officials used science to sugarcoat the pills residents were supposed to swallow about the water. As for activists' own claims about water quality, rendering them in scientific terms gave them weight that experiential knowledge—no matter how extensive—lacked when viewed through the technocratic lens of officialdom. It was not that the claims became *truer,* but rather *less arguable*—even *in*arguable. As LeeAnne Walters liked to say: "You can't argue with science."[2]

The problem was that there *were* arguments about science—lots of them. Activists argued with the science put forward by officials and scientists they mistrusted. Officials contested scientific claims made by activists and scientists alike. And scientists quarreled not only with activists and officials, but also among themselves. Assertions about the inarguability of scientific knowledge served mainly to make these clashes more violent, for they were used to sharpen spears on multiple sides.

Within this knotty epistemic terrain, the scientific value of particular claims was often less important than the perceived credibility of the people making them. New fronts of struggle opened up around efforts to construct, protect, and, at times, *de*construct credibility.[3] As discussed in chapter 5, it was a challenge for Flint activists to establish themselves as credible knowers even when the subject of their knowledge was their own personal experience. Staking a claim to scientific knowledge presented another layer of difficulty. Activists had to navigate thickets of technical jargon, comply with exacting standards of evidence,[4] and yoke their assertions about the water to scientifically verifiable "facts" that captured only imperfectly their sense of its full risks and harms. They also had to alter their demeanor at times, showing that they could be calm and logical when speaking in a scientific register even as they bristled with indignation at the smug condescension of officials.[5]

Brandishing science effectively in the service of the cause was difficult to do without help. No matter how much activists built up their own lay expertise, and no matter how dispassionately they presented their evidence, it was always possible their claims would fail to make an impact without the backing of established scientific authorities. Some allies with claims to varying degrees of scientific expertise were close at hand—people like Laura Sullivan, to whom activists turned at various times for advice and assistance, as well as a few other residents with backgrounds in chemistry and water. The expertise activists were able to muster from within their personal networks only went so far, however, as captured in the anecdote of Sullivan the mechanical engineer having to improvise an explanation of the health effects of lead exposure (see chapter 6). Furthermore, the data activists were able to compile on their own, while plenty compelling when viewed through lay eyes, lacked the statistical bite to pierce the official narrative about Flint's water problems being localized and fleeting. The combination of limited resources within the community and the hardened resolve of officials to avoid taking action meant that activists could not "afford" but to accept expert help from wherever it came.[6]

While assistance from the outside could enhance the strength of the movement, however, it could also make activists vulnerable. Whenever activists partnered with an outsider, Claire McClinton told me, they had to ensure they maintained their "independence." Would-be allies had to recognize that activists were already operating with their "own agenda," and that "helping" meant figuring out how to support that agenda.[7]

Alliances with experts could be difficult to fit into this paradigm. They involved inequalities of resources, access, and influence that could be disempowering if not carefully managed, as well as institutional and financial entanglements on the expert side that could divide loyalties and bring unwelcome outside influences into the picture. Even experts who purported to play a support role and let local activists take the lead were rarely free of their own agendas or fully committed to the principle of local control. One reason was that experts tended to derive their sense of entitlement to speak about matters of local concern from their own expertise, rather than from the wishes of their local partners. In the event of disagreement, this meant they sometimes spoke for themselves rather than the movement, in ways that could potentially undermine activist objectives as well as activists' own representations of their struggle and social reality.

In their eagerness—and at times, desperation—for help, activists did not linger on the potential downsides of expert alliances, or even perceive them, necessarily. The relationships they entered into were informed by the imperatives of the moment and extemporaneous assessments of their benefactors' motivations and personal character. At first, it seemed those assessments had been sound: between early 2015 and early 2016, they brought several outside expert figures to Flint, all of whom appeared to have the interests of residents at heart, and all of whom moved pieces of the movement's agenda forward.

As time went on, however, it became clear that power handed over to expert allies under conditions of crisis could be just as unaccountable, and just as vulnerable to abuse, as the emergency state power they had been fighting since 2011. In fact, these two species of power seemed to be drawing ever more closely together, as the state neutralized the disruptive effect of outside expertise by bringing it into the fold of the official response to the crisis. The scientific idiom activists had used, with the assistance of their allies, to crack the case of Flint's contaminated water became the state's preferred language for bringing that case to a close—well before activists (and residents more broadly) were prepared to do so.[8]

At the center of this dynamic was Marc Edwards, the ultimate example—for many Flint activists, anyway—of the expert-scientist-ally turned enemy collaborator. His devolution from "hero" to "zero" in their eyes (to borrow Tony Palladeno's always-colorful phrasing) was not only the most spectacular, it also sucked every other lay-expert alliance into its orbit in one way or another, shaping, in the process, the activists' attitudes toward science and expertise more generally. Unsurprisingly, Edwards and the activists had two completely different explanations for the decline of his reputation in Flint. As activists saw it, Edwards "changed," falling prey to the allure of power, fame, and money—or simply his own egotism—and selling them out in the process. As Edwards saw it, he was perhaps the most steadfast character of all, maintaining a stoic commitment to the truth no matter how inconvenient, as allegiances shifted all around him and he was shot full of arrows by dishonest, unfair, and politically-motivated people. He began to describe the situation in Flint as "science anarchy," with the unifying and objective qualities of science replaced by "tribal" loyalties and "subjective," "unscientific," "postmodern social justice."[9]

For Edwards, it was all a sign, apparently, that what he once called the "netherworld" of activism was less penetrable by the luminous rays of scientific truth than he had originally hoped.[10] The scientist who began by defending his own "activism" to fellow members of his profession,[11] and was heralded as an apostle of a more democratic and inclusive science, ended up suggesting that "as a scientist you can't really engage with activism unless it's a ... public emergency."[12] Activists were just too prepared to part ways with the truth when it didn't suit them, and to crucify those who attempted to steer them back onto the right path.

While activists were never as enamored with the idea of scientific truth as Edwards—an important part of their struggle, always, was validating other ways of knowing—by no means did they see any inherent conflict between science and activism. As often as not, they framed their criticisms of him in scientific terms, maintaining that his science was biased, faulty, or, more often, simply incomplete. They strongly suspected that Edwards, along with the Michigan Department of Environmental Quality (MDEQ) and the EPA, was exaggerating the scientific consensus about the improvements to Flint's water quality for political reasons: the sooner the water was declared "safe," the sooner all involved could move on. More generally, having learned to think of Flint's water infrastructure as an unwieldy, complicated, open system, they were suspicious that knowledge of that system could ever really be "closed." They had grown too used to surprises—lead appearing in unexpected places, new contaminants cropping up, main breaks and leaks and all manner of things bubbling from the tap. Besides, there were still questions residents had about the water and its effects on their health that had not been answered to their satisfaction. There were political reasons, no doubt, for activists' tendency to resist consensus and closure when it came to the safety of the water, but there were also more sophisticated epistemologies at play than activists were typically given credit for.

It made a difference that activists themselves had been involved in the production of scientific knowledge. They operated with heightened awareness of how science gets made, freshly awake to the infrastructure of knowledge production just as they were to the infrastructure under their feet. When they encountered a scientific claim, they saw not just the claim itself but the personalities, the practices, the institutions, the money, and the interests wrapped up with it. They had also come to perceive the artificiality of definitions of "science" and "scientist," and it emboldened them to contest uses of those terms they believed were overly narrow and self-serving. Activists did not have to deny the truth in science to see that science also involved power—that it mattered who got to define it, who got to decide how it was used, and who got to declare scientific controversies "over."

When activists began to witness erstwhile expert allies contributing to politically convenient closures—by deploying their own credibility or

attacking the credibility of others—without any kind of democratic process
behind them, they once again felt the lash of power that was unaccountable and unresponsive, and it stung all the more, in this case, because they
had helped to create it.

Bob Bowcock and the Appeal to Expertise

On January 20, 2015, a post appeared on Facebook that sent a shiver of excitement through the activist community. After receiving numerous pleas for
help from Flint activists, Erin Brockovich, *the* Erin Brockovich, was denouncing the city's "dangerous, undrinkable drinking water." Shortly thereafter,
she promised to send her longtime right-hand man, water consultant and
former water utility manager Bob Bowcock, to assess the situation firsthand.

Bowcock visited Flint for four days in mid-February. Parts of his visit had
an official flavor: he met with Mayor Walling, Public Works Director Howard
Croft, and Councilman Wantwaz Davis and was granted a personal tour of
the water treatment plant. He also, however, cemented a lasting reputation as
a friend of the activists, marching side by side with them through the freez-
ing cold on Valentine's Day in a scarf borrowed (in good Californian fashion)
from Laura Sullivan. Addressing the marchers with a bullhorn, he affirmed
the importance of activism: "Your attendance on this very, very cold day is
important. You're demonstrating leadership to everyone in this community
that this water issue is a problem that can be solved with community action."

After the march, Bowcock laid out his initial impressions of the water situation at a well-attended talk at Saints of God Church. In some ways, his message was sharply at odds with what the activists were saying at that point
about the water. Most significantly, he did not think it necessary to abandon
the river as a drinking water source. In the short term, he said, some "very,
very simple" changes to the water treatment process—like dialing down the
chlorine, discontinuing the lime-softening process, and introducing an activated carbon barrier—would improve matters considerably. (Notably, what
Dayne Walling took away from his conversation with Bowcock was that
the situation was "manageable."[13]) Given how committed activists were to
returning to Lake Huron water, it was the first disconcerting example of an
expert ally unexpectedly undermining a nonnegotiable demand.

In other ways, though, Bowcock bolstered the activists' position. He told
them that for anyone to say the water was safe was "just not honest," that

there could be a big difference between the quality of the water leaving the treatment plant and the water coming out of the tap, and that water with a noticeable color or smell was indeed a concern from a health standpoint (contrary to what other "experts" had said at the disastrous town hall the preceding month). He also warned that there could be contaminants in the water the city was overlooking or not acknowledging. There were hundreds of unregulated disinfection byproducts (DBPs), for example, that were just as dangerous as the four trihalomethanes residents had been told about. There were species of bacteria, like legionella, that weren't being tested for. And the fluoride added to the water at the treatment plant, while not officially considered a contaminant, could just as well be: Bowcock said it was making the water more corrosive and was "a huge waste of money" besides. He warned that household filters would "polish" the water aesthetically but would not make it safe and advised residents to take warm baths rather than hot showers to avoid steam inhalation.[14]

On February 17, Bowcock sent a letter to Walling and the City Council with sixteen recommended changes to the city's water treatment and distribution processes. They turned out to be very similar to the recommendations made the next month by Veolia, which received $40,000 of taxpayer money for its trouble. It was a point of pride with the activists that the person they brought in *pro bono* had effectively scooped the Veolia report, and it taught them that they could marshal experts every bit as competent as those put forward by officials—*more* competent, even. Bowcock, after all, seemed to be tuned in to contaminants that weren't being taken seriously by other experts, particularly fluoride. Shortly after Veolia released its final report (which nowhere mentioned the word "fluoride"[15]), and inspired by what Bowcock had said about the chemical a few weeks earlier, Water You Fighting For? organized a "take the poison out" press conference and rally focused on fluoride's corrosivity and purported health dangers.

Bowcock's mixture of alarming intimations of neglected risks and straightforward advice to the water utility gained him an audience with both activists and officials, but ultimately he made more of an impression on the former than the latter. Although he stayed in touch with Howard Croft, who for some time thereafter would call him looking for guidance, his recommendations mostly, in his estimation, "fell on deaf ears."[16] Ironically, it was precisely the fact that he was not listened to that was useful to the activists: it was yet another indication that the city was not committed to or capable of getting the chemistry of the river water right and needed to switch sources entirely. It was also a source of commonality between activist and expert: Bowcock, too, had tried to get officials to change course but was not taken seriously.

When Bowcock left Flint after his short visit, he did so with what would prove to be enduring credibility with the activists. Although the fit between his perspective and theirs was imperfect, he had come at their behest, without any professional or financial incentive for doing so, and helped to initiate them into a still-new world of technical discourse around water. He had gone about his business in an unassuming way, without any sign of an agenda or desire for the spotlight ("It can't be mine and Erin's issue," he told me. "It *has* to be the community's issue."[17]) He had celebrated the activists precisely for their *activism*, and even joined in it (though he and Brockovich later declined to get involved in the Coalition for Clean Water's legal injunction or endorse Karen Weaver for mayor).

Bowcock remained in regular touch with activists behind the scenes, providing advice and support on a sometimes daily basis. His failure to get much movement out of officials, however, while in some sense good for his street credibility, did not solve the immediate problem: getting off the river. It would take an alliance with another expert to do that.

Marc Edwards, "Citizen Science," and the Limits of Lead

When Marc Edwards took up Flint's cause in the summer of 2015, he was already well known to the scientific community as a leading expert on lead corrosion. During his involvement in the Washington, D.C., lead-in-water crisis of the early 2000s, some mythologized him as a scientific superhero who used the powers of science to assist communities in distress (a sketch from a grateful D.C. resident, hung on his office wall, depicted him as "Corrosion Man").[18] Edwards received national recognition at the time for his work. He was profiled in *Time* magazine (where he called the elimination of lead in drinking water "a cause to die for"),[19] awarded a MacArthur "Genius Grant," and dubbed, simply, "The Water Guy."[20]

Edwards himself, however, remembered the D.C. experience as one of impotence and failure. Not only were residents exposed to lead for years before the story broke, it took even longer to prove that the city's attempt at a solution (partial service line replacement) was making the problem worse and that the Centers for Disease Control and Prevention (CDC) analysis of D.C. children's blood lead levels (showing no change despite huge exposures) was wrong. Although there was ample evidence of official malfeasance, none of the people harmed ever received reparations. In the origin story Edwards gave his Flint intervention, D.C. was the prologue in which the hero watches helplessly as those he has tried to save meet their doom—and vows never to let it happen again.

Flint was a second chance: it was shaping up to be "another D.C.," but there was still time to spare residents a great deal of harm.[21] Edwards was determined, however, to go into Flint with the right "narrative," one in which the heroes and the villains were sharply delineated.[22] The villains, as in D.C., were the dark forces of "institutional scientific misconduct"—an epidemic (said Edwards) within the state and federal agencies charged with protecting public health.[23] These agencies were swarming with "weak, unethical cowards" because their "perverse" incentive structure put loyalty to the agency over loyalty to the human race.[24] Instead of treating science as a "public good," they used it "to fool people"[25] whenever doing so meant saving face or avoiding inconvenient remedial action. And they did not take kindly to people exposing their way of operating—a lesson Edwards learned the hard way in D.C. when the EPA canceled its subcontract with him for lead testing.[26]

The heroes, by contrast, were those who dispelled government obfuscation with fearless scientific inquiry and put science in the service of the public, without consideration for professional or material gain. Edwards liked to say that he and his team had gone "all in for Flint,"[27] "dropp[ing] everything" to come to the city's aid at a time when no one from the area with comparable expertise was offering to help.[28] He described the intervention to me as a "suicide mission" that required putting his "career on the line," not to mention considerable expenditures of resources, time, and energy.[29] At one point, Edwards estimated that the team had spent $300,000 out of pocket to make its work in Flint possible,[30] and put in the equivalent of six years' worth of man-hours. The team was so strapped for cash, he claimed, that its $850,000-per-year lab operation—funded largely by grants he said he now had precious little time to apply for—was becoming unsustainable.[31] The motif of altruistic sacrifice on behalf of Flint residents by an uncommon breed of scientist infused the story the Flint Water Study team told about its own intervention, and it created the impression that the criticism later directed at Edwards was not only unfair but also ungrateful.

Edwards also had a place for the activists, of course, within his science-centric Flint narrative: they were the "citizen scientists" who had put together a first-rate ground operation and distinguished themselves by their intuitive grasp of the scientific method. As far as I could tell, Flint activists did not have any previous familiarity with the term "citizen scientist." As LeeAnne Walters told me, "I did not coin myself a citizen scientist. That was coined on me.... That wasn't something I put out there."[32] While Walters came to embrace the designation, others were less comfortable with it. Claire McClinton balked when I asked her if she identified with the term, screwing up her face. The thought of deriving an identity from the Virginia Tech collaboration, which was "just sampling," as she put it, seemed absurd. As far as she was concerned, the sampling effort was simply one prong of the struggle among others—it in no way defined the struggle or the people waging it. The way she made sense of the term "citizen science" was to think of it as a "political term about the activism of the people," expressing the determination of residents to take matters into their own hands.[33] The real significance of citizen science, in other words, was not the "science" part but the democratic initiative that made it possible. Edwards's framing of Flint activists as citizen scientists was one sign among others that he was attempting to write them into his own preconceived narrative rather than figuring out how *he* fit into *theirs*. In this dynamic were seeds of later controversies.[34]

Given the unfamiliarity of the term "citizen science" to Flint activists, Edwards and his team had considerable influence over how it was defined and applied. They employed it like a badge of honor, a compliment they paid to their most valued collaborators, at first applying it freely to all the activists who participated in the original sampling effort. As these activists fell off the Virginia Tech bandwagon, however, whittling the Flint wing of the team down to LeeAnne Walters and a few allies, Edwards increasingly held Walters up as *the* citizen scientist *par excellence*. (The other activists, he told me, were "heroic in their own way" but didn't have her "poster child" qualities.[35]) The more Walters's personal journey from resident to activist to citizen scientist came to be seen as the summation of the grassroots side of the Flint Water Study's intervention—even as her support of Edwards and part-time residence in Flint began to marginalize her within the activist community—the more Edwards's version of citizen science looked like a success. Every award Walters received, all the way up to the prestigious

Goldman Environmental Prize (the "Nobel" of environmental activism), enhanced his credibility, too—at least, with outsiders.[36]

If Edwards and the Flint Water Study team could bestow the honorable designation of citizen scientist, they could also take it away. The most striking case was that of Melissa Mays, an important contributor to the original sampling effort who became one of Edwards's most vocal critics. As relations soured, Edwards began to depict her as Walters's foil, as the anti–citizen scientist: whereas Walters was ethical, honest, and rigorous, willing to follow the science of the water wherever it led, Mays was an unscrupulous liar, who exemplified the kind of fearmongering and refusal to face facts Edwards believed was plaguing the activist community. There were signs that the revocation of Mays's citizen science card was even retroactive: in a presentation subtitled "Ut Prosim in Action" (after Virginia Tech's motto of service), Flint Water Study's Siddhartha Roy used a cropped photo of the original sampling team that cut her out of the picture.[37]

One of the most important vehicles Edwards used to promote his citizen science frame and narrative of the water crisis as a whole was the website established by the Virginia Tech team, Flintwaterstudy.org. Its main inspiration was WASAwatch, a website founded in 2009 that became an important means of disseminating information to residents about the D.C. water crisis and its aftermath as well as influencing the local water utility (WASA[38]) and federal agencies like the CDC, which paid close attention to the site. There was a qualitative difference between the two sites, however: WASAwatch was controlled by local residents and activists, with Edwards playing a behind-the-scenes support role, whereas Flintwaterstudy.org was controlled by Edwards and his team, and what happened with it was out of the activists' hands.[39] This is not to say the activists weren't glad of its existence, at least at first. As Nayyirah Shariff told me, they even "built it up and legitimized it," helping to turn it into the place to go for breaking news about the crisis. The problem was that after the site "flipped" (a shift she dated to January 2016), becoming a platform for commentaries that clashed with the activists' point of view and eventually for public attacks on activists, their allies, and fellow scientists, there was little anyone could do about it.[40]

Although these structural imbalances of power over framing and communication were present from the beginning of Virginia Tech's involvement in Flint, the wave of grassroots credibility on which Edwards and the team rode in made it easy to overlook them at first. Not only was Edwards, like Bob Bowcock, an independent outsider stepping up to help and willing to work with activists, he was much more aggressive about calling out the officials who activists felt were stonewalling them. Of course, his intervention was also far more involved and effective than Bowcock's, at least with respect to the short-term goal of getting off the river. The storybook version of that intervention, heavily promoted by the Flint Water Study team itself, depicted the resulting collaboration as a triumph of grassroots initiative, benign expert support, and "stunning" accomplishment.[41] It seemed at first that it had been genuinely empowering to the activists, who took pride in having led a sampling operation impressive in its sophistication, scale, and impact, and having done science "better" than trained scientists. The compliment fed into the populism at the heart of the water movement's conception of democracy: in a city turned over to authoritarian technocrats due to the supposed deficiencies of its residents, laypeople had taken the science of the water into their own hands and wowed the experts with their competence.

The success of the collaboration, however, also had an empowering effect on the expert. The media showered Edwards with attention and the STEM community showered him with accolades, awards, and opportunities, holding up his work in Flint as a "gold standard" to be emulated elsewhere.[42] Although Edwards seemed to revel in the idea that he was a maverick and an outsider, all the attention and esteem gave him considerable influence over mainstream perceptions of the water crisis—including, critically, perceptions of whether or not the crisis was "over." Edwards became the default scientific authority outsiders rushed to for comment whenever there was a new development in Flint, accumulating the kind of *a priori* credibility—one might describe it as "credibility excess"[43]—that put competing perspectives at an automatic disadvantage.

When Edwards had his guns trained on the state, activists saw his credibility as an asset to the movement, consciously cultivating it by talking up his scientific expertise, his independence, and the trust he had earned from residents. While their endorsement could not by itself vindicate Edwards's science—it would take Dr. Mona Hanna-Attisha's blood lead study to do that—it went a long way toward building up his national reputation as someone who put science in the service of the "public good."[44] The idea that grateful Flint residents had embraced Edwards as their champion became an invitation for outsiders to play up his "heroic" qualities.[45]

By the time I began attending activist meetings in early 2016, however, cracks were already beginning to appear in Edwards's credibility with the activists. Now that Edwards was the scientific face of the lead crisis, Governor Snyder decided it would be better to take him on as a partner than risk incurring more of his wrath, appointing him in January to the state committee overseeing the crisis recovery effort in Flint. Edwards became a trusted advisor and even—according to a rumor circulating within the activist community—the governor's "friend." Right around the time when activists started calling for Snyder's arrest, Edwards began singing his praises, describing him as "very, very committed to getting this fixed for the city of Flint." Once Snyder learned of Hanna-Attisha's blood lead data, Edwards said, he "immediately intervened to remove the health threat," effectively putting an end to the public health crisis as early as October 2015. He also brought in international experts to look at Flint's infrastructure and "studied the Lead and Copper Rule" so carefully that he could be classed as one of the "top experts" in the country on the rule.[46]

Edwards's attitude toward the EPA followed a similar trajectory. At first he was fiercely critical of the agency: during his Congressional testimony in early 2016, he passed up no opportunity to excoriate it, much to the delight of his Republican questioners. (Snyder, during his own testimony, followed suit.) As activists learned more about Edwards's rocky history with the EPA, and his right-wing political leanings, it got some of them thinking: what if his main motivation for getting involved in Flint was actually to continue a personal and political vendetta against the agency?

Although Edwards initially went after the EPA with guns blazing, however, he became increasingly laudatory of the agency right around the time it gave him an $80,000 grant to retest homes for lead: whatever its initial failings, it was now doing "good work" and "effectively assisting with the recovery."[47] Edwards insisted that his change of heart began earlier, with the resignation of EPA Region 5 Administrator Susan Hedman and the agency's embrace of Miguel del Toral, but for the activists the timing, once again, seemed more than just coincidental.

It is possible, though, that none of this would have mattered—not the kind words for mistrusted people and agencies, or the willingness to accept money from them—if the activists had not felt like Edwards's message about the water was taking an unwelcome turn. The main value Edwards had to the water movement—and in this sense he was no different from Bowcock—was that he breathed authority into its message that the water was not safe. Up through October 2015, the political importance of that claim was that it formed the basis of activists' demands to leave the river. From October onward, its political implication was that Flint was still in crisis and still needed help. The claim was not *merely* political, however, but also an expression of the deeply felt belief of activists and many, many residents of the city.

It was Edwards's particular interpretation of *why* the water was not safe that proved to be a liability. What brought the Virginia Tech team to Flint was, of course, lead—far from the first contaminant to spark concern among residents and one that only gradually became a priority for the water movement during the spring and summer of 2015. The main significance of lead to the activists was that it was perking up the ears of officials who were otherwise ready to be done talking about the river. Shifting attention to lead made good strategic sense from this perspective, but it had a downside whose consequences became progressively clear: lead explained little to nothing about what residents had actually experienced or were experiencing. It was not responsible for the "aesthetic" issues with the water (color, taste, smell), or skin rashes, or hair falling out, or respiratory illness, or a variety of other health symptoms residents attributed to the water. The existence of these symptoms gave activists strong reason to believe that lead was not the only or even the main thing harming residents. However, if the strategic value of lead caused them to look past this difficulty—at least temporarily—Edwards had stronger incentive for Flint to be understood, fundamentally, as a *lead-in-water crisis*. Characterizing the crisis this way had the effect of making his expertise preeminently relevant, especially after scientists with other kinds of expertise began sampling in Flint. And most importantly, from a narrative perspective, it set Flint up to be the redemptive sequel to D.C.

Despite Edwards's focus on lead, he wanted residents to know that he was well aware of their health symptoms and on the lookout for other contaminants of concern. When his team came to Flint for a short visit in the middle of the activists' sampling effort and did some sampling of its own, it left, he said, "no stone unturned."[48] Initially, the team raised some concerns about bacterial growth because of the abundance of iron in the water but, after further research, reported nothing alarming in the way of pathogens. The team also corroborated the city's claim that TTHMs had fallen to levels well within the acceptable range. (As for the period of time when TTHM levels were high, the team affirmed that "in the grand scheme of things, worse things can happen."[49]) These results led to a fateful determination, relayed at the September 2015 town hall at which the team debuted its findings directly to residents: the water was "safe for bathing and showering."[50]

As long as the team was supplying a knockout punch in the form of high lead results, the activists could tolerate these kinds of statements for the time being; the lead issue by itself was enough of a bombshell to bolster greatly the demand to leave the river as well as a robust set of demands for remediation and reparations. But for Edwards, seemingly—and for the state, which came to consider him the main authority on the subject—the city's ninetieth percentile for lead became the preeminent indicator of whether or not the water was "safe." And within months of the switch back to Detroit water, system-wide lead levels were dropping.[51] All indications, Edwards suggested, were that a D.C.-scale tragedy had been averted. He chalked up the positive trend to the reestablishment of a passivation layer through the addition of orthophosphates (on his advice) at the water treatment plant: in layman's terms, the pipes were "healing," preventing the further leaching of lead. So much so, he submitted—to much shock and derision among activists and residents—that removing them did not have to be a top priority given all of Flint's other infrastructural needs.[52]

Statements of this kind had a whiplash effect on residents who had come to see lead service lines as acute threats to their health. Edwards himself had taught residents to imagine that they were drinking their water through a "lead straw," a straw with the capacity to leach soluble lead and, at unpredictable times, particulate lead that could send their blood lead levels soaring if ingested. Using the water, he had said, was like playing "Russian roulette."[53] It was little consolation, then, to hear that the water was getting back to normal on average, since that was no guarantee that any particular glass of water was lead free. For Edwards, however, the remedy for such worries was simple: point-of-use faucet filters, which by January 2016 were available, for free—a "generous" act, he told me[54]—at state-sponsored distribution sites in every ward of the city. Until the day that all the lead pipes were replaced, he said, Flint residents could, like D.C. residents, "learn to live with lead in water."[55]

While Edwards would not flatly assert that the water was "safe," he began to stress that the water in Flint was as safe as, or safer than, municipal water in most other parts of the country. At one point, he claimed that filtered Flint tap water was "every bit as good if not better than the quality of … bottled water."[56] In response to these kinds of statements, activists seized upon every

Figure 7.1
Banner outside a Flint home. Christina Murphy.

high lead result from an individual home as evidence that he was wrong: the
water was *not* getting better (or was even getting worse), and the lead crisis was
far from over. At other times, though, the same activists would say they had
no argument with the overall lead picture Edwards was painting, or even that
they weren't worried about lead anymore. Instead, they argued that the real
problem was with contaminants *other* than lead that Edwards was neglecting
to take seriously because they contradicted his sanguine narrative of Flint as
a "success story."[57] Conflating the water crisis with the lead crisis seemed like
a dismissal by implication of all the ailments unrelated to lead that residents
continued to complain of (and that had, in many cases, turned them into
activists in the first place). With national outrage over Flint running high by

early 2016, these ailments were being treated with more respect than ever—it was a child with rashes, after all, who was chosen to symbolize the crisis on the cover of *Time*.[58] Attributions of symptoms like rashes to the water, however, still lacked a scientific foundation, and activists knew by now that compiling anecdotal evidence of the water's dangers would only get them so far. Once again, they would seek to infuse their experience of harm with the weight of science, and with trust in Edwards dwindling, they would do it not with his help, but with the help of yet another "expert" outsider.

Water Defense and the Boundaries of Science

Scott Smith, like Bob Bowcock, was closer to the world of activism than academia. He, too, was the "expert" arm of a small advocacy group associated with a high-profile celebrity: Water Defense, a nonprofit founded by the actor Mark Ruffalo in 2010. Water Defense grew out of Ruffalo's involvement in the anti-fracking movement, and much of its work revolved around this cause. It was an oil spill, however—the March 2013 rupture of the ExxonMobil-owned Pegasus Pipeline in Mayflower, Arkansas—that brought Ruffalo and Smith together. Smith was in Mayflower doing volunteer water sampling and finding oil where ExxonMobil said it wasn't. Intrigued by his work, Water Defense reached out through social media and struck up a dialogue that eventually led to a position with the organization.[59]

What stood out about Smith was not just his revealing sampling results, but the instruments he used to obtain them. A Harvard MBA, Smith's background was in the plastic foam business. In 2006, the New York factory housing his foam company was heavily damaged in a flooding event that deluged it in sewer backup and oil-contaminated water.[60] After the flood, Smith became "obsessed with coming up with a simple solution to filter oil from water." Over the next several years, he invested $5 million in the development of a foam-based product that would fit the bill.[61] The result was OPFLEX®, described by Smith as "the World's only proven Open-Cell Elastomeric Foam technology to filter oil from water and other contamination from the surface water including the entire water column."[62] The material's secret, Smith maintained, was its "biomimicry" of the human lungs, absorbing some substances while repelling others. More specifically, it was "oleophilic," attracting oil like a magnet, and "hydrophobic," repelling water after cleansing it of contaminants.

Prior to founding Opflex Solutions in 2011, Smith began taking his proto-types to disaster sites around the country and the world to test—and, at the same time, demonstrate—their efficacy. In the process, he had a catharsis that expanded his sense of what the material might be used for. In 2010, the Deepwater Horizon oil spill brought him to the Gulf of Mexico, where BP made some experimental use of his foam during its cleanup effort (a proud moment that Smith, years later, clearly viewed as signaling the arrival of his invention).[63] As he was "working side by side with fishermen and people in the communities of the Gulf of Mexico," he "realized the world was rely-ing on instantaneous water testing—taking water samples for a split second from the surface of the water." The problem with this method of testing was that it "was giving false negatives of dangerous oil-related chemicals." It suddenly dawned on Smith that OPFLEX® could be deployed not only for cleanup purposes, but as an "environmental indicator" capable of detect-ing chemicals that would otherwise go unnoticed. From that moment on, he recalled, his life "changed forever." He realized that he "had a duty and obligation to inform people" about the importance of what he described as "cumulative" water testing. Unlike "instantaneous," grab-sample testing, Smith claimed that testing water with his sponge-like material mimicked the body's exposure to contaminated water over time, offering a video of what was in water rather than a snapshot. It increased the likelihood, he said, of picking up contaminants that might be randomly missed by grab samples, at levels of accumulation analogous to what people encounter while swimming, bathing, or showering.[64]

Ruffalo was attracted to the technology for its potential to provide a fuller index of water contamination.[65] His vision was to use OPFLEX® to develop a "national open-source mapping of the nation's headwaters" cata-loguing baseline contaminant levels.[66] Such a map would make it easier to gauge the severity of contamination events, but it would also have an empowering effect on communities, opening their eyes to "the true state of their water based on proven, scientific data."[67] OPFLEX®'s low price point and ease of use would also enable "civilian scientists to test the water," decreasing reliance on testing by industry and the EPA and "arming the public with a technology that can't be gamed."[68]

Water Defense wore its science-and-technology-meet-real-life philosophy on its sleeve. Smith emphasized that part of what made his foam special was that he had developed it out in the field, not in a traditional laboratory. In a joint interview in June 2014, he and Ruffalo explained that Water Defense was "unique in that our laboratory is the real world. We go into a community, listen to their concerns, and help them diagnose and then solve [their] specific water contamination problems."[69] Just as loose as the organization's definition of a "laboratory" was its of a "scientist": it presented Smith, a businessman and activist with no particular scientific training, as its "Chief Scientist," and occasionally as its "Chief Chemist."

In a video posted on January 9, 2016, Smith debuted a new configuration of his OPFLEX® foam: the "Water Defense WaterBug." While Smith's other foam devices were designed for large-scale water cleanup and were thus large themselves (like his "synthetic eel grass" and "megapads"), the WaterBug was small and sleek—one could imagine using it in everyday settings.[70] Demonstrating its absorbent properties, in the video Smith articulates the logic of WaterBug sampling in language Flint residents would hear repeatedly over the next several months:

> Typical water testing that is used to declare water "safe" for communities is based on testing the water for a split second. That doesn't make sense. We don't encounter water for a split second. We don't swim in the water for a split second, we don't bathe for a split second, we don't shower for a split second. So why are we relying ... our health and human safety on testing that tests water for a split second?

He then rattles off a number of ominous-sounding chemicals he says he has found with his foam in bathtubs and sinks all over the country: trimethylbenzene, toluene, xylene—chemicals all the more insidious for being "clear, colorless, [and] odorless." "It is simply unacceptable," he opines, "for people to have to bathe, shower, cook, or drink water with any level of these toxic chemicals."

Three weeks later, after connecting with Melissa Mays through a mutual contact, he arrived in Flint. Another video documents Smith's four-day visit. It opens on the night of January 29, 2016, in Smith's room at the local Holiday Inn Express. He explains that he has been instructed by hotel staff not to drink the water but reassured that it is safe for bathing and showering. "The question is," he asks the camera rhetorically, "if water is not safe to drink, why is it safe to bathe and shower in?" He proceeds to extract a device from a glass jar—an aquamarine sponge, shaped like a Koosh ball with thicker tentacles, that he introduces as "the Water Defense WaterBug." What makes the device distinctive, he informs the viewer, placing it under the open faucet of the hotel bathtub, is its ability to "mimic the way we all encounter water."

The next clip finds Smith setting out at sunrise to take another sample—this time, of the Flint River. His "mission," as he puts it, is to "get baseline Flint River readings" for "the full gamut of potential chemicals of concern." Speaking in a car on the way to the sampling site, he explains that "once we have ... these baseline readings, we can then have an index and we can trace that throughout homes we test, hotels we test, schools we test, and so on." After arriving at a convenient bridge, Smith throws a larger version of the sponge over the side. Thirty minutes later, he hoists it back up and cuts several tentacles off for analysis before returning the device to the river to soak for 24 hours.

What Smith does not explain in the video is how he proposes to trace an "index" of chemicals from the river to residents' taps, given that the city had stopped using Flint River water in October of the previous year. The *non sequitur* seemed to suggest that Smith had not been following the news coming out of Flint closely enough to realize that the city was back on Lake Huron water. Although Smith would later, in his own defense, cite other reasons why it was useful to have a baseline reading,[71] Marc Edwards would point to the gaffe as one reason, among others, to question his competence.

However, that controversy was still in the future. *Prima facie*, there was much about Smith that was alluring to activists looking for more evidence of the water's impurity. His focus on the "cumulative" effects of contaminants in bath and shower water could help to explain health problems like rashes and hair loss, problems being treated—or so many residents felt—condescendingly and dismissively by officials (a much-maligned poster put out by the state and county health departments cheerily proclaimed, "Hey Flint! It is safe to wash!" with a picture of two smiling babies in a bubble bath).[72] Furthermore, Smith had the appeal of being an outsider independent of the agencies now funding Edwards—a masterless warrior (in his self-description, "Water Warrior One"), free to follow the evidence where it led him. Melissa Mays became Smith's closest ally, developing the kind of loyal and defensive relationship with him that LeeAnne Walters had with Edwards, but I heard numerous activists, after meeting Smith for the first time, speak of their intuitive trust in him and sense that he was on their side. Some activists did raise concerns that Smith was trying to make money by scaring residents, using the crisis as a showcase for a proprietary technology from which he could, in theory, profit. But Smith was generally seen as far less compromised by his ties to the business world than Edwards was by his ties to state and federal agencies; ironically, while the activists accused the tenured professor of being motivated by money, they painted the businessman as an altruist who, like Bob Bowcock, had merely responded to pleas from the community for help and had no ulterior motive. It was a sign that Smith's reputation as an activist committed to the cause of clean water would take primacy in their minds over his business background.

Smith found another important anchor of support in a less obvious corner of the community: the plumbers of United Association Local 370. The plumbers were already highly regarded for their contributions to the water crisis response,[73] but the specific issue that brought Smith to the union hall during his first visit to Flint was water heaters: he wanted to sample them, but didn't trust himself to open them. On that simple basis, a collaboration was born. United Association (UA) plumbers Harold Harrington and Ben Ranger would accompany Smith to residents' homes and assist with his sampling and the installation of shower filters. Smith took to sporting a UA 370 jacket and posting grave-faced pictures of himself and the plumbers to Facebook during sampling visits, continual reminders that they were on his side.[74]

As with Edwards, however, what ultimately mattered more than who Smith chose to work with was what he had to say about the water. And what he had to say was, to put it simply, sensational. Within two weeks of Smith's first visit to Flint, Water Defense put out a press release that led with a gripping hook: "There is much more than lead in the water in Flint, Michigan." Not only had Smith found "dangerous levels of lead in bathwater" (16 parts per billion [ppb], to be exact), but also "dangerous levels of volatile chemicals including chloroform, methylene chloride, and other trihalomethanes in bathroom sinks and showers." Appended to the release were more than two hundred pages of test results provided by the independent lab ALS Environmental, where Smith's samples had been analyzed.[75]

Press coverage of these claims was spotty at first, but picked up during Smith's next visit, which coincided with the Flint Democratic presidential debate and found him accompanied by a delegation that included Mark Ruffalo, Van Jones and Vien Truong (co-founder and CEO, respectively, of the green economy group Green for All), and billionaire philanthropist Tom Steyer. On March 7, activists from the Flint Rising coalition (whose story is told in the next chapter) arranged a joint press conference that took advantage of the national spotlight and star power on hand to amplify Smith's message. From a podium in the basement of St. Michael's Church (the coalition's headquarters), Ruffalo warned that "you've got a lot more contaminants in this water than what you're being told about." During his own remarks, Smith said it was "absolutely incomprehensible ... how anybody with any responsibility could make any kind of statement that this water is safe to bathe and shower in."[76]

The same day, standing on a bridge over the Flint River and ringed by Flint Rising activists, Smith delivered what he called "breaking news": he had found levels of "chloroform and trihalomethanes" as high as 95 ppb at the home of a family with a three-year-old suffering from persistent rashes, and 900 ppb of dichlorobenzyne at the home of Harold Harrington (whose wife was plagued by rashes, hair loss, and respiratory problems, and whose dog had mysteriously died)—more "irrefutable" scientific data to add to his earlier findings. Smith said he was seeing levels of contaminants, particularly chloroform, that were the worst he had ever encountered across sixty-two disasters—contaminants other samplers were missing entirely because they were fixated on lead and copper and weren't testing hot water. He also gave residents reason to believe that efforts to "heal" the water system would not be effective, due to the difficulty of coating damaged galvanized pipes with orthophosphates.[77]

Over the next two months, as Water Defense further solidified its relationship with the activists,[78] the stream of bad news coming from Smith continued. I was present for his talk at a Flint Rising community meeting in early April, at which he summarized findings from WaterBug and grab sampling at twenty houses. He continued to find high levels of DBPs, he told us (a full eighteen samples taken with the WaterBug had come back over the federal limit), but there was even more to worry about. At a time when officials, guided by Edwards, were desperately trying to increase water usage to distribute orthophosphates and chlorine more efficiently throughout the water system, he warned that flushing the pipes would aerosolize chemicals (including lead) and put residents at risk of inhaling them. (As support for this claim, he cited the work of "expert" toxicologists and "experts in plumbing systems" and distributed an arcane scientific paper from 1993 on the volatilization of lead.) Smith also cautioned that the extra orthophosphates being dumped in the system could have the "unintended consequence" of causing low blood pressure, saying he had heard from a "multitude" of people suffering from the problem.[79]

With all the many red flags Smith threw up between February and May—not to mention his assertion that the contamination in Flint was the worst he'd ever seen—it came as a surprise to me when he later claimed that he had never said the water was unsafe. It sent me back to the video of his presentation at the church, and to the media coverage of his earlier statements (which invariably implied or stated outright that Smith was calling the water unsafe for bathing and showering).[80] When I pored over Smith's actual words, I realized there had been a streak of agnosticism running through them all along. At the church he had said (and there were other, similar, instances) that "Water Defense would never say that Flint water is unsafe for bathing or showering; we are just saying we do not know." Perhaps my powers of observation simply failed me, but I found it telling that this statement had escaped me the first time. After all, the activists were seizing upon Smith's findings as proof of the water's dangers and of officials' continuing dishonesty—this was their version of Smith's "breaking news" and it was broadcast far and wide throughout the activist community, over social media, and beyond. Smith's position on the water was treated as one of a piece with the position taken by Bob Bowcock, who said unequivocally on a Flint-themed episode of the *Steve Harvey Show* around this time that the water in Flint was *not* safe for bathing and showering. Melissa Mays would repeatedly contrast Edwards's alleged treachery with Bowcock's and Smith's loyalty to residents and willingness to give them the straight story. As far as I could tell, Smith did little to discourage these kinds of interpretations. Consequently, his statements about "not knowing" seemed like technicalities—it was plain to see that, in practice, they were not nearly enough to prevent the activists from arriving at dire conclusions about the meaning of his findings.

For all his criticisms of official pronouncements about the water's safety, however, Smith did not come to town looking to pick a fight. On the contrary, he hoped his sampling would command the respect of the scientists already at work in Flint and earn himself a voice in the conversation about the city's water quality. He was particularly hopeful for the approval of the EPA, which had previously recognized his foam as being of some use in water cleanup. As the issues raised by Smith began to make headlines, the agency promised to look into them, even as it continued to tell residents it was safe to bathe and shower. But if Smith had reason to feel encouraged by this nibble of official interest in (or at least acknowledgement of) his findings, he soon encountered a formidable foe among the scientific authorities on Flint's water in the person of Marc Edwards.

By March, Edwards had learned enough about Smith to have formed an exceedingly low opinion of him. Smith's "ludicrous claims," he told me, could not have come at a worse time. As officials at the EPA and other agencies puzzled over how to respond to Smith, he said, energy was being siphoned off from the core recovery effort (i.e., lead remediation), and the temporary goodwill of state and federal agencies was being squandered.[81] Edwards did not immediately call Smith out, however. Initially, there was talk of some sort of conference call between the two of them and the activists. Despite efforts at mediation by Bob Bowcock and Erin Brockovich, however, the various parties could not agree on terms, Smith backed out, and the idea fell through. In the meantime, activists began to invoke Smith's results as evidence that Edwards was not telling the whole truth about the water. LeeAnne Walters pleaded with Edwards to make some sort of public statement about Smith and Water Defense.[82]

What Edwards responded with was more than just a statement—it was a scornful and unsparing takedown that impugned Smith's message, motivations, and scientific pretensions. In scathing, satirical posts to Flintwaterstudy. org, Edwards wrote that Smith (whom he called "SpongeBob Scarepants") had "exploited the fears of traumatized Flint residents, whose unfortunate prior experience taught them to carefully listen to views of outsiders who question authority." He compared Smith's tendency to set off alarm bells before paradoxically professing neutrality on the question of the water's safety to yelling "FIRE!" in a crowded theater and then, during the ensuing stampede, "I DO NOT KNOW IF THERE IS A FIRE!"[83] Aside from unnecessarily complicating the recovery effort, Edwards said, Smith's alarmism was frightening residents away from proper hygiene, contributing to a surge in gastrointestinal illness that reached epidemic levels over the summer. The claim (later contradicted by the CDC's conclusions about the outbreak[84]) was angrily denounced by activists as victim blaming for its implication that residents' own washing habits were making them sick.

Edwards was similarly uncharitable in his assessment of Smith's motives: Smith was an ambulance-chasing huckster who was using the water crisis as a platform for a "product launch."[85] More than one product was, apparently, on offer, actually: in addition to the WaterBug, in May, Smith began marketing his open-cell sponge technology as a filtration device under the name AquaFlex™, having earlier hinted to the activists of the possibility of bringing "green jobs" to the area by "working with the plumbers' union and the residents" to create "solar-powered filtration" systems.[86] The two technologies would, presumably, complement each other: after one revealed contamination missed by other sampling methods, the other could be used to remove it. Over Smith's protestations that he had never had any intention of trying to sell Flint residents anything, Edwards's contact at the *Huffington Post* described him as an "opportunistic sponge salesman."[87]

As for the scientific merits of Smith's sampling, these Edwards savaged mercilessly. Given that Smith's WaterBug had not been properly vetted by the scientific community, he said, it was impossible to compare it against standard methods of sampling: it "could give results two, five, ten, or even one hundred times higher than the EPA standard, and it would say nothing at all about the regulated safety of Flint water."[88] Edwards also pointed to evidence that Smith did not understand the importance of controls to the scientific method—he had sampled airborne water particles in residents' showers, for example, but hadn't thought to sample the air before turning on the water. More broadly, Smith lacked control *cities*: despite his insinuations that Flint was particularly bad off relative to other disaster-stricken parts of the country, he didn't have the hard data to show it was true. And the data being collected by others, using tried and tested methods, directly contradicted the notion that there was anything unusual going on with DBPs in Flint. To make the point, Edwards arranged a press conference with Shawn McElmurry of Wayne State University—an environmental engineer doing his own sampling in Flint—and David Reckhow of the University of Massachusetts—a leading expert on DBPs—to explain that there was nothing strange about either the type or quantity of DBPs being found in Flint's water.[89] In fact, as Edwards put it, the levels were "typical of a very good tap water."[90]

Edwards did not stop at panning the WaterBug and scoffing at the rough edges around Smith's sampling endeavors. He went after Smith's credentials, too. Again and again, Edwards came back to the fact that Smith did "not appear to have any scientific degree,"[91] suggesting that this disqualified him from speaking with any kind of authority about the science of the water. He had enlisted McElmurry and Reckhow to help him smother Smith's claims under a blanket of academic science and slam the door shut on his attempt to insert himself into official conversations about the water.[92] Smith, by Edwards's reckoning, was no "citizen scientist" (a term Smith began to apply to himself), much less a worthy mentor to budding citizen scientists in Flint, but a "pseudoscientist," a *poseur* who had come to town masquerading as an expert and profaning the good name of science in the process.[93]

Of all Edwards's criticisms of Smith, this one provoked the most indignation from the activists: hadn't they, despite their lack of scientific training, just been praised to the skies for doing science "better" than the professionals? How could Smith's lack of credentials be a deal-breaker? LeeAnne Walters insisted to me that the activists' sampling had been qualitatively different because it was carried out under the guidance of a leading scientific expert. But Smith, as he never tired of pointing out, had his expert support too (notably, Judith Zelikoff of the New York University School of Medicine), and his samples—which included traditional grab samples in addition to WaterBug data—were analyzed at a legitimate lab. One could question his way of communicating about the safety of the water, or the merits of the WaterBug, or point out mistakes he had made, but to dismiss everything he did and said as bunk because he didn't have a degree? It seemed like pure elitism, an attack on citizen science itself, with every jab at Smith glancing off the activists, too.[94] In the midst of a heated exchange with members of the Edwards camp on Facebook, Melissa Mays wrote sarcastically: "Since the citizens did the first three hundred Virginia Tech tests, not Marc himself, that first round of testing must be completely invalid because none of us had PhDs. Makes sense." She went on to quote the Wikipedia definition of "scientist," which implies that any "individual who uses the scientific method" may qualify.[95] (Smith himself greatly played up the apparent snobbishness of Edwards's appeal to authority, depicting him, in a series of photographs posted to social media, as a plush, star-bellied Sneetch.)

When Mays and other activists rallied around Smith, then, they were not only defending him, but defending themselves—defending their own competence, defending their ability to judge who was trustworthy and who wasn't, and defending (once again) their view of reality, their staunch belief that there *was* something abnormal about the effects of bathing and showering in Flint water, and that there *were* contaminants being missed by other sampling methods. They were also defending their right to know as much as possible about their water, and condemning any paternalistic insinuation that they could not handle the truth—that they would inevitably overreact to negligible threats or misuse data they thought confirmed their fears or served their political objectives. In this connection, another means Smith used to differentiate himself—the fact that he made detailed lab reports for the homes he tested publically available, each consisting of around fifty pages of raw data—became an ever more important mark of distinction. Smith and his allies argued that this gesture of transparency was an indication of his respect for residents' intelligence and judgment, in contrast to Edwards's apparent belief that residents were easily bewildered and spooked.

In October, I personally tried to convince Edwards that the approach he was taking with Smith was counterproductive. Yes, he had landed some blows: Smith had pushed his WaterBug into the background (saying it was "under on-going review"[96]), moderated some of his claims, and changed the way he tended to identify himself (preferring "Chief Technology Officer and Investigator" to "Chief Scientist"), and he no longer got the kind of media attention he did when he first came to town. Edwards, however, was clearly overestimating the extent to which he had discredited Smith. He was under the impression, for example, that Bob Bowcock thought Smith was "insane" (unaware, until I told him, of Bowcock's even more extreme statements about bathing and showering[97]), but Bowcock ultimately came down on Smith's side, appearing in a video in which he and Brockovich extolled Smith's efforts in Flint to put science into the hands of everyday people. And Smith continued to make inroads in his quest for respectability: Mark Durno, the head of the EPA's response in Flint, agreed to sample with him side by side and presented with him at an EPA roundtable, and a member of Snyder's Cabinet Office invited him to visit MDEQ's lab. By this time, Smith was not only full of praise for the EPA, but had concluded that even the state was starting to come around.

The irony in Edwards's attack on Smith was that it had the unintended consequence of greatly prolonging the latter's involvement in Flint. It turned out (I had not realized it at first, for he had not broadcast the fact) that Smith had come to Flint in the middle of shooting a documentary centered on his disaster-hopping travels throughout the United States and the world. He did not anticipate his stop in Flint lasting for more than a couple of weeks, but when Edwards attacked him, Flint became the place where he had to make a stand and defend his reputation. I got the impression in my own conversations with Smith that he was irked at having gotten bogged down in Flint, and was looking for some way to exit the situation gracefully. This turned out to be an important factor during the next chapter of the science wars.

The Battle over Bacteria

The conflict between Edwards and Smith revolved mainly around DBPs, but there was another type of contaminant lurking in the background, one that also offered some hope of explaining unexplained illnesses and impeding the rush to declare the crisis over: bacteria. Residents had been wary of bacteria ever since the boil water advisories of 2014, but the state's admission in January 2016 that cases of Legionnaires' disease had boomed during the two summers prior took these concerns to a new level. It was the strongest evidence yet that the water could actually *kill* people, and residents looked ahead to the summer months with trepidation. So did the state. The revelations about Legionnaires' had gotten the attorney general talking about possible manslaughter charges for some state employees, and officials in Lansing were terrified that they would have to deal with another slew of cases as the weather warmed.

To get out ahead of any potential problem, the state recruited Shawn McElmurry from Wayne State University to carry out a study of legionella contamination, awarding him a $4.1 million grant to be overseen by the Michigan Department of Health and Human Services (MDHHS). McElmurry was already in the process of forming the Flint Area Community Health and Environment Partnership (FACHEP), a multiuniversity team of researchers working with grants from the National Institutes of Health and the National Science Foundation to study the water system's recovery and the point-of-use filters being distributed to residents. For help with community engagement around these various studies, McElmurry enlisted Laura Sullivan and, in April, me, writing us both into the legionella grant.

I accepted the assignment with some hesitation. I was hard at work at the time trying to integrate myself into the activist scene, and signing on to a state-funded study was hardly going to boost my credibility with people who saw the state as their number-one enemy. It would not be easy for Sullivan and I to convince the activists that the study was shaping up to be serious and important work worth paying attention to or even getting involved in (for it, too, had a large "citizen science" component).[98] Our initial idea, to arrange small-group conversations between the activists and core members of the team, went nowhere: the activists wouldn't even respond to messages about it, and acted annoyed when Sullivan unexpectedly invited some members of the team to a Flint Rising community meeting. Activists already had their expert (or at least counterexpert) of choice in Scott Smith, and were extremely skeptical, understandably, that state-sponsored research would result in anything but whitewashing.

Still, FACHEP was doing work that piqued at least some interest, even early on: like Smith, it was looking for contaminants other than lead and sampling hot water heaters as well as hot water in showers. Pointing out that Edwards also made a point of sampling hot water heaters around the same time, Harold Harrington told me that it seemed like Smith's methods were catching on, with the scientists following the lead of the so-called "pseudo-scientist."[99] This perceived overlap of FACHEP's work with Smith's created at least some possibility of winning over the activists allied with him.

I did not see much hope of this happening, however, without directly, and respectfully, engaging Smith. My preference was to have members of FACHEP, the Virginia Tech team, and the EPA sit down with Smith in some sort of a public setting and have a civil conversation about his data. I figured that under these conditions Smith would self-moderate his claims and we could move on from Edwards's unhelpful barrage of *ad hominem* insults to a more substantive discussion of residents' concerns. Sullivan and I spent two months trying, behind the scenes, to arrange a panel of this nature, without success: there was little appetite for wading into the waters that Edwards and Smith had bloodied with their mutual animosity. Ironically, as Sullivan and I worked diligently to give Smith what he wanted—a seat at the table—he and Melissa Mays came to the conclusion that we were aligned with Edwards, or at least hostile to Water Defense, and kept their distance from us for the next several months.[100]

In the meantime, we were still faced with the conundrum of how to convince the activists (and, more broadly, residents) of the credibility of FACHEP's work, particularly the legionella study. After the failure of our initial overtures, there were two things the team needed to prove, as I saw it: first, that it could accept money from the state while retaining its independence, and second, that it had something to say about the water that was worth hearing. On the first front, it helped that McElmurry had negotiated strict conditions to ensure the study's integrity, but it didn't stop the state from attempting to corral the study in a politically acceptable direction. Tortuous contract negotiations delayed the start of sampling until the warmest summer months had passed (and with them, the most suitable conditions for studying bacterial growth). It appeared to the core members of the team that the state was fearful their work would show cases of Legionnaires' disease were being underreported, or that the outbreaks of 2014 to 2015 were caused by the switch to the river. Carrying out even the work we had contracted for proved to be a continual battle, leading to combative exchanges with the MDHHS[101] and repeatedly putting the future of the project in jeopardy. When the team refused to compromise some key parts of the study, Rich Baird, Governor Snyder's close advisor and his man on the ground in Flint, told us that we were not giving our "customer" (i.e., the state) what it wanted, and that there were "other" teams waiting in the wings (i.e., Virginia Tech) that would. At one point, it looked virtually certain that the state would pull the project's funding and we would all end up in court.

As frustrating and time consuming as all the drama was, it did bolster the team's credibility with residents and activists by suggesting that FACHEP was not simply taking orders from the state. I took it as a good sign when, at a Flint Democracy Defense League meeting, Claire McClinton and Nayyirah Shariff expressed their willingness to help generate some popular pressure to move the study forward. What really began to arouse activists' sympathies, however, was their burgeoning realization that FACHEP's message about the safety of the water was going to be different from that of Edwards.

Several of FACHEP's early findings suggested that bacterial contamination was still a potential concern in Flint. Legionella was not present in the water system in large quantities, but the type of legionella (serogroup 6) showing up in samples was virtually invisible to urine antigen tests, raising the possibility (just as the state feared) that cases of Legionnaires' disease were being missed in clinical settings. Furthermore, chlorine residuals at the tap were minimal to nonexistent in some homes (between 10 and 20 percent of them), creating a favorable environment for bacterial growth. And early results from the point-of-use filter study suggested that the filters could pose a threat to Flint's most at-risk residents. Scientists had long known that bacteria proliferated in such filters, but McElmurry and Nancy Love of the University of Michigan, the leaders of the filter study, were finding significant amplifications of opportunistic bacterial pathogens linked with upper respiratory infections, as well as bacteria typically associated with the mammalian gut (suggestive of some sort of fecal contamination). Among the bacteria found were species listed by the World Health Organization as being especially dangerous because of their resistance to antibiotics.[102]

The filter issue was full of political significance. The state was determined to get out of the business of providing free bottled water, and the most obvious means to this end was to make filters available to all residents and argue that the water could be safely consumed through them. To raise the issue of bacteria in the filters at all, given popular fears about bacteria in general, was an obstacle to that agenda. Residents could see right on the boxes the filters came in that they did not filter out bacteria, but no official attempt was made (to my knowledge) to inform the community about the implications of filter use for bacterial exposure. In fact, the state seemed determined for the filters to remain "black boxes," actively seeking to prevent FACHEP from sampling filter cartridges for legionella.[103] Consequently, when the team informed residents that the filters actually exacerbated bacterial contamination, it came as a surprise—yet another piece of information they would like to have known but no one saw fit to tell them.[104] FACHEP even quantified the growth by providing participants in its filter study with heterotrophic plate count data showing the extent to which bacteria had proliferated from the influent to the effluent side of the filters.

In the results letter it sent to participants, FACHEP stressed that even high quantities of bacteria are not necessarily harmful, using the example of yogurt as a reference point. The unforeseen discovery of potentially pathogenic bacteria, however, threw a wrinkle into this message. Given everything residents had experienced, it seemed like they were entitled to know about the findings while there was still time to take extra precautions, even though the results were preliminary and analysis ongoing. At the same time, the team certainly did not want to oversell the risks and cause unnecessary anxiety in people who had plenty of it to deal with already.

As we debated the finer nuances of risk communication internally, Marc Edwards contacted McElmurry in early December with a request. Based on Virginia Tech's latest findings, he was prepared to declare Flint water as safe as municipal water in other cities and wanted the FACHEP team to sign off on a statement acknowledging that water quality had improved substantially. The request was hardly a surprise by that point. Edwards had already given indications that he was determined to treat as nonissues the very subjects of FACHEP's ongoing research. In August 2016, he made his claim about filtered water being as good as, if not better than, bottled water. In October, he claimed to me that Flint and Genesee Counties had seen the lowest numbers of Legionnaires' cases that year in their history, looked surprised when I told him how many cases there had actually been, and then explained the numbers away as a product of more vigilant monitoring.[105] In November, he made his claim about filtered water being as good as, if not better than, bottled water.[106] The thrust of these remarks seemed to be that the science of the water was settled (for Edwards and his team had settled it), implying that any further research was superfluous and any suggestion of lingering risks irresponsible.

McElmurry told Edwards that a sweeping statement about Flint's water quality would be premature and declined to endorse the proposed statement. Although it seems Edwards was already positioning his narrative about the water to undercut FACHEP's work, from that point on my impression was that he was watching us like a hawk. It was plain that all the business about bacteria, just like Smith's warnings about DBPs, was interfering with his attempts to bring the story of his intervention in Flint to a triumphant conclusion.[107]

Edwards was not the only one watching FACHEP's next moves. Scott Smith, too, had begun to take a keen interest in the team's work. Although he had not given up on proving his earlier claims about DBPs (he was now doing control sampling in other cities and posting to social media about the "non-detects" he was getting outside of Flint), his emphasis began to shift to bacteria after two pathogenic species turned up in his samples. He was hopeful that FACHEP's far more extensive research would corroborate this finding and thereby bring it more scientific legitimacy. He also seemed to sense that FACHEP's work was opening up an escape hatch for him, presenting an opportunity to pass the torch of "more-than-lead" credibility to us and thereby moderate expectations that he would continue to conduct regular sampling in Flint (he told me that his work in Flint was "done" and that he saw our team as picking up where he was leaving off). Scarred by his experience with Edwards, however, and still unconvinced of our sympathies, he first had to make sure he was not going to get burned. In the lead up to our first community meeting in mid-December 2016, at which we planned to roll out our preliminary findings directly to residents, Smith called me almost daily as he tried to feel out whether he could safely get behind FACHEP. Because the team would not (indeed could not, by the terms of our contract) share nonpublic data with him, declaring his support for FACHEP was a bit of a gamble, premised largely on his perception of my trustworthiness. Nevertheless, it was a gamble he decided to take, and he began the delicate process of convincing his allies, particularly Melissa Mays and the plumbers, to attend our meeting with open minds.

They did indeed attend, but when they arrived skepticism was etched so deeply into their faces that I could tell we would have our work cut out for us winning them over. As soon as the scientists on the team began to speak, Mays began furiously scribbling away (I figured she was planning some sort of retort). But gradually, as I darted around the room from her to the plumbers to the tables full of other activists (for a good number of them had turned out), emphasizing the takeaway points, her demeanor softened. Our message was moderate and full of caveats, but at least we were not proclaiming the water "safe" and were expressing an ongoing commitment to look further into the concerns we (and residents) had identified.

"It was nice to hear that things aren't all better," Mays told the press afterwards, "because that's what we're used to hearing—that things are better, that things are all fine."[108] From that point on, she and many of the other activists began to cite the work of "Wayne State" (for this was the name by which the team was popularly known) alongside the work of Smith as having revealed inconvenient truths about the water. Smith, for his part, decided that FACHEP's findings resoundingly confirmed his own. He threw his symbolic support behind the team and praised our work effusively on social media.

The changing landscape of scientific credibility in Flint was illustrated vividly the next month during a key town hall about water. The timing of the town hall—a day after officials and scientists met for a closed-door summit in Chicago to hash out a "consensus" about the state of the water—reflected an all-too-familiar pattern: the "experts" settle the technical side of the water question without public input or oversight before imparting the end product, scrubbed of all residue of debate and disagreement, to an essentially passive audience. The activists, however, were determined not to be passive. Some of them had traveled to Chicago to protest the closed-door summit outside of EPA Region 5 headquarters. Now, for the town hall, which was to feature the experts from the summit, they had devised a craftier means of expressing their discontent, distributing empty water bottles that members of the audience were to crinkle whenever they disagreed with something being said. Edwards, appearing via webcam, touted the water system's recovery over some of the most emphatic crinkles of the night. Even Miguel del Toral received his fair share for making similar comments (not coincidentally, it was the last public appearance I saw him make in Flint). When McElmurry and Love presented about FACHEP's work, however, the activists sat in respectful silence.

By that time, it appeared Edwards's next campaign would be against FACHEP, beginning with a critique of the team's messaging about the filters. The essence of his critique was that it was irresponsible to provide residents with heterotrophic plate count data—it only frightened them needlessly—and even more irresponsible to suggest that the filters might be creating new health risks.[109] The kinds of bacteria raising eyebrows, he insisted, were commonly found in water. Worried that Edwards was "backing himself into a corner" by rushing to judgment before all the data were in, McElmurry and Love tried to get him to reconsider his position on a conference call in the lead up to the Chicago summit. "That just failed," Love recalls. "He just didn't wanna hear it."[110] Instead, at the summit, Edwards accused FACHEP of causing "much of Flint" to lose faith in the filters, offering only anecdotal evidence. In fact, it was well known that large numbers of residents had always mistrusted the filters.[111] Not even Edwards's couple of diehard defenders in Flint used them, and ironically, it was one of them who first sounded the alarm over social media about the issue of bacterial proliferation after getting a results letter from FACHEP, explaining to a member of the Virginia Tech team who tried to talk her down that her preference was to be extra careful about bacterial exposure.

In public presentations, Edwards began to cite a World Health Organization statement to the effect that an increase of bacteria in filters does "not indicate the existence of a health risk," while leaving out the statement's critical caveat: "*so long as the entry water meets acceptable water microbial quality norms*" (emphasis added).[112] The idea that Flint water might still be microbiologically compromised, a possibility FACHEP continued to take seriously, entailed the no-longer-allowable assumption that there was still something *ab*normal about the water situation in Flint. Edwards also began to stress that filter use was common around the country, as if the elective use of filter technology by a typical filter-using household raised the same considerations as the citywide, emergency deployment of a device largely unfamiliar to, and unwanted by, residents—for political as well as public health reasons.[113] Filter use in Flint was not, in other words, obviously comparable to filter use elsewhere, nor could it be reduced to a merely technical issue of the proper functioning of the filters.[114] Finally, Edwards teamed up with the National Sanitation Foundation to launch a separate, state-funded filter study in Flint and control cities, in an apparent effort to lay a firmer foundation for his criticisms. The collaboration failed totally, and all the samples taken were destroyed due to problems with the sampling methodology—a fact not communicated to the residents who opened their homes for the study (I was one of them), who waited and waited in vain for an update. Meanwhile, the Genesee County Medical Society and Genesee County Health Department recommended that "children less than 6 years old, pregnant women, and individuals with weakened immune systems should continue using only bottled water"—or boil filtered water before drinking it.[115]

As FACHEP began to prepare for its second round of legionella sampling in the spring of 2017, Edwards grew increasingly hostile. After being confronted in person by angry activists (including Quincy Murphy, a member of FACHEP) accusing him of downplaying concerns about bacteria, and criticized on Facebook by Laura Sullivan, Edwards gave McElmurry an ultimatum. FACHEP, he said, had "repeatedly made false statements and spread rumors, that promote FACHEP at the expense of the State and VT." He ordered McElmurry to put out an "unambiguous" statement disavowing Murphy's and Sullivan's supposed falsehoods or he would "correct the record publicly" to "the utmost of [his] abilities."[116] When McElmurry took the position that Flint residents, speaking as residents (as both Murphy and Sullivan were), had a right to express themselves, Edwards launched what would become a two-year-plus-long campaign to delegitimize FACHEP and its members.

He began by co-filing, with LeeAnne Walters, a Freedom of Information Act (FOIA) request for a wide range of internal FACHEP emails, in an apparent fishing expedition. Edwards and Walters portrayed the FOIA as part of an attempt to help a resident obtain sampling data on her house.[117] To try to massage tensions and address the resident's concerns, I initiated two days' worth of diplomacy with Walters, with whom I had up to that point been on friendly terms. Soon thereafter, however, Edwards and Walters decided, for the first time, to call out the team by name.[118] This they did in a clumsy, lo-fi video streamed over Facebook in collaboration—in yet another irony—with an out-of-town activist with a reputation for purveying conspiracy theories about the water. From that point on, Edwards became much bolder in his public criticisms of the team, referring to its members as "unscrupulous" and depicting us in keynote addresses as fledgling birds incompetently bumbling our way through research that was out of our league.[119]

The baby-bird metaphor became more difficult to sustain after the team published results from its legionella work in top journals in early 2018, including a paper in *Proceedings of the National Academy of Sciences* (*PNAS*) that linked the Legionnaires' disease outbreaks of 2014 to 2015 to low chlorine residuals within households after the switch to the Flint River.[120] Arguing that FACHEP had failed to give proper credit to the Virginia Tech team's work on legionella, Edwards and colleagues immediately, and unsuccessfully, challenged the paper. It was *his* team's work, Edwards claimed, that had first demonstrated the connection between the outbreaks and the source change and hypothesized the chlorine connection, and FACHEP was trying to rewrite history by giving itself credit for the discovery.

If Edwards had difficulty perceiving the difference between FACHEP's research (which included rigorous statistical analysis of the legionella/chlorine correlation) and his own (which lacked such analysis), the state did not. The MDHHS was already prepared to attack the papers upon publication[121] after FACHEP refused to submit to the state's insistence that the team continue its work under the supervision of an "independent" water research institute with prior ties to the Snyder administration.[122] The reason for the state's power play soon became apparent, as the *PNAS* article (unlike Virginia Tech's work on legionella) made a major political splash in the preliminary hearings of MDHHS Director Nick Lyon and Chief Medical Executive Eden Wells, who faced involuntary manslaughter charges for failing to alert the public about the Legionnaires' threat.

If activists had any lingering doubt that Edwards's interests and the state's were now aligned, it was dispelled when he was called to testify in defense of Lyon and Wells in March 2018.[123] Whereas FACHEP members had testified to Lyon saying things in meetings like "everyone has to die of something," and to his and Wells's efforts to prevent certain kinds of research, Edwards spoke glowingly about his own interactions with them and their commitment to public health in Flint.[124] He also took the opportunity to criticize FACHEP's work.[125]

Almost as soon as Edwards left the stand, a post in the form of an exposé, targeted at Shawn McElmurry, appeared on Flintwaterstudy.org under the title "FACHEP vs. The People of the State of Michigan." It accused McElmurry of misleading the state about his past work in Flint and stealing a former graduate student's model of the city's water system in a plot to procure grant money made available by the water crisis, concluding that McElmurry was potentially "guilty of perpetrating, one of the most insidious cases of scientific misconduct ever, in relation to procurement of disaster relief research funding."[126] In conjunction with the blog post, Edwards filed a complaint against McElmurry's professional engineer's license (later dismissed for lack of evidence) and promised that similar exposés were to come on Nancy Love and Laura Sullivan. When I declared on Facebook that we would not be bullied by him, he called me out by name, too, and accused us all of "gorg[ing]" ourselves "at the FACHEP funding trough."[127]

Edwards also said on the website that FACHEP's legitimacy was now "completely tied" to McElmurry's proving his claims about his earlier work in Flint.[128] It was another sign of how thoroughly divorced Edwards's understanding of credibility was from that of the Flint activists and residents I knew. Whereas there was plenty of community interest now in FACHEP's findings, there was almost none whatsoever that I could detect—certainly among activists—in what McElmurry did or did not do in Flint prior to the water crisis. In fact, Edwards's attack, in conjunction with his earlier testimony for Lyon and Wells, provoked the fiercest backlash against him yet. One prominent activist who had never spoken out against Edwards before excoriated him up and down social media for doing the work of the state by trying to destroy McElmurry's reputation, posting a headshot of Edwards struck through with a red "no symbol" and bracketed by the words "Your 'Welcome to Flint' Card has been REVOKED!! GET OUT AND DON'T COME BACK!!"

Accountability in a "Post-truth World"

As late as the summer of 2018, Edwards maintained that it was only ever "a few folks" who were resistant to his message about the water and driving the criticisms of him.[129] That claim did not comport even remotely with my observations on the ground. From 2016 onward, I observed, in public and private settings, a steady stream of concerned, perplexed, and outraged reactions to his statements and behavior. Significantly, I encountered these reactions not only within Flint's activist community (where LeeAnne Walters was Edwards's "only friend,"[130] as Claire McClinton put it) but within other communities I had contact with as well, including the medical and academic communities, and even within the EPA. Beginning in 2017, I started to hear variations on the claim that Edwards was going to "crash and burn."[131]

In May 2018, in a historic development, sixty residents signed a letter in protest of Edwards's attack on FACHEP and behavior toward the community generally, sending it to a variety of professional engineering and scientific associations and calling for an independent investigation.[132] Edwards, denouncing what he called the letter's "many false claims"[133] and depicting it as a plot to smear him by Melissa Mays and two of his former activist colleagues from D.C. (who had also become vocal critics), pledged to track down each of its signatories individually and ask them whether they agreed with its every last word.[134] After multiple academics with knowledge of the situation expressed a desire to help, I worked with them to put together another letter, affirming the right of residents to be heard and condemning any attempt to intimidate and silence them.[135] Edwards's response was to accuse the twelve academic signatories of jealousy[136] and to attribute the support letter to a "cancer" infecting the social sciences that needed to be "exposed and dealt with."[137]

Edwards and Siddhartha Roy also went on the offensive against Mays. After she shared a picture through Facebook of a fire hydrant spewing brown water and mistakenly said it was current, they deputized a sympathetic resident (technically, Walters was not their *only* friend) to "investigate" and document the fact that the hydrant had not been opened in months. They then built two Flintwaterstudy.org posts around the notion that Mays and a few other individuals were stirring up fears about the water still being unsafe (a belief that was, in fact, still the conventional wisdom throughout a huge swath of the community).[138] It did not matter, apparently, that the claim about the photo did not originate with Mays, that thousands of other people had also shared it, or—most tellingly—that the very resident doing the "investigating" had also posted the picture and said it was taken a few days before, in a similar effort to show that the crisis was not yet over.

Mays was an obvious target for a head-on attack of this nature, not only because she was such a scathing critic but also because Edwards and Roy knew she was a controversial figure within the community, with detractors who would gloat over her misfortune even if they agreed with her about the water. A FOIAed email later revealed, however, that the Flint Water Study team was targeting a wider range of activists and groups behind the scenes. In November 2017, Edwards and Roy enlisted a student to compile a record of social media posts from groups and persons of "interest" that included "falsehoods" about the water, claims about health harms, and criticisms of the team (Edwards specifically requested a screenshot "anytime they call each other heroes, or complain about the money or awards [Mona, Lee-Anne, VT] we are getting"). When Roy and the student floated the idea of creating a "fake" page to collect the information surreptitiously, with a stock image instead of an authentic headshot, Edwards seems to have done nothing to dissuade them.[139] Edwards later claimed that such a page was never used, and defended the data collection as part of a paper on the dissemination of misinformation through social media. Fake page or no fake page, however, from the activists' perspective it was a shocking revelation that those who continued to speak out most forcefully about the water were being actively surveilled, not to mention discredited in academic publications. One activist felt harassed enough that she expressed her intent to file a personal protective order against Edwards.

The list of targets specified in the emails suggested that Edwards and Roy were still focused on the Scott Smith–Melissa Mays alliance as the Pandora's box that unleashed "science anarchy" on Flint, for all had been vocal about being sampled by Smith. It made the next twist in the Scott Smith subplot even more counterintuitive. In July 2018, a guest blog post appeared on Flintwaterstudy.org featuring a mea culpa purportedly written by Smith, in which he detailed the mistakes he had made in Flint and the lessons he had learned from them. Edwards and Roy held it up as a model of responsibility in a "post-truth world,"[140] calling Smith "intellectually honest,"[141] and citizen science guru Caren Cooper (who had just been written into a $1.9 million EPA grant awarded to Edwards and his team[142]) praised the two sides for reconciling and "uniting for #CitizenScience!"[143] It was a vindication for Edwards, with the added benefit of stripping Mays of one of her chief allies in the middle of a broader campaign to isolate and discredit her.

From the ground in Flint, however, the whole thing looked awfully suspicious. Shortly after the post went live, Smith began telling people that he had not wanted to write it, that he had been threatened by Edwards and Roy, and that he disliked Edwards as much as anyone else.[144] When draft versions of the post leaked, it became clear that Edwards himself had written a substantial portion of the confession. Changing Smith's "lessons learned" (the phrasing of the original draft) to "*citizen science* lessons learned," Edwards put a number of admissions into Smith's mouth, including that Smith had caused "a lot of pain and suffering for everyone involved" by avoiding dialogue in early 2016, and that it was "possible, and even likely" that his manner of presenting his data had "changed" residents' "bathing and showering habits." Edwards also seems to have come up with some of the "lessons" himself, including the lesson that "confrontations" are sometimes necessary and that scientific authority is valuable.[145] In his original draft, Smith seems to have been fishing for at least some contrition from Edwards. Writing that "launch[ing] devastating personal attacks without adequately vetted true and accurate facts can be very painful for many people and cause permanent reputational and financial damage if not corrected properly," Smith asked Edwards to consider handling such situations differently in the future.[146] The request did not make the cut, however, and Edwards continued to act as though his hands had been tied when he began publicly shaming Smith in 2016.

The situation became even more bizarre and confusing when Smith, even as he maligned Edwards in some contexts, began working as a mole for him. He contacted multiple signatories of the residents' complaint letter to ask if they knew their names were on it, sent Edwards years' worth of email exchanges he'd had with residents, and passed along an in-progress paper shared with him as a courtesy by a signatory to the academic support letter. He also exploited the trust of an activist who had participated in an FDDL meeting where the issue of Edwards had come up, milking her for information before concocting a totally fabricated account of what Laura Sullivan and I had said at the meeting and sending it to Edwards, who forwarded it to colleagues.[147] The resurrection of Scott Smith as a duplicitous double agent, then, only wreaked more havoc within the community, exacerbating activists' sense of betrayal and directly contributing to the circulation of new falsehoods.

The developments with Smith coincided with Edwards's most aggressive sally against activists yet: a $3 million defamation lawsuit against Melissa Mays and the two D.C. activists he accused of having helped to compose the residents' complaint letter. The lawsuit sent a ripple wave of shock through the community. Residents started to warn each other—tongues only half in cheek—about speaking out against Edwards, for fear that more people would be sued.

Although no one could have anticipated how bad things would get, Nayyirah Shariff lamented that activists had not placed stricter terms on their collaboration with Edwards from the start. She told me she considered it a "personal failure": more than any of the other activists who decided to partner with the Flint Water Study team, she knew how academic research was supposed to proceed in marginalized communities. She was familiar with the history of the Tuskegee Experiment, which she invoked when Edwards began to turn on members of the community. Even the original sampling effort, she said, should have included stronger protections: human subjects training, approval by Flint's community-based review board, and a consent form for sampling. More broadly, there should have been a memorandum of understanding between Edwards, his team, and their resident collaborators, with "built-in accountability measures."[148] Without such measures in place, the power Edwards exercised—whether he was making authoritative pronouncements about the water or using his sizable platform as a bully pulpit to tear others down—was as unchecked as the power of any emergency manager.

Where power is effectively unchecked, the disposition of the individual exercising it becomes the key factor in determining whether it is abused. In this connection, activists regularly remarked on what they saw as Edwards's imperiousness: his tendency to appoint himself to crusading roles, to speak with airs of authority about areas outside his expertise, and to disparage the contributions of other researchers who did not align themselves strictly with his perspective. Of Edwards's campaign against "bad actors," Shariff joked that she wanted to see the notes from the meeting at which he was delegated that role.[149] Of his attacks on other scientists with differences of opinion about the condition of Flint's water, Claire McClinton asked, rhetorically, "Who died and made him king of all scientific data?" The community, she said, did not need him to be the "arbiter of sound science."[150]

And Edwards certainly, she said, had "no business" suing residents, or otherwise attacking them—it was an attempt to "demoralize" people that fed directly into the state's efforts to minimize the crisis and shut down lingering concerns. "This is *Flint*," McClinton told me. "If you're trying to silence people's voices, it's not gonna work."[151]

The Fight Is (Not) Over

When the Virginia Tech Flint Water Study team introduced itself to the world in the summer of 2015, it said its first aim in Flint was "To support *citizen scientists* concerned about public health."[152] At that time, no one could have imagined what the consequences would be for residents and their allies who failed to live up to Marc Edwards's definition of "citizen science," or for other researchers who dissented from his views about how science was to be conducted and communicated. I found that Edwards's own explanation for the breakdown of relations—that deep-seated anti-expertise and post-truth sentiment had taken root in Flint,[153] supplemented by a catastrophic breakdown in trust and intensified by the allegedly unscrupulous behavior of activists, their allies, and other researchers—was inadequate, limited by its erasure of the power dynamics involved in his own intervention.

Certainly, challenging the "expertise" of those who said the water was safe *was* a central part of the activists' fight in Flint—as Quincy Murphy put it to me, "that's how we broke the door down."[154] And residents *had* lost a great deal of trust, even in people who were probably worthy of it. However, activists bristled at the suggestion that lingering concerns about the water were the products of an anti-expertise, antiscience, mistrustful worldview. Such concerns were not about not trusting people, Claire McClinton said—after all, there *were* people residents trusted, they just happened to be people other than Edwards—but about unanswered questions and indications of risk within the science produced about the water.

McClinton, like many of the other activists, believed the more people looking into the water, the better.[155] One tragic effect of the atmosphere of hostility and suspicion clouding the conduct of scientific research in Flint was that lines of inquiry of great significance to residents were greatly hindered or stalled out entirely. A citizen science project I spent months developing with a member of the Virginia Tech team who disagreed with Edwards about bacteria fell apart after Edwards began to attack FACHEP. Time that could have been spent on science was sucked up by credibility struggles, and much to my frustration the core members of FACHEP—battered alternately by the state and by Edwards—became reticent about making any public statements at all about the team's work.[156] While the team developed close relationships with the city's chief public health advisor and the Genesee County Medical Society—critical voices in the conversation about public health in Flint—it was too focused on watching its step and triple checking its results (knowing they were likely to be attacked) to develop a full-bodied presence in the community. Most tragic was that the worthy project of building close, collaborative relationships between community members and scientific experts had to take a backseat, at least in the short term, to confronting, in the behavior of Edwards, another crisis of unaccountable power. It was one among other reasons why the activists felt their fight had to continue.

The idea that there might still be reason to keep fighting was, ultimately, the source of the starkest contrast between Edwards and the activists. Edwards told me in the fall of 2016 that the fight for Flint was "pretty much over"—there were no more "doors" to break down (to adopt Quincy Murphy's metaphor), for officials were now embracing "good" science and trying to do the right thing. In fact, the response to the crisis as a whole was as close to a model as one could imagine, he said, with the state going above and beyond the call of duty.[157] The problem was that the city's "warriors," who had earlier played a constructive role, were finding it difficult to transition into "peacetime." They were not only on the wrong side of the science of the water, in other words, but they were at this point fighting for nothing—not least of all when they fought against him.[158]

It was news to the activists, however, that "peace" in their city had been realized and that there was nothing left to fight for in Flint. Whatever Edwards believed, it was their deep conviction that Flint had not yet been made "whole," not even close. The next chapter in the struggle for justice, they insisted, had yet to be written, and this time they were more determined than ever to write it themselves.

8   From Poisoned People to People Power: Fighting for Justice, Expanding Democracy

We're protagonists in our own liberation struggle.
—Nayyirah Shariff, Flint Rising meeting, Flint, MI, May 18, 2017

When Flint's pro-democracy activists and budding water warriors joined forces, it was to expose the injustice of their poisoned water and force officials to take action. When they launched the second phase of their fight, after Detroit water had begun to flow through Flint's pipes again and talk turned from "reconnection" to "recovery," it was to ensure that residents got the justice they deserved moving forward. Justice meant, firstly, *accountability*: punishment of those responsible for the crisis and reform of the government agencies that failed to protect public health. Justice meant, secondly, *reparations*: the replacement of damaged infrastructure and full funding of the health care, nutrition, and education necessary to repair the harm done to bodies and minds.

Justice also had a lot to do with *how* the recovery effort happened, with who was in charge of setting priorities, making decisions, and determining when the overall mission had been accomplished. The important questions from this perspective were: To what extent would the response to the crisis be shaped by the very people and agencies that had caused it in the first place? What kind of say would residents have over how resources coming into the city were managed? Who would get to decide when Flint had been made "whole"?

The water activism of the next two-and-a-half years was informed by the strong belief that justice was not being done in Flint. Officials had yet to pay any legal price for their actions, the money coming in was inadequate to address the full scope of the need (as defined by residents), and the state continued to demonstrate—at least in the activists' view—contempt for the people it had poisoned and a determination to shirk responsibility. It was, activists argued, replacing the pipes at far too slow a rate, wasting money (along with its nonprofit allies) on initiatives of little benefit to residents, and looking for every opportunity (usually the latest favorable lead result from the Michigan Department of Environmental Quality [MDEQ] or Virginia Tech) to draw down its presence in Flint, all while operating behind a façade of community "partnership." Even with all the national attention the crisis was getting, and all the pressure being put on officials to do right by Flint, the general feeling within the grassroots community was that the city would have to fight for everything it got. Although many of the activists had already been immersed in water activism for over a year when I first joined up with them in January 2016, I felt like they were just getting started, gearing up for an even bigger fight than that which they had just won.

Just as the struggle for democracy that began in 2011 fed into the struggle for clean, affordable water, the struggle for "water justice" (a term activists sometimes used to tie together their various demands) fed back into the broader struggle for democracy. In linking the crisis to emergency management, the activists landed their heaviest blow against the emergency manager (EM) system since the overturning of Public Act 4 in 2012. As their political narrative of the crisis went mainstream, Flint's EMs, as well as the architects of the EM law, had to answer for themselves. Asked during his Congressional testimony whether the law had "failed"—at least in this instance—Governor Snyder was surprisingly candid: it was, he said, "a fair conclusion."[1] All three state bodies that subsequently investigated the crisis determined that the law needed to be fundamentally reformed.[2]

The crisis also stimulated the state to start devolving back to the city the powers it had retained after the last of Flint's EMs stepped down in April 2015. Mayor Weaver, who had sided with the activists in calling for the full restoration of local control,[3] got the rest of her powers back in January 2016, after Snyder stressed that building a "strong relationship" with her was critical to the recovery effort.[4] Three weeks later, she used those powers to fire Natasha Henderson, the city administrator given enhanced say over decision making by EM Ambrose upon his resignation. The City Council had a harder time convincing the state that it ought to have *its* powers restored, too, but finally, in May, they were reinstated on a provisional basis.[5]

To be sure, home rule was *not* yet back in effect in Flint. The veto power of the Receivership Transition Advisory Board (RTAB) still hung over all business conducted by city officials. When RTAB used its power to bar the city from suing the state for the latter's role in the crisis, or overturned a council resolution to suspend the placement of liens on homes for nonpayment of water bills, it was a slap in the face to residents' self-determination and a reminder of who really exercised sovereignty in Flint.[6] If the activists' fight for representative democracy was not yet over, however, there was no doubt that the political fallout from the crisis helped to advance it considerably.

The recalibration of state and local power prompted by the crisis, as well as the substantial federal involvement in Flint from January 2016 onward, dramatically shifted the political opportunity structure in which the activists were operating.[7] Traditional channels of political influence were now far more open than before, and there was actual money on the table at the state and federal levels. Activists began to spend a considerable amount of time in Lansing and Washington, D.C., speaking directly with representatives and pushing for more aid. They also lobbied for longer-term, structural changes, including stricter regulations on water quality and water monitoring, protections around water affordability and accessibility,[8] and more federal funding for public water systems.[9] With local officials now able to exert more influence over city affairs, activists also began to place more emphasis on holding them accountable, turning some of their energies toward pressure, and at times protest, of both Mayor Weaver and the City Council.

All things considered, the situation activists faced in early 2016 was pregnant with an unusual degree of political possibility—far more than existed in 2015, when all they had to organize around was the "impossible" demand to abandon the river. The prospect of realizing other, more winnable, victories became a key basis for further organizing, with activists striving to mobilize residents and sympathetic outsiders around a series of targeted battles. The demands activists made, however, continued to overflow the opportunity structure that presented itself (at least as a "reasonable" person might have outlined it). The lesson learned from the battle over the river was that the hardheaded resolve of even a small group of people could move mountains, and having the wind at their backs only made the activists more ambitious. But while the new "impossible" demands they introduced helped to keep the spirit of activism alive within the movement, at times they also complicated efforts to organize residents in sustainable and effective ways.

In addition to opening up new political opportunities, the national attention the water crisis attracted made new resources available to Flint activists, as the broader activist community in Michigan and beyond turned Flint into one of its top priorities and expressions of solidarity and support began to flow into the city. Relationships with outside activist and advocacy groups greatly enhanced the capacity of local activists and enabled a variety of initiatives that would otherwise not have materialized or would have been difficult to sustain. But here, too, activist culture helped to determine how activists responded to the possibilities in front of them. The intense localism and populism of the grassroots in Flint made accepting—much less asking—for help from the outside an uneasy prospect, and there were times, I observed, when activists opted for autonomy over assistance. Empowering people in a city like Flint to save themselves, however, required that activists not only mobilize resources already available to them, but create *new* capacity within the community—a far more difficult prospect.

Activists like the members of the newly formed Flint Rising coalition, with which I was closely involved from February 2016 forward, viewed such community capacity-building as the next chapter in the fight for democracy in Flint. They saw in the thousands of residents who were now alert, mobilized, and brimming with a newfound sense of agency latent "people power" calling out to be organized, and capable of being directed at much more than just the needs created by the water crisis. Their meetings were not only strategy sessions about water: they were spaces in which residents were encouraged to imagine the kind of society they wanted to live in, to practice interacting in ways that prefigured that society, and to develop the skills they would need to realize it. It was all in the name, said Nayyirah Shariff (who would become Flint Rising's director), of "expanding" democracy, rather than simply "defending" it.[10] Democracy from this perspective was not merely synonymous with representative government and home rule, but more radical, a vision that looked beyond the water crisis to the transformation of the city as a whole (which was, after all, "pretty messed up before, too," as Shariff put it).[11] That vision was not to be ideologically predetermined in every detail, however, but rather developed though an open-ended process of grassroots deliberation and praxis—a process we might call, following Kathleen Blee, "democracy in action."[12]

Developing broad-based consensus around even short-term objectives proved to be a challenge, however. Because organizational capacity in Flint was so minimal to begin with, it was difficult to keep residents mobilized and conversing with each other in a concerted way on a consistent basis. Individual activists developed powerful voices and connections to networks that stretched far beyond Flint, but while they carried the story of the crisis far and wide and did impressive advocacy work outside of the city, collective action on the home front was often spotty and *ad hoc*. Efforts by Flint Rising to build up a more sustainable presence by professionalizing its operation and securing stable sources of funding produced new opportunities but also new controversies. Often, when critical moments of decision came, there was no clear place within the grassroots to turn for guidance and leadership. While activists successfully revived the "spirit" of the water movement every so often, especially during the nostalgia-tinged water source change anniversary events in April of each year, it was a continual struggle to keep the movement's flesh on the bone.

For all these reasons, there is no storybook version of water activism in Flint in the years after the switch back to Detroit water. While outsiders celebrated and even romanticized the water movement, treating activists more often than not with great deference and respect, the view of the movement from the inside was far messier and more complex. There were notable accomplishments but also quite a few missed opportunities. And the intensely "DIY" sensibility of Flint activists—while inspiring for its *chutzpah*—was, it seemed to me, also a liability at times, complicating relationships with allies, stretching activists thin, and fostering an inflated sense of what could be achieved through uncompromising assertions of popular will.

Although I do think that a shared sensibility colored activism in Flint across different groups and phases of the water movement, however, I also came to realize that it manifested itself in diverse ways. Behind the projection of confidence and unity that originally struck me about the activists, I found that their sense of themselves as political agents, and their sense of the identity of the movement as a whole, was in a state of ongoing flux and construction. Activists new and old were engaged, not only in a struggle for water, justice, and democracy, but in a struggle to figure out how to *be* activists within the political landscape created by the crisis, and the collective course they charted through that territory was a subject of continual, and sometimes contentious, negotiation.

The Feds Will Not Save Us: The Need
for a Grassroots Crisis Response[13]

One of the most important matters to settle in early 2016 was who, on the
official side, would lead the crisis response, for it was against this backdrop
that the activists would have to decide on their next moves. During the
preceding year, activists had called repeatedly for the "feds" to step in and
take the reins away from the state. Now that the water crisis was beginning
to get national attention, the prospects for federal intervention seemed
brighter than ever. The collective national conscience was bristling at the
sight of American citizens—*not*, as was repeatedly stressed, the denizens of
a "Third World" country—hauling cases of water home through the snow
because they could not drink what came out of their taps. The will to do
something to help Flint was clearly taking shape.

The activists were determined to use Flint's moment in the spotlight to
convince the world of the state's criminal indifference to their plight and
make their case for more federal help. A characteristic example was the
#ArrestSnyder rally of January 8, which also happened to be my *entrée* into
the water movement. The rally came at a critical time, three days after the
state's declaration of emergency, when we were waiting expectantly to see
how President Obama would respond. We gathered on the lawn of City Hall
(the closest thing to an agora in Flint), in the fading light of a dreary, rainy
day. Organized by Water You Fighting For? in conjunction with activists
from the Detroit-based People's Water Board, Detroit Light Brigade, and We
the People of Detroit (who came bearing a U-Haul full of water), the event
had drawn a large number of people, perhaps two hundred,[14] and I had to
peer under and around umbrellas to get a glimpse of the featured speakers.
Melissa Mays and Nayyirah Shariff stood at the center of it all, backlit by
floodlights and ringed by cameras, rallying the crowd, as an activist wear-
ing prison clothes and an oversized Snyder head milled about and members
of the Detroit Light Brigade projected the words "Water is a human right"
onto the side of the Genesee County Jail across the street.

Shariff reminded everyone of what it would mean to residents if they
had to depend on the State of Michigan for help: the abused would be at
the mercy of the abusers who had "demeaned and demonized" them, disregarded the federal laws instituted to protect them, and failed to act with

"urgency" when it was proved their lives were in danger. The state's efforts since October to demonstrate good faith—like the forced resignations of MDEQ director Dan Wyant and spokesperson Brad Wurfel—were, she said, "PR" moves, and Governor Snyder's apology for the state's role in the crisis, issued a week earlier, was too little too late (he could take it and "flush it"). The residents of Flint were still in search of "justice, accountability, and reparations," and they were more likely, Shariff implied, to get them from the federal government than from the state.

A week later, President Obama declared a federal state of emergency in Flint, and a variety of federal agencies stepped forward to offer their services. The US Department of Health and Human Services, the official federal point agency in Flint, provided public health support, while the Federal Emergency Management Agency (FEMA) took over the provision of bottled water, filters, and test kits at the water point of distribution sites (PODs). The Centers for Disease Control and Prevention began looking into blood lead levels, Legionnaires', and rashes, and the Environmental Protection Agency (EPA), after having resisted getting involved for months, took charge of the rehabilitation of the water system. It was a strong showing, if a little late in coming, but it was missing one key element: the disaster declaration the activists were looking for.[15] Federal agencies would remain in a support role, leaving residents more dependent than they wanted to be on the people they believed had poisoned them. Any federal money earmarked for Flint would be routed through the state, to be dispensed at the state's discretion. The arrangement was intolerable to the activists, who refused to give up their demand for disaster status, reiterated at almost every water meeting and event I attended over the next two-and-a-half years.

The face of the state response on the ground was Rich Baird, longtime friend and advisor to Snyder (his official title within the administration was "transformation manager") and "the governor incarnate in Flint," as Claire McClinton put it.[16] Baird, next to Snyder himself, was the person activists most loved to hate, the lightning rod for much of the ire they did not aim directly at Snyder. No matter how many times he professed his affection for the city (as a Flint native), or his sympathy with residents' anger and frustration, activists saw him as a scheming, dissimulating, serpentine character. Though his naturally ruddy face would grow even redder when he was (as sometimes happened) publically berated by them, he seemed resigned to it and determined to finesse his way through the hostility rather than attempt to shut it down, joking behind closed doors about the delicate "dance" he had to do whenever he hosted community meetings.[17]

The activists saw Baird as the conduit through which the state insinuated itself into almost everything that happened in Flint, including all aspects of the crisis response.[18] Baird was not working alone, however: filling out the front lines of the official response were a variety of nonprofit organizations that already had a presence in Flint. Every Thursday afternoon, the regional director of the Red Cross emceed a "Community Partners" meeting that brought these organizations together, along with representatives of government agencies, to discuss the status of various recovery initiatives. These meetings were the subject of much derision among the activists. Although technically open to anyone who cared to attend, they were not well publicized, and until activists raised a stink, they could not be recorded, giving the impression that the entities participating in them preferred to operate out of the public eye. A year into the recovery effort, some activists—and, I would venture to guess, the vast majority of residents—still did not even know of the existence of the meetings.

Most of all, though, the activists scoffed at the name "Community Partners." The people at the meetings, they said, were thoroughly "out of touch" with the "real" community of Flint, and were perpetually coming up with "hare-brained schemes" that were tone-deaf to what residents actually needed and wanted. I even heard the Community Partners coalition described as a kind of colonial body, originating in the determination of the "oppressors" to have "people who look like them" lead the recovery.[19] The whole approach also bore an unmistakable family resemblance to the emergency management paradigm: the state, acting through a Snyder appointee, was working with local members of the "nonprofit industrial complex," rather than residents themselves, to shape the city's future.[20] Tellingly, Claire McClinton described her efforts to unite the grassroots water groups at their own coalitional meetings as the "anti-Community Partners."[21]

Grasping for Unity

More specifically, what McClinton was hoping to do was to *re*unite the groups that had been part of the water struggle from the "beginning." The Coalition for Clean Water (CCW) had never really consciously decided to disband, but after the realization of its main objective, its constituent groups had started to drift apart. The Concerned Pastors, so instrumental in bringing the groups together initially, largely faded into the background, giving the Weaver administration space to stake out a leadership role (occasionally they reappeared to defend Weaver when she came under attack). When members of the original coalition spoke to the media (and some of them were in high demand now), they spoke for themselves or their groups rather than the coalition as a whole. They were also pulled in different directions by external networking opportunities and pushed apart by personal animosities that were kept in check, for the most part, when everyone was fighting the same fight. Without the CCW's precision of purpose, different groups were beginning to articulate different demands and objectives, at a time when it seemed imperative to present a united front to the world. Opportunities for collaboration were being lost simply because one group did not know what the other was doing.[22]

Despite the oft-heard lament that people were not working together, efforts to restore unity did not get very far. When I first met Laura Sullivan, in February, she was attempting to reassemble the activists from the CCW to help establish a citizens' advisory board that would give residents more influence within the official recovery effort. The board, as she envisioned it, would set priorities for the order of pipe replacements (deciding which houses should be first in line), investigate new claims of harm from the water (ensuring they got the proper attention from scientific authorities), and keep tabs on the way private donations were being managed. The idea stalled out, however, when some of the activists declined to participate.

Claire McClinton's efforts were a variation on the same theme of reunification, but they were focused on a more modest goal: a "Two Years Too Long" rally on the second anniversary of the switch to the Flint River. In this instance, most of the people asked to participate did so, their solidarity symbolized in a much-praised image on the back of the event's official T-shirt: a jigsaw puzzle, shaped like the city of Flint, with each group represented by one of the pieces. The participants even managed to settle upon three consensual demands: the extension of Medicare benefits to all residents and former residents exposed to the water, the declaration of a federal disaster in Flint, and the abolition of the EM system. On the day of the rally, we congregated, as usual, at City Hall, where about fifty activists made a respectable show of strength in their matching black-and-white shirts, and representatives of the different groups took turns speaking to the crowd through a bullhorn.

The general feeling at the debriefing session afterward was that the event had been a success. It had few lingering effects where coalition building was concerned, however. Although McClinton continued to call "Two Years Too Long Coalition" meetings through the rest of the year, attendance was random and often sparse. And while she continued to hold up the three demands as a triumph of consensus, it did not stop other groups from coming up with demands of their own.

The appearance of a 501c4 group calling itself, simply, the "Flint Coalition" created further complication. The Flint Coalition did not have the same genealogical relationship to earlier water activism—instead, it was closely associated with an interfaith community and educational center on the north side of town, and had more of a professional bent than the other groups. It came out with five "points" in January that included demands for a disaster declaration and an external auditor to monitor the funds coming into Flint.[23] Later, it proposed a four-point plan for pipe replacement. This group and the others proceeded along more or less wholly different tracks despite the overlap of some of their goals. One fleeting point of contact was established in June, however, when the coalition invited environmental justice doyenne Lois Gibbs to lead a strategy session, extending invitations to other groups and presenting it as an opportunity to build broad consensus. McClinton, Nayyirah Shariff, and Melissa Mays all attended, and Gibbs did a fine job of running the meeting, but it was awkward nonetheless. Without a strong understanding of the dynamics in the room, Gibbs made a well-intentioned attempt to get everyone to agree on a list of objectives, implying all the while that the Flint Coalition would take the lead in rallying the various groups together. The buy-in, however, simply wasn't there on the activists' part. When I tried to insert into the conversation some of the demands they had articulated in other contexts, their unamused looks from the other side of the room made me think I should have kept my mouth shut. After one follow-up meeting (which only Shariff attended), the groups went their separate ways.

The Birth of Flint Rising

While these abortive attempts at coalition building were going on, another group was making a bid to be the epicenter of grassroots activism in Flint, a group that grew out of an intensive effort to bring word of the water crisis, and emergency water assistance, to the local Spanish-speaking community. In late

January, San Juana Olivares-Macias, chair of the Genesee County Hispanic/ Latino Collaborative, came to the realization that many Spanish-speaking residents still had no idea the water they were drinking was unsafe—a reflection of the dearth of Spanish-language communications about the water (when Olivares first checked the state's water crisis website for materials to distribute, everything was in English). Some of those who *did* know about the crisis had first learned of it from relatives in Mexico who saw coverage on the news. Furthermore, the modicum of information that had trickled down to the community was, in many cases, hurting more than it was helping: many of those who had heard the water was "bad" (a rumor was going around about a body being found in the river) were boiling it, further concentrating whatever lead was present and rendering it even more dangerous. Heart-wrenching stories began to appear in the press of mothers who continued to feed their infants lead-tainted formula through the fall months of 2015, as English-speaking residents were scrambling to attach filters to their faucets and stocking up on bottled water.[24] Even after the water PODs opened in January, many members of the community—especially the undocumented—were wary of using them because staff at some sites were asking for ID (a practice eventually exposed and ended by activists). And when anyone who looked official came knocking with offers of assistance, many refused to answer the door, fearful of immigration raids.

As the problem was coming into focus, Olivares got in touch with Art Reyes III, a former student of community organizing guru Marshall Ganz and organizer with the Center for Popular Democracy. Reyes had deep roots in Flint (his father was one of the leading figures within the local United Automobile Workers [UAW]) and the crisis presented an opportunity to put his training to good use in his hometown. In collaboration with Nayyirah Shariff and local activist and artist Desiree Duell, Olivares and Reyes organized a door-to-door canvass on the east side of Flint, where most of the city's Hispanic population was concentrated. During their first weekend of canvassing, they found that around 95 percent of Spanish-speaking residents they made contact with were unaware that the city had a lead problem or that lead posed a special threat to children.[25] The discovery only heightened their sense of urgency: over the next month, they enlisted the help of hundreds of volunteers and knocked on some eight thousand doors.[26]

As the canvassing gathered momentum, the activists began to target a wider swath of residents, extending their reach into public housing complexes and North Flint (predominantly African American and the most blighted and economically depressed side of the city). They partnered with the group Crossing Water, a rapid-response team of social workers and volunteers who followed up with residents in need of water, filters, or support services. They also began to talk about what else they could do with the momentum they were gathering and the contacts they were making in the community. The result of this conversation was a decision to brand themselves as a new group—a new "coalition," in fact: Flint Rising.

In February, Flint Rising made its official debut. In addition to keeping up the canvassing, it began inviting residents to attend weekly community meetings on Saturday mornings in the basement of St. Michael's Church. Over the next several months, I attended almost every one of these meetings, often accompanied by my wife and son. It seemed like the place to be: the canvassing operation was truly impressive and professionally managed (I went on some canvasses myself), evincing a level of organizational competence not always in evidence in Flint, the organizers were experienced and knowledgeable, and the meetings were often (though not always) well attended. Furthermore, Flint Rising explicitly presented itself as the umbrella organization that was bringing together the city's grassroots groups, and "St. Mike's" church as the only place where anything really noteworthy water related was going on at the grassroots level.

At first I had a difficult time figuring out what the "coalition" was, however. The only local group that was unambiguously on board, from what I could tell, was the Flint chapter of Michigan Faith in Action—an affiliate of the national community organizing network People Improving Communities through Organizing (PICO)—which had its offices in the church.[27] The Flint Democracy Defense League (FDDL), often cited as being a member of the coalition, had only one real point of contact with it (Shariff), and I knew from attending FDDL meetings that there was some skepticism within the group of Flint Rising's sudden appearance on the scene. Shariff later told me that some block clubs and pastors had also been involved early on, but from what I could tell, Flint Rising's self-identification as a coalition of local groups was more aspirational than it was empirically accurate.

The real coalition that formed the backbone of Flint Rising, I gradually realized, was a network of progressive political, community organizing, and labor groups based outside Flint that looked at the small group of Flint activists involved as the coalition's "local steering committee." Not until I was added to Flint Rising's internal listserv months later did I come to appreciate how instrumental these groups had been in supporting, or even making possible, much of what Flint Rising had done up to that point, and I found it curious that their involvement was generally elided (at least it seemed that way to me) at the community meetings, the main interface between Flint Rising and residents. There were, after all, strong reasons for partnering with these groups, for they brought with them valuable skills, connections, and resources: Michigan Voice took the lead in coordinating canvassing, Progress Michigan arranged press conferences and media "clapbacks" every time a major piece of water crisis news broke, unions like AFSCME, the SEIU, and the UAW helped with event turnout and transportation, and Michigan United helped set the coalition on a path toward establishing its own 501c3 and 501c4 funds. A variety of other groups—groups like Food and Water Watch, Clean Water Action, America Votes, the Sierra Club, the American Civil Liberties Union (ACLU), and the Michigan Nurses Association—also contributed in ways that extended the coalition's reach and enhanced its effectiveness.

The relationship local Flint Rising activists had to this extensive network of organizations was no small part of why they were able to command respect from influential and powerful people. When then-presidential candidate Hillary Clinton stopped through in early February, they managed to arrange a face-to-face meeting between her and two core organizers. When Surgeon General Vivek Murthy came to town a week later, they took him along on follow-up visits to homes they had canvassed. When Mark Ruffalo and other notables visited on the eve of the presidential debate in March, Flint Rising activists held a joint press conference with them and helped to tour them around town.

Flint Rising's connections also gave it more political clout whenever the coalition lobbied for more state or federal assistance.[28] Lobbying efforts got particularly intense in late spring 2016, when a battle emerged over a $127 million state appropriation for Flint that looked like it might not get through the State House before the summer recess. The fear that the state would not come through with the resources Flint needed was very real at the time: the NAACP had threatened "civil disobedience" if the state did not come up with a plan for pipe replacement,[29] and on several occasions I heard people seriously considering the possibility of rioting. Flint Rising's collaboration with state-level lobbying organizations, however, helped create more direct, and arguably more constructive, ways of applying pressure. Activists worked with these groups to organize a full-court press to get the bill passed, flooding key Republican leaders with phone calls, busing residents to Lansing for press conferences and prayer vigils in the Capitol rotunda, and hand delivering letters to legislators. When the House finally approved the bill in June, activists had no doubt their efforts had made the difference, and they held up the campaign as one of the movement's major victories.

Both Reyes and Shariff insisted to me that no one had made an intentional effort to mask or downplay the role of outside groups in Flint Rising. Given the activist culture they were operating within, however, it was clear why they were not eager to portray Flint Rising as a coalition comprised mainly of outsiders. For one thing, it would have elicited the kinds of suspicions regularly directed by residents at people and groups purporting to speak for the community but not 100 percent "Flint." (Even some Flint Rising activists worried about the ratio of residents to outsiders involved in the coalition's internal deliberations: one asked me to start participating in conference calls to create more balance.) More importantly, drawing attention to the role of outside groups in the coalition would have clashed with the message that became an increasingly central theme of Flint Rising's community meetings: the message that Flint residents had the power to do things for themselves.

Community Organizing and Activism

Flint Rising was not the only group talking about popular empowerment, of course, but the language it used to do so was distinctive, drawn from a body of thought and practice developed by professional community organizers. According to the community organizer credo, the overriding objective of the organizer is not to do *for* people but to help people do for themselves by building "people power." People power, as understood by the organizer, is a product of relationships between individuals living in geographical proximity that can be parlayed into collective action. Where these relationships do not yet exist, the organizer's job is to help establish them. The main tool used for this purpose is the "one-to-one," a face-to-face "facilitated and strategic conversation" with individual residents aimed at identifying where their self-interest lies, convincing them that it can be furthered by banding together with their neighbors in collective action, and securing a commitment from them to attend organizing meetings or contribute in some way to advancing a collective struggle.[30] In this way, a community is transformed into a "constituency," a group of people "standing together to realize a common purpose."[31]

Where social needs and injustices exist within a community, the organizer's goal is to help people change their situation rather than merely cope with it.[32] This is what differentiated Flint Rising's canvassing from most other operations providing immediate water relief. The coalition looked at canvasses as opportunities to bring people into the movement by spreading the word about community meetings and identifying residents with leadership qualities who could be groomed into neighborhood-level organizers. By instilling organizing skills and putting residents to work in their own corners of the city, Flint Rising's intention was to create "distributed leadership," a decentralized network of mutually accountable people and groups sharing power and responsibility and working toward common goals. Once organized in this way, residents would have a formidable apparatus at their disposal that they could direct at any number of short- and long-term objectives. It would fundamentally alter the balance of power in Flint, undermining the hegemony of local elites and enabling residents to act for themselves whenever elected officials were unwilling or unable to act on their behalf.

It was essential, from Shariff's perspective, that Flint residents lead the organizing effort on the ground. Oftentimes, she pointed out to me, organizing work is done by college-educated, predominantly white people paid to come into a community from the outside. In theory, by building local capacity, such organizers gradually render themselves obsolete. Shariff's hope, however, was to obviate the need for them altogether by training up residents mobilized by the water crisis.[33] Sometimes she or Sharon Allen of Michigan Faith in Action would incorporate mini-trainings into community meetings, leading us through "power analysis" or "strategy development," or familiarizing us with rules-of-thumb well known to organizers (e.g., "self-interest moves people," "power concedes nothing without a demand," "follow the money," "real power is hidden," "no permanent allies or enemies"). The problem with trying to train people during the community meetings, however, was that turnout was so erratic there was little chance of producing a cumulative effect. To offer more substantive guidance to individuals with the potential to become "neighborhood captains" (I was one of two people to volunteer for Ward 7), Art Reyes led a day-long organizer training in May 2016.

When Reyes led trainings, the influence of Marshall Ganz was especially evident, particularly Ganz's emphasis on the utility of storytelling as an organizing tool.[34] Stories, Reyes told us, are excellent mechanisms for provoking an emotional response and stirring people to action. To begin with, an organizer has to have a prepackaged personal story about being called to action that models the kind of agency he or she seeks to elicit in others (this story can be used to lead off one-to-ones and other personal interactions with potential recruits). The constituency as a whole has to have a story of "us," establishing a common identity rooted in shared values and experiences. It also has to have a story of "now," establishing why collective action is imperative, what needs to be done, and what the future will look like if action is successful.

Reyes also taught us to be on the lookout, especially when canvassing, for members of the community with moving personal stories of their own that could be strategically useful to the coalition. Such stories had become hot commodities in the national media, where they were now granted great epistemic weight, presented nonjudgmentally as capturing essential truths about what was going on in the city. Flint Rising took advantage of this dynamic in its first major public event: a "People's Hearing" in March, to which it invited Governor Snyder —not to speak, but to sit and listen to residents talk about their experiences, in what Shariff described as an "inversion of the emergency management paradigm."[35] (When Snyder declined to attend, she used a stand-in, puppet version of him to "receive" the coalition's demands.)

The lineup of speakers at the People's Hearing—mothers, people of color, members of the Hispanic community and the deaf community—reflected another important development: with all the respect residents' experiences were now commanding, it was possible for even politically and culturally marginalized voices to speak and be heard. In some ways, personal qualities that had previously been epistemic liabilities—motherhood, or skin color, for example—were now assets enabling certain kinds of people to speak about the crisis with special gravitas. It was an opportunity to redefine what "Flint" looked like to the wider world and, simultaneously, assuage some of the bitterness created by the early prominence of white activists.

There is no better example than Flint Rising's embrace of Nakiya Wakes, an African American, single mother living below the poverty line, whose story was one of the most dramatic to come out of the water crisis. Wakes had experienced many of the same problems with the water as other residents—rashes, hair loss, smelly and discolored water—but her account of how the crisis had affected her children set her apart. Since the city's original change of water source, her son Jaylon, who had tested positive for elevated blood lead levels, had developed serious behavioral problems and been suspended from school an incredible fifty-six times. Wakes also attributed the deaths of two unborn children to the water. Five weeks after learning she was pregnant in early 2015, she went to the emergency room with complications and discovered she had miscarried. A follow-up visit, however, revealed that another heart was beating inside her womb: she had been pregnant with twins all along. Wakes called it her "miracle baby." At thirteen weeks, however, more problems arose and she returned to the ER. After five days of hemorrhaging brought her to the brink of death, the second pulse, too, fell silent. Devastated, Wakes returned home from the hospital to find a blue flyer about total trihalomethanes (TTHMs) in her mailbox. It was the first she had heard of the water being dangerous, particularly to pregnant women. Although she would later conclude that lead, rather than TTHMs, was the most likely culprit, the upshot was the same: the water had taken her babies.

Flint Rising seized upon Wakes's story and coalition partners worked to amplify it by arranging speaking opportunities and encouraging media coverage. Wakes related her water crisis experience regularly at activist events and actions and was featured in the *New York Times*, CNN, and a Hillary Clinton campaign ad. But most extraordinary of all, unlike those who first came forward with stories about the water, not once did Wakes feel like she was disbelieved. Just the opposite: she marveled at how many people had been touched by her story and had expressed their sympathies to her. No one asked her for scientific proof or a medical endorsement of her claims—the pathos and humanity of her words were enough.[36]

Flint Rising not only created opportunities for Wakes to speak, it trained her *how* to speak. Because Wakes was new to public speaking (at first, she told me, she felt a "frog" in her throat every time), coalition partner Progress Michigan worked on helping her script what she would say and build confidence in her own abilities, as it did with other select individuals whose stories fit the message the coalition wanted to project.[37] Just how conscious the speakers themselves were of their role in the organizers' strategy is debatable, however. I inadvertently created controversy within Flint Rising's inner circle when I revealed to Wakes (thinking she already knew) that

Figure 8.1
Stories of residents featured on the Flint Rising website. Flint Rising.

some of the organizers had envisioned her story as a substitute, of sorts, for that of another poor, African American mother whose health problems had prevented her from participating. Incidents like this led some within Flint Rising to question the transparency of the strategizing going on within the coalition. One activist—who was conscious that her role for the coalition's PR purposes was that of the poor, *white* mother—told me that "people who don't have any experience are being used."[38]

One could argue that "using" people is simply part of the art of the community organizer: at one community meeting, Shariff explained that an "assertive" approach to organizing involved trying to "lure" people by appealing to their self-interest and "guilt trip[ping]" them by assigning them responsibilities—without letting on that they were being "hustled."[39] But the idea that organizing involves distinctions between the hustlers and the hustled, the organizers and the organized, raises questions about its compatibility with principles of democracy like transparency, equality, and participatory decision making. It also makes the question of *who* is doing the organizing—and whose interests they are serving—all the more important.

In conversations with some local Flint Rising activists, it became clear that they felt the outside groups within the coalition were trying to organize *them*, using the local steering committee—and the opportunity provided by the water crisis—to advance their larger organizational agendas. These "outside interests," one activist worried, were controlling the "framing" and "representation" of the work being done on the ground in Flint, under the guise of merely facilitating that work.[40] I even heard the dynamic compared to emergency management, in that outsiders were invoking their own purportedly superior skillset to justify infringing on the self-determination of local residents.

Officially, however, the coalition was operating with an agenda shaped by demands that had been "distilled," Shariff told me, from what residents were calling for "out there in the community":[41] a 100 percent refund for water bills dating back to April 2014 and bill forgiveness until the water was safe ("We Don't Pay for Poison"), replacement of Flint's damaged infrastructure—all the way to the tap—using Flint labor ("Fix What You Broke"), and health and education services for all children, adults, and seniors in the community ("Our Families Deserve to Be Healthy"). Few in Flint would have denied that these demands were just, and some of the victories Flint Rising claimed—especially the passage of the state supplemental bill—clearly advanced them, giving residents tastes of victory that organizers usually consider critical to any sustained organizing effort.[42] They were not always practical demands to organize around, however. At a Flint Rising meeting in June 2017, for example, I was in a breakout group that was supposed to come up with strategies to push for the "We Don't Pay for Poison" demand. It was so farfetched by that point, however, to think that the state would pay 100 percent of residents' water bills (given that a few months earlier it had ended even its temporary 65 percent credit) that it was not possible to have a meaningful conversation about how to proceed.

It was not just Flint Rising that was having trouble operationalizing its stated goals: in the heady days after the switch back to Detroit, when the activists felt like they "had 'em by the balls" (as one put it[43]), certain demands sunk into the DNA of the movement that were long shots to begin with and only grew further divorced from political "reality" as time went on. The ubiquitous disaster area demand—even though it seemed so self-evidently just to so many people—was perhaps the best example. If there had ever been a moment when Flint might have been granted such a declaration, or some sort of special federal dispensation that circumvented the Stafford Act, it had long since passed by April 2017, when, as the spokesperson for the now-*Three* Years Too Long rally, I reiterated the demand to local media. My own position (when I removed my spokesperson's cap) was that it was counterproductive to persist in demands that had such little hope of being realized—demands that had come into being at the peak of the activists' feeling of power and possibility but had since outlived their usefulness. At the same time, giving them up was, admittedly, an uncomfortable prospect, for it would inevitably look like an admission of defeat. More importantly, it would contradict the lesson activists learned during the first phase of the water struggle: if you demand the impossible loud and long enough, you just might get it. When I debated the matter with Claire McClinton, she told me that her preference was to "throw caution to the wind," not to pay any mind to what polite society deemed to be possible or reasonable.[44] It put anyone counseling pragmatism in a tricky spot: who wanted to be responsible for deflating an "impossible" hope that might be the next one to come true?

Related to this tension between political opportunities and movement demands was a persistent tension—most evident within Flint Rising—between organizing and activism. While the logics of organizing and activism are not necessarily incompatible when the capacity exists to sustain both simultaneously,[45] when capacity is limited, prioritizing one often means neglecting the other.[46] An illustrative example of this tradeoff arose after the founding of a constituent group within Flint Rising in spring 2016 that took the name Flint Mom Power. My wife was one of a few people present at the inaugural meeting of the group, where it was decided that its chief mission would be to organize local moms around issues of public education. Almost as soon as this decision was made, however, the group's energies were completely redirected into planning a week of water-related direct actions during the month of May. What resulted were some of the more memorable, attention-getting actions of the water crisis—particularly, a die-in at the water treatment plant featuring mothers and grandmothers clad in white jumpsuits smeared with red paint over the reproductive organs to symbolize harms done to women by lead. But from my wife's perspective, the sudden substitution of (rather militant) activism for organizing was like a bait and switch: the practical work she had signed up for had to be totally suspended to make the actions possible, and she drifted away from the group, not to return. A similar dynamic emerged later in the year, when Flint Rising was in the middle of a concerted

Figure 8.2
America's Heartbreakers action at the Flint Water Treatment Plant (May 16, 2016).
MLive, Flint Journal.

effort to organize the city ward by ward, but got sidetracked by the announcement of new water shutoffs, which seemed to call for an urgent response.
(I cannot deny my own complicity in this instance, for I was one of the people
calling for direct action.) At a community meeting in December that was supposed to be part of the organizing effort, attendees were told that Flint Rising's
next steps would be actions around shutoffs—actions which, for various reasons, were never followed through on.

The Dilemmas of Professionalism: Flint Rising 2.0

After the week of direct action in May 2016 and the passage of more state aid for Flint in June, Flint Rising began a process of reinvention. In August, it received a $250,000 grant from the Kellogg Foundation for "building an organizing infrastructure" to address the water crisis.[47] The money allowed for the hiring of a director, organizers, and canvassing staff. It touched off a heated debate among the Flint-based activists over who was most qualified for the positions and how the hires should be made.

When the dust settled (but only after some activists went their separate ways), Nayyirah Shariff emerged as Flint Rising's director. She saw it as an opportunity to reset the group (for it was now officially a *group* rather than a coalition), to make it more independent from outside groups and take it in a more radically democratic direction. Although she was required by the terms of the grant to adopt the title of "Director," she challenged the other activists to think outside the box of the "nonprofit industrial complex," recommending that the group eschew top-down hierarchies in favor of an approach that built egalitarian, democratic values into the group's organization and decision-making processes. Flint Rising's objective, as Shariff conceived of it, was not merely to organize around the group's official demands, but "to pilot the type of society we want to live in."[48] As she started to bring on staff, she strove to create an organizational culture of cooperative decision making. She trained the team members in conflict resolution[49] and assigned them readings to facilitate deeper thinking about the group's purpose and mission—readings on water democracy,[50] on nonviolent struggle,[51] on the difference between "serving" people and cultivating democratic citizenship,[52] on the famously egalitarian Landless Workers' Movement in Brazil.[53] These were signs, as I saw it, that Flint Rising was beginning to evolve beyond the Machiavellianism of the community organizing paradigm into a group that was more prefigurative in nature, more humanistic, more oriented toward the ideal of the "beloved community" (a term Shariff began to use with some frequency).[54]

Shariff tried to bring the same spirit to Flint Rising's rebooted community meetings, which after a six-month hiatus resumed in December. The meetings, she told me, were intended to help residents become the agents of their own liberation by creating "spaces" of "self-governance" in which they could collectively talk through the challenges facing them, develop their own solutions, and experience, viscerally, what authentic democracy feels like. Shariff had no illusions, however, that everyone who turned out— motivated, as they usually were, by water concerns and lacking political experience—was coming in with the kind of refined political consciousness she was trying to develop in her staff. She viewed Flint Rising as an organization that could meet newly mobilized residents where they were at, foregrounding the issues most immediate to them, but also working to "train people up" by helping them to see not only *that* things were "bad" (because most needed no convincing), but *why* they were bad, and what could be done to address them on a structural level. This entry-level approach to bringing residents up to speed politically was, to Shariff's mind, one of the things that distinguished Flint Rising from the FDDL: the FDDL, she said, was like a "senior thesis," trading in sophisticated political analysis that went over the heads of most residents, whereas Flint Rising was "freshman orientation," aiming to draw people in who were incensed about the water but still getting their political bearings.[55]

As Flint Rising became more professional in its structure and operation, however, it became in some ways even more opaque than previously. While it held regular internal staff meetings, its community meetings were much more sporadic, scheduled to cap off systematic canvassing efforts within individual wards. Given that canvassing was now conducted by professional staff rather than the eclectic influx of volunteers who had sustained it through the first half of 2016, Flint Rising's day-to-day operations were self-contained and less accessible to people who wanted to feel like they were part of the group. Just as Flint Rising's earlier reliance on outside groups chafed against its self-conception as the center of grassroots empowerment in Flint, the constraints of functioning on a 501c3 model coexisted uneasily with its ambition to be the avant-garde of popular democracy. Although Shariff was consciously trying to push against the limits of that model, she was fully aware, she told me, that the "revolution" would not be made by grant-funded organizations and that Flint Rising was no exception. Ultimately, she hoped, more radical groups would arise that Flint Rising could help to get off the ground by providing them with meeting space and skills training—acting, in a sense, as an incubator for the seeds that others wished to plant.[56]

The Elusive Dream of (Water) Democracy

Activists began 2016 fiercely critical (as always) of the state, but confident they could wring resources from it, hopeful for a boost from the federal government, and decidedly more optimistic about city administration after the replacement of Dayne Walling with Karen Weaver. By the end of the year, the situation had changed. Activists continued to call the state out for failing to commit itself fully to the recovery effort—at one point, Flint Rising activists delivered over a thousand "you owe me" messages in water bottles to Governor Snyder's office, listing all the ways residents were still waiting for justice— but now their focus was on preventing the state from pulling out of Flint entirely. With system-wide lead levels dropping, the general feeling was that the state was eager to declare the water restored and put the crisis behind it. One particular point of contention was the water PODs: after the end of the federal declaration of emergency in August, the state had taken over responsibility for them, and in early 2017, state officials announced a two-phase plan to shut them down. With full replacement of Flint's lead and galvanized service lines still at least three years away, and with residents still suspicious of point-of-use filters, the prospect of losing free bottled water (which the Genesee County Medical Society continued to recommend for physically vulnerable residents) caused a great deal of consternation and anger. Once again, Flint Rising was on the scene, sponsoring "pop-up pickets" at PODs that were slated to close. Activists also drew attention to the fact that, as Flint residents had their bottled water taken away, Nestlé—a company with ties to the Snyder administration and the largest bottler of water in the world, with wells all over Michigan—was at the same time sucking thousands of gallons out of the ground every minute for a pittance, not far from Flint.[57]

One brake on the state's withdrawal was a major legal victory in November 2016: a federal court order, in a case brought by Melissa Mays, the Concerned Pastors, the Natural Resources Defense Council, and the ACLU, forcing the state to deliver bottled water to residents without functioning filters on their taps. The state immediately began fighting the order—a spokesperson for Snyder said complying with it would take a "herculean effort … on the magnitude of a large-scale military operation" and would redirect resources away from where they were most needed.[58] A settlement in March 2017 ultimately excused the state from water delivery and established a timeline for the POD closures, on the condition that the state commit $87 million

Figure 8.3
You Owe Me bottles delivered by Flint Rising activists to State Capitol. *MLive, Flint Journal.*

to pipe replacement and send teams to every home to check on the status of residents' filters. Reaction to the settlement was mixed within the activist community: people were glad to have more resources but displeased that the settlement gave the state an exit plan, and some accused the plaintiffs of presuming to speak for residents without soliciting their opinions or even informing them about the progress of the suit.[59]

The federal government was also showing signs of closing the books on Flint. The city got a large windfall of federal aid in December 2016 with the passage of a $170 million federal funding package—still less than the activists were hoping for, and, as Claire McClinton put it, laden with "strings attached as far as the eye can see"[60]—but with this, Flint scraped the bottom of the federal barrel. The same month, the House Committee on Oversight and Government Reform ended its investigation of the water crisis. Some federal agencies, chiefly the EPA, continued to maintain a presence in Flint, but it grew increasingly skeletal.

With less to fight for at the state and federal levels, and with the city back in possession of most of its power, events at City Hall began to take on more importance. Well into 2016, the activists rallied around Mayor Weaver as their chief ally (along with Councilman Eric Mays) within city government. As time went on, however, some activists began to feel like the focus on the state as the root of all evil was distracting from what they saw as the failures and abuses of Weaver's administration. The city was continuing to enforce its ordinances on water shutoffs and liens for nonpayment of water bills, for example, despite the fact that nonpayment was still for many residents a matter of principle. Furthermore, in April 2017, at a mayor-sponsored town hall on water swarming with police, six activists were arrested for disorderly conduct after minor disruptions. Following this incident, some activists began to speak of the need to resist "fascism" in Flint—not the "fascism" of state appointees, now, but of the Weaver administration.[61]

The first chinks in Weaver's armor had appeared earlier, however, when she became embroiled in the controversy over the most momentous decision to be made about the future of Flint's water. With the city back on Lake Huron water, the question was whether it would switch, as planned, to getting that water through the Karegnondi Water Authority (KWA) pipeline upon its completion (now slated for summer 2017), or find some way of remaining on the Detroit system, now operated by the regional Great Lakes Water Authority (GLWA). Anti-KWA sentiment was by now very strong within the activist community, shaped by the beliefs that hidden fracking interests were driving the project, that it was a privatization ploy, that it would undermine both Flint's and Detroit's financial stability, that it had already put Flint in a vulnerable position relative to the city's creditors, and that it was one of the main causes of the water crisis. It was when Mayor Weaver, backed into a political corner, made good on the city's promise to help finance the KWA pipeline's construction that some of the activists began to speak out against her publicly for the first time.

In April 2017, however, Weaver made a stunning announcement: the city's water consultant, John Young, had negotiated a deal that would allow Flint to stay with GLWA at a lower cost than if it opted for the KWA. It seemed too good to be true, especially since it involved GLWA taking on Flint's bond debt, and no one knew quite what to make of it at first. As the activists learned more about the terms of the deal, realizing that it would lock Flint into a thirty-year contract with no guaranteed wholesale rate or say in rate setting, they grew almost as opposed to it as they were to the KWA. No one seemed to have much of an alternative, though. Some insisted that the city renegotiate a shorter-term contract, even though thirty years was the industry standard and the chances of GLWA's budging on the issue were slim. Some of the same activists who were vehemently opposed to the KWA began saying that Flint *had* to have its own treatment plant, destined to be mothballed if the city chose GLWA but a central part of the KWA plan (since the plan required the city to treat raw water). More generally, activists insisted that Flint ought to have a "Flint-controlled" water system, but without a strong sense of what that would consist of, given the available options. While everyone could agree on the need for a better contract, beyond that, activists' vision of an alternative, more democratic, water future was thin at best, and outside of a collective letter of concern,[62] there was no real attempt to organize around even the contract demand.

Perhaps this state of aporia is one reason why so much excitement was generated by the news that activists who had fought against the Dakota Access Pipeline alongside residents of the Standing Rock Indian Reservation were coming to Flint. Just over a week before the mayor made her water recommendation, a group of these out-of-town activists, joined by a few locals (some of whom had been to Standing Rock themselves), established a settlement called Camp Promise in Kearsley Park, on the east side of Flint. The camp grew steadily over the next several weeks as more itinerant activists flocked to the city, having heard through activist networks that the crisis in Flint was no better and that residents were still desperately in need of help. Convinced of this before even arriving, they brought with them a militant mentality, fused to a sketchy understanding of the subtleties of the crisis and local politics. They became a combative presence at City Council meetings and town halls—without always, it seemed to me, having a strong sense of who it was they were combatting.[63]

When outside "help" came in the form of activists like these—whose sensibilities, tactics, and apparent commitment to the cause resonated strongly within the local activist scene—Flint activists were quick to accept it. They stood up for the camp when city police threatened to evict the campers and started spending a good deal of time hanging around the campfire, as Camp Promise became another venue to which people were invited to come hear residents' "stories." For a while, it looked as though there might be a true fusion of the insiders and the outsiders. There was one moment in particular that for me, and I think for others as well, signified that budding synthesis. On the day of our Three Years Too Long march and rally,

I helped lead a group of marchers from a staging area on the north side of Flint along a three-mile route to City Hall, laboring much of the way under the weight of a huge banner, covered in expressions of solidarity, that had traveled, it proclaimed, "From Baltimore to Standing Rock to Flint." As we approached the heart of downtown, we saw that, off to our left, another contingent that had left for City Hall from Camp Promise was fortuitously converging on the same spot at the same time. As the two streams fused, and the march suddenly doubled in size at the perfect moment, there was a feeling of exuberance and camaraderie in the air.

Alas, it did not last. The campers began feuding with each other, leading a breakaway faction to form another community it called the "Wolves' Den" in a private residence.[64] Campers also started feuding with local activists, making comments to the effect that Flint residents did not seem like they had any real desire to fight for themselves. After everything the activists had been through, no insult could have stung more. Some of Camp Promise's former enthusiasts began promoting an online petition calling for the camp to be led by a Flint resident.

The appeal of Camp Promise was somewhat mystifying to me, but it was also instructive. The way some of the activists would wax poetic about it and proselytize for it, urging people to come see it for themselves, bore out its self-description: it really was a beacon of "promise," at least for a while. Clearly there were longings for durable spaces of freedom and community that other groups weren't managing to satisfy. The idea that such spaces could appear all of the sudden (literally, overnight) seemed to have a kind of enchanting appeal—more so, anyway, than the idea that such spaces are hard-won products of diligent organizing, accreting little by little over time, through the reshaping of existing institutions and the building of relationships within established geographies. The "promise" of Camp Promise lay also, it seemed, in the idea that the camp might revive the spirit of the water movement, as symbolized by the "sacred" fire at its center that was supposed to keep burning until the activists' demands were met and the crisis was finally over.

Insofar as this spirit was still alive in early 2018, as my ethnographic work began to draw to a close, it was still searching for a suitable body. Activists continued to do important work outside Flint—speaking, lobbying, forging ties to new activist networks (like the revived Poor People's Campaign led by Reverend William Barber II)—but the grassroots in Flint remained largely an "alphabet soup" (as one person put it to me) of different groups working on different things and only marginally cognizant of each other. Flint Rising, the group with the most ambitious vision of bringing residents together and empowering them in lasting ways around a transformative agenda, kept a low profile during the second half of 2017. After a series of internal controversies, some staff members quit and the group's canvassing ground to a halt. The organizers who remained—Nayyirah Shariff, Melissa Mays, and Gina Luster—had a hard time between the three of them keeping the group afloat, as financial backers began to check in ever more eagerly for updates and people in the community began to wonder what had happened.

The situation was summed up well when the group reappeared in February 2018, calling a hastily arranged meeting designed to focus on a concrete, seemingly manageable objective: preparing residents to submit public comment about proposed revisions to Michigan's state-level Lead and Copper Rule. Shariff opened the meeting by telling the fifteen or so people in attendance that Flint Rising was "rooted in the belief that those who are directly impacted should be driving the work." It soon became clear, however, that a small group of people had already been working on the issue ("for twenty months," as Mays put it) without bringing other residents into the conversation, or actively informing them about it. Now, at the tail end of the revisions process, Flint Rising was offering residents a crash course in the relevant background as well as talking points to reiterate to the MDEQ. The arrangement might have worked if people had felt ownership for what the core members of the group were doing in other venues, but some activists in the room came to the meeting determined to raise concerns about the group's patchy interface with the community. Sue Whalen, a former Flint Rising staff member, rose to ask why the group had not stayed in touch with the people it had made contact with over the previous two years, or people who had worked for the organization in the past. It felt "disempowering," she said—like people were being "used." Tony Palladeno, chiming in to support her, said that Flint Rising had left people "hanging."[65]

What began as one of the more focused activist meetings I had been to in Flint quickly unraveled, as Whalen's and Palladeno's dissenting comments touched off a cascade of remarks having little to do with the agenda at hand. As the meeting veered off course, Tru Saunders spoke up with a call to action that harkened back to her audacious stand in front of City Hall in the winter of 2015. "All this stuff you guys are coming up with," she said (referring to the "paperwork" distributed to the meeting's attendees), was already known to officials, and reiterating it would not make any difference. What was really needed was to "shut some stuff down." A "24/7 protest" was in the works, she informed everyone, located in the same spot where she had once stood alone in the cold—this time, with people rotating in and out, day and night, a human version of the ever-burning flame.[66]

The Way Forward

These were the extremes that activists in Flint had the challenge of working within: the need to rally around the immediate, smaller-scale opportunities spit out by the slowly turning wheels of justice, and the need to demonstrate, continuously, the authenticity of a movement that prided itself on breaking down barriers through feats of personal and political will. The synthesis of organizing and activism that Flint Rising was striving for had the potential, I thought, to reconcile those priorities at the group level, if only it could be sustained logistically. But such a synthesis must also be integrated into the political identities of the people that such groups seek to mobilize, who must come to see everything from policy work, to power building, to protest as expressions of the same political agency. For that kind of political maturation to take place requires spaces more stable and nurturing than those that Flint Rising—or any other group, for that matter—was able to provide.

If Flint's water activists were tough and stubborn, heirs to the city's great fighting tradition, it was evident to me by the spring of 2018 that many of them also flirted regularly with feelings of helplessness and despair— feelings shaped by living in a city that for some time had been a victim of history more often than a maker of it, struggling for its very existence against economic collapse, political dissolution, and the creep of entropy eroding it from the inside out. Four years after the first inklings of a water movement began to appear, activists felt both that they had won extraordinary victories, and that, somehow, "nothing" had changed and no solution to the city's problems was in sight. They continued to stress that Flint's water was undrinkable, that little was being done to fix the problem, and that officials did not care whether residents lived or died.

The 24/7 protest never happened, but Flint was not done fighting yet. In April, two pieces of news broke that simultaneously brought the activists' struggle full-circle and kindled it anew. On the 4th, Governor Snyder announced that he was officially ending all vestiges of state receivership in Flint: home rule was, at last, restored. Then, on the 6th, in a development that did not seem coincidental, the state announced that it was closing the city's remaining water PODs, marking the end of state-provided bottled water. Five days later, I joined two busloads of activists on an emergency trip to the State Capitol. We rallied on the Capitol steps and disrupted the state legislature with chants of "DO YOUR JOBS! OPEN THE PODS! WATER FOR FLINT, *NOT* NESTLÉ!" On the 25th, the four-year anniversary of the switch to the Flint River, we were back, protesting outside the offices of the MDEQ, as state police blocked the front doors and hazy faces grinned at us through the windows above.

And thus, the fight for water, for justice, for a democratic future beyond emergency management, went on: in fits and starts, through concord and disagreement, walking a fine line between the pride, and the peril, of self-determination.

Conclusion

Water has a way of encouraging us to think about society at its most elemental level. The provision of clean, safe water is one of the cornerstones of civilization, a precondition of everything else that human beings have achieved or can achieve. More than with any other essential natural resource, accessing water depends upon intricate forms of social coordination: to transport it, to treat it, to sell it, to monitor its quality, to return it to nature after it has passed through human bodies and infrastructures. Our use of water depends also on whether or not, when told we can drink it by the authorities that watch over us, we believe. How we deliver clean, safe water, who is most likely to get it, and whether or not we feel we can trust it when it arrives may not tell us everything we need to know about the societies we live in, but tells us a great deal.

Within the American political tradition as it has come down to us, democracy is equally elemental. It is supposed to be the foundation of our common identity, the basis of our political decision making and of our culture. It is supposed to embody our principles, the value we place on freedom, on equality, on human life. And we are supposed to have faith that even when democracy is hard, even when it doesn't produce the outcomes we seek, it is still the best available form of human association.

Claire McClinton liked to say that for people not to have clean water, and not to have democracy—in the twenty-first century, in the United States of America—was "unthinkable."

Ironically, it is often the unthinkable that most makes us think. It is in those moments when the taken-for-grantedness of everyday life is shattered that the foundations of our social existence are exposed to view. When the water that we use to make our coffee and bathe our children is poisoned by "policy," it is marked with the failures of our social institutions, and with the social injustices that force some more than others to bear the brunt of those failures. And sometimes the failures are so big, the injustices so glaring, that things actually change.

After Flint, some things changed. Cities around the country started proactively identifying and replacing their lead lines. Utilities started offering free water testing to residents and refining their corrosion control protocols. The Environmental Protection Agency sped up its ongoing efforts to revise the Lead and Copper Rule.[1] State regulatory agencies heightened their vigilance. Drinking water infrastructure became—at least officially—a national priority.

Whether Flint will help to provoke similar changes in the area of municipal democracy remains to be seen. In October 2017, the US Supreme Court dashed one of activists' last hopes of bringing down Michigan's emergency manager law through the legal system when it declined to consider whether the law was constitutional.[2] This decision left in effect the Sixth Circuit Court's affirmation of the principle that states have "absolute discretion" over the powers granted to "political subdivisions."

If the water movement in Flint proved anything, however, it was that there are other kinds of power that matter, too. Even in an utterly disenfranchised city, where elected representatives are little more than figureheads and where the most sacred emblem of democracy, the vote, is profaned by futility, it is still possible for the "people" to make their power known. The people of Flint made their power known whenever they organized a rally or a march, whenever they delivered petitions or carried out direct actions, whenever they pushed their own "narrative" of the crisis or commandeered the language and methods of science to show that the official narrative was false.

Some interpreters of what happened in Flint have described it as a "miracle," a chance concatenation of capable grassroots leaders and well-placed allies rarely seen in other environmental justice struggles and not likely to be duplicated.[3] The activists I knew resisted that notion. They saw the water movement as a reawakening of the plucky, democratic spirit that had always formed a part of the city's identity—the spirit that had carried the sit-down strikers through the winter of 1937, that had brought advocates of fair housing to City Hall with their sleeping bags, that had steeled the opponents of the Genesee Power Station against the further pollution of their air. The renewal of that spirit could not have come at a more critical time—not only because lives depended on it, but also because the city was in need of a definitive rebuke to the idea that it could not manage on its own.

Paul Jordan, the lifelong Flint resident who stood in front of City Hall in 2011 to announce the first legal challenge to Public Act 4, described the water crisis to me as a "quantification of the risk of the loss of democracy." In any "sane world," he mused, the crisis would "increase the value of democracy."[4]

Some in Flint had always been convinced of that value. Others had learned it the hard way: in the medium of skin, and hair, and brain, and lung. What they had also learned, however, was that "democracy" could not simply be quashed by fiat. It was not just an absence in Flint, expunged through the abrogation of representative institutions, but a presence—a presence that the people of Flint themselves were actively creating, driven by pathos as much as politics, in an example to the world of what the democratic spirit looks like when imbued with the urgency of life itself.

Notes

Preface and Acknowledgments

1. RealtyTrac, "U.S. Residential Property Vacancy Rate Drops 9.3 Percent," February 9, 2016, https://wpnewsroom.realtytrac.com/news/u-s-q1-2016-u-s-residential-property-vacancy-analysis/.

2. In 2006, the Flint public school system was the eighth largest in the state. By 2015, it had fallen to fifty-fourth. Julie Mack, "Michigan's 30 Largest School Districts Now Compared to 2006," *MLive*, May 12, 2016, https://www.mlive.com/news/index.ssf/2016/05/michigans_30_largest_school_di.html.

3. Richard O. Boyer and Herbert M. Morais write of the strikers that "it was their firmness that built the CIO, that made a hundred other unions possible, that cracked the open shop, that filled the common people, the working people, with a great thrill and resolve." *Labor's Untold Story*, 303. For general accounts of the strike, see Kraus, *The Many and the Few*, and Fine, *Sit-Down*.

4. The democratic potential contained in the sit-down strike, a constant touchstone for Flint activists, is highlighted by Jeremy Brecher: "The principles under which [workers] could govern their own activity can be seen in the self-organization of the sitdown strikers.... All those who worked together simply met in assembly and made the decisions that affected their common activity, and all were responsible for doing their share of carrying the decisions out. ... They could have run not only the sitdown but the factory itself in this way." *Strike!*, 306.

5. One of the images created by activists to advertise what turned out to be a seminal water march in February 2015 was superimposed on a photograph of the sleep-in protestors. It read: "Lest we forget. These people would not accept the idea they were inferior. Don't forget the '67 Sleep-ins! First in the nation to ban housing discrimination." And: "Fighting for people's rights is a Flint tradition."

6. See Clark and Kramer, "'An Equal Opportunity Lie.'"

7. The EPA ruled against claims of environmental racism in this case, but the facility was never built. See Buford and Lombardi, "Steel Mill That Never Was," and Dawson, "Lessons Learned from Flint, Michigan."

8. Hillary Clinton, in particular, sought to distinguish herself as a champion of the city. She later suggested that her "advocacy for the heavily African American community of Flint" may have "alienated white voters in other parts of Michigan," and cost her the state in both the primary and general elections. Clinton, *What Happened*, 214.

9. See, for example, Clark, *The Poisoned City*, and Hanna-Attisha, *What the Eyes Don't See*.

Timeline

1. Ron Fonger, "Flint Council Votes to Do 'All Things Necessary' to End Use of Flint River," *MLive*, March 23, 2015, https://www.mlive.com/news/flint/index.ssf/2015/03/flint_council_votes_to_do_all.html.

2. Randy Conat, "Coalition Wants Flint to Return to Detroit Water," ABC12, June 5, 2015, https://www.abc12.com/home/headlines/Coalition-wants-Flint-to-return-to-Detroit-water-306325041.html.

Introduction

1. For a detailed breakdown of Flint's water rates, see Raftelis Financial Consultants, Inc., *Flint Water Rate Analysis Final Report*.

2. In addition to Flint, the KWA is comprised of the City of Lapeer and the counties of Genesee, Lapeer, and Sanilac. Mayor Dayne Walling claimed that "Flint would save $19 million over eight years" as well as seeing "the additional benefits of partial ownership and economic development" by joining the KWA. Genesee County Drain Commissioner Jeff Wright promised, similarly, that "the city would pay roughly $6.4 million annually for water service if it joined the pipeline—a nearly $4 million savings on what it pays Detroit for water." See Dominic Adams, "'Biggest Decision for City in Decades' Is Proposal to Join Regional Pipeline, Says Flint Mayor," *MLive*, March 16, 2013, https://www.mlive.com/news/flint/index.ssf/2013/03/flint_mayor_dayne_walling_says_10.html.

3. Melissa Mays, personal interview with author, Flint, MI, February 17, 2016.

4. Dominic Adams, "Flint to Spend $171,000 for Engineering to Treat Flint River Water While KWA Pipeline Is Built," *MLive*, July 8, 2013, https://www.mlive.com/news/flint/index.ssf/2013/07/flint_to_spend_171000_for_engi.html.

5. Dominic Adams, "Closing the Valve on History: Flint Cuts Water Flow from Detroit after Nearly 50 Years," *MLive*, April 25, 2014, https://www.mlive.com/news/flint/index.ssf/2014/04/closing_the_valve_on_history_f.html.

6. Stephen Busch, Lansing and Jackson district supervisor in the Office of Drinking Water and Municipal Assistance at the MDEQ, quoted in Adams, "Closing the Valve on History."

7. Ron Fonger, "State Says Flint River Water Meets All Standards but More than Twice the Hardness of Lake Water," *MLive*, May 23, 2014, https://www.mlive.com/news/flint/index.ssf/2014/05/state_says_flint_river_water_m.html.

8. Adams, "Closing the Valve on History."

9. Dominic Adams, "Flint Mayor Takes to Twitter to See How Residents Like Flint River Water," *MLive*, April 28, 2014, https://www.mlive.com/news/flint/index.ssf/2014/04/switch_to_flint_river_for_city.html.

10. Ron Fonger, "Flint Water Supervisor Warned State of Problems before Switch to River," *MLive*, February 12, 2016, https://www.mlive.com/news/flint/index.ssf/2016/02/flint_water_supervisor_warned.html.

11. Governor Rick Snyder himself called the crisis his "Katrina." Ron Fournier, "Snyder Concedes Flint is His 'Katrina,' a Failure of Leadership," *National Journal*, January 18, 2016.

12. In June 2016, Attorney General Bill Schuette filed civil charges against private contractors Lockwood, Andrews, and Newnam, Inc., and Veolia, alleging professional negligence and, in Veolia's case, fraud.

13. Counts, "How Government Poisoned the People of Flint."

14. Ron Fonger, "Emergency Manager Calls City Council's Flint River Vote 'Incomprehensible'," *MLive*, March 24, 2015, https://www.mlive.com/news/flint/index.ssf/2015/03/flint_emergency_manager_calls.html.

15. Some may question my use of the term "movement" to refer to the relatively small and loosely integrated network of water activists in Flint. I have adopted the term, in part, because it connotes an overarching continuity of purpose across the ebb and flow of activism, the formation and dissolution of various alliances, and the activities of different groups. More importantly, it reflects my determination to accord respect to the self-definition of the activists, who insisted that they were part of a "movement" and not just a "moment." Whether Flint's water activism qualifies as a "movement" in a sociological sense I leave up to the reader to decide.

16. The fact that I was a resident of Flint for a large portion of the time span encompassed in this book gave my research some of the strengths and limitations of "native ethnography." On one hand, my resident status accorded me some automatic credibility and allowed me access to people and spaces I would not otherwise have had. On the other hand, as a mostly trusted "insider," I sometimes felt obliged to guard insider "intimacies" and pressured to avoid airing the activists' dirty laundry (see Rolston, *Mining Coal and Undermining Gender*, 29). In this book, I have had

to walk a fine line between my desire to be candid about the activist movement and my desire to preserve personal relationships, with long-term residence in the city in mind. I would argue, however, that my own entanglement in controversies within the activist community has given me a sense of entitlement to speak more freely than I may have if I were observing the etiquette of a guest, an ally, or a sympathetic outsider. It is worth noting, also, the ways in which my ethnographic work was less than fully "native": I was working within a newly adopted community into which I was still very imperfectly integrated, without prior kinship relations or friendships to use as resources. In this respect, many of the challenges I faced were similar to those faced by a traditional ethnographer.

17. This criticism focused on a letter written by Kettering University President Robert McMahan and sent to parents and alumni on January 18, 2016, which stressed that the water at Kettering was safe and sought to correct "misinformation" about the nature of the lead contamination and extent of the confirmed harms.

18. In an added twist, though not one of any real consequence for my credibility within the community, my institution's namesake, Charles Kettering, is generally credited with the introduction of lead into gasoline—an innovation meant to solve the problem of "engine knock" but having the effect of dispersing the toxic metal into the environment through car exhaust. The blood lead level of the average American plummeted after leaded gasoline was phased out in the 1970s and 1980s, but the legacy of the contamination persists to this day, especially in tainted soil.

19. Goffman, *On the Run*, 237.

20. Desiree Duell, personal interview with author, Flint, MI, August 24, 2016.

21. See the work of the We the People of Detroit Community Research Collective, "Mapping the Water Crisis."

22. Fortun, *Advocacy after Bhopal*, 1.

23. One limitation of my research is that I did not travel with the activists on most of their numerous trips to Lansing, Washington, D.C., or the places around the state and country where they were invited to speak. Thus, my field site did not range over the full scope of the territory traversed by the activists.

24. Steffen Dalsgaard argues that "if his or her interlocutors use Facebook, so should the ethnographer." "The Ethnographic Use of Facebook in Everyday Life," 97. I came to see Facebook (more so than Twitter) as an extension of the community, "holistically entangled" (as Dalsgaard puts it) with offline interactions, and therefore critical to understanding them (98).

25. Juris, "Practicing Militant Ethnography," 164–166.

26. I follow Myron Aronoff and Jan Kubik in regarding the essence of ethnography as "participant observation, a disciplined immersion in the social life of a given group of

people," and in-depth interviews as supplementary to this activity. Aronoff and Kubik, *Anthropology and Political Science*, 28.

27. The endnotes in this book reflect the fact that I have made extensive use of local news sources for basic factual information about the crisis and its surrounding context. I am fully aware of their limitations. While I have not knowingly included any inaccurate claims from these sources, I have not done the extensive investigative work that would be required to thoroughly vet each and every one. I use these sources not necessarily because they offer the final word on what "really happened," but because they are useful in establishing the context in which activists exercised political agency in Flint. Although activists were often skeptical of local news coverage of the crisis, their understanding of what was going on at any particular time was heavily mediated by that coverage, especially as relayed in the steady stream of breaking news posts to Facebook.

28. Because the crisis and the people working to resolve it received substantial press coverage from late 2015 on, almost everyone quoted or otherwise referenced in this book is already on record expressing their thoughts about the crisis, and I have sometimes drawn from these secondary sources rather than my own interviews for choice quotes. The existence of this extensive public record is one of the reasons why I have made the carefully considered decision to refer to my sources (with their permission) by their real names rather than pseudonymizing them. There is another important reason, however. While preserving anonymity is sometimes a necessary means of protecting people whose safety or reputations would be compromised by identification, it also has the unfortunate effect of depriving "ordinary" people of the credit they deserve for their activism. Powerful public figures get named because their prior visibility makes it impossible and unnecessary not to name them; however, too often, the real protagonists of the stories academics tell must content themselves with indirect recognition. Not so in this book.

29. It should be clear by now that I arrived at these themes reflexively, in dialogue with activists, rather than adopting the positivist method of investigating preconstituted "facts." On reflexive science, see Burawoy, "The Extended Case Method."

30. For a similarly broad way of conceiving of water justice, see Zwarteveen and Boelens, "Defining, Researching and Struggling for Water Justice." The authors argue that "definitions and understandings of justice cannot be based only on abstract notions of 'what should be,' but also need to be anchored in how injustices are experienced. They need to be related both to the diverse 'local' perceptions of equity and to the discourses, constructs, and procedures of formal justice" (147).

31. Sze and London, "Environmental Justice at the Crossroads," 1347. Jeffrey Juris explains that one of the goals of militant ethnography is "to facilitate ongoing activist (self-)reflection regarding movement goals, tactics, strategies, and organizational forms" ("Practicing Militant Ethnography," 165). David Graeber suggests that the

ethnographer can even engage in a kind of "utopian extrapolation," "teasing out the tacit logic or principles underlying certain forms of radical practice, and then, not only offering the analysis back to those communities, but using them to formulate new visions." *Possibilities*, 310.

32. Examples include, but are not limited to, Levine, *Love Canal*; Brown and Mikkelsen, *No Safe Place*; Checker, *Polluted Promises*; Lerner, *Diamond*; and McGurty, *Transforming Environmentalism*.

33. I take inspiration from Erikson's counsel that "there are times when the need for generalizations must yield to the urgency of passing events, times when the event must tell its own story." *Everything in Its Path*, 12. Bent Flyvbjerg reminds us in "Five Misunderstandings about Case-Study Research" that good case study narratives "typically approach the complexities and contradictions of real life," and that "a particularly 'thick' and hard-to-summarize narrative is not a problem. Rather, it is often a sign that the study has uncovered a particularly rich problematic" (21).

34. Harvey, "Militant Particularism and Global Ambition," 83–84.

35. As Kim Fortun writes, one of "the most stubborn dilemmas of advocacy" is "the need to render one's object of concern in all its particularity so that justice is not lost to grand schemes and glossy claims—while, at the same time, showing how 'the problem' one is concerned about crosscuts time and space, demanding a systemic response." *Advocacy after Bhopal*, 14.

36. See especially Mohai, "Environmental Justice and the Flint Water Crisis."

37. Karen Bakker, for example, argues that the notion that water is a "human right," often presented as antithetical to the privatization of water, is in fact compatible with it. For discussion, see Sultana and Loftus, *The Right to Water*.

38. See Swyngedouw and Heynen, "Urban Political Ecology, Justice and the Politics of Scale."

39. Swyngedouw and Kaika, "Urban Political Ecology," 472.

40. Swyngedouw and Kaika, 472.

41. Pellow, *Garbage Wars*, 3.

42. To illustrate the consequences of proceeding from the "inside out," it is instructive to consider the application of the concept of "environmental racism" to the water crisis. The term has been used by many commentators to describe the crisis, with the suggestion that Flint's majority-minority demographics help to explain everything from the decision to use the Flint River to the official skepticism that greeted residents' early concerns about the water. What I encountered on the ground among activists, however, were complex feelings about race that included, in some cases, outright hostility to racial framings of the crisis and, in many others, the desire

to emphasize other demographic factors (particularly class) in preference to race (see chapter 5). While considerations of race of course factor centrally into many aspects of the story I tell in this book, I have for the aforementioned reasons chosen not to make environmental racism one of the book's orienting concepts.

43. I was not able to conduct any kind of sustained investigation into why most residents did *not* engage in water activism (à la, e.g., Bell, *Fighting King Coal*). It was a common lament among the activists that more people did not turn out to meetings, rallies, and marches. Some had visions of mobilizing thousands or even tens of thousands of residents, but aside from a core group of hardcore activists who were almost always involved in something or other, people came and went. While some were active as early as spring 2014, others did not show up to a meeting until 2017. Flint's relative lack of social capital undoubtedly played a role in limiting the scope, consistency, and impact of local water activism. What I call "activism" in this book, however—focusing on relatively traditional forms of collective action—was but a piece of the overall mobilization of Flint residents around the crisis. It is important to recognize, with Anna Lora-Wainwright in *Resigned Activism*, that "activism" more broadly defined comes in diverse forms, many of which are invisible—even, often, to the ethnographer. It is also worth pointing out that some who call themselves "activists" do little, seemingly, to earn the designation, while others who are very "active" are uncomfortable with it. Of those who were most involved in water activism in Flint, a handful were longtime activists who self-identified as such and felt a strong sense of connection to other activists past and present. Most, however, were novices who wore the label "activist" uncomfortably, as if it was a new piece of clothing still being broken in. Some came to embrace the label fully and consistently, others more hesitantly and sporadically.

44. Swyngedouw and Heynen, "Urban Political Ecology, Justice and the Politics of Scale," 909.

45. Harvey, *Spaces of Hope*, 241.

46. What activists meant by "local control" encompassed, roughly, what is meant by the term "home rule," a term that I will use when referring to the right of municipalities to determine their own forms of government, pass ordinances, and run their own affairs more generally. The term "home rule" was less familiar to the average activist, however, and did not, from what I could tell, resonate as strongly as its more intuitive alternative.

47. Claire McClinton, personal interview with author, Flint, MI, September 11, 2018.

48. This was the language used by Simone Lightfoot, Director of National Urban Initiatives at the National Wildlife Federation, at the second annual environmental justice summit in Flint, March 2018.

49. See Finewood and Holifield, "Critical Approaches to Urban Water Governance," and Susskind, "Water and Democracy."

50. Cameron Harrington calls for the "realignment away from viewing collaborative governance as a depoliticized process of negotiation where shared and/or competing visions of water management are peaceably managed." "The Political Ontology of Collaborative Water Governance," 265.

51. Jaime Hoogesteger, for example, has highlighted the importance of "contentious actions" in moving from "mere participation in government programs to becoming active in the elaboration and implementation of water policies even in the absence of formal participatory spaces." "Democratizing Water Governance from the Grassroots," 83.

52. On rendering water "technical" as a way of depoliticizing it, see Joy, Kulkarni, Roth, and Zwarteveen, "Repoliticising Water Governance." See also Swyngedouw, "The Antinomies of the Postpolitical City." On the notion of "rendering technical" more generally, see Li, "Rendering Society Technical." Jason Corburn points out that "deliberative forums … rarely have found a way to avoid granting science and technical expertise a privileged position in the discourse." *Street Science*, 43.

53. In a review of literature on the subject of regionalization in the mid-90s, political scientist Janice Beecher noted that "The strong desire to maintain local control" was a "significant barrier to regionalization." *The Regionalization of Water Utilities*, 3. More recent research suggests that this desire continues to act as a barrier: e.g., Hansen, "Community Water System Regionalization and Stakeholder Implications."

54. Penny Harvey and Hannah Knox, for example, describe infrastructures "as dynamic relational forms" with "political implications" (*Roads*, 4–5), while Nikhil Anand writes that "Infrastructures are neither ontologically prior to politics nor are they merely effects of social organization. Infrastructures are flaky accretions of sociomaterial *processes* that are brought into being through relations *with* human bodies, discourses, and other things" (*Hydraulic City*, 13).

55. The point was influentially made by Susan Leigh Star in "The Ethnography of Infrastructure." Nikhil Anand applies the idea to Flint in "The Banality of Infrastructure."

56. Graham, *Disrupted Cities*, 3.

57. For a useful account of large technical systems, see Hughes, "The Evolution of Large Technical Systems."

58. This is one of the central insights of recent ethnographies of infrastructure. For examples, see Björkman, *Pipe Politics*; Von Schnitzler, *Democracy's Infrastructure*; and Anand, *Hydraulic City*.

59. Furlong, "Small Technologies, Big Change."

60. Much has been said about the democratizing implications of citizen science. In "When Citizen Science Meets Science Policy," Eric Kennedy, for example, writes that citizen science "is part of a much larger call for renewed and reinvigorated forms

of democracy," and that its democratizing quality "is found in the emerging push to include previously marginalized communities in government decision-making and scientific processes; to increase participation in democratic processes among youth and other communities; to make data and research more openly accessible and freely available" (46). Citizen science, Kennedy continues, "pushes for a science that is inclusive, open, and transparent. It calls for the remaking of expert processes in ways that invite new members to the table, and that allow avenues for all communities to feel ownership and opportunity when it comes to scientific processes. And it holds research—especially publicly funded research—to account through demands for open access, open data, and open lines of communication with researchers and users. Ultimately, it aspires to open pathways for participation in science, and to influence decision making, to anyone who seeks them." Citizen science is "subversive," he argues, because it makes "participatory methods ... the norm" (47).

61. Cooper and Lewenstein, "Two Meanings of Citizen Science," 59.

62. Cooper and Lewenstein, 59.

63. At least some of his inspiration seems to have come from the account of narrative found in Olson, *Houston, We Have a Narrative*.

64. Eventbrite, event description entry, "Citizen Science and the Flint Water Crisis: Triumph, Tragedy, and Misconduct," American University, February 8, 2018.

65. Even the application of the term "citizen science" to the collaboration is to some extent a reflection of these incongruities. There are a number of other terms in existence that arguably do a better job of capturing the kind of community-driven research typical of environmental justice activism, including "participatory action research," "activist-mobilized science," and "street science." See Baum, MacDougall, and Smith, "Participatory Action Research"; Conde, "Activism Mobilising Science"; and Corburn, *Street Science*.

66. Ottinger, "Social Movement-Based Citizen Science," 90.

67. Ottinger, 91.

68. Conde, "Activism Mobilising Science," 68.

69. Harding, "Rethinking Standpoint Epistemology." Additionally, coproductionist accounts of science challenge us to consider whether *any* science is truly value neutral or immune to social influences. See Jasanoff, *States of Knowledge*.

70. For application of the concept in an environmental justice context, see Allen, *Uneasy Alchemy*.

71. Some have suggested that science conducted under these conditions is inherently "post-normal." See, for example, Bidwell, "Is Community-Based Participatory Research

Postnormal Science?" Drawing from the influential work of Silvio Funtowicz and
Jerome Ravetz, Bidwell writes that post-normal science takes more than just traditionally defined scientific facts into consideration, including "community values, history,
personal experiences, and other types of information not traditionally considered
legitimate in research on environmental health" (748).

72. Pellow, "Popular Epidemiology and Environmental Movements," 309.

1 Flint First

1. Hanna-Attisha, LaChance, Sadler, and Schnepp, "Elevated Blood Lead Levels,"
283–290.

2. Associated Press, "Doctors Warn Flint of High Lead Levels in Tap Water," *Detroit
News*, September 24, 2015, https://www.detroitnews.com/story/news/local/michigan
/2015/09/24/flint-plans-advisory-curbing-exposure-lead/72725736/.

3. Mona Hanna-Attisha, press conference, Hurley Medical Center, Flint, MI, September 24, 2015.

4. All quotes from the testimony of Hanna-Attisha are derived from the author's field
notes and the video record of the Meeting of the Joint Committee on the Flint Water
Public Health Emergency, University of Michigan–Flint, Flint, MI, March 29, 2016.

5. Snyder is quoted in Chad Livengood and Keith Laing, "Flint Aid Fight Escalates as
Federal Funding Stalls," *Detroit News*, April 15, 2016.

6. See the House Fiscal Agency memo from March 7 for a summary of allocated and
requested funds around this time. Memorandum by Mary Ann Cleary, Michigan
House Fiscal Committee, "Flint Water Emergency Appropriations," revised April 29,
2016, https://www.house.mi.gov/hfa/PDF/Alpha/Flint_Water_Emergency_Memo.pdf.

7. For another statement of Hanna-Attisha's argument for prioritizing Flint, see
Hanna-Attisha, "The Future for Flint's Children."

8. Technically, Hanna-Attisha said that "no other *state* was poisoned by policy" rather
than no other *city*. I later confirmed with her that she misspoke, having intended to
say "city." This is clearly what the audience took her to mean.

9. Pastor Alfred Harris, personal interview with author, Flint, MI, February 28, 2017.
The Saint Paul quote is from Romans 8:28.

10. For another nationwide comparison of blood lead levels, see Shah et al., "Blood
Lead Concentrations," 218–223. It is also worth mentioning that while Flint's lead
levels spiked temporarily due to an unusual confluence of circumstances, communities suffering from more typical forms of lead exposure through paint and soil see
high rates year after year. One important caveat in assessing the quantity of harm
in Flint, however, is that the impact of elevated blood lead is not linear—low doses

have been found to have a larger proportional impact (i.e., increasing BLLs from 1 to 2 μg /dL is worse than increasing 10 to 11 μg /dL). Lanphear et al., "Low-Level Environmental Lead Exposure," 894–899. For overviews of changing understandings of the prevalence and significance of childhood lead poisoning, see Christian Warren, *Brush with Death*, and Markowitz and Rosner, *Lead Wars*.

11. Marc Edwards, talk at Hurley Medical Center, Flint, MI, December 2, 2015.

12. Edwards, "Fetal Death and Reduced Birth Rates," 739–746.

13. Some suggested that lead ingested through drinking water would simply be urinated out of the body without entering the blood. After a flawed CDC study seemed to show no detrimental effects in D.C., Edwards did his own study that confirmed a correlation between high lead in water and high blood lead. Edwards, Triantafyllidou, and Best, "Elevated Blood Lead," 1618–1623.

14. Milloy, "EPA's Lead Heads."

15. "Political Insider Bill Ballenger Fired after Questioning If Flint Water Is a Crisis, Saying It Didn't Hurt Him," CBS Detroit, January 20, 2016, https://detroit.cbslocal.com/2016/01/20/michigan-political-analyst-fired-after-criticizing-flint-water-crisis-as-a-hoax/. Ballenger maintained that neither he nor anyone in his neighborhood experienced issues with the water and disputed the claim that children testing positive for elevated lead were exposed through water.

16. Ron Fonger, "Flint Water Crisis Was 'Overplayed,' Michigan DEQ Exec Tells Investigator," *MLive*, June 1, 2016, https://www.mlive.com/news/index.ssf/2016/06/high-ranking_michigan_deq_offi.html. Reynolds called Sygo's account of the incident that led to this accusation "a complete fabrication." Another MDEQ employee, Bryce Feighner, said that residents had been hurt more by "hype" than they had by their water; see Garret Ellison, "Treating River Water Would Not Have Prevented Flint Crisis, DEQ Official Says," *MLive*, April 28, 2017, https://www.mlive.com/news/index.ssf/2017/04/bryce_feighner_mdeq_flint_wate.html.

17. Ballenger, in fact, was fired from his position as a contributor to the *Inside Michigan Politics* newsletter.

18. Other than a "public relations crisis," that is, which Ari Adler, a communications staff member in Governor Snyder's office, warned that the situation was shaping up to be in January 2015. Jake May, "Debunking 4 Claims."

19. Ron Fonger, "Flint Residents Call for Investigative Hearings into 'Water Crisis,'" *MLive*, January 5, 2015, https://www.mlive.com/news/flint/index.ssf/2015/01/state_deq_high_levels_of_disin.html.

20. Snyder requested $96 million in federal aid for service lines, water, and filters. See Chad Livengood and Jonathan Oosting, "Snyder to Appeal Obama's Denial of Flint Disaster Zone," *Detroit News*, January 17, 2016.

21. Activists were especially interested in the precedent set in Libby, Montana, where the federal government extended Medicare coverage to the whole community, irrespective of age, to help compensate for harms caused by asbestos contamination from vermiculite mining. In Flint, Medicaid was temporarily expanded to cover everyone in the city under twenty-one as well as pregnant women. See Smith, "Why Medicare for Libby and Medicaid for Flint?" For an overview of the Libby affair, see Schneider and McCumber, *An Air That Kills*. The authors describe Libby as "the single worst event the EPA had ever encountered" due to the pervasiveness of the contamination and its terrible human toll, including hundreds of deaths from asbestosis (162).

22. Pastor Alfred Harris, interview, February 28, 2017.

23. Nayyirah Shariff, "Flint: As 2 Unelected Emergency Managers Are Charged over Water Poisoning, Will Gov. Snyder Be Next?," interview by Amy Goodman, *Democracy Now!*, December 21, 2016.

24. One person to use this concept explicitly was environmental justice scholar Paul Mohai in testimony to the Michigan Civil Rights Commission. Mohai said that Flint had experienced a "severe environmental and health burden" that was "an environmental injustice by itself." Hearings on the Flint Water Crisis before the Michigan Civil Rights Commission (September 8, 2016). Written Testimony of Paul Mohai, Professor of Natural Resources and the Environment, University of Michigan.

25. Schlosberg, *Environmental Justice and the New Pluralism*, 12.

26. The ability to quantify harm, particularly bodily harm, is especially important under conditions of economic and political disenfranchisement, when establishing an entitlement to state resources to rectify injuries can offer a kind of "biological citizenship," a place within an otherwise disinterested body politic. See Petryna, *Life Exposed*.

27. Even in well-known and seemingly clear-cut cases of environmental catastrophe and contamination, like the nuclear accident at Chernobyl and the leaching of buried chemical waste at Love Canal, New York, the relationship between exposure to contaminants and subsequent health impairments is often highly ambiguous. For an excellent account of the ambiguities of epidemiology of this kind, see Fagin, *Toms River*.

28. James Felton, "Family Upset over Lack of Legislation on Lead Limit," WNEM, September 16, 2016.

29. Emily Lawler, "43 Flint Residents Identified with Elevated Lead Levels So Far, Urged To Take Precautions," *MLive*, January 7, 2016, https://www.mlive.com/lansing-news/index.ssf/2016/01/43_flint_residents_identified.html.

30. Gómez et al., "Blood Lead Levels." The authors note that "whereas the GM [geometric mean] BLL increased during the Flint River water switch, the increase was no greater than the random increase noted from 2010 to 2011, and GM BLLs in Flint

have since returned to historical lows" (6). For an earlier challenge to Hanna-Attisha's work, see Campbell, Hanna-Attisha, and LaChance, "Flint Blood Lead Levels," e6.

31. Hanna-Attisha, "Don't Downplay Lead Problems." Gómez and his coauthors admit that within their sample "no child tested was young enough to be formula dependent. Therefore, changes in BLLs in the very young from water used in formula preparation during 2014–2015 Flint River water switch cannot be determined." For an analysis more compatible with that of Hanna-Attisha's, see Zahran, McElmurry, and Sadler, "Four Phases." Hanna-Attisha was also involved in an effort to assess whether lead exposure caused a decline in fertility rates in Flint. Although her own study petered out, two other studies on the same topic touched off yet another debate. In a working paper, two economists, Daniel Grossman and David Slusky, claimed that the uptick in miscarriages and fetal deaths during Flint's time on the river was "horrifyingly large" ("Effect of an Increase in Lead," 32). The DHHS, however, challenged the methodology of the study (Paneth, "Review") and reported its own preliminary finding that there was no adverse effect on birth outcomes whatsoever (Ron Fonger, "'Serious Concerns' about Study Claiming Flint Water Increased Fetal Deaths," *MLive*, September 28, 2017, https://www.mlive.com/news/flint/index.ssf/2017/09/state_ques tions_study_that_cla.html). For a revised version of Grossman and Slusky's paper, see Grossman and Slusky, "The Impact of the Flint Water Crisis on Fertility."

32. Gómez and Dietrich, "The Children of Flint."

33. Jan Worth-Nelson, "Citizens to Hurley Board: 'Lead-Exposed' Word Change 'Preposterous,' and Devastating to Trust," *East Village Magazine*, May 31, 2018.

34. Unified Coordination Group, *Flint Rash Investigation*. It is important to note the limitations of the CDC study, which failed to incorporate case controls that would have allowed for meaningful comparisons. While the study raised the possibility that rashes developed while Flint was on the river may have resulted from excessive chlorination, it was unable to confirm this retrospectively.

35. Zahran et al., "Legionnaires' Disease Outbreak."

36. "Numerous Flaws Found in Flint Area Community Health and Environment Partnership Journal Articles," Michigan.gov, February 5, 2018, https://www.michi gan.gov/som/0,4669,7-192-29942-459450--,00.html.

37. Byrne et al., "Serogroup 6 *Legionella pneumophila*."

38. Reports by *Bridge* magazine in January 2017 and PBS Frontline in July 2018 seemed to validate popular suspicions that many cases diagnosed as generic pneumonia were in fact Legionnaires'. *Bridge* suggested that, given the abnormally high number of deaths from "pneumonia" during that time span (an average of 88.5 per year, contrasted with 53 in 2013), the actual number of deaths from Legionnaires' was likely much higher. Dawsey, "Soaring Pneumonia Deaths." For Frontline's coverage, see Ruble et al., "Flint Water Crisis Deaths."

39. Leonard N. Fleming, "Expert in Flint Case: Man Didn't Die from Legionnaires'," *Detroit News*, March 23, 2018.

40. For a general treatment of psychological harm and environmental contamination, see Edelstein, *Contaminated Communities*.

41. Residents sometimes spoke of an entire city suffering from post-traumatic stress disorder (PTSD). And, in fact, there was data to support that characterization: a county health survey conducted in the middle of the crisis found that negative perceptions of water quality were indeed correlated with PTSD symptoms. Kruger, Cupal, Kodjebacheva, and Fockler, "Perceived Water Quality." A study done by the CDC in May 2016 found that 38.0 percent of Flint residents surveyed reported having poor mental health compared to 12.9 percent of the total population of Michigan. Centers for Disease Control and Prevention, *Community Assessment for Public Health Emergency Response (CASPER)*.

42. Abby Goodnough and Scott Atkinson, "A Potent Side Effect to the Flint Water Crisis: Mental Health Problems," *New York Times*, April 30, 2016; Marion V. Day, "Flint Water Crisis Has Physical and Psychological Impact," *MLive*, February 29, 2016, https://www.mlive.com/news/flint/index.ssf/2016/02/flint_water_crisis_has_physica.html; and Melikian, "Psychological Damage."

43. Drum, "Lead."

44. Liu, "Marc Edwards."

45. Marc Edwards, "Research Update: Corrosivity of Flint Water to Iron Pipes in the City—A Costly Problem," September 29, 2015, http://flintwaterstudy.org/2015/09/research-update-corrosivity-of-flint-water-to-iron-pipes-in-the-city-a-costly-problem/.

46. Pruett, "Rebuild Flint the Right Way."

47. The estimate is from Pruett, "Rebuild Flint the Right Way." See also Mark Guarino, "New Crisis for Flint Residents: Cost of Home Damage Caused by City Water," *Washington Post*, January 22, 2016.

48. Zahran, McElmurry, and Sadler, "Four Phases."

49. A report in February 2017 found that "home values in Flint have risen over the past two years, despite the water crisis the city is facing." Mark Bullion, "Flint Housing Market Rebounds amid Water Crisis," ABC12, February 1, 2017, https://www.abc12.com/content/news/Flint-housing-market-rebounds--412476443.html. Homeowners faced other difficulties, though, like the need to prove their water was safe before they were eligible for new loans. Daniel Goldstein, "Lead Poisoning Crisis Sends Flint Real-Estate Market Tumbling," *MarketWatch*, February 17, 2016.

50. Tony Palladeno Jr., quoted in "Green for All, Flint Residents: Absence of Governor Snyder in List of Flint Charges Is Criminal," Green for All, April 20, 2016, https://www.greenforall.org/flint_criminal_charges.

51. Nakiya Wakes quoted in Sara Sidner, "Michigan Governor's Aides Pushed for 'Urgent' Fix to Flint Water Crisis," CNN, February 28, 2016, https://www.cnn.com /2016/02/28/us/flint-governor-emails/index.html.

52. Nayyirah Shariff and Marc Edwards, "'Gov. Snyder Should Be Arrested': Flint Residents Demand Justice over Water Poisoning," interview by Amy Goodman, *Democracy Now!*, January 8, 2016.

53. Paul Egan, "Gov. Rick Snyder Blames 'Career Bureaucrats' for Flint Water Crisis," *Detroit Free Press*, March 17, 2016.

54. Schuette's motives were widely questioned by activists who suspected his gubernatorial ambitions were behind his crusading rhetoric.

55. "Charges Brought against 6 More in Flint Crisis," MSNBC, July 31, 2016, https:// www.msnbc.com/msnbc-news/watch/charges-brought-against-6-more-in-flint-crisis -735643203814?v=raila&.

56. Paul Egan and Elisha Anderson, "Emergency Managers, City Officials Charged in Flint Water Crisis," *Detroit Free Press*, December 20, 2016.

57. Jackman, "Bill Schuette Is Indicting Emergency Managers."

58. For example, the 1983 General Accounting Office study of hazardous waste sites in EPA Region IV (General Accounting Office, "Siting of Hazardous Waste Landfills and Their Correlation with Racial and Economic Status of Surrounding Communities," June 1, 1983); United Church of Christ Commission for Racial Justice, *Toxic Wastes and Race in the United States*; Environmental Protection Agency, *Environmental Equity*; and the pioneering scholarship of Bunyan Bryant and Paul Mohai (*Race and the Incidence of Environmental Hazards*). For discussion of some of the controversy around early studies focusing on distributive injustice, see Taylor, *Toxic Communities*, ch. 2.

59. Young, *Justice and the Politics of Difference*, 23.

60. Principles #5 and #7. For other examples, see Schlosberg, *Defining Environmental Justice*, 65–67. Luke Cole and Sheila Foster write: "The Environmental Justice Movement … has answered the participation question clearly and decisively. The Movement's principles and practice have focused on the idea that communities should speak for themselves, that those who must bear the brunt of a decision should have an equal and influential role in making the decision." *From the Ground Up*, 106.

61. For an application of a slightly different typology of justice to the water crisis, see Perreault, Boelens, and Vos, "Introduction."

62. For useful background, see Benz, "Toxic Cities."

63. See Moss, "Environmental Justice"; Ward, "The Promise of Jobs"; and Cole and Foster, *From the Ground Up*, 124–125. See also Robin Bravender, "Civil Rights

Advocates Despair after Decades of Agency Inaction," *E&E News*, February 19, 2015; Stephens, "The Flint River Lead Poisoning Catastrophe"; and Carpenter, "How the EPA Has Failed."

64. Dorka, *EPA Final Genesee Complaint Letter*, 7. Only one other agency, a California state agency, has been found in "preliminary" violation of the EPA's antidiscrimination regulations since 1994. See "Agreement between Cal. Dep't of Pesticide Regulation and U.S. EPA, Angelita C. v. Cal. Dep't of Pesticide Regulation (Aug. 24, 2011)," https://www.ejnet.org/ej/angelitac-settlement.pdf.

65. Dorka, *EPA Final Genesee Complaint Letter*, 3. The EPA found that the absence of these protections had especially negative consequences for African Americans, people with low English proficiency, and people with physical impairments.

66. Dorka, *EPA Final Genesee Complaint Letter*, 27–28.

67. Dorka, 1.

68. Dorka, 30.

69. The state announced the formation of an Environmental Justice Work Group on February 15, 2017, in direct response to "recommendations from the Flint Water Advisory Task Force and the Flint Water Interagency Coordinating Committee's Policy Subcommittee." See "Environmental Justice Work Group Seeks to Improve State Guidelines and Policy," Michigan.gov, February 15, 2017, https://www.michigan.gov /snyder/0,4668,7-277--405091--,00.html.

70. Gosman, Written Testimony, 10.

71. The "Environmental Justice Work Group Report: Michigan as a Global Leader in Environmental Justice" appeared in March 2018. One of the report's findings was that "the present statutes, regulations, policies, and procedures of the State deprive local governments of utilizing their authority to function for the common good. By substituting its authority for local authority, the State preempts the initiative and responsibilities of local government and curtails any meaningful public involvement in government decision making." The report recommended eliminating "limitations placed on local governments" that hinder the latter's ability "to identify or correct environmental justice problems within their locales" (22).

2   How Did It Happen?

1. *Bridge Magazine* Staff, "Disaster Day by Day." For a compilation of *Bridge Magazine*'s work on the crisis, see Campbell, *Poison on Tap*.

2. Progress Michigan, "Snyder Cherry Picks Flint Water Crisis Emails," January 20, 2016, http://www.progressmichigan.org/2016/01/snyder-cherry-picks-flint-water-crisis -emails/.

3. Dan Kildee, "Statement by Congressman Dan Kildee on Gov. Snyder Declining to Testify on Flint Water Crisis," February 8, 2016, https://dankildee.house.gov/media/press-releases/statement-congressman-dan-kildee-gov-snyder-declining-testify-flint-water.

4. Michigan's notoriously lax sunshine laws (the state was ranked dead last for transparency in a 2015 Center for Public Integrity report) facilitated official obscurantism by exempting communications involving the Governor's office and state legislators from Freedom of Information Act requests. Even state agencies subject to the laws operated within a culture of disregard for such requests. In one instance, the Mackinac Center sued the MDEQ after waiting 121 days for crisis-related documents it was told would take mere hours to process. Some argued that the general atmosphere of inscrutability at the state level emboldened officials to act incautiously and directly contributed to causing and prolonging the crisis. See, for example, Byrnes, "Amid the Flint Water Crisis."

5. Comments from Gerald R. Ford School of Public Policy, University of Michigan panel event, October 24, 2016.

6. For discussion, see chapter 6, "Plot in Narrative," in Scholes, Phelan, and Kellogg, *The Nature of Narrative*, and chapter 9, "Story and Discourse in the Analysis of Narrative," in Culler, *The Pursuit of Signs*.

7. The inevitable ambiguities of environmental contamination events have a way of bringing out the relativity of narratives, as no one account can capture such events in their full complexity. See Mazur, *A Hazardous Inquiry*.

8. See Ganz on the need for movements to construct a "story of now" in "What Is Public Narrative?"

9. On the importance of movements struggling over the terms of public discourse, see Woodly, *The Politics of Common Sense*. As Woodly writes, "Changing public discourse changes power relations, and altered power relations change politics—the principles and policy that are at stake in the struggle over who shall govern and how.... A movement that effectively alters the terms of discourse can overcome considerable opposition and structural disadvantages to achieve sustained, meaningful change" (1).

10. In the social movements literature, frames tend to be treated as conscious conceptual structures that are used by actors in pursuit of strategic ends. This chapter deals with the activists' efforts to construct what Snow and Benford call a "diagnostic" frame that defines a problem and assigns blame, in the service of what they would call "prognostic" and "motivational" frames. See "Ideology, Frame Resonance, and Participant Mobilization." For a general overview of the framing literature, see, by the same authors, "Framing Processes and Social Movements."

11. Brass fixtures made before 2014 could have up to 8 percent lead content and still be considered "lead free."

12. For the connection between low chlorine residuals and bacterial growth, see Zahran et al., "Legionnaires' Disease Outbreak."

13. Marc Edwards, "Why Is It Possible that Flint River Water Cannot Be Treated to Meet Federal Standards?," August 24, 2015, http://flintwaterstudy.org/2015/08/why -is-it-possible-that-flint-river-water-cannot-be-treated-to-meet-federal-standards/.

14. Marc Edwards in Wisely, "Flint River Water."

15. Although environmental engineer Shawn McElmurry acknowledged that "common sense tells you that the Flint River is not your first choice of drinking water" (in John Wisely and Robin Erb, "Chemical Testing Could Have Predicted Flint's Water Crisis," *Detroit Free Press*, October 10, 2015), he, too, concluded that there was "no reason" the river water "could not have been treated properly and used safely." In Jim Lynch, "DEQ: Flint Water Fix Should Have Come by 2014," *Detroit News*, January 21, 2016.

16. In Wisely and Erb, "Chemical Testing."

17. Masten, Davies, and McElmurry, "Flint Water Crisis," 26.

18. Wisely, "Flint River Water."

19. Olson et al., "Forensic Estimates of Lead."

20. Marc Edwards, "Investigation of MDEQ's New 'Corrosion Control' Claim Reveals More Deception and Incompetence: Where Is the EPA?," October 4, 2015, http:// flintwaterstudy.org/2015/10/investigation-of-mdeqs-new-corrosion-control-claim -reveals-more-deception-and-incompetence-where-is-the-epa/.

21. See, for example, Olson, "Science behind the Flint Water Crisis." The MDEQ itself used this language when it issued a *mea culpa* in October 2015. See Ron Fonger, "DEQ Replaces Water Official after State Acknowledges 'Mistake' in Flint," *MLive*, October 19, 2015, https://www.mlive.com/news/flint/index.ssf/2015/10/top_state_water_offi- cial repla.html.

22. In Fonger, "DEQ Replaces Water Official." The "mistake" was so befuddling, however, that even some who were sympathetic to the technical narrative, like EPA on-scene coordinator Mark Durno, were willing to believe that more sinister motives may have been a factor. It was either "ignorance," he told me, or "some malicious reason" that "could have had to do with money." Mark Durno, phone interview with author, October 10, 2017.

23. Ron Fonger, "Documents Show Flint Filed False Reports about Testing for Lead in Water," *MLive*, November 12, 2015, https://www.mlive.com/news/flint/index. ssf/2015/11/documents_show_city_filed_fals.html.

24. Mark Brush, "Expert Says Michigan Officials Changed a Flint Lead Report to Avoid Federal Action," Michigan Radio, November 5, 2015. For a water system to be in com- pliance with the action level, 90 percent of homes tested must be below 15 ppb lead.

25. On June 25, 2015, MDEQ water quality analyst Adam Rosenthal wrote to employees at the Flint Water Treatment Plant that he was concerned that preliminary sampling had come in over the federal action level and hoped that subsequent samples would bring the city's ninetieth percentile back down. His remarks looked more incriminating in light of a 2008 email in which he suggested, in reference to lead levels in another city, tossing out a high result to avoid having to give "public notice." Ryan Felton, "Michigan Official Suggested Gaming Water Tests to 'Bump out' Lead Results," *Guardian*, April 27, 2016.

26. Susan Masten, personal interview with author, East Lansing, MI, December 5, 2017.

27. Milman and Glenza, "33 US Cities."

28. Vock, "In Flint's Aftermath."

29. This pledge ran into resistance on the part of Republican legislators citing the higher costs of compliance it would impose on municipalities. Jonathan Oosting and Michael Gerstein, "GOP Leaders Oppose Snyder's Lead Water Rule," *Detroit News*, March 23, 2017. At the federal level, Representative Dan Kildee sponsored a bill that would take the EPA action level down to 5 ppb by 2026.

30. It was the first element of what he described as the "perfect storm" that caused the crisis:

a) Chronic underinvestment in water infrastructure
b) Underappreciation of the role of corrosion control in sustaining urban potable water systems
c) Increased corrosion due to higher chloride in Flint's new source water
d) Failure to appropriately monitor for lead and opportunistic premise plumbing pathogens

See the Virginia Tech team's National Science Foundation Rapid Response Research grant proposal: Siddhartha Roy, "Our VT Team Wins $50,000 Grant from the National Science Foundation to Study Flint Water," September 14, 2015, http://flintwaterstudy.org/2015/09/our-virginia-tech-research-team-wins-a-50000-grant-from-the-national-science-foundation-to-study-flint-water/.

31. Sarah Schuch, "Flint Residents Should Be Drinking Flint River Water by Mid-April, Officials Say," *MLive*, March 12, 2014, https://www.mlive.com/news/flint/index.ssf/2014/03/flint_residents_should_be_drin.html. In April 2017, Robert Kaplan of EPA Region 5 estimated the necessary cost to upgrade the plant adequately at around $100 million. Ron Fonger, "Top EPA Official: 'No Reasonable Operator' Would Have Used Flint Water Plant," *MLive*, April 19, 2017, https://www.mlive.com/news/flint/index.ssf/2017/04/epa_regional_director_says_spe.html.

32. Paul Egan, "Water Plant Official: Move to Flint River 'Bad Decision,'" *Detroit Free Press*, March 29, 2016.

33. Matthew Dolan, "Flint Water Woes Reach beyond Lead in Drinking Supply," *Detroit Free Press*, June 5, 2016.

34. Ron Fonger, "Flint DPW Director Says Water Use Has Spiked after Hundreds of Water Main Breaks," *MLive*, April 22, 2015, https://www.mlive.com/news/flint/index.ssf/2015/04/flint_dpw_director_says_water.html. Bryce Feighner of the MDEQ broke with consensus, and garnered the opprobrium of the scientific community, when he argued that water main breaks and other infrastructural problems were the main source of the water's corrosivity (because they necessitated more chlorination), that orthophosphates would not have prevented the crisis, and that the city was largely to blame for what happened. See Ron Fonger, "Treating River Water Would Not Have Prevented Flint Crisis, DEQ Official Says," *MLive*, April 22, 2017, https://www.mlive.com/news/index.ssf/2017/04/bryce_feighner_mdeq_flint_wate.html. For Marc Edwards's response, see Ron Fonger, "Water Expert: 'No Known Relationship' between Main Breaks, Lead in Water," *MLive*, April 28, 2017, https://www.mlive.com/news/flint/index.ssf/2017/04/water_expert_no_known_relation.html.

35. For background on the use of lead in plumbing, see Troesken, *The Great Lead Water Pipe Disaster*.

36. A spring 2016 report by Rowe Engineering estimated that Flint's water infrastructure as a whole needed upward of $214 million in repairs. See Dolan, "Flint Water Woes."

37. Tom Pelton, "What Flint and Baltimore Share in Common: Dangerously Neglected Plumbing," WYPR, January 20, 2016, http://www.wypr.org/post/what-flint-and-baltimore-share-common-dangerously-neglected-plumbing.

38. American Society of Civil Engineers, *ASCE 2017 Infrastructure Report Card*. See also US Government Accountability Office, *Water Infrastructure*.

39. For the lead service line estimate, see Cornwell, Brown, and Via, "National Survey." For the estimated cost, see Matthew Dolan, "U.S. Could Face a $300B Lead Pipe Overhaul, Agency Warns," *Detroit Free Press*, March 4, 2016.

40. Olsen and Fedinick, "What's in Your Water?" See also Food and Water Watch, "U.S. Water Systems."

41. See 21st Century Infrastructure Commission, "21st Century Infrastructure Commission Report."

42. Ron Fonger, "Flint Water Line Replacements Have 22 Percent Failure Rate," *MLive*, May 17, 2017, https://www.mlive.com/news/flint/index.ssf/2017/05/1_in_5_flint_water_service_lin.html.

43. Frank Witsil, "Governor Rick Snyder Seeks to Map Michigan's Infrastructure," *Detroit Free Press*, April 3, 2017. Like Snyder's proposal to lower the lead action level, his proposals to step up investment in state infrastructure ran into pushback from Republican legislators.

44. As Michigan State University professor Janice Beecher put it, "At a very personal level for everyone, regardless of roles and responsibilities, the fundamental lesson is 'do your job.' Do what you were trained and hired to do because the public and the public interest depend on it, and the consequences of neglecting your duty can be dire." In McGuire et al., "Roundtable—The Flint Crisis."

45. Flint Water Advisory Task Force, *Final Report*, 29.

46. Paul Egan, "Gov. Rick Snyder Blames 'Career Bureaucrats' for Flint Water Crisis," *Detroit Free Press*, March 17, 2016.

47. Abby Goodnough, "Governor Snyder: E.P.A. Prolonged Flint Disaster," *New York Times*, March 17, 2016.

48. For example, in Josh Hakala, "Flint's Struggles Began with GM's Move to Suburbs in 1940s, Historian Says," Michigan Radio, February 8, 2016.

49. Highsmith, "Flint's Toxic Water Crisis."

50. Highsmith.

51. Highsmith, *Demolition*, 131.

52. Highsmith, 133.

53. Highsmith, 16.

54. See Dandaneau, *A Town Abandoned*. For further insight, see Jones and Bachelor, *The Sustaining Hand*.

55. Dandaneau, *A Town Abandoned*, 251.

56. Melissa Naan Burke, "EPA Email: Let's Not 'Go out on a Limb' for Flint," *Detroit News*, March 15, 2016.

57. In his account of the development of the waste management industry, David Pellow emphasizes "the importance of the *history* of environmental racism and the processes by which it unfolds." *Garbage Wars*, 7. For another model historical approach, consider the fusion of environmental and social history in Hurley, *Environmental Inequalities*.

58. "Crystal Clear: The Flint Water Crisis," panel discussion at the University of California, Irvine, March 10, 2016. For the definitive account of the "urban crisis," with direct relevance to Flint, see Sugrue, *Urban Crisis*.

59. Quote from Flint activist Tony Palladeno. See Steve Carmody, "Civil Rights Commission Draft Report Does Not Recommend Lawsuit in Flint Water Crisis," Michigan Radio, January 24, 2017.

60. Michigan Civil Rights Commission, *The Flint Water Crisis*, iv.

61. Michigan Civil Rights Commission, 84.

62. Michigan Civil Rights Commission, 84–85.

63. Michigan Civil Rights Commission, 117.

64. Michigan Civil Rights Commission, 119.

65. Michigan Civil Rights Commission, 124.

66. Michigan Civil Rights Commission, 128.

67. The MCRC did compensate for this somewhat, however, when it submitted an amicus brief in support of a writ of certiorari filed with the US Supreme Court in the case of *Bellant vs. Snyder*: see Sarah Cwiek, "Michigan Civil Rights Commission Urges U.S. Supreme Court to Review Emergency Manager Law," Michigan Radio, April 25, 2017. The MCRC released a one-year follow-up report on March 26, 2018, in which it described its recommendations as "aspirational rather than practical" and acknowledged that they would "require not only legislative, structural, and institutional changes, but equally important cultural, interpersonal, and even intrapersonal changes." Arbulu and Levy, "One-Year Update," 1.

68. "Coalition of Clean Water's Demands in Light of Serious Lead in Water Issues," Flintwaterstudy.org, September 20, 2015, http://flintwaterstudy.org/infor mation-for-flint-residents/demands/.

69. Marc Edwards, interview on Washington Journal, C-SPAN, February 29, 2016.

70. Ron Fonger, "Former Flint EM Says He Was 'Unjustly Persecuted' for Flint Water Crisis," *MLive*, March 15, 2016, https://www.mlive.com/news/index.ssf/2016/03 /former_flint_em_says_he_was_un.html.

71. The quote is from a tweet on March 6, 2016 (@onetoughnerd).

72. Chad Livengood and Jonathan Oosting, "Snyder to Flint: 'I'm Sorry and I'll Fix It,'" *Detroit News*, January 20, 2016.

3   Poisoned by Policy

1. PA 72 was an extension of PA 101 of 1988. PA 101 allowed EFMs for municipal governments; PA 72 of 1990 extended this to school districts.

2. Beata Mostafavi, "What Happened Last Time? A Look Back at Flint's 2002 State Takeover," *MLive*, November 10, 2011, https://www.mlive.com/news/flint/index .ssf/2011/11/what_happened_last_time_a_look.html.

3. Other "safety nets" built into PA 4 included requirements that all local governments balance their budgets and submit deficit reduction plans when deficits arose, as well as provisions for extra borrowing as a means of eliminating deficits. See the

report prepared for the Mackinac Center for Public Policy by Hohman, "Proposal 1 of 2012."

4. Office of Governor Rick Snyder, "Emergency Manager Legislation Will Give State Early Warning of Impending Trouble, Help Local Governments," press release, March 16, 2011, https://www.michigan.gov/snyder/0,4668,7-277-57577-252799--,00.html.

5. See, e.g., Representative Al Pscholka, quoted in Jonathan Oosting, "Michigan Decides 2012: Public Act 4 Emergency Manager Ballot Proposal," *MLive*, September 24, 2012, https://www.mlive.com/politics/index.ssf/2012/09/michigan_decides_2012_emergenc.html.

6. Berfield, "Financial Martial Law."

7. Candidates for EM positions have to possess at least five years' worth of business or government experience and complete a short training sequence. While these qualifications go beyond what an average citizen needs to run for office, whether they are sufficient to prepare EMs to exercise such broad powers has been much disputed by the law's critics. See Jeff Green and Jonathan Keehner, "Threat of Municipal Bankruptcy Makes Michigan Train Financial SWAT Teams," *Bloomberg News*, April 18, 2011.

8. The other notable restrictions PA 4 placed on EMs were arguably more favorable to residents: EMs were unable to reduce pension payments (these being protected by the state constitution) or unilaterally raise taxes.

9. Claire McClinton quoted in the ACLU documentary *Here's to Flint*. David Fasenfest writes that the first objective of the austerity measures imposed by EMs is to "preserve the financial interests of lenders and bond holders without exploring how those interests may have created the problem in the first instance." Fasenfest, "A Neoliberal Response," 4.

10. Kristin Longley, "Flint Could Be Test Case if New Emergency Financial Manager Bill Becomes Law," *MLive*, February 24, 2011, https://www.mlive.com/news/flint/index.ssf/2011/02/flint_could_be_test_case_if_ne.html.

11. For an overview of Flint's economic condition at this time, see Doidge et al., "The Flint Fiscal Playbook," and Scorsone and Bateson, "Long-Term Crisis." Figures on the median sales price of Flint homes are taken from a CNN analysis of RealtyTrac data. See Patrick Gillespie, "Flint, Michigan: A Hollow Frame of a Once Affluent City," CNN Money, March 7, 2016, https://money.cnn.com/2016/03/06/news/economy/flint-economy-democratic-debate/index.html.

12. Minghine, "The Great Revenue Sharing Heist."

13. Peter Luke, "Gov. Rick Snyder Signs Michigan Business/Income Tax Overhaul into Law," *MLive*, May 25, 2011, https://www.mlive.com/politics/index.ssf/2011/05/gov_rick_snyder_signs_michigan.html.

14. Lederman, "Flint's Water Crisis Is No Accident."

15. Flint Democracy Defense League, "The State of Flint under Emergency Management," read aloud in council chambers, Flint, MI, March 3, 2014.

16. Translating the activists' argument into legal scholar Richard Schragger's terms, the withdrawal of state revenue sharing stripped Flint of its *actual capacity* to govern itself, creating the conditions under which the removal of Flint's *formal authority* to govern itself could be justified. Schragger, *City Power*, 5.

17. Flint Financial Review Team, "Report of the Flint Financial Review Team," 4, accessed June 15, 2017, https://www.michigan.gov/documents/treasury/Flint-Review TeamReport-11-7-%2011_417437_7.pdf. Site no longer available.

18. Flint Financial Review Team, "Report of the Flint Financial Review Team," 3.

19. Flint Financial Review Team, 6.

20. Flint Financial Review Team, 8.

21. Eng, "Editorial."

22. Josh Freeman, personal interview with author, Flint, MI, May 16, 2017.

23. Kristin Longley, "Emergency Financial Manager Recommended for Flint Same Day Mayor Dayne Walling Re-Elected," *MLive*, November 10, 2011, https://www.mlive.com/news/flint/index.ssf/2011/11/emergency_financial_manager_re.html.

24. Longley, "Emergency Financial Manager."

25. See Ford, "Dayne Walling."

26. It is worth noting that the state retained the power to overrule such choices.

27. For a fuller account of emergency management in Flint, and activists' responses to it, see Nickels, *Power, Participation, & Protest.*

28. See Mona Hanna-Attisha's statement from chapter 1.

29. "Gov. Snyder's Staff Responds to Questions about Flint Water Crisis," *MLive*, May 3, 2016, https://www.mlive.com/news/index.ssf/2016/05/gov_snyders_staff_responds_to.html.

30. Later charged by Attorney General Schuette with false pretenses, Croft was the main official at the city who helped push the water treatment plant into operation prematurely, insisted the water was safe, and resisted switching the city back to Detroit water.

31. Flint Water Advisory Task Force, *Final Report*, 2. And elsewhere: "The Flint water crisis occurred when state-appointed emergency managers replaced local representative decision making in Flint, removing the checks and balances and public accountability that come with public decision making" (1).

32. Hammer, "The Flint Water Crisis, the Karegnondi Water Authority and Strategic
–Structural Racism," 37.

33. One major question to arise in retrospect was whether state actors were acting
chiefly out of "economic" considerations or "political" ones. It could be argued that
these motivations were inextricably intertwined, particularly under a corporate-
friendly administration that had come into office pledging to run government like
a business. However, in the discourse around the crisis, economic and political
motivations were often differentiated. By some accounts, the crisis was the result of
shortsighted penny pinching by officials who thought more like accountants than
public servants. Others held that the crisis had nothing to do with money, and was
instead part of an effort to further a more insidious political agenda. I treat both
positions, however, as part of the political narrative because of their shared emphasis on the core themes considered in this chapter: the denial of local democracy and
the determination of state actors to impose a preconceived agenda on Flint, even as
the water situation began to spiral out of control.

34. Attorneys for EMs Earley and Ambrose sought to exploit this ambiguity when
they argued, against a class-action suit brought by activists, that EMs were local
officials. Gus Burns, "Emergency Managers Weren't State Employees, Lawyers
Argue in Flint Water Lawsuit," *MLive*, January 9, 2018, https://www.mlive.com
/news/detroit/index.ssf/2018/01/flint_water_lawsuit_likely_to.html. According to
the theory of emergency management, the interests of the state and the interests
of cities overlap because the state has a stake in the health of its cities. Insofar as
that theoretical congruence breaks down in practice, however, there is always the
possibility that an EM officially charged with doing what's best for the city will in
fact do what's best for the state (and/or private interests with influence over the
state). A report issued by the House Judiciary Committee Democratic Staff noted
that even an internal Department of Treasury analysis found EMs would likely use
the broad powers granted by the EM law "for their own gain" rather than in the
interests of the local unit of government (House Judiciary Committee Democratic
Staff, "Democracy for Sale," 9). In a sympathetic account of the logic of emergency
management, legal scholar Clayton Gillette contends that "by addressing the
political underpinnings of fiscal distress, takeover boards may be more capable of
satisfying the interests of local residents for public goods than local elected officials, and may also represent the interests of nonresidents and creditors who are
not considered by those officials." However, he continues, "The same conditions
that invite intervention by central officials capable of countering the consequences
of flawed local decision making also permit takeovers by less benevolent officials
whose interests align poorly with those of the stakeholders in municipal fiscal
health.... It is plausible that where the interests and local residents, state residents,
and creditors diverge, a state-appointed takeover board may not identify its objective with the interests of the first group. Perhaps that result is acceptable on the
assumption that the takeover board internalizes the interests of all those affected

by local fiscal distress. But there is a risk that takeover boards serve the interests of the state in more nefarious ways than marginally favoring creditors over local residents." Gillette, "Dictatorships for Democracy," 1, 11, 70, https://lsr.nellco.org /cgi/viewcontent.cgi?article=1373&context=nyu_lewp.

35. Flint Democracy Defense League, "The State of Flint."

36. Flint Democracy Defense League, "The State of Flint."

37. The claim that emergency management violates a human right to democracy was part of the basis for a petition to the Inter-American Commission on Human Rights submitted by Claire McClinton and a legal team from Loyola University on behalf of myself and a number of other residents: "Petition Alleging Violations of the Human Rights of Citizens of Flint, Michigan," November 27, 2017. One can also consider the question of whether there is a "right" to democracy from a domestic perspective. As Richard Schragger writes, despite the absence of a guarantee to local democracy in the US Constitution, constitutional scholars like nineteenth-century Michigan Supreme Court Chief Justice Thomas Cooley "argued persuasively that representative local government was a matter of 'absolute right' and could not be overridden by state legislative fiat." That notion lost popularity in the twentieth century, however, as cities came to be seen as "venal and corrupt," and as suspicions of local politics gave rise to a technocratic ideal of city government more amenable to top-down decision making. Schragger, "Flint Wasn't Allowed Democracy." State takeovers, then, were envisioned as "a technocratic solution to a political defect." Schragger, *City Power*, 242.

38. Highlighting the role of the city in creating the crisis was a conscious strategy on the part of Snyder's communications staff. See Jim Lynch, "Emails: Wide Support on Flint Switch from Detroit Water," *Detroit News*, February 26, 2016.

39. Pscholka said he was getting "Christmas lists" from Flint officials and that there would be no "blank checks" written by the state: "This was a local decision to take themselves off the Detroit system and join this pipeline, and that's what started this whole series of events." Anthony Pollreisz, "Pscholka to Flint: No Blank Checks from State to Solve Water Crisis," WKZO-AM, January 14, 2016.

40. For the official history of the Detroit water system, see Daisy, *Detroit Water and Sewerage Department*. For another take, see Green, "Detroit's Water System."

41. Wright, "The Flint Water Crisis, DWSD, and GLWA," 5. In Hammer's "Flint Water Crisis, KWA and Strategic-Structural Racism: A Reply to Jeff Wright," he points out that the DWSD, like other public utilities, is legally prohibited from turning a profit, and required to price its water according to the cost of delivery.

42. Wright, "The Flint Water Crisis, DWSD, and GLWA," 4.

43. Wright, 7.

44. See Ron Fonger, "50 Years Later: Ghosts of Corruption Still Linger along Old Path of Failed Flint Water Pipeline," *MLive*, November 12, 2012, https://www.mlive .com/news/flint/index.ssf/2012/11/ghosts_of_corruption_still_lin.html.

45. Wright, "The Flint Water Crisis, DWSD, and GLWA," 8.

46. Councilman Scott Kincaid said that for Flint to treat raw water at its own treatment plant would put it in "control" of its "own destiny." Shaun Byron, "Flint Council to Take up Proposed Pipeline Deal at Monday Meeting," *MLive*, March 20, 2013, accessed June 15, 2017.

47. Kristin Longley, "Here Are 7 Things to Know about Flint's Water Treatment Plant," *MLive*, October 12, 2012, https://www.mlive.com/news/flint/index.ssf/2012/10/here _are_7_things_to_know_abou.html.

48. Wright, "The Flint Water Crisis, DWSD, and GLWA," 8.

49. Wright, 10. Although officials in Flint seemed to buy Wright's argument about rates (see May, "Debunking 4 Claims"), members of the Flint Water Advisory Task Force determined that the KWA had never offered any significant cost savings and that local support for the project was a product of the desire for water independence. Counts, "Flint Water Crisis Got Its Start."

50. In January 2013, KWA received final approval from the Army Corps of Engineers to begin construction.

51. Jeff Wright, "Response to Bill Johnson and DWSD's Position on KWA," Genesee County Drain Commission press release, March 21, 2013.

52. See Kristin Longley, "Flint City Council Members Seek to Halt Emergency Financial Manager," *MLive*, September 10, 2012, https://www.mlive.com/news/flint /index.ssf/2012/09/flint_city_council_members_see.html.

53. Tucker, Young, Jackson, Tull, Inc., *City of Flint Water Supply Assessment*.

54. Ron Fonger, "Detroit Claims Karegnondi Water Pipeline Plan in Genesee County 'Rife with Financial Discrepancies,'" *MLive*, March 19, 2013, https://www .mlive.com/news/flint/index.ssf/2013/03/detroit_claims_karegnondi_wate.html.

55. ROWE Professional Services Company, *Review of December 21, 2012 Presentation*.

56. Wright, "The Flint Water Crisis, DWSD, and GLWA," 23.

57. Some suspected Dillon of delaying his recommendation so he could make it under the new law, an accusation the Treasury Department denied. Dominic Adams, "State Treasury Department Expects Flint Water Source Recommendation 'Soon'," *MLive*, March 20, 2013, https://www.mlive.com/news/flint/index.ssf/2013/03/state_treasury _department_expe.html.

58. Wright, "The Flint Water Crisis, DWSD, and GLWA," 32.

59. Wright, 31. "As Drain Commissioner," he writes, "I insisted that the City Council vote because I believed that the City's permanent water source should be decided by Flint's elected representatives" (32).

60. Hammer, "Reply to Jeff Wright," 13.

61. Hammer, "The Flint Water Crisis, the Karegnondi Water Authority and Strategic–Structural Racism," 17. Wright says that Hammer's interpretation is wrong: "It wasn't close to done. At that time, Flint did not know what it wanted to do. Flint did not agree to buy water from KWA until April 2013. Between January 3, 2012, and April 2013, Flint negotiated with both DWSD and KWA. It also continued to consider going to the Flint River permanently. A done deal is not done until all parties to it agree that it is done" (Wright, "The Flint Water Crisis, DWSD, and GLWA," 19).

62. Hammer, "The Flint Water Crisis, the Karegnondi Water Authority and Strategic–Structural Racism," 12.

63. As Hammer points out, "no effort was made to help Flint finance these costs." "Reply to Jeff Wright," 23.

64. Dominic Adams, "Flint River Now an Option for Drinking Water Following Detroit's Termination of Contract," *MLive*, July 23, 2013, https://www.mlive.com /news/flint/index.ssf/2013/07/city_readying_water_plant_to_t.html. Former councilman Sheldon Neeley, despite lodging an affirmative vote, told me that retrospectively he did not think the council's vote was adequately informed. Sheldon Neeley, personal interview with author, Flint, MI, December 9, 2017. Former council president Josh Freeman, on the other hand, told me that the council had plenty of opportunities to study the KWA issue, that it was discussed many times, and that any claim about being rushed into a decision was a "lie." Freeman, interview, May 16, 2017.

65. The analysis hinges on a January 2012 email sent by KWA engineer John O'Malia describing EM Brown's intention to use such a strategy, calling it a "precaution." Hammer, "The Flint Water Crisis, the Karegnondi Water Authority and Strategic–Structural Racism," 19.

66. Hammer, "The Flint Water Crisis, KWA and Strategic-Structural Racism," 14.

67. Dominic Adams, "Flint City Council Approves Resolution to Buy Water from Karegnondi, State Approval Still Needed," *MLive*, March 25, 2013, https://www .mlive.com/news/flint/index.ssf/2013/03/flint_city_council_approves_re.html.

68. Allie Gross, "Docs Reveal Flint's EM Agreed to Buy $1M Worth of Extra Water from the KWA—This Was Never about Saving Money," *Detroit Metro Times*, February 27, 2016.

69. Dominic Adams, "Flint City Council Modifies Water Pipeline Proposal, Sends Measure Back to Committee," *MLive*, March 18, 2013, https://www.mlive.com/news /flint/index.ssf/2013/03/flint_city_council_modifies_wa.html.

70. Hammer, "The Flint Water Crisis, KWA and Strategic-Structural Racism," 20.

71. Flint Democracy Defense League, "The State of Flint."

72. Guyette, "A Deep Dive."

73. Lynch, "Emails."

74. Paul Egan, "Records: Mich. Gov. Office in Loop on Flint Drinking-Water Decision," *Detroit Free Press*, November 22, 2015.

75. Jeff Wright and Ed Kurtz, "Joint Statement by Jeff Wright and Ed Kurtz Regarding Detroit's Final Offer on Water Service," Genesee County Drain Commission press release, April 16, 2013.

76. Jim Lynch and Jennifer Chambers, "Flint Crisis Charges Raise Scrutiny of EM Law," *Detroit News*, December 20, 2016.

77. Hammer, "Reply to Jeff Wright," 19.

78. Chad Livengood, "Ex-DEQ Staffer Denies 'Sweetheart' Flint Deal," *Detroit News*, May 12, 2016.

79. Wright, "The Flint Water Crisis, DWSD, and GLWA," 12. One KWA attorney mentioned ensuring that Flint had "debt capacity in the future" as a motivation. Paul Egan, "'Sweetheart' Bond Deal Aided Flint Water Split from Detroit," *Detroit Free Press*, May 11, 2016.

80. Hammer, "Reply to Jeff Wright," 18.

81. Charges available from www.michigan.gov/documents/ag/FINAL_Earley_et_al_ Complaint_and_Warrant_121916_546055_7.pdf.

82. Hammer, "The Flint Water Crisis, KWA and Strategic-Structural Racism," 20–21.

83. Genesee County's backing was critical in getting the bonds a good rating, and thus a manageable interest rate. Ron Fonger, "Rating Agencies Take Notice as Genesee County Pledges to Cover Flint's Pipeline Borrowing," *MLive*, April 1, 2014, https:// www.mlive.com/news/flint/index.ssf/2014/04/genesee_countys_pledge_to_cove .html.

84. Dayne Walling maintained that "the terms of the agreement are standard for a long-term capital project." Paul Egan and Matthew Dolan, "Official: Flint Will 'Lose Everything' if It Leaves KWA," *Detroit Free Press*, June 11, 2016.

85. Egan and Dolan, "Official."

86. As activist Quincy Murphy put it, "Really, to tell you the truth, I really think this emergency manager was put in place for the City of Flint to make sure the KWA [went forward]." Jim Lynch, "Flint Residents Criticize Staying with KWA Pipeline," *Detroit News*, May 18, 2016.

87. Allie Gross, "Emails Reveal Flint EM and State Advised Not to Join the KWA—It Was Never about Saving Money," *Detroit Metro Times*, February 13, 2016.

88. Maynard, "The Flint Water Crisis." The Young Turks also got in on the speculation, focusing on Snyder's corporate donors. Jordan Chariton, "Why Flint Water CRISIS Has Troubling Ties to Rick Snyder's Pro-Fracking Donors," Medium, March 28, 2017, https://medium.com/@marketing_75534/why-flint-water-crisis-has-troubling -ties-to-rick-snyders-pro-fracking-donors-a02119fa8b1f.

89. Leonard N. Fleming, "Flint's Weaver: Stick with Detroit Water," *Detroit News*, April 18, 2017. Flint activist Melissa Mays told me that DWSD "fell apart" because KWA took away its largest customer, "And now it's regionalized to the Great Lakes Water Authority [GLWA]." "Both [the KWA and GLWA] are regionalized systems," she pointed out, which "opens the door to privatization, which is the worst thing that could possibly happen to us. But I think that was the state's plan all along." Melissa Mays, personal interview with author, Flint, MI, February 17, 2016.

90. See Kornberg, "The Structural Origins of Territorial Stigma."

91. The quote is taken from Walling's responses to questions from the Michigan Joint Select Committee on the Flint Water Public Health Emergency, available from www.senate .michigan.gov/ committees/files/2016-SCT-FLINT-03-29-1-08.PDF.

92. Kristin Longley, "Water Pipeline vs. Flint River: City of Flint Studying Its Drinking Water Options," *MLive*, January 22, 2011, https://www.mlive.com/news/flint/index .ssf/2011/01/water_pipeline_vs_flint_river.html. Councilman Sheldon Neeley was blunt: "My preference is for whatever option is going to save us the most money."

93. Longley, "Water Pipeline vs. Flint River."

94. ROWE Professional Services Company, *Analysis of the Flint River*.

95. Jeff Wright claimed that "many in Flint wanted to use the river permanently and pay for the maximum improvements" ("The Flint Water Crisis," 13). At the very least, some local politicians wanted residents to appreciate the value of the water treatment plant as one of the city's major assets. Councilman (and later State Representative) Sheldon Neeley, for example, took groups on tours of the water plant so they could see its capabilities firsthand and sample treated river water. On one of these tours in October 2012, he lamented the widespread belief that "the Flint River is an awful source of water," insisting that "it's not awful. It's safe to drink." He also pointed out that in the recent past Flint had used river water for a short period during repairs to the DWSD main, with no apparent ill effects or complaints from residents. Kristin Longley, "Flint Water Plant in Spotlight as City Weighs Drinking Water Options," *MLive*, October 12, 2012, https://www.mlive.com/news/flint/index.ssf/2012/10/flint_water_plant_heralded _as.html. Neeley told me that in talking up the treatment plant to residents he was in no way advocating that the city use the river or any other specific water source. Neeley, interview, December 9, 2017.

96. Dayne Walling, responses to Michigan Joint Select Committee.

97. Even after local officials rejected the possibility, EMs Brown and Kurtz both eyed the river as a cheaper long-term water source. In his first Flint Deficit Elimination Action Plan, Brown noted the cost savings that could be realized by using the river, which "would allow for funds to upgrade the plant, provide funds to enable a concentrated effort on reducing water leakage, and make debt service payments on the Financial Stabilization Bonds" (quoted in Hammer, "The Flint Water Crisis, the Karegnondi Water Authority and Strategic–Structural Racism," 23). Kurtz considered using the river in late 2012 as a long-term source but consulted with the MDEQ and rejected the idea as infeasible. Guyette, "Exclusive: Gov. Rick Snyder's Men Originally Rejected Using Flint's Toxic River."

98. Kristin Longley, "Flint Asks Detroit for Permission to Blend Treated Flint River Water with Water from Detroit," *MLive*, October 9, 2012, https://www.mlive.com /news/flint/index.ssf/2012/10/flint_asks_detroit_for_permiss.html.

99. Former council president Josh Freeman penned a forceful response to Earley's misrepresentation of the council vote: "At no time have the elected leaders of the city of Flint voted to use the Flint River as our primary drinking source. The documented facts show the decision to move to the Flint River was made solely by emergency managers sent to run the city on behalf of the state of Michigan." Joshua Freeman, "City Council President: Emergency Manager Set Flint on Path to River Water," *MLive*, October 29, 2015, https://www.mlive.com/opinion/flint/index.ssf/2015/10/city _council_president_emergen.html.

100. City of Detroit, Water and Sewerage Department, "Water War Undermines Flint-DWSD Relations," news release, April 1, 2013, http://voiceofdetroit.net/wp-content /uploads/water_war_undermines_flint-dwsd_relations-2013-14.pdf.

101. Ron Fonger, "Detroit Was 'Mad, Angry, Vindictive' in Flint Water Talks, Former EM Claims," *MLive*, May 2, 2017, https://www.mlive.com/news/flint/index .ssf/2017/05/former_flint_em_told_congress.html.

102. Freeman, interview, May 16, 2017.

103. Hammer, "The Flint Water Crisis, the Karegnondi Water Authority, and Strategic–Structural Racism," 22. Wright's retort: "Leaving aside whether the termination notice caused officials in Flint to believe DWSD would really try to cut off drinking water (some did believe DWSD might), it certainly caused them a great deal of anxiety. They seriously thought that DWSD might actually force them to turn to the Courts to enjoin a shutoff. Also, the termination notice caused them to think about their alternatives, what they could do in response to the notice. Many Flint officials were truly offended by the letter" ("The Flint Water Crisis, DWSD, and GLWA," 22). "They also feared the notice might be a ruse to allow DWSD to raise their rates for years after April 17, 2014, which it was" (23).

104. Darnell Earley, Emergency Manager, email to Sue McCormick, Detroit Water and Sewerage Department, March 7, 2014.

105. Ron Fonger, "20 Percent Increase: Detroit Hikes Price of Water for Genesee County Suburbs," *MLive*, July 7, 2014, https://www.mlive.com/news/flint/index .ssf/2014/07/20_percent_price_hike_detroit.html.

106. The Flint Water Advisory Task Force was clear in its final report: "Emergency managers, not locally elected officials, made the decision to switch to the Flint River as Flint's primary water supply source" (*Final Report*, 7). See also *Bridge Magazine*'s vetting of this claim: Michigan Truth Squad, "Who Approved Switch to Flint River? State's Answers Draw Fouls," *Bridge Magazine*, January 21, 2016.

107. In Wright's words, "It was in this resolution on June 26, 2013, that the City of Flint decided to go to the River. GCDC, KWA, and I had nothing to do with that decision" ("The Flint Water Crisis, DWSD, and GLWA," 24).

108. In its final report, the Flint Water Advisory Task Force wrote that "Flint EM Ed Kurtz authorized use of the Flint River as a water source for Flint, as clearly indicated by his approval of a sole-source contract for the engineering firm Lockwood, Andrews, and Newnam (LAN) to prepare the Flint [water treatment plant] for full-time treatment of Flint River water," *Final Report*, 40.

109. Ron Fonger, "Former Flint EM: 'My Job Did Not Include Ensuring Safe Drinking Water,'" *MLive*, May 2, 2017, https://www.mlive.com/news/flint/index.ssf/2017/05/ former_flint_em_my_job_did_not.html.

110. Hammer maintains that while the KWA decision was "political," "the decision to use the Flint River and the question of how to finance necessary improvements to the [water treatment plant] were driven by financial concerns" ("The Flint Water Crisis, the Karegnondi Water Authority and Strategic–Structural Racism," 23). The City of Flint's own 2014 Annual Water Quality Report stated that "the use of the Flint River as a source water for the City of Flint Water Treatment Plant" was "driven largely by economics and the financial state of the City." In January 2016, the media confusingly conflated the debate over the cost savings of switching to the KWA with the cost savings of switching to the river temporarily. Articles began to appear claiming that the switch to the river was not, in fact, about saving money, but what was meant was that the switch to the *KWA* was not—at least according to DWSD's critique of the project— about saving money. For example, Allie Gross, "New Emails Reveal the Switch to the Flint River Was Not about Saving Money," *Detroit Metro Times*, January 25, 2016.

111. Ron Fonger, "Company Says Flint EM Told Employees: Keep Water Work to Minimum Required," *MLive*, June 29, 2016, https://www.mlive.com/news/index .ssf/2016/06/flint_consultant_says_former_e.html.

112. Ron Fonger, "Flint Water Problems: Switch Aimed to Save $5 Million—But at What Cost?," *MLive*, January 23, 2015, https://www.mlive.com/news/flint/index .ssf/2015/01/flints_dilemma_how_much_to_spe.html.

113. March 2015 memo to Deputy Treasurer Wayne Workman, quoted in May, "Debunking 4 Claims." Jerry Ambrose summed up the logic of the switch in his Congressional testimony: "You know, the long and short of it is, they came back and said, yes, we can make this work for a short period of time.... We realized that that would generate some financial savings for us over the next couple years.... And so we said, I mean, why would we not try it?" Ron Fonger, "Flint Emergency Manager Told Congress He Never Met or Talked to Gov. Snyder," *MLive*, January 23, 2017, https://www.mlive.com/news/flint/index.ssf/2017/01/flint_emergency_manager_told_c.html.

114. See ROWE Professional Services Company, *City of Flint Water Reliability Study*.

115. For a polemical (and not entirely accurate) account of the water crisis as a product of austerity and the "politics of disposability" associated with it, see Giroux, *America at War with Itself*. For the connection between austerity and public health, see Stuckler and Basu, *The Body Economic*.

116. Fonger, "Former Flint EM." Note that Darnell Earley seems to have taken a different position: "The EM obviously is the person responsible for making sure that those things get done, and I've always accepted that." US House Committee on Oversight and Govt. Reform March 15, 2016 Transcript, p. 32, https://www.flint watercommittee.com/wp-content/uploads/2016/05/FLINT-HEARING-OF-MARCH -15-FINAL-with-cover-sheet.pdf.

117. Fonger, "Flint EM Told Employees."

118. Flint Water Advisory Task Force, *Final Report*, 27.

119. As Dayne Walling told *East Village* magazine: "I can't see any scenario where myself and Flint City Council would have supported going back to the Flint River; and that's probably not based on any science. ... The perceptions of the Flint River in this community—it's getting better for fishing and canoeing—but beyond that the idea of drinking the Flint River water is something that most people in this community start off not liking.... I don't think elected officials could've made that decision." Quoted in Ford, "Dayne Walling."

120. As Mays put it, "You can push the button any time and get water—good water." Ron Fonger, "Flint Residents Say They'll Meet to Fight High Prices, 'Plummeting Water Quality'," *MLive*, January 5, 2015, https://www.mlive.com/news/flint/index .ssf/2015/01/flint_residents_say_theyll_mee.html.

121. Ron Fonger, "Detroit Water Chief Says She's Willing to Sell Emergency Water to Flint—No Strings Attached," *MLive*, January 26, 2015, https://www.mlive.com /news/flint/index.ssf/2015/01/detroit_water_chief.html.

122. As Jerry Ambrose said, "It's not possible to just push a button and go back." Ron Fonger, "Flint Emergency Manager Says There Are Two Big Reasons Not to Reconnect Detroit Water," *MLive*, January 29, 2015, https://www.mlive.com/news /flint/index.ssf/2015/01/flint_extends.html.

123. Bishop Bernadel Jefferson, personal interview with author, Flint, MI, May 17, 2017. When Earley sold the asset, he did so against the protestations of the City Council, which voted against the sale 7 to 2 (but was unable, under the terms of PA 436, to come up with an alternative that was equally financially advantageous). The activists' opposition to the sale stemmed, in part, from the feeling that the county was taking advantage of Flint and that at most the pipe should be leased. Ron Fonger, "Flint City Council Turns down $3.9 Million Offer for Water Pipeline," *MLive*, May 20, 2014, https://www.mlive.com/news/flint/index.ssf/2014/05/flint_city_council.html.

124. As Curt Guyette ("A Deep Dive") put it, "That stipulation sealed the city's fate, locking it into using the river water."

125. The council voted to support the loan but was not informed of the critical condition imposed by Ambrose. Emily Lawler, "State Loan Prohibited Flint from Rejoining Detroit Water System," *MLive*, March 2, 2016, https://www.mlive.com/news/index.ssf/2016/03/state_loan_prohibited_flint_fr.html.

126. Including hiring for top executive positions, the resolution of litigation and labor disputes, and the budget process. Ron Fonger, "Exiting Flint Emergency Manager Issues Final Orders on Transition," *MLive*, May 6, 2015, https://www.mlive.com/news/flint/index.ssf/2015/05/departing_flint_emergency_mana.html.

127. Laura Sullivan, personal interview with author, Flint, MI, November 14, 2016.

128. May, "Debunking 4 Claims." Similarly, the Treasury Department predicted that if Flint were to switch back to DWSD for eighteen months, it would end up costing the city $18 million.

129. *Bridge Magazine* Staff, "The Latest on What Key Snyder Aides Knew about Flint and When," *Bridge Magazine*, March 1, 2016.

130. Email from Dennis Muchmore to Brad Wurfel, Dennis Muchmore, David Murray, and Sara Wurfel, February 5, 2015.

131. Email from Terry Stanton (of the Treasury Department) to Brad Wurfel, Dennis Muchmore, David Murray, and Sara Wurfel, February 5, 2015.

132. Bebow, John. "How Snyder's Chief of Staff Wrestled with Flint Water, with Few Victories," *Bridge Magazine*, March 2, 2016.

133. In Congressional testimony, Ambrose said, paraphrasing, that "it has less to do with the vote that they took than with the manner in which they took it." Ron Fonger, "Congressman Wants Federal Criminal Investigation of Three Former Flint EMs," *MLive*, January 18, 2017, https://www.mlive.com/news/flint/index.ssf/2017/01/congressman_wants_federal_pros.html.

134. Peter Hammer concludes that "Flint residents had knowledge of the water crisis almost immediately upon the switch to the Flint River, but they lacked the power

to influence the decision making of the Emergency Managers, Treasury, [MDEQ], or the Governor" ("The Flint Water Crisis, the Karegnondi Water Authority and Strategic–Structural Racism," 35).

135. Hammer, "The Flint Water Crisis, the Karegnondi Water Authority and Strategic–Structural Racism," 39.

136. See, for example, Schmitt, *The Concept of the Political*; Agamben, *State of Exception*; and the considerable commentary these works have inspired.

137. Anderson, "Democratic Dissolution."

138. Anderson, 610.

139. Honig, *Emergency Politics*, xv.

4   The Pro-Democracy Struggle in Michigan and the Prehistory of the Water Movement in Flint

1. Nayyirah Shariff, personal interview with author, Flint, MI, April 20, 2016.

2. The transcript of Snyder's speech is available from www.legislature.mi.gov/ (S(dpua wbkxbzdov3qy5ixuwdqu))/documents/2011–2012/Journal/House/htm/2011-HJ-01 -19-004.htm.

3. "Hundreds Protest Emergency Manager Bills," *Lansing State Journal*, March 9, 2011. There was much discontent around the proposed budget as well. Claire McClinton told the *Flint Journal* that "it boils down to the same thing—our government is taking care of corporations and they're not taking care of working class people who make the community what it is." Kayla Habermehl, "Local UAQ Joining State Budget Protest," *Flint Journal*, March 15, 2011.

4. Available from www.michigan.gov/documents/snyder/EMF_Fact_Sheet2_347889_7 .pdf.

5. Berfield, "Financial Martial Law in Michigan."

6. Activists sometimes framed the struggle against the law as part of a new civil rights movement, implying that in Michigan, African Americans had to struggle for their right to vote (or at least their right to vote for people who would exercise actual power) all over again.

7. Quoted in Steve Neavling, "Michigan Civil Rights Leaders Plan an Occupy Protest at Gov. Rick Snyder's Home on Martin Luther King Jr. Day," *Detroit Free Press*, December 13, 2011.

8. Savage, "Michigan GOP."

9. See Savage, "Michigan Rising."

10. Krista Gjestland, "Protesters Gather for March outside Gov. Snyder's House," *News-Herald*, January 17, 2012, http://www.thenewsherald.com/news/protesters-gather -for-march-outside-gov-snyder-s-house-with/article_172ede4a-1b7e-55e1-8c06-2b72 e6237ab7.html.

11. Klein, *The Shock Doctrine*. Commenting on Michigan's PA 4 on *Democracy Now!* in March 2011, Klein described it as "a frontal assault on democracy. It's a kind of a corporate coup d'état at the municipal level." For further reflections on the relationship between neoliberalism and democracy, see Brown, *Undoing the Demos*.

12. Patrick Sullivan, "Dictatorship or Democracy? Push to Repeal the Emergency Manager Law Goes Local," *Northern Express*, June 26, 2011.

13. Greg Bowens, phone interview with author, January 30, 2017.

14. Brandon Jessup, phone interview with author, January 27, 2017.

15. American Civil Liberties Union of Michigan, "ACLU Seeks Records about Emergency Financial Manager Law," April 7, 2011, http://www.aclumich.org/article/aclu -seeks-records-about-emergency-financial-manager-law.

16. See coverage on *Eclectablog* by Chris Savage: "Imposition of an Emergency Manager"; "Think Emergency Managers Are Only for 'Black' Schools and Cities?"; and "Another Michigan City."

17. Erik Kain, "Teachers and Tea Partiers Unite to Repeal Michigan Emergency Manager Bill," *Forbes*, April 6, 2011.

18. Bishop Bernadel Jefferson, interview with author, Flint, MI, May 17, 2017.

19. Kristin Longley, "Report: Font Expert Says Emergency Manager Law Petitions Had Correct Size," *MLive*, June 8, 2012, https://www.mlive.com/news/flint/index.ssf /2012/06/font_expert_says_emergency_man.html.

20. Bob Mabbitt, personal interview with author, Flint, MI, June 15, 2017.

21. Nayyirah Shariff, personal interview with author, Flint, MI, July 6, 2017.

22. Alec Gibbs, phone interview with author, February 10, 2017.

23. Jonathan Oosting, "Snyder Signs Replacement Emergency Manager Law: We 'Heard, Recognized and Respected' Will of Voters," *MLive*, December 27, 2012, https:// www.mlive.com/politics/index.ssf/2012/12/snyder_signs_replacement_emerg.html.

24. Oosting.

25. The appropriation, amounting to $5,780,000, was ostensibly to cover EM salaries and other costs of administering the law.

26. The first challenge to the constitutionality of the law, to my knowledge, was that levied in April 21 by two pension boards representing Detroit public employees:

the Detroit General Retirement System (for general employees) and the Police and Fire Retirement System. See Savage, "Benton Harbor/Emergency Financial Manager."

27. Joining in the suit were the Goodman & Hurwitz PC (on behalf of the National Lawyers' Guild), the Center for Constitutional Rights, and lawyers associated with AFSCME: Herb Sanders and Miller Cohen. As in the case of the repeal, AFSCME's involvement represented a critical endorsement by organized labor. But AFSCME Council 25 Legal Director Herb Sanders insisted that the legal challenge was about fundamental matters of right and wrong rather than traditional union politics.

28. *Brown et al. vs. Snyder et al.*

29. Kristin Longley, "Flint Resident Joins Effort against Michigan's Emergency Financial Manager Law," *MLive*, June 22, 2011, https://www.mlive.com/news/flint /index.ssf/2011/06/flint_resident_joins_effort_to.html.

30. Center for Constitutional Rights, "MI Citizens Take Emergency Manager Law to Court, Citing Unconstitutional Power Grab," June 22, 2011, https://ccrjustice.org /home/press-center/press-releases/mi-citizens-take-emergency-manager-law-court -citing.

31. John Philo, phone interview with author, February 3, 2017.

32. *Phillips et al. vs. Snyder et al.*

33. "Order Granting in Part and Denying in Part Defendants' Motion to Dismiss (document no. 41) and Denying Defendants' Motion to Stay Proceedings (document no. 47)," available from www.voiceofdetroit.net/wp-content/uploads/Steeh-rulgin -EM-lawsuit-11–19.pdf.

34. Bolstering the case for discrimination was evidence that fiscally troubled black cities were more likely to get EMs than fiscally troubled white cities. The predominantly white cities, like Allen Park and Hamtramck, that *had* received EMs had asked the state for them. See Kirkpatrick and Breznau, "The (Non)Politics of Emergency Political Intervention," and Lee et al., "Racial Inequality," 1–7. The Detroit Branch of the NAACP also filed a lawsuit alleging infringement on African Americans' voting rights. See Khalil AlHajal, "NAACP Lawsuit Claims Emergency Manager Law Violates Voting Rights of Half Michigan's African Americans," *MLive*, May 13, 2013, https://www.mlive .com/news/detroit/index.ssf/2013/05/naacp_lawsuit_claims_emergency.html.

35. Philo, interview, February 3, 2017.

36. The decision outlined a variety of ways in which citizens could express their will under emergency management: "Citizens can still advocate for the removal of state-appointed managers and can vote out local officials who allowed the emergency, legislators who approved the law or the governor who made the appointment." Jonathan Oosting, "Appeals Court Upholds Mich. Emergency Manager Law," *Detroit News*, September 12, 2016.

37. This argument did not go far with residents trapped in the gerrymandered blue districts around Michigan's major urban centers, who were at an inherent disadvantage within state electoral politics. See Ted Roelofs, "Gerrymandering in Michigan Is among the Nation's Worst, New Test Claims," *Bridge Magazine*, April 13, 2017.

38. Oostin, "Appeals Court." For another perspective, see Nick Krieger, "What's Next for Opponents of Michigan's Emergency Manager Law?," Fix the Mitten, September 13, 2016, https://www.fixthemitten.com/blog/whats-next-for-opponents-of-michig ans-emergency-manager-law.

39. In March 2017, they filed a writ with the Supreme Court. Ron Fonger, "Supreme Court Could Decide if Michigan EM Law Violates Voting Rights Act," *MLive*, March 31, 2017, https://www.mlive.com/news/flint/index.ssf/2017/03/supreme_court_asked _to_hear_mi.html. In October, the court declined to hear the case. Todd Spangler, "U.S. Supreme Court Rejects Challenge to Michigan's Emergency Manager Law," *Detroit Free Press*, October 2, 2017. Attorneys then moved forward with the racial discrimination claim. Brian McVicar, "Michigan's Emergency Manager Law Is Racist, Lawsuit Argues," *MLive*, December 6, 2017, https://www.mlive.com/news/index.ssf/2017/12 /michigans_emergency_manager_la.html.

40. Philo, interview, February 3, 2017. "From the time we filed that first case … to today," he said, "there's been a complete flip in the public perception of that law. It's hard to find people who defend it anymore."

41. When Kevyn Orr took office in Detroit in March 2013, for example, he was "cautious," John Philo told me, compared to EMs in other cities who had come in like "bulls in the china closet." Philo, interview, February 3, 2017.

42. Video of Sanders's comments is available from https://www.youtube.com/watch ?v=Gu3fHnSmnmM.

43. Speaking of the relationship between an EM and elected officials at a training session for prospective EMs, Harris said, "You don't have to do *anything* with these guys. … The fact of the matter is, the city manager is now gone—I am the city manager. I replaced the finance director. So I'm the finance director and the city manager. I am the mayor and I am the commission and I don't need them. All I need is the expertise." Savage, "Benton Harbor."

44. Savage, "Protest Rick Snyder."

45. Savage, "Some Thoughts."

46. Claire McClinton, personal interview with author, Flint, MI, June 7, 2017.

47. For a general history of the city that highlights its relations with its predominantly white neighbor St. Joseph, see Kotlowitz, *The Other Side of the River*.

48. Mahler, "Now That the Factories Are Closed."

49. For example, his stacking of the local planning commission and redevelopment authority with individuals friendly to his agenda. See Savage, "MI Gov. Rick Snyder's Takeover." With the help of some misleading national coverage by Rachel Maddow, the issue of PA 4 came to be conflated with the issues surrounding the park (which was leased out years before PA 4 went into effect). The park served a useful lightning rod for activists, however, as they sought tangible ways of illustrating the dangers of PA 4. In Flint, activists would make use of controversies around public assets in much the same way.

50. Brendan Savage, "Occupy the PGA Marches in Downtown Benton Harbor to Protest Senior PGA's Use of Park Land," *MLive*, May 26, 2012, https://www.mlive.com /news/index.ssf/2012/05/occupy_pga_marches_in_downtown.html.

51. Reverend Pinkney's association with the League of Revolutionaries for a New America was one of the things that tied him to McClinton. The league's national monthly, *People's Tribune*, served as one of the chief organs for Flint activists and McClinton (a longtime contributor) in particular during the water crisis. For a highly sympathetic account of Pinkney, see Bassett, *Soldier of Truth*.

52. McClinton, interview, June 7, 2017.

53. An interesting question is why the state's first takeover of Flint in 2002 did not provoke similar resistance. Paul Jordan remembers the actions of EFM Ed Kurtz as being more "surgical," limited to "budget control." Elected officials were "shackled" but not "totally disabled" and "there wasn't a sense of being totally disenfranchised." Paul Jordan, personal interview with author, Flint, MI, December 21, 2016. Claire McClinton told me that there was "some resentment but not resistance." McClinton, interview, June 7, 2017.

54. Reverend Dr. Reginald Flynn, "A Letter from the Flint City Jail," *People's Tribune*, August 7, 2012.

55. See Kristin Longley, "Judge Overrules Flint Emergency Manager's Order on Retiree Prescription Drugs; City Appealing Decision," *MLive*, January 7, 2013, https:// www.mlive.com/news/flint/index.ssf/2013/01/judge_overrules_flint_emergenc .html.

56. Shariff, interview, April 20, 2016.

57. Shariff, interview, April 20, 2016.

58. See Kristin Longley, "Flint Emergency Manager Michael Brown Talks Public Safety, Taxes, Water Pipeline at First Public Meeting," *MLive*, February 2, 2012, https://www.mlive.com/news/flint/index.ssf/2012/02/flint_emergency_man ager_michae_12.html. Activist Melodee Mabbitt remembers that Brown would get "laughed out" of some places by hostile members of the audience. Melodee Mabbitt, personal interview with author, Flint, MI, June 15, 2017. Shariff described public

meetings under emergency management as a kind of charade. She recounted one instance in particular when she and other activists had to "mic-check" Brown at a public hearing to expose the fact that he had already adopted the budget on which he was inviting public comment. Shariff, interview, April 20, 2016.

59. Shariff, interview, April 20, 2016.

60. Kristin Longley, "Group Protests Flint Emergency Manager on Flint City Hall Lawn," *MLive*, April 30, 2012, https://www.mlive.com/news/flint/index.ssf/2012/04 /group_protests_flint_emergency.html. Morten's 2013 play *State of Emergency* chronicles the pro-democracy movement from a Flint perspective, featuring some of the Flint activists as characters.

61. The performance also riffed on the "no taxation without representation" theme prominent within the pro-democracy movement. As Shariff pointed out, "Our Flint income taxes are due April 30. As things stand now, because we have an emergency manager, we will have no say in how those taxes are spent." "FLINT PROTEST: Michigan Emergency Manager Law (P.A. 4) Amounts to 'Taxation without Representation,'" announcement available from http://publicdevelopment.blogspot.com/2012/04/flint -protest-michigan-emergency.html.

62. As part of the deal, which preceded Uptown's much-anticipated relocation of the Flint Farmer's Market (the management of which was taken over by Uptown in 2002 when the city could no longer afford it), the city agreed not to support the establishment of any other farmer's market in the city. Melodee Mabbitt led a petition drive to try to stop the relocation of the market, and the development of a market in north Flint in defiance of the agreement became a focus of residents on that side of town. See Morckel, "Patronage and Access to a Legacy City Farmers' Market."

63. "They're stealing small today so they can steal big tomorrow," said Councilman Sheldon Neeley after the food bank deal. Kristen Longley, "Flint Emergency Manager Allows Food Bank to Pave Part of Brennan Park for Parking Lot in Exchange for Upgrades," *MLive*, August 23, 2012, https://www.mlive.com/news/flint/index.ssf/2012 /08/flint_emergency_manager_grants.html.

64. Khalil AlHajal, "Food Bank Faces Some Opposition in Leasing Part of Brennan Park for Hunger Center Parking Lot," *MLive*, June 14, 2012, https://www.mlive.com /news/flint/index.ssf/2012/06/food_bank_faces_some_oppositio.html. Residents did not prevent the lease but they did get the food bank to build another playground in the park.

65. Scott Atkinson, "Flint's Santa Has a New Job as a Temp after Years of Secluded Retirement," *MLive*, February 27, 2015, https://www.mlive.com/news/flint/index .ssf/2015/02/the_true_story_of_one_santa_cl.html.

66. As Alec Gibbs put it to me, the activists were looking for "key entry points for public acts that would draw attention to [emergency management]" (Gibbs, interview, February 10, 2017). Activists were also trying to bring attention to the ways in which emergency management in Flint, as in Benton Harbor, was being used to

advance a local agenda of what Kettering University anthropologist Laura Jordan calls "neoliberalism writ small." See Jordan, "Neoliberalism Writ Large and Small." The activists of the FDDL claimed that "most of the time the emergency manager answers to Uptown Reinvestment and all of its shell corporations." Flint Democracy Defense League, "The State of Flint under Emergency Management," transcript of speech delivered at Flint City Hall, March 3, 2014.

67. Flint Democracy Defense League, "The State of Flint under Emergency Management."

68. Flint Democracy Defense League, "The State of Flint under Emergency Management."

69. The human right FDDL singled out as a priority in its visioning statement was the right to "safe, clean, accessible, and affordable drinking water and sanitation." That right was rendered moot, the group maintained, when people did not have a say in government or in the price they paid for their water.

70. Longley, "Flint Emergency Manager Michael Brown."

71. Nayyirah Shariff, personal interview with author, Flint, MI, July 6, 2017.

72. Dominic Adams, "Flint Group Wants Public Vote on Using Tax Money to Pay for Water Pipeline," *MLive*, October 11, 2013, https://www.mlive.com/news/flint /index.ssf/2013/10/residents_want_to_vote_on_pote.html.

73. I was unable to ask Wright to comment on this claim, as he did not respond to my request for an interview.

74. Ron Fonger, "Attempt Fails to Force Public Vote in Flint on Using Tax Money to Pay for Water Pipeline," *MLive*, November 26, 2013, accessed July 1, 2017.

75. McClinton, interview, June 7, 2017.

76. Kristin Longley, "Flint Water, Sewer Rates Increasing 35 Percent," *MLive*, August 16, 2011, https://www.mlive.com/news/flint/index.ssf/2011/08/flint_water_sewer _rates_increa.html.

77. Kristin Longley, "Flint Water Rate Hikes Lead to Influx of Well Drilling Inquiries," *MLive*, May 6, 2012, https://www.mlive.com/news/flint/index.ssf/2012/05 /drill_baby_drill_flint_water_r.html. EM Brown tried to justify the city's retail rate hikes by pointing to wholesale rate hikes by Detroit, as well as infrastructural issues like water loss (the city was losing about 30 percent of water to leaks at the time). But the activists framed the issue of water rates differently: rates were being raised not "to cover the cost of water," but to "plug the deficit" created by Snyder's pro-business tax cuts and withdrawal of revenue sharing. Flint Democracy Defense League, "The State of Flint under Emergency Management."

78. As of December 2012, the city consistently averaged about 120 shutoffs for nonpayment each week. See Kristin Longley, "Agencies Fielding Pleas for Help with

Higher Flint Water Bills," *MLive*, December 26, 2012, https://www.mlive.com/news/flint/index.ssf/2012/12/higher_flint_water_rate_leads.html.

79. Molly Young, "Flint Officials Confirm 'Massive' Water Theft Investigation, Crackdown," *MLive*, September 17, 2014, https://www.mlive.com/news/flint/index.ssf/2014/09/flint_officials_confirm_massiv.html. The city continued to pay for these investigations even after the water was deemed unsafe to drink in October 2015. Gary Ridley, "Flint EM Spent More than $52K on Theft Probes after Water Was Deemed Unsafe," *MLive*, February 10, 2016, https://www.mlive.com/news/flint/index.ssf/2016/02/flint_em_spent_more_than_52k_o.html.

80. Kristin Longley, "Flint Raising Rental Home Water Deposits to $350," *MLive*, February 25, 2013, https://www.mlive.com/news/flint/index.ssf/2013/02/flint_raising_rental_home_wate.html.

81. Dominic Adams, "Flint Monthly Water and Sewer Bills Highest in Genesee County by $35," *MLive*, June 1, 2014, https://www.mlive.com/news/flint/index.ssf/2014/06/post_386.html.

82. The city's water revenue was still, somewhat mysteriously, considerably lower than projected, and the utility was still not managing to cover its costs. Dominic Adams, "Flint Still Looking for Leaks in Revenue Stream for Water and Sewer Service," *MLive*, April 15, 2014, https://www.mlive.com/news/flint/index.ssf/2014/04/water_rate_increases_loom_for.html. See also Dominic Adams, "Flint Water Rate Questions Abound on Eve of Switch away from Detroit and to River," *MLive*, April 17, 2014, https://www.mlive.com/news/flint/index.ssf/2014/04/questions_abound_on_water_rate.html.

83. For an overview of the relationship between Detroit and Flint activists, see Howell, Doan, and Harbin, "Detroit to Flint and Back Again."

84. Interviewed by Laura Bonham and Egberto Willieson, Move to Amend Reports, September 1, 2014, http://www.blogtalkradio.com/movetoamend/2014/08/01/move-to-amend-reports-wlaura-bonham-egberto-willies.

85. "Claire McClinton Speaking after the Water March 08 08 2014," August 10, 2014, video, 3:47, https://www.youtube.com/watch?v=lL3l0CNWoSI&index=3&list=PLwOo_suOzHOEnK4hruzAqtNNcFp-Leo6p.

86. "Nayyirah Shariff Speaking after the Water March 08 08 2014," August 10, 2014, video, 1:30, https://www.youtube.com/watch?v=1vtjKI7AbUg.

87. "Eric Mays Speaking after the Water March 08 08 2014," August 10, 2014, video, 7:56, https://www.youtube.com/watch?v=3bpb_4pVsdY&list=PLwOo_suOzHOEnK4hruzAqtNNcFp-Leo6p&index=6.

88. Under the terms of PA 436, elected officials in Flint had the option of voting out an EM after eighteen months with the support of six council members and the

mayor. Mays was able to rally five of his colleagues around the idea, but encountered resistance from Mayor Walling. Gary Ridley, "Flint City Council Members Rally for Removal of State-Appointed Emergency Manager," *MLive*, October 6, 2014, https://www.mlive.com/news/flint/index.ssf/2014/10/flint_city_council_members_cal.html.

5 The Rise of the Water Warriors

1. Mays, "Flint Mom Shares the Heartbreak."

2. Mark Bashore, "Despite Health Issues, Flint Activist Plays Pivotal Role," WKAR, April 27, 2016, http://www.wkar.org/post/despite-health-issues-flint-activist-plays-pivotal-role#stream/0.

3. I have taken the actual quotes from the above-cited interview with The Stir. Other details of Mays's story are from Melissa Mays, personal interview with author, Flint, MI, February 17, 2016.

4. Melissa Mays, interview with Jack Olmstead, GMO Free News, November 17, 2015.

5. LeeAnne Walters, testimony to the Michigan Joint Select Committee on the Flint Water Public Health Emergency, Flint, MI, March 29, 2016.

6. Numerous details in this section are taken from LeeAnne Walters, personal interview with author, Flint, MI, October 11, 2016.

7. See Smith, "This Mom Helped Uncover."

8. Lurie, "Meet the Mom."

9. Otiko, "Residents Say."

10. Environmental contamination that disrupts the rhythm of everyday life and invades the private realm of home and family often leads to the political mobilization of individuals with little to no experience with politics. See Cole and Foster, *From the Ground Up*, 152.

11. I cannot here mount a full methodological defense of this manner of proceeding. Suffice to say that I believe a phenomenological approach to theorizing the development of political agency is especially relevant to environmental contamination events and consistent with the ethnographic approach described in the introduction. For examples of the application of phenomenological analysis to the experience of environmental contamination, see Dorya et al., "Lived Experiences"; Dorya et al., "A Phenomenological Understanding"; and Seamon, "Lived Bodies." For phenomenology and the ethnographic study of the meanings of illness, see Kleinman, *The Illness Narratives*. I have also taken some inspiration from the discussion of phenomenology and political theory in Krupp, "Phenomenology."

12. On the concept of "political etiology," see Hamdy, "When the State and Your Kidneys Fail." On analyzing suffering as the embodiment of structural violence, see Farmer, *Pathologies of Power*.

13. These terms, and other descriptive details in this section, are derived primarily from an analysis of posts to the Flint Water Class Action Facebook page from fall 2014 to winter 2015.

14. Ron Fonger, "City Adding More Lime to Flint River Water as Resident Complaints Pour in," *MLive*, June 12, 2014, https://www.mlive.com/news/flint/index.ssf/2014/06/treated_flint_river_water_meet.html.

15. See Zahran, McElmurry, and Sadler, "Four Phases of the Flint Water Crisis," and Christensen, Keiser, and Lade, "The Effects of Information Provision."

16. Christina Zdanowicz, "Flint Family Uses 151 Bottles of Water per Day," CNN, March 7, 2016, https://www.cnn.com/2016/03/05/us/flint-family-number-daily-bottles-of-water/index.html.

17. For a useful analysis of the significance of water within the gendered space of the household, see Kaika, *City of Flows*, ch. 4. In her congressional testimony before the House Oversight and Government Reform Committee on February 3, 2016, Lee-Anne Walters dramatized the psychological effect of her family's loss of confidence in the security of their own home: "My home used to be a place of comfort and safety for my family. It used to be what a home should be: a place of peace and protection from the outside world. That was taken from us—and not just from my family but from every home and every citizen in Flint. Now my home is known as 'ground zero.'"

The idealized imagery of a happy, healthy family life disturbed by the intrusion of new and unanticipated threats played an important role in residents' efforts to convey the significance of the water crisis to those who had not personally experienced it. Just as traditional environmentalism has often relied upon a romanticized vision of unspoiled nature in order to present environmental destruction as desecration, residents like Walters made use of a similar narrative of harmony shattered, with the home figured as a sacred space defiled by destructive external forces.

18. Mays, "Flint Mom Shares the Heartbreak."

19. Some scholars have estimated that as many as 70 percent of the members of local and statewide environmental justice groups are women. See, for example, Brown and Ferguson, "Making a Big Stink," 149.

20. See Belenky, Clinchy, Goldberger, and Tarule, *Women's Ways of Knowing*. For mothers, specifically, see Ruddick, *Maternal Thinking*. For a useful discussion, see Code, *What Can She Know?*, ch. 1. For an example of the application of the "ways of knowing" framework to environmental justice, see Brown and Ferguson, "Making a Big Stink." I do not wish to enter into the contentious debate about whether this

epistemological characterization is accurate, only to put it forward as a hypothesis that would help to explain women's prominent role in environmental justice struggles.

21. See Gibbs, *Love Canal*, and Harr, *A Civil Action*. There is debate within the social movements literature over whether mothers, particularly those with young children, are more likely than women generally to be concerned about local environmental contamination. See Hamilton, "Concern about Toxic Wastes," and responses to Hamilton's work—for example, Blocker and Eckberg, "Environmental Issues as Women's Issues."

22. Bishop Bernadel Jefferson, personal interview with author, Flint, MI, May 17, 2017.

23. Jefferson, interview, May 17, 2017.

24. Maegan Wilson, personal interview with author, Flint, MI, September 15, 2016.

25. Laura Gillespie MacIntyre, personal interview with author, Flint, MI, August 29, 2016.

26. For useful accounts of perceptions of risk, see Douglas and Wildavsky, *Risk and Culture*; Beck, *Risk Society*; and Adams, *Risk*. For an illuminating case study, see Auyero and Swistun, *Flammable*.

27. Although the near-ubiquitous dichotomy between victimhood and agency has sometimes been challenged by political theorists (e.g., Nussbaum, *Upheavals of Thought*), it is less common to argue that a sense of victimhood might actually *enhance* agency. For exceptions, see Stringer, *Knowing Victims*; Jacoby, "A Theory of Victimhood"; and Jeffery and Candea, "The Politics of Victimhood." For an account of the water crisis that preserves the traditional distinction between victimhood and agency, see Jackson, "Environmental Justice?"

28. Similarly, in *Life Exposed*, Petryna writes of the importance of Chernobyl victims being seen as "recognized suffers of the state" as a basis for making political demands (xx).

29. Brown, Morello-Frosch, Zavestoski, and the Contested Illnesses Research Group, *Contested Illnesses*, 22.

30. Brown et al., *Contested Illnesses*, 22.

31. For examples, see King, "Michigan Gov. Rick Snyder"; Eligon, "A Question of Environmental Racism in Flint"; Craven and Tynes, "The Racist Roots of Flint's Water Crisis"; Ross and Solomon, "Flint Isn't the Only Place With Racism in the Water"; New York Times Editorial Board, "The Racism at the Heart of Flint's Crisis"; Wernick, "This Professor Says"; Pulido, "Flint, Environmental Racism, and Racial Capitalism"; Mascarenhas, "The Flint Water Crisis"; Zimring, *Clean and White*; and Benz, "Toxic Cities." Flint's congressional representative Dan Kildee went so far as to claim that

race was "the single greatest determinant of what happened in Flint." Quoted in
Eligon, "A Question of Environmental Racism in Flint." Robert Bullard has influentially
defined environmental racism as "any policy, practice, or directive that differentially
affects or disadvantages (whether intended or unintended) individuals, groups, or
communities based on race or color." Bullard, *Dumping in Dixie*, 98. On environmental
racism in general, see Cole and Foster, *From the Ground Up*; Taylor, *Toxic Communities*;
and Bullard, *Confronting Environmental Racism*.

32. For example, Hill, *Nobody*.

33. Susan J. Douglas, "Without Black Lives Matter, Would Flint's Water Crisis Have
Made Headlines?," *In These Times*, February 10, 2016. The Black Lives Matter "Solidarity Statement with Flint, Michigan," released in January 2016, made the point that
"Black people in America—especially those living in rural and poor areas—have long
been denied the same access to clean drinking and water for bathing and sanitation as
everyone else. The crisis in Flint is not an isolated incident. State violence in the form
of contaminated water or no access to water at all is pervasive in Black communities."

34. Nakiya Wakes, personal interview with author, Flint, MI, September 7, 2016.

35. For an intriguing parallel, consider the 1974 blaxploitation film *Three the Hard
Way*, in which white supremacists plot to eliminate the black residents of three
major American cities (including Detroit) by poisoning their municipal water sup-
plies with a chemical mixture that only affects the black population.

36. Michigan Civil Rights Commission, *The Flint Water Crisis*, 2. For commentary, see
Kaffer, "It's Time to Speak Up." Part of the problem with making a civil rights charge
stick, MCRC Chair Agustin Arbulu explained to me, is the American legal system's
insistence upon proof of malicious intent (i.e., in this case, racial animus). In my own
comments to the commission after the release of its report, I argued that it was a mistake to jump to the conclusion that present-day discrimination is merely "implicit"
and unintentional in the absence of legally incriminating instances of racism, for it
means overlooking the phenomenon of *covert* bias—i.e., biases of which an individual
is conscious and acts upon but are not openly admitted. My comments are referenced
in Worth-Nelson, "Longstanding Systemic Racism." Peter Hammer took the analysis of structural racism a step further by proposing the idea of "strategic-structural
racism": while structural racism explains present-day patterns of injustice through
a historical lens, "strategic racism" refers to the actions of contemporary actors who
take advantage of those patterns. Although calling racism "strategic" would seem to
imply conscious wrongdoing, Hammer maintains that anyone who profits economically or politically off of racial disadvantage or prejudice is acting as a "strategic" racist,
"regardless of whether the actor has express racist intent," and argues that some of
the key decisions leading up to the Flint water crisis—notably, the financial finagling
involved in the construction of the Karegnondi Water Authority pipeline—evidence
precisely this kind of strategically racist action. Hammer, "The Flint Water Crisis, the
Karegnondi Water Authority and Strategic–Structural Racism," 2.

37. Carly Hammond, "EXCLUSIVE: Flint Official Says Water Crisis Caused by 'Ni**ers Not Paying Their Bills,'" Flint Talk, June 4, 2017, http://www.flinttalk.com/viewtopic .php?p=80342.

38. Melissa Naan Burke, "EPA Email: Let's Not 'Go out on a Limb' for Flint," *Detroit News*, March 15, 2016.

39. Matthew Dolan, "Residents Raise Race as Factor in Flint Water Crisis," *Detroit Free Press*, April 28, 2016.

40. On one occasion, in the lead-up to an action at the Michigan State Capitol, we had to drop one of our planned chants ("Water is a human right, not just for the rich and white!") because of the vociferous objections of an activist—a white woman, but backed up by multiple black activists—who complained that it was "so racist" because it implied (she felt) that people like her were not victims of the water.

41. Walters, interview, October 11, 2016.

42. Salmon, "American Genocide."

43. Gina Luster, personal interview with author, Flint, MI, September 7, 2016.

44. Undated conversation with Claire McClinton. For a class-oriented socialist critique of the MCRC's conclusions, see Brewer, "Michigan Blames Flint Water Crisis."

45. Mays, interview, February 17, 2016.

46. Abel Delgado, interview with author, Flint, MI, December 7, 2016.

47. Desiree Duell, interview with author, Flint, MI, August 24, 2016.

48. Luster, interview, September 7, 2016.

49. Ron Fonger, "Flint Councilman Equates Water Troubles to 'Genocide' by Governor," *MLive*, April 6, 2015, https://www.mlive.com/news/flint/index.ssf/2015/04/flint _councilman_claims_govern.html.

50. Steve Carmody, "Flint Councilman Stands by 'Genocide' Charge," Michigan Radio, April 10, 2015.

51. Wantwaz Davis, interview with author, Flint, MI, November 11, 2017.

52. Author's field notes, Flint Democracy Defense League meeting, August 27, 2016.

53. This is from a social media post by someone I wish to keep anonymous. Facebook, February 17, 2017.

54. Sam Gringlas, "Will the Water Crisis Finally Secure More than Band-Aids for Flint?," *Belt Magazine*, June 27, 2016.

55. Author's field notes, Water Is Life: Strengthening the Great Lakes Commons (conference), Woodside Church, Flint, MI, September 29, 2017.

56. Duell, interview, August 24, 2016, and Laura Gillespie McIntyre, personal interview with author, Flint, MI, August 29, 2016.

57. Fricker, *Epistemic Injustice*, 1.

58. Figures taken from census data.

59. Fricker, *Epistemic Injustice*, 36.

60. For influential accounts of the concept, see Taylor, "The Politics of Recognition"; Young, *Justice*; Honneth, *The Struggle for Recognition*; and Fraser, "Rethinking Recognition."

61. Lawrence Reynolds, interview with author, Flint, MI, July 12, 2017.

62. Mays, interview, February 17, 2016.

63. Walters, interview, October 11, 2016.

64. I take the distinction from the classic discussion by Mills in *The Sociological Imagination*.

65. Rauch, "When Your Water Poisons Your Children."

66. As Brown and Mikkelsen define it, popular epidemiology is "the process by which laypersons gather scientific data and other information and direct and marshal the knowledge and resources of experts to understand the epidemiology of disease." *No Safe Place*, 125–126. The authors describe the phenomenon as "an extremely significant advance for both public health and popular democratic participation" (127).

67. One might describe this as converting a collective experience of illness into a *politicized* illness experience that links disease to the "social determinants of health." Brown, *Toxic Exposures*, 30.

68. Mays, interview, February 17, 2016.

6   Demanding the Impossible

1. Gertrude Saunders, "Flint City Council 012615," January 26, 2015, video, 1:36:51, https://www.youtube.com/watch?v=Z-7MmKfjanI.

2. Claire McClinton, interview with author, Flint, MI, June 7, 2017.

3. In John Dryzek's terminology, emergency management has very little inbuilt "deliberative capacity." Dryzek, "Democratization as Deliberative Capacity Building."

4. Dryzek, "Democratization as Deliberative Capacity Building."

5. Brown, "Popular Epidemiology and Toxic Waste Contamination."

6. Even when activist interventions were discursively oriented—seeking to reframe the water situation as a "crisis," for example—they had a coercive rather than a

deliberative character, aiming to counteract the discursive power of others. For discussion of this tactic, see Dodge, "Environmental Justice and Deliberative Democracy." Contemporary theorists of deliberation have begun to evaluate activism from the perspective of deliberative democratic "systems," in recognition of the fact that activities relevant to the deliberative health of a body politic take place at many sites, and may themselves lack traditionally deliberative virtues. See especially Mansbridge et al., "A Systemic Approach to Deliberative Democracy." Given the "inside-out" orientation of this book, I instead adopt the *anti*-systemic perspective of the activists, evaluating their activities as efforts to contest not only particular policies but also the underlying logic of the emergency manager system. The activists certainly did not see the EM system as a "deliberative system" they had any interest in trying to improve.

7. One could argue that, in some ways, residents were "impossible subjects" under emergency management to begin with. For a parallel to another kind of "impossible activism" carried out from a marginalized position, see Nyers, "Abject Cosmopolitanism."

8. These details are culled from 1,600 pages of emails released to *The Detroit News*. See Chad Livengood, "Emails: Flint Water Warnings Reached Gov's Inner Circle," *Detroit News*, February 26, 2016.

9. Dayne Walling, interview with author, Flint, MI, March 9, 2016.

10. All quotations in this and the following paragraphs are from video records of the water quality meeting, Flint City Hall, Flint, MI, January 21, 2015.

11. Ron Fonger, "Flint Water Advisory Committee Formed by Mayor, Emergency Manager," *MLive*, February 17, 2015, https://www.mlive.com/news/flint/index.ssf/2015/02/40-member_citizen_water_commit.html.

12. "I was trying to create a forum for community dialogue that was more like the participatory process we had around the master plan," Walling told me. "I was the one who pushed for the community advisory meetings, the creation of a technical task force. I was the one who demanded that these groups meet in public ... that the public be able to attend and participate, just like we had done with the master plan." Walling, interview, March 9, 2016.

13. Nayyirah Shariff, who served on two master plan advisory groups, told me that their apparent participatory qualities masked hidden interests operating behind the scenes, particularly those associated with the Uptown developers. She came away from the experience "very dissatisfied," concluding that the master planning process was another attempt to apply a false democratic veneer to life under emergency management in Flint. Nayyirah Shariff, interview with author, Flint, MI, April 20, 2016. I heard similar comments on the master plan from Desiree Duell, another participant in the process, who told me that the end result was "not completely authentic." Desiree Duell, interview with author, Flint, MI, August 24, 2016.

14. McClinton, "No Safe Affordable Water."

15. Ron Fonger, "Water Consultant Recommends Flint Make Changes in Treatment, Distribution," *MLive*, March 4, 2015, https://www.mlive.com/news/flint/index .ssf/2015/03/flint_water_consultant_tells_c.html.

16. Laura Sullivan, interview with author, Flint, MI, March 25, 2016.

17. When this was pointed out in the press, Florlisa Fowler and Nayyirah Shariff reacted in different ways. Fowler: "I wrote [the mayor] an email, requesting an invitation—politely.... I asked if he could pick me or another group member.... We should have at least one." Shariff: "My concern with this whole process is what will be the purpose of the committee? ... When I looked at most of those groups [that were invited] they've been silent [on the water issues]." Others made the all-important point that many of the people on the committee didn't live in Flint. Ron Fonger, "Some Flint Water Activists Didn't Get Invitation, but Mayor Says Advisory Committee Could Expand," *MLive*, February 17, 2015, https://www.mlive.com/news /flint/index.ssf/2015/02/flint_water_activists_dont_get.html.

18. Jiquanda Johnson, "Flint Water Advisory Committee's First Meeting Erupts in Shouting Match," *MLive*, March 5, 2015, https://www.mlive.com/news/flint/index. ssf/2015/03/flint_residents_say_committee.html.

19. A clip featuring this remark is included in the ACLU documentary *Here's to Flint* (Curt Guyette and Kate Levy, *Here's to Flint*, ACLU of Michigan, March 8, 2016, 44:54).

20. Ron Fonger, "Flint Water Committee Meets, but Some Residents Don't See Progress," *MLive*, March 19, 2015, https://www.mlive.com/news/flint/index.ssf/2015/03 /flint_water_committee_meets_bu.html.

21. Ron Fonger, "Flint Mayor Ready to Talk about Changing Water Advisory Committee Format," *MLive*, March 24, 2015, https://www.mlive.com/news/flint/index .ssf/2015/03/flint_mayor_ready_to_talk_abou.html.

22. Ron Fonger, "Lead Revives Flint's Dormant Expert Committee on Water," *MLive*, October 5, 2015, https://www.mlive.com/news/flint/index.ssf/2015/10/flints _expert_committee_on_wat.html.

23. Walling, interview, March 9, 2016.

24. Laura Sullivan's feeling, informed by her interactions with Walling and observations of him in closed-door meetings, was that he was not actually committed to having a conversation about the water, treating it as a nonissue. Generally speaking, activists attributed his dispassionate demeanor not to his stated belief in a civil and cooperative politics, but to either a weakness of will or to his being a collaborator with the state. Sullivan also recalls numerous instances of other officials putting on an amiable face in public settings but treating residents' concerns with condescension and

contempt in private ones, apparently convinced that residents' health symptoms were either psychosomatic or being exaggerated for cynical reasons. She remembers feeling embarrassed when she encountered these attitudes, having at first reassured the activists that those in charge were paying attention and trying to do the right thing. In one instance, when Howard Croft was rolling his eyes about residents' rash complaints, she told him that "you are in charge of more than the water, you are in charge of people's trust in the water, and if you have such disregard for their concerns, there's no way in the world you'll ever have their trust." Laura Sullivan, interview with author, Flint, MI, November 14, 2016.

25. Young, "Activist Challenges to Deliberative Democracy," 684.

26. As Jason Corburn points out, a *coproduction* model of expertise, in contrast to this unidirectional flow of expert knowledge, requires a "deliberative politics" in which local knowledge is valued and participation solicited. Corburn, *Street Science*, 41. Resident knowledge of water quality at the tap was critical to an understanding of the situation, Laura Sullivan told me, because no one "at the plant level had any clue that there were actually things showing up in the water downstream because of the interaction of that water with our pipes." Laura Sullivan, interview with author, Flint, MI, November 14, 2016.

27. Walling, interview, March 9, 2016.

28. Ron Fonger, "Flint Residents Call for Investigative Hearings into 'Water Crisis'," *MLive*, January 5, 2015, https://www.mlive.com/news/flint/index.ssf/2015/01 /state_deq_high_levels_of_disin.html; Ron Fonger, "Flint Democracy Defense League Plans Four Meetings on City's Water Problems," *MLive*, January 29, 2015, https:// www.mlive.com/news/flint/index.ssf/2015/01/flint_democracy_defense_league_1 .html.

29. Nayyirah Shariff, Facebook post, January 5, 2015. In another post from February 23, 2015, Shariff wrote that "we don't do hierarchies; we are all members." On the importance of "free spaces" to democratic movements, see Evans and Boyte, *Free Spaces*.

30. Eric Dresden, "Flint Residents Protest Drinking Water Problems outside City Hall," *MLive*, January 12, 2015, https://www.mlive.com/news/flint/index.ssf/2015/01 /clean_water_is_a_right_and_a_p.html.

31. At least this is the way the story of the group's origins was told originally. After the contentious breakup between Mays and Walters (explained in the next chapter), and after the third member of the group drifted away from water activism and began to excoriate both of them, Mays began to say that the group had been formed by herself and her husband, Adam.

32. William E. Ketchum, "People Take to Streets to Protest Flint Water Quality," *MLive*, February 14, 2015, https://www.mlive.com/news/flint/index.ssf/2015/02/flint_residents _protest_citys.html.

33. Ron Fonger, "Flint Pastors Tell State Officials: Get Us off Flint River Water Now," *MLive*, February 5, 2015, https://www.mlive.com/news/flint/index.ssf/2015/02/flint _pastors_tell_state_offic.html.

34. Later, it was revealed that the conference had cost Reverend Alfred Harris a spot on the Receivership Transition Advisory Board. "I take that as a great compliment," Harris said. "If it cost me, it cost me. They understood my interest was strictly for the people ... not what the state wanted me to do." Ron Fonger, "Pastors Paid Price from Governor's Staff for Activism in Flint Water Crisis," *MLive*, February 29, 2016, https://www.mlive.com/news/flint/index.ssf/2016/02/pastors_paid_price_from _govern.html.

35. Coalition for Clean Water, "Coalition for Clean Water."

36. The coalition did not come to a perfect consensus, however. For Tru Saunders, the "hook" stretched credulity—it implied that the city was continuing to distribute water that its own data showed was harmful, even though the city did not see it that way. Although Saunders believed as much as anyone that the water was bad, she accused the coalition of dishonestly misrepresenting the city's position, and, after an argument, left the group and did not come back. Gertrude Saunders, interview with author, Flint, MI, June 6, 2017.

37. Randy Conat, "Coalition Wants Flint to Return to Detroit Water," ABC12, June 5, 2015, https://www.abc12.com/home/headlines/Coalition-wants-Flint-to-return-to -Detroit-water-306325041.html. Surrounded by activists on the steps of the Genesee County Circuit Court, attorney Trachelle Young argued that the range of problems with the water evident over the preceding months was suggestive of a "structural problem." It was better to return to Detroit, which had indicated its willingness to accept a short-term arrangement "with no obligations and no strings attached," than it was to continue to entrust the health of residents to the inexperienced operators of Flint's water system. Gary Ridley, "Lawsuit Seeks End to Flint River Drinking Water, Return to Detroit," *MLive*, June 5, 2015, https://www.mlive.com/news/flint/index .ssf/2015/06/lawsuit_seeks_end_to_flint_riv.html. See also Coalition for Clean Water, "Coalition for Clean Water."

38. The suit ran into difficulties when US District Judge Stephen J. Murphy III determined that the coalition's legal argument was "completely undeveloped." Ron Fonger, "Judge Won't Force Flint to Return to Buying Detroit Water," *MLive*, June 23, 2015, https://www.mlive.com/news/flint/index.ssf/2015/06/judge_says_flint_doesnt _have_t_1.html. For follow-up coverage, see Ron Fonger, "Water Coalition Drops Federal Claim, Flint Calls Lawsuit 'Baseless,'" *MLive*, July 16, 2015, https://www.mlive .com/news/flint/index.ssf/2015/07/water_coalition_drops_federal.html; and Ron Fonger, "Lawsuit Aimed at Forcing Flint to End Use of Flint River Dismissed," *MLive*, September 15, 2015, https://www.mlive.com/news/flint/index.ssf/2015/09/lawsuit _aimed_at_forcing_flint.html.

39. Ron Fonger, "Flint Mayor Accepts Petitions but Not Call to End Use of Flint River," *MLive*, August 31, https://www.mlive.com/news/flint/index.ssf/2015/08/flint_mayor _accepts_petitions.html.

40. Guyette, "Corrosive Impact."

41. Miguel del Toral, personal interview with author, Flint, MI, May 6, 2016.

42. See Curt Guyette and Kate Levy's short film for the ACLU of Michigan, "Hard to Swallow: Toxic Water in a Toxic System in Flint," 2015.

43. Lindsey Smith, "Leaked Internal Memo Shows Federal Regulator's Concerns about Lead in Flint's Water," Michigan Radio, July 13, 2015.

44. A Freedom of Information Act request for the city's sampling data filed by Curt Guyette proved these fears to be well founded when it revealed that the city's nine-tieth percentile had been falsified through the conscious exclusion of two critical data points.

45. Laura Sullivan, personal interview with author, Flint, MI, November 14, 2016.

46. Sullivan, interview, November 14, 2016.

47. Laura Sullivan, personal interview with author, Flint, MI, March 25, 2016.

48. Email from Dennis Muchmore to Harvey Hollins, August 5, 2015.

49. Email from Harvey Hollins to Dennis Muchmore, August 5, 2015. As part of bringing the water issue to "closure," Muchmore and Hollins offered to donate 1,500 filters to residents through the Concerned Pastors (rather than the Coalition for Clean Water, *per se*). The condition was that the pastors tell people the filters had come from an "anonymous donor." Ron Fonger, "Concerned Pastors planning water filter giveaway in Flint," *MLive*, August 26, 2015, https://www.mlive.com /news/flint/index.ssf/2015/08/concerned_pastors_say_theyll_a.html. There was some controversy over the way in which the filters were distributed. For some activists, particularly those who had prior suspicions of the Concerned Pastors, the "hush-hush filters" episode became evidence of the pastors' inclination toward backroom deals and excessively cozy relationships with political elites.

50. LeeAnne Walters, personal interview with author, Flint, MI, October 11, 2016.

51. A National Science Foundation Rapid Response Grant awarded to the Virginia Tech team in September 2015 would ultimately cover the cost.

52. Curt Guyette, personal interview with author, Flint, MI, December 8, 2016.

53. Walters, interview, October 11, 2016.

54. Siddartha Roy, interviewed by Philip Silva, "The Flint Water Crisis Illuminated by Citizen Science," The Nature of Cities podcast, February 29, 2016, https://www .thenatureofcities.com/2016/02/29/the-flint-water-crisis/.

55. Marc Edwards, Siddhartha Roy, and William Rhoads, "Lead Testing Results for Water Sampled by Residents," September 2015, http://flintwaterstudy.org/information-for-flint-residents/results-for-citizen-testing-for-lead-300-kits/.

56. Coalition for Clean Water joint press conference, Flint City Hall, September 15, 2015, available from https://www.youtube.com/watch?v=xwg5L3mYUEI.

57. Ron Fonger, "Feds Sending in Experts to Help Flint Keep Lead out of Water," *MLive*, September 10, 2015, https://www.mlive.com/news/flint/index.ssf/2015/09/university_researchers_dont_dr.html.

58. Ron Fonger, "Watch: Flint News Conference on Lead in Water Issues," *MLive*, September 25, 2015, https://www.mlive.com/news/flint/index.ssf/2015/09/watch_live_flint_lead_in_water.html.

59. Molly Young, "Clean Water Activists Demand Detroit Reconnection in Flint after Lead Study," *MLive*, September 28, 2015, https://www.mlive.com/news/flint/index.ssf/2015/09/coalition_for_clean_water_dema.html.

60. The petition was cosponsored by the ACLU and the Natural Resources Defense Council. See "Petition for Emergency Action under the Safe Drinking Water Act, 42 U.S.C. § 300i, to Abate the Imminent and Substantial Endangerment to Flint, Michigan Residents from Lead Contamination in Drinking Water," October 1, 2015, https://www.nrdc.org/sites/default/files/petition-for-emergency-action-under-the-safe-drinking-water-act-20170302.pdf.

61. Ron Fonger, "State Offers City Cash for Filters, but No Break from Flint River," *MLive*, October 2, 2015, https://www.mlive.com/news/flint/index.ssf/2015/10/state_rolls_out_flint_water_pl.html.

62. Ron Fonger, "Pastors Threaten Lawsuit over Flint River Water, Demand Reconnection to Detroit System," *MLive*, April 8, 2015, https://www.mlive.com/news/flint/index.ssf/2015/04/pastors_threaten_lawsuit_over.html.

63. The cost was $12 million, $6 million of which would be provided by the state, $4 million by the Charles Stewart Mott Foundation, and $2 million by the City of Flint.

64. Damon Maloney, "Concerned Pastors, Residents Claim Victory over Return to Detroit Water," ABC12, October 8, 2015, https://www.abc12.com/home/headlines/Concerned-pastors-residents-claim-victory-over-return-to-Detroit-Water-331475132.html.

65. Dayne Walling, interview with author, Flint, MI, March 9, 2016.

66. Susan Hedman of EPA Region 5 had told Walling that the city and county were already doing (with help from the state and the nonprofit sector) everything the EPA might have ordered them to do. Walling, interview, March 9, 2016.

67. Ron Fonger, "Karen Weaver Makes History, Elected Flint's First Woman Mayor," *MLive*, November 4, 2015, https://www.mlive.com/news/flint/index.ssf/2015/11 /karen_weaver_makes_history_ele_1.html. Walling told me that, in his view, "the activism certainly had an effect on the election." Walling, interview, March 9, 2016.

68. Guyette, "Flint's State of Emergency Is a Sign."

69. Walling, interview, March 9, 2016.

70. Melissa Mays and Nayyirah Shariff acted as advisors to the screenwriters of the movie (*Flint*). Despite being major characters in the film, LeeAnne Walters refused to participate officially and Claire McClinton told me she was never contacted by the producers (or the other activists involved).

71. For an especially egregious example—though one among many, many others—see Campbell, *Poison on Tap*.

7   The Water Is (Not) Safe

1. Coalition for Clean Water joint press conference, Flint City Hall, September 15, 2015, available from https://www.youtube.com/watch?v=xwg5L3mYUEI.

2. For example, in Ashley O'Brien, "Transformed by Water and Politics, Walters Fights On," *East Village Magazine*, November 16, 2015.

3. Relevant here are Steven Epstein's insights about debates over science as "credibility struggles." Epstein defines credibility as "the believability of claims and claims-makers ... the capacity of claims-makers to enroll supporters behind their arguments, legitimate those arguments as authoritative knowledge, and present themselves as the sort of people who can voice the truth" (*Impure Science*, 3). The credibility of a speaker, he writes, "can rest on academic degrees, 'anointment' by the media, or the speaker's access to esoteric forms of communication; the credibility of any knowledge claim can depend on who advances it, how plausible it seems, or what sort of experimental evidence is invoked to support it" (3). The central role of credibility in the reception of scientific knowledge reflects the extent to which the communication and transmission of that knowledge is dependent upon trust. See Hardwig, "The Role of Trust in Knowledge."

4. On scientific standards as potential barriers to lay participation in science, see Ottinger, "Buckets of Resistance."

5. LeeAnne Walters estimates that they succeeded about 85 percent of the time. Interview with author, Flint, MI, October 11, 2016.

6. Claire McClinton, interview with author, Flint, MI, September 6, 2018.

7. McClinton, interview, September 6, 2018.

8. Governor Snyder pledged that "no arbitrary decision would be made" about when the water was safe and that the state "would let the science take us to that conclusion." Office of Governor Rick Snyder, "City of Flint's Water Quality Restored, Testing Well below Federal Action Level for Nearly Two Years," press release, April 6, 2018, https://www.michigan.gov/snyder/0,4668,7-277-57577_57657-465766--,00.html.

9. Quoted in Wang, "The Engineered Crisis in Flint."

10. Marc Edwards, "Lead in Drinking Water and Public Health: A Scientist's Descent into the Activist Netherworld," talk delivered at Goddard Space Flight Center, Greenbelt, MD, February 2, 2009.

11. See the exchange between Edwards, David Sedlak, and a number of other interlocutors, beginning with Sedlak's editorial "Crossing the Imaginary Line" and including Marc A. Edwards, Amy Pruden, Siddhartha Roy, and William J. Rhoads, "Engineers Shall Hold Paramount the Safety, Health and Welfare of the Public—but Not If It Threatens Our Research Funding?," October 10, 2016, http://flintwaterstudy. org/2016/10/engineers-shall-hold-paramount-the-safety-health-and-welfare-of-the-public-but-not-if-it-threatens-our-research-funding/. Edwards claimed at one point that the Virginia Tech team "ended up leading a lot of the activism that occurred in Flint" ("The Crowd and the Cloud Live Aftershow," April 13, 2017, Facebook video, 1:02:52, https://www.facebook.com/crowdandcloudTV/videos/1953213671579827/).

12. Marc Edwards, interview on *The Tom Sumner Show*, July 27, 2018.

13. Ron Fonger, "Erin Brockovich Investigator Says Tweaks Can Fix Flint River Water," *MLive*, February 11, 2015, https://www.mlive.com/news/flint/index.ssf/2015/02/erin _brockovich_investigator_s.html.

14. Bowcock's talk is available from https://www.youtube.com/watch?v=k3nh1 P12huQ.

15. See Veolia, *Flint, Michigan Water Quality Report.*

16. Bob Bowcock, phone interview with author, December 1, 2016.

17. Bowcock explained to me that he and Brockovich, as a two-person team, have to be "selective" about which of the many contamination cases around the country they get involved in (about five hundred requests for help come in each day, he said). Among their criteria for intervention is that an affected community has to be "forming an organization," with community members "starting to meet in people's homes and … starting to want to take action." In cases where residents are trying to get an organizing effort off the ground but "don't understand the science," Bowcock comes in as a consultant "to help the community take some immediate action to at a minimum remediate some of the problems occurring," preferring to work with the water utility but resorting to coercive measures like legal injunctions when necessary. Bowcock, phone interview, December 1, 2016.

18. May, "Marc Edwards: Corrosion Man."

19. August, "The Plumbing Professor."

20. Home-Douglas, "The Water Guy."

21. Colby Itkowitz, "The Heroic Professor Who Helped Uncover the Flint Lead Water Crisis Has Been Asked to Fix It," *Washington Post,* January 27, 2016.

22. Marc Edwards, interview with author, Ann Arbor, MI, October 26, 2016.

23. Edwards, "Institutional Scientific Misconduct."

24. Burke, "Flint Water Crisis Yields Hard Lessons."

25. Marc Edwards, interview with RT America, February 26, 2016.

26. See Home-Douglas, "The Water Guy."

27. Russell, "Clean Water Warrior Wins."

28. As Edwards put it to C-SPAN, "we dropped everything and ... tried to even the odds on behalf of Flint residents so they could find out the truth about their drinking water." Washington Journal, February 29, 2016.

29. Edwards, interview, October 26, 2016.

30. Marc Edwards and Siddhartha Roy, "Is Unfiltered Flint Water Safe to Drink?— New FAQ for Flint Residents," May 4, 2017, http://flintwaterstudy.org/2017/05/faq -may-2017/.

31. Robby Korth, "Virginia Tech Water Study Team Faces Financial Struggles," *Roanoke Times,* April 13, 2016.

32. Walters, interview, October 11, 2016.

33. McClinton, interview, September 6, 2018.

34. In conceptualizing his intervention in Flint, Edwards took inspiration from a former collaborator, medical anthropologist Yanna Lambrinidou, and the course they once taught together at Virginia Tech, "Engineering Ethics and the Public: Learning to Listen." In my view, the Flint Water Study team's aggressive promotion of the "citizen science" frame, which contributed to the underlying narrative disconnect between its account of the water crisis and that of the activists, was one among other impediments to the kind of deep, ethnographic listening espoused by Lambrinidou. As the relationship with Edwards went downhill, I repeatedly heard activists say that Edwards was *not* listening to people within the community. Worried that Edwards was usurping resident voices in Flint, Lambrinidou became an outspoken critic of his intervention. See her "On Listening, Science, and Justice" and "When Technical Experts Set Out to 'Do Good,'" as well as Kolowich, "The Accidental Ethicist," and Hohn, "Flint's Water Crisis."

35. Edwards, interview, October 26, 2016.

36. On the tendency to treat Walters as the face of the grassroots struggle in Flint, see Jackson, "The Goldman Prize Missed the Black Heroes of Flint."

37. Siddhartha Roy, presentation at 2017 McComas Staff Leadership Seminar, Virginia Tech, Blacksburg, VA, April 26, 2017, https://vtechworks.lib.vt.edu/handle/10919 /80929.

38. "WASA" is the District of Columbia Water and Sewer Authority.

39. Steven Epstein points out that a social movement's "possession of its own media institutions" is critical to its ability to construct its own credibility. *Impure Science*, 22. The closest the activists came to this was the Water You Fighting For? website, but posts to Flintwaterstudy.org had much greater reach, even within local social media networks.

40. Nayyirah Shariff, interview with author, Flint, MI, September 15, 2018.

41. Edwards and Pruden, "We Helped Flint Residents," 12057.

42. Cooper and Lewenstein, "Two Meanings of Citizen Science," 59. The awarding institutions that chose to honor Edwards and his team rarely, if ever (from what I could tell), took the time to talk to members of the community or look more deeply into the details.

43. On the ways in which credibility excess "undermin[es] and creat[es] obstacles for dissenting voices" and exacerbates epistemic injustice, see Medina, "The Relevance of Credibility Excess," 18.

44. See Edwards and Roy, "Academic Research in the 21st Century." Edwards's frequent invocations of the "public good" made for a head-scratching complement to his ideological inclinations, which included affection for the egoist hero-worship of Ayn Rand (he was known to recommend *Atlas Shrugged* to his colleagues and even give copies as gifts). As is well known, Rand did not believe the concept of the "public" was coherent to begin with, much less the concept of a public "good." See Rand, *The Virtue of Selfishness*.

45. Itkowitz, "The Heroic Professor."

46. Washington Journal on C-SPAN interview, February 29, 2016. For a somewhat more guarded Edwards, see Gary Ridley, "'Beginning of the End for Flint Water Crisis Health Disaster, Edwards Says," *MLive*, August 11, 2016, https://www.mlive .com/news/flint/index.ssf/2016/08/flint_in_beginning_of_the_end.html.

47. Edwards and Roy, "Is Unfiltered Flint Water Safe to Drink?"

48. Pam Radtke Russell, "Clean Water Warrior Wins 2017 ENR Award of Excellence," *Engineering News-Record*, April 13, 2017.

49. Marc Edwards, "Flint's New GAC Treatment Filter Is Helping Meet EPA's THM Standards," August 31, 2015, http://flintwaterstudy.org/2015/08/flints-new-gac-treatment-filter-is-helping-meet-epas-thm-standards/.

50. The presentation is available at http://flintwaterstudy.org/2015/09/distribution-of-lead-results-across-flint-by-ward-and-zip-codes/.

51. By the end of 2016, the official consensus was that the city's ninetieth percentile for lead was solidly below the federal action level. Ron Fonger, "Virginia Tech: Testing Shows 'Amazing' Flint Water Improvements," *MLive*, December 2, 2016, https://www.mlive.com/news/flint/index.ssf/2016/12/virginia_tech_testing_shows_fl.html.

52. One person told me that Edwards made such a remark publicly as early as January 2016, although I did not hear it myself. The main controversy came toward the end of the year, when a news article appeared that highlighted this position. For his response to the fallout, see Marc Edwards, "Understanding Flint's Water Infrastructure Crisis: Water Infrastructure Inequality in America," December 9, 2016, http://flintwaterstudy.org/2016/12/understanding-flints-water-infrastructure-crisis-water-infrastructure-inequality-in-america/; and Marc Edwards, "The Flint Infrastructure Crisis: Two Dinners with Flint Residents," December 19, 2016, http://flintwaterstudy.org/2016/12/the-flint-infrastructure-crisis-two-dinners-with-flint-residents/.

53. Matthew Dolan, "Researcher: Flint Water 'Like Russian Roulette'," *Detroit Free Press*, April 12, 2016.

54. Edwards, interview, October 26, 2016.

55. Marc Edwards, interview on Washington Journal, C-SPAN, February 29, 2016.

56. Marc Edwards, Flint Water Study team press conference, August 11, 2016. https://youtu.be/77CW8rBq2oo?t=2558

57. Holly Fournier, "Edwards' Team Shows Dramatic Drop in Flint Lead Levels," *Detroit News*, December 2, 2016.

58. Regina H. Boone, "Free Press Photo Helps Define Flint Tragedy for Nation," *Detroit Free Press*, January 21, 2016.

59. Darcey Rakestraw, "Exclusive: Water Defense Video Shows Tar Balls, Oil Slicks near Kern County Irrigation Site," Food and Water Watch, May 26, 2015, https://www.foodandwaterwatch.org/news/exclusive-water-defense-video-shows-tar-balls-oil-slicks-near-kern-county-irrigation-site.

60. Dana C. Silano, "SBA Recognizes Local Business Owner for Flood Recover Efforts," *Times Telegram*, April 29, 2008. See also Smith's Opflex Solutions bio, available from www.cctechcouncil.org/wp-content/uploads/2012/09/PDF-Scott-Smith-Bio.pdf. Opflex eventually became embroiled in a dispute over rent and, ironically, environmental cleanup at its former New York headquarters, eventually relocating

to Indianapolis: Jeff Swiatek, "Rent Dispute in N.Y., Tax Abatement in Indy for Foam Maker," *Indystar*, April 30, 2015.

61. "Cellect Plastics LLC Signs 5-Year $30 Million Contract for Global Supply of Opflex™ The Green Stuff™ with ClearWater Environmental Technologies Inc.," *Business Wire*, July 30, 2010, https://www.businesswire.com/news/home/2010073000 6059/en/Cellect-Plastics-LLC-Signs-5-Year-30-Million.

62. From Smith's LinkedIn profile, accessed June 2017, www.linkedin.com/in/scott -smith-1b100776/.

63. See the nod to Smith's work in *USA Today*: Julie Schmidt, "After BP Oil Spill, Thousands of Ideas Poured in for Cleanup," November 15, 2010.

64. Valerie Mohler, "Meet the Man Mark Ruffalo Hand-Picked to Fight for Clean Water: Q&A with Water Defense Chief Scientist Scott Smith," DiscountFilterStore. com, March 12, 2014, http://blog.discountfilterstore.com/blog/mark-ruffalo-hand -picked-scott-smith-clean-water-fight/.

65. See "Mark Ruffalo, Back Again on Reddit. Let's Talk Water Defense with Scott Smith," *Reddit*, May 6, 2015, https://www.reddit.com/r/IAmA/comments/351yxe/mark _ruffalo_back_again_on_reddit_lets_talk_water/.

66. Rakestraw, "Exclusive."

67. "Mark Ruffalo, Back Again on Reddit."

68. Rebecca Ford, "Mark Ruffalo on the Hulk's Future, the Dangers of Fracking and 'Smear Campaigns' against Actor Activists," *The Hollywood Reporter*, October 30, 2014. The second quote is from a video subsequently removed. See also Cliff Weathers, "Mark Ruffalo and Scott Smith Boldly Fight for Clean Water," Alternet, June 13, 2014, https://www.alternet.org/environment/mark-ruffalo-and-scott-smith-why-dir ect-action-critical-keeping-our-water-safe. During an April 2016 community meeting in Flint, Smith stoked residents' sense of empowerment by saying, "Everyone should be proud—this is about the community leading it, and just maybe, maybe, all these other experts, and the EPA and your own agencies are gonna learn from *you*." Author's field notes, Scott Smith presentation, St. Michael's Church, Flint, MI, April 9, 2016.

69. Weathers, "Mark Ruffalo and Scott Smith."

70. In a 2015 year-end recap of Water Defense's work, Ruffalo wrote that the WaterBug would "empower individuals and groups to address their own local water concerns" and help "create the most comprehensive independent source of water quality data available to the public." Ruffalo, "Our Work in 2015."

71. "Our Work," Flint Water Defense Info, available from https://flintwaterdefense info.wordpress.com/information/our-work/.

72. Joe Guillen, "State Removes Criticized Flint Water Poster," *Detroit Free Press*, January 9, 2016.

73. In January 2016, the union purchased and distributed $20,000 worth of bottled water. Later, they mobilized plumbers from all over the area to install filters and new faucets free of charge.

74. The partnership with the plumbers also became a way for Smith to illustrate the value of putting water sampling technology and know-how into the hands of nonexperts. As the plumbers shadowed Smith, they were struck by the simplicity of his sampling procedures. As Harold Harrington put it to me, "If I'da known back then what I know now I'da been out testing the water, cause I'd seen the brown water coming out of my house. But I listened to officials that were supposed to know better. That's why I think you should have the knowledge. ... You should be able to go test your own water. I mean, it's not rocket science ... but nobody knows how to do it." The impulse to make sampling more widespread led to an idea: plumbers spent every day working on water infrastructure—why not enable them to assess the quality of the water running through it? In April, Water Defense and the UA entered into a national agreement whereby Smith would train UA plumbers in water sampling so that they could offer it as a service to their customers. Harold Harrington, interview with author, Flint, MI, October 27, 2016.

75. "Nonprofit: Concerning Levels of Chemicals Found in Water," WNEM, February 18, 2016.

76. Stephanie Parkinson, "Actor Mark Ruffalo Calls on Obama to Declare National Disaster in Flint Water Crisis," NBC25News, March 7, 2016, https://nbc25news.com/news/local/actor-mark-ruffalo-calls-on-obama-to-declare-national-disaster-in-flint-water-crisis. Later, Flint Rising partnered with Ruffalo and Green for All on a petition calling for Governor Snyder to comply with their demands. Roberto Acosta, "Mark Ruffalo, Van Jones Petition in Flint Water Crisis to Fix Service Lines," *MLive*, March 28, 2016, https://www.mlive.com/news/flint/index.ssf/2016/03/mark_ruffalo_van_jones_start_p.html.

77. Kristin Aguirre, "Actor Mark Ruffalo Reveals New Findings in Contaminated Flint Water," NBC25News, March 9, 2016, https://nbc25news.com/news/nbc25-today/actor-mark-ruffalo-reveals-new-findings-in-flint-water. Smith later claimed vindication when Edwards admitted that orthophosphates were not working well on galvanized pipes. Once again, from the activists' perspective, their independent "expert" was out in front of the academicians. See Ilse Hayes, "More Troubles for Flint Residents: Interior Galvanized Pipes Also Need Replacement," NBC25News, February 6, 2017, https://nbc25news.com/news/nbc25-today/more-troubles-for-flint-resid more-troents-interior-galvanized-pipes-also-need-replacement.

78. Josh Sidorowicz, "Flint Families Pleading to Speak with Gov. Snyder while in D.C.," Fox17, March 16, 2016, https://fox17online.com/2016/03/16/flint-families-pl eading-to-speak-with-gov-snyder-while-in-d-c/.

79. Author's field notes, Scott Smith presentation, St. Michael's Church, Flint, MI, April 9, 2016.

80. For example, "Smith warned residents that it is not safe to bathe in the water because it had not been tested for the full spectrum of chemicals." Amanda Emery, "Water Defense Investigator Talks Bathing during Flint Water Crisis," *MLive*, April 9, 2016, https://www.mlive.com/news/flint/index.ssf/2016/04/water_defense_inves tigator_tal.html.

81. Marc Edwards, interview with author, Ann Arbor, MI, October 26, 2016.

82. LeeAnne Walters, interview with author, Flint, MI, October 11, 2016.

83. Marc Edwards, "A-List Actor but F-List Scientist: Mark Ruffalo Brings Fear and Misinformation to Flint," May 16, 2016, http://flintwaterstudy.org/2016/05/a-list -actor-but-f-list-scientist-mark-ruffalo-brings-fear-and-misinformation-to-flint/.

84. As CDC medical epidemiologist Jevon McFadden put it, "The epidemiological evidence from the shigellosis outbreak investigation does not support the hypothesis that it was caused by altered hygienic practices such as changes in bathing or hand washing." Email correspondence with Yanna Lambrinidou, April 18, 2017.

85. Marc Edwards, "In Flint Water Disaster Response, Ruffalo is a Bad Actor," May 23, 2016, http://flintwaterstudy.org/2016/05/in-flint-water-disaster-response-ruffalo -is-a-bad-actor/.

86. "Aquaflex Update: Water Expert Scott Smith Launches Aquaflex™, Brings Clarity to Water Crisis," *Business Wire*, May 13, 2016, https://www.businesswire.com/news /home/20160513005406/en/Aquaflex-Update-Water-Expert-Scott-Smith-Launches.

87. Delaney, "Mark Ruffalo's Water Nonprofit."

88. Edwards, "A-List Actor but F-List Scientist." Note the qualification: *regulated* safety. Part of Smith's appeal to the activists was precisely that he was testing in *un*regulated parts of the home—showers, bathtubs, hot water heaters—for which EPA standards did not exist. His credibility did not stand or fall with them, then, based on how his numbers compared to existing regulations.

89. Rebecca Williams, "Water Experts Say Non-Profit Group's Flint Water Test Lacks Credibility," Michigan Radio, June 7, 2016.

90. Edwards, "A-List Actor but F-List Scientist."

91. Edwards, "A-List Actor but F-List Scientist."

92. See also Allen et al., "Showering in Flint, MI."

93. Marc Edwards and Siddhartha Roy, "Citizen Science in Flint: Triumph, Tragedy and Now Misconduct?," September 26, 2017, http://flintwaterstudy.org/2017/09 /citizen-science-in-flint-triumph-tragedy-and-now-misconduct/. Firm distinctions

between science and pseudo-science have famously eluded generations of philosophers of science. For discussion, see Gordin, *The Pseudoscience Wars*. It is useful in this context, perhaps, to think of efforts to make such distinctions as "boundary-work" aimed at the construction of scientific authority. See Gieryn, "Boundary-Work and the Demarcation of Science."

94. See, in this connection, Edwards's pillorying of The Young Turks's Jordan Chariton for the latter's Smith-inspired attempt at water sampling. Marc Edwards, "EXCLUSIVE! Mark Ruffalo's WATER DEFENSE Sampling Methods Revealed," May 9, 2017, http://flint waterstudy.org/2017/05/exclusive-mark-ruffalos-water-defense-sampling-methods-reve aled/.

95. "Scientist," Wikipedia entry, https://en.wikipedia.org/wiki/Scientist.

96. "Our Work," Flint Water Defense Info.

97. Edwards told me to provide him with the evidence of Bowcock's statements about bathing and showering and he would "call [him] out." I decided that helping Edwards open up a new front in his campaign against so-called bad actors was not in the best interests of the community, and I never followed up with the relevant information. Author's email correspondence with Marc Edwards, October 26, 2016.

98. Numerous residents worked on the project as water samplers, community navigators, and community health resource specialists. Although the study did not originate in the community, it also had a "citizen science" component in the sense that the team trained lay residents (including me) to assemble sampling kits and collect samples. All participating residents received IRB training and were considered "key personnel" (i.e., integral to the success of the research).

99. Harrington, interview, October 27, 2016.

100. That conclusion was based on Sullivan's tangible distaste for Smith (she initially thanked Edwards for calling him out) in addition to circumstantial evidence, like Edwards CCing us on an email prior to a Flint Water Study press conference (an email that ended up in Mays's hands).

101. Jiquanda Johnson, "Flint Leaders Upset after State Asks City Official to Leave Water Meeting," *MLive*, March 3, 2017, https://www.mlive.com/news/flint/index .ssf/2017/03/state_asks_flint_official_to_l.html.

102. See "Global Priority List of Antibiotic-Resistant Bacteria to Guide Research, Discovery, and Development of New Antibiotics," www.who.int/medicines/publica tions/ WHO-PPL-Short_Summary_25Feb-ET_NM_WHO.pdf.

103. Eden Wells, chief medical executive at MDHHS, told the team that sampling the filters was a "red line" it could not cross. Ron Fonger, "Witness Says State Fought Testing Flint Faucet Filters for Legionella," *MLive*, November 15, 2017, https:// www.mlive.com/news/flint/index.ssf/2017/11/prof_says_state_officials_obje.

html. McElmurry later testified that MDHHS Director Nick Lyon objected to filter sampling because he "did not want to find more legionella" in Flint. Ron Fonger, "Witness Says MDHHS Director Didn't 'Want to Find More Legionella' in Flint," November 17, 2017, https://www.mlive.com/news/flint/index.ssf/2017/11/prof _felt_mdhhs_director_didnt.html. For a useful discussion of the concept of "black boxes," see Latour, *Science in Action*. See also the notion of "undone science" in Hess, *Undone Science*.

104. For background on the microbial colonization of filters, drawing from Ann Arbor data, see Wu et al., "The Microbial Colonization of Activated Carbon." See also Nriagu et al., "Influence of Household Water Filters."

105. For he and the team's final take on the number of cases that year (sixteen), see Rhoads et al., "Distribution System Operational Deficiencies," 11986.

106. Edwards, Flint Water Study team press conference, August 11, 2016.

107. In published papers, Edwards began to date the crisis as 2014–2016. For an example, see Parks et al., "Potential Challenges."

108. Oona Goodin-Smith, "Water Filters Could Increase Bacteria in Flint Water, Researchers Say," *MLive*, December 14, 2016, https://www.mlive.com/news/flint /index.ssf/2016/12/state-provided_water_filters_i.html.

109. When FACHEP released its recommendations for best practices with the filters, it did not tell residents not to use the filters, but rather to flush them for fifteen seconds before use to clear out the highest concentrations of bacteria. On Flint-waterstudy.org, Edwards endorsed the recommendation but referred to it conde-scendingly as a "reminder," pointing out that filter manufacturers already advised flushing. Flint residents, however, had never been officially instructed to flush the filters previously. "Supporting Wayne State University and University of Michigan's Flushing Reminder," May 12, 2017, http://flintwaterstudy.org/2017/05/supporting -wayne-state-university-and-university-of-michigans-flushing-reminder/.

110. Nancy Love, interview with author, Ann Arbor, MI, July 26, 2017.

111. Skepticism around the filters cropped up almost immediately: Carrie Laine, "Brita Spokesperson Disputes Concerns over Water Filters," WNEM, October 7, 2015." One major concern was that the levels of lead being detected in some homes were higher than 150 ppb, the highest level for which the filters were certified: Matthew Dolan, "EPA: High Lead Levels in Flint Exceed Filters' Rating," *Detroit Free Press*, January 29, 2016. Although EPA testing determined that the filters were able to handle even very high lead levels, residents still mistrusted them—according to a phone poll taken five months into the filter distribution, some 70 percent of residents: Paul Egan, "Poll: Flint Residents Don't Trust Water Filters," *Detroit Free Press*, June 2, 2016. See also Sarah Hulett, "In Flint, Trust in Filters—and Government— Elusive," Michigan Radio, June 30, 2016.

112. World Health Organization, "Heterotrophic plate count measurement in drinking water safety management," *WHO Public Health Expert Report* (April 2002), 4, http://www.who.int/water_sanitation_health/dwq/WSH02.10.pdf.

113. The unfamiliarity of filters factored into another problem: their improper use. As emphasized by Michael Hood of the humanitarian group Crossing Water: "'Anywhere from 50 to 70 percent of folks that we're seeing have filters that are not working,' Hood says, adding that it's irresponsible to tell people it's safe to drink filtered water when so many people aren't using filters correctly. 'They are broken. They are not installed properly. Don't have faucets that accommodate them. Or they (Flint residents) can't read the instructions because there's a very high illiteracy rate in the city of Flint.'" Hulett, "In Flint."

114. For coverage of some of the issues with the filters—technical and otherwise— see Brian Barrett, "The Flint Water Crisis Is Bigger than Elon Musk," *WIRED*, July 12, 2018; and Auditi Gupta, "State Water Filters Prove Lacking in Flint, a City 'Full of Forgotten People,'" *Rewire News*, August 16, 2018.

115. Genesee County Health Department, "Reminder Regarding Flint Water Emergency Declaration and Recommendations," press release, May 16, 2018, https://gchd.us/wp-content/uploads/2018/05/GCHD-FLINT-WATER-ER-DECLARATION-RECOMMENDATIONS_5.16.18.pdf.

116. Email correspondence between Marc Edwards and Shawn McElmurry, May 27, 2017.

117. The implication that FACHEP was withholding information from residents was, said Nancy Love, "100 percent untrue." Love, interview, July 26, 2017. At least some of the frustration the resident felt with the team was understandable, however. It was taking far longer than expected to analyze definitively (or as definitively as possible) some of the bacterial samples—a product of limited funds, limited manpower, and technical challenges in the lab. The delay was a gift to Edwards and Walters, who could use it to argue that the team either did not know what it was doing or was not being forthcoming about the results it had in its possession. This issue aside, only one of the eleven items in the FOIA had anything to do with the resident's sampling results—the others being designed, seemingly, to dig up dirt on the team, particularly on Laura Sullivan (an increasingly outspoken critic of Edwards). When Wayne State was slow to comply with the request, Edwards teamed up with the right-wing think tank Mackinac Center to sue the university. It was another scandal within the activist community—while Edwards was "hollerin' about ethics," Claire McClinton said, he himself made the "unethical" decision to work with the "architects of the emergency manager [law] that created the Flint water crisis." McClinton, interview, September 6, 2018.

118. Walters also proposed to do a GoFundMe to raise $10,000 in support of the FOIA for the nonexistent documents the resident was demanding (a proposal Edwards

distanced himself from as soon as she mentioned it). After I stressed to Walters at length that I thought the GoFundMe would be unethical, she backed off the idea.

119. Marc Edwards, keynote address at Microbiology of the Built Environment Conference, Washington, DC, October 24, 2017.

120. Byrne et al., "Prevalence of Infection-Competent Serogroup 6 *Legionella pneumophila*," and Zahran et al., "Assessment of the Legionnaires' Disease Outbreak."

121. MDHHS Response to Flint Area Community Health and Environment Partnership, Proceedings of the National Academy of Sciences Article, February 5, 2018, www.michigan.gov/documents/mdhhs/MDHHS_Response_to_FACHEP_Proceedings_of_the_National_Academy_of_Sciences_Article_FINAL_613088_7.pdf; MDHHS Response to Flint Area Community Health and Environment Partnership, American Society for Microbiology mBio Article, February 5, 2018, https://www.michigan.gov/documents/mdhhs/MDHHS_Response_to_FACHEP_American_Society_for_Microbiology_mBio_Article_rev_21318_613639_7.pdf; KWR Watercycle Research Institute, "Assessment of the Study on Enhanced Disease Surveillance and Environmental Monitoring in Flint, Michigan," October 2017, https://www.michigan.gov/documents/mdhhs/171108_KWR_2017.081_final_report_scoping_mission_DEF_613090_7.PDF.

122. FACHEP broke things off with the state entirely in December 2017, turning down $900,000 in grant money.

123. When Judge David Goggins decided to bind Lyon over for trial in August, despite Edwards's sympathetic testimony, activists were overjoyed. I was there in the packed courtroom when Goggins delivered his decision, prompting tears and exclamations of "*Thank you!*" from the activists in attendance. Disgusted that Edwards was on the other side during this critical moment in activists' fight for accountability, Claire McClinton called it the clearest indication yet that he had "join[ed] the enemy." McClinton, interview, September 6, 2018.

124. Ann Pierret, "Virginia Tech Researcher Praises Michigan Department of Health and Human Services," ABC12, March 26, 2018, https://www.abc12.com/content/news/Virginia-Tech-researcher-sings-praises-of-Nick-Lyon-during-testimony-477978693.html; Ron Fonger, "Researcher Says Wells Tried to Find the Truth in Flint Water Crisis," *MLive*, March 27, 2018, https://www.mlive.com/news/flint/index.ssf/2018/03/edwards_files_complaint.html.

125. *The People of the State of Michigan vs. Nicolas Leonard Lyon*, 2018; statement of Edwards, *The People of the State of Michigan vs. Eden Victoria Wells*, 2018; statement of Edwards.

126. Marc Edwards and Siddartha Roy, "Considering the Unimaginable: Did McElmurry Completely Fabricate His Story of Work 'IN FLINT' from 2010–2014?," March 31, 2018, http://flintwaterstudy.org/2018/03/considering-the-unimaginable-did-mcelmurry-completely-fabricate-his-story-of-work-in-flint-from-2010-2014/.

127. Edwards and Roy, "Considering the Unimaginable."

128. Marc Edwards, comment on "Wayne State University Response to Questions," April 4, 2018, http://flintwaterstudy.org/2018/04/wayne-state-university-response -to-questions/.

129. Edwards, interview on *The Tom Sumner Show*, July 27, 2018.

130. McClinton, interview, September 6, 2018.

131. Gina Luster, interview with author, Flint, MI, November 1, 2017.

132. The letter is available from flintcomplaints.com.

133. Marc Edwards, "Citizen Engineering Comes to Flint—Disrupting Communities by Undermining Engineering Expertise," June 2, 2018, http://flintwaterstudy.org/2018/06 /citizen-engineering-comes-to-flint-disrupting-communities-by-undermining -engineering-expertise/. The two main examples Edwards singled out as constituting deliberate defamation are instructive. He said it was defamatory to claim that "Mr. Edwards has repeatedly spoken and written about how there are no bacteria or dangerous pathogens in Flint residents' water." When seen from residents' perspective, however, the claim was entirely understandable. Residents were repeatedly told, beginning in 2015, that the Flint Water Study team was finding "no" *legionella pneumophila* in Flint's water: see Emily Garner, "Results from Field Sampling in Flint (Aug 17–19 2015): Opportunistic Pathogens," August 29, 2015, http:// flintwaterstudy.org/2015/08/results-from-field-sampling-in-flint-aug-17-19-2015 -opportunistic-pathogens/; Fournier, "Edwards' Team Shows Dramatic Drop" ("In November [2016], we were not able to detect any culturable Legionella inside the house at all"); Ann Pierret, "Latest Virginia Tech Flint Water Tests Show Safe Lead Levels, No Legionella Bacteria," ABC12, September 15, 2017, https://www.abc12. com/content/news/Virginia-Tech-expert-declares-qualified-end-to-water-crisis -in-Flint-444683013.html. Edwards and his team were of course entitled—and indeed, obligated—to report their results to the community, whatever they were. The point is that the message residents heard from him was that there was "no" *legionella pneumophila* in the water, whereas the message they heard from others, namely FACHEP, was that there was at least some. Edwards, during his testimony on behalf of MDHHS director Nick Lyon, wondered from the stand why FACHEP was "sampling so extensively where the legionella were not [present]," but the bacteria *were* present in homes—in 12 percent of the homes the team sampled in 2016, for example. Edwards also scoffed at the idea that there might be harmful bacteria in the filters, saying there was "no evidence" that the filters were "dangerous" (*The People of the State of Michigan vs. Nicolas Leonard Lyon*, 2017; statement of Edwards), despite the risks the Genesee County Medical Society said the bacteria posed to vulnerable populations.

The other claim that particularly rankled Edwards was that he had portrayed residents as being "dumb" and "dirty" for supposedly making themselves sick by changing their bathing and showering habits. (He told me in October 2016 that he was "very angry" about the accusation and had never said anything that could be construed that way. Edwards, interview, October 26, 2016.) The claim was not, of course, meant to be an exact quote, but rather an interpretation of the upshot of Edwards's own claim about the implications of residents' changing personal hygiene practices—a claim for which activists (and the CDC) felt there was insufficient evidence and which they thought was insulting.

While I felt the phrasing of the letter could have been improved in places, I also felt that its claims represented authentic, evidence-based perceptions and interpretations of Edwards's words and actions, rendered in the rhetorical style typical of activist culture in Flint. I did not see the letter, therefore, as dishonest or as a deliberate attempt to defame (the signatories had, in fact, risked defamation themselves by stepping into Edwards's line of fire). The letter was also a potentially powerful vehicle for publicizing concerns that activists (and other residents) had been raising for years but that had received little to no attention from the outside world. For these reasons, I signed it after it was posted online. Edwards's objections to the letter, incidentally, were posted to the same website for anyone to see.

134. Worth-Nelson, "Activists' Letter Aims Grievances." I knew by then from over two years of ethnographic work that the list of signatories only scratched the surface of the discontent residents felt toward Edwards. I knew numerous people who chose not to sign the letter simply because of its tone, or, alternately, because of their personal distaste for Melissa Mays, whose participation Edwards successfully foregrounded in his efforts to discredit the letter.

135. The letter is available from flintaccountability.org.

136. Nidhi Subbaraman, "A Scientist Is Suing Flint Activists for Defamation. They Say His Ego Is out of Control," Buzzfeed News, July 26, 2018, https://www.buzzfeed news.com/article/nidhisubbaraman/marc-edwards-flint-lawsuit.

137. Robby Korth, "Virginia Tech's Flint Research Professor Accuses Ex-colleagues of Defamation," *Roanoke Times*, July 26, 2018.

138. See Marc Edwards and Siddhartha Roy, "Is This Flint Photo from 2015?," June 29, 2018, http://flintwaterstudy.org/2018/06/is-this-flint-photo-from-2015/; and Marc Edwards and Siddhartha Roy, "Highlights of a Typical Week of 'Citizen Engineering' in Flint," July 5, 2018, http://flintwaterstudy.org/2018/07/highlights -of-a-typical-week-of-citizen-engineering-in-flint/.

139. Bill Moran (@BillMoranWins), "Day 65 Cont.: Virginia Tech's Marc Edwards, who is suing a Flint Mom for $3 million, has his students create fake Facebook pages to monitor Flint activists," Twitter, September 5, 2018, 10:57 a.m., https://twitter .com/billmoranwins/status/1037393379102113795?lang=en.

140. Flint Water Study (@flintwaterstudy), "Mr. Smith @WaterWarriorOne's example is something we should all applaud and emulate. It is so refreshing, in this post-truth

world, to see someone admit mistakes and take responsibility," Twitter, July 13, 2018, 12:16 p.m., https://twitter.com/flintwaterstudy/status/1017850284213702656.

141. Introduction to Scott C. Smith, "Lessons I Learned in Flint and Clarifying the Facts," July 11, 2018, http://flintwaterstudy.org/2018/07/scott-smith-flint-guest-post/.

142. Prior to the grant collaboration, Cooper nominated Edwards for the American Association for the Advancement of Science's "Freedom and Responsibility" award, which he won in February 2018.

143. Caren Cooper (@CoopSciScoop), "Bravo! for a courageous step & cheers to uniting for #CitizenScience!," Twitter, July 12, 2018, 6:25 a.m., https://twitter.com /CoopSciScoop/status/1017399599689097216.

144. According to an attorney retained briefly by Smith, the latter had explored the possibility of suing Edwards for defamation just a few days earlier. See Bill Moran, "The Tale of Honest Iago: Marc Edwards' New Pet 'Unethical Opportun- ist' Scott Smith," Medium, July 27, 2018, https://medium.com/@BillMoranWrites /the-tale-of-honest-iago-marc-edwards-new-pet-unethical-opportunist-scott-smith -c04f7bbac76e.

145. Scott Smith, "Draft Lessons I Learned in Flint ME edits 06-18-18" (unpublished manuscript, June 18, 2018), Word file. Smith originally wrote, "In no way did I ever claim to have a PhD or be trained as [a] PhD or other officially trained scientist." Edwards changed it to, "In retrospect, I should not have approved and used a title implying that I was a trained scientist." Scott Smith, "Draft Lessons I Learned in Flint and Clarifying the Facts 06-24-18 ME scs redlines 06-26-18," (unpublished manuscript, June 26, 2018), Word file.

146. Scott Smith, "Draft Lessons I Learned in Flint and Clarifying the Facts 06-24-18 ME scs redlines 06-26-18."

147. Scott Smith, "Forgot to Tell You that You and I Are Tied Together with Devos Family and Mott Family Foundation," email to Marc Edwards, July 16, 2018, for- warded to Susan Masten, Amy Pruden, Siddhartha Roy, and Kasey Faust.

148. Shariff, interview with author, September 15, 2018. How the Virginia Tech team's intervention in Flint came to be described as a "gold standard" despite its lack of these protections is a curious aspect of the STEM community's eager embrace of Edwards.

149. Shariff, interview, September 15, 2018.

150. McClinton, interview, September 6, 2018.

151. McClinton, interview, September 6, 2018.

152. "The Virginia Tech Research Team," n.d., http://flintwaterstudy.org/about-page /about-us/. Emphasis in original.

153. Edwards, "Citizen Engineering Comes to Flint." Much of this analysis hinged on the supposed influence of Donna Riley, dean of engineering education at Purdue University, who happened to be a friend of Yanna Lambrinidou. See Marc Edwards et al., "Bizarre Attack on FlintWaterStudy, Rigor, and Purdue Slide Rules: An Epic Failure to Measure Up," January 16, 2018, http://flintwaterstudy.org/2018/01/bizarre-attack-on-flintwaterstudy-rigor-and-purdue-slide-rules-an-epic-failure-to-measure-up/. To my knowledge, Riley had no personal involvement in Flint whatsoever, and her only comment on the record explicitly about Edwards or Virginia Tech was the rather sympathetic one she gave to the *Chronicle of Higher Education* in Kolowich, "The Accidental Ethicist."

154. Quincy Murphy, interview with author, Flint, MI, May 27, 2018.

155. The idea that it was in the interest of the community to have multiple voices speaking to the science of the water reflected the sense that "controversies enrich democracy"; as Callon, Lascoumes, and Barthe write, controversies generate a fuller inventory of actors, problems, and solutions, promote learning as laypeople and experts learn from each other, break down simple oppositions, and make new compromises and alliances possible. *Acting in an Uncertain World*, 28. When health symptoms are imperfectly explained by scientific understanding, efforts to shut down scientific controversy can, in Steven Epstein's words, seem like the "stifling of democratic openness of opinion and the authoritarian imposition of closure." This is why empowering communities through science necessitates that community members have a say about "how scientific controversies end." *Impure Science*, 29. See also Irwin's distinction between "Enlightenment" and "critical" science in *Citizen Science*.

156. It should be said, however, that FACHEP's attempt to cultivate a low profile was also part of a concerted effort to avoid attracting too much credit or attention for its work—a reaction against the Flint Water Study team's heavy self-promotion. When FACHEP's legionella papers were published, for example, several members of the team battled the media people at their respective universities to tone down the standard celebratory press blast touting the contributions of university faculty, maintaining that the focus should be on Flint.

157. "If you wanted to say, like, what would a fair sort of solution look like it'd be something like Flint," he told me. Edwards, interview, October 26, 2016. In all my interviews and ethnographic interactions, I did not encounter a resident of Flint who agreed with this view.

158. Edwards, interview, October 26, 2016.

8 From Poisoned People to People Power

1. Rick Snyder, testimony to House Oversight and Government Reform Committee, March 17, 2016, https://www.flintwatercommittee.com/wp-content/uploads/2016/05/FLINT-HEARING-OF-MARCH-17-FINAL-with-cover-sheet.pdf. Snyder continued

to tout what he considered the successes of the EM law in other Michigan cities, but did not seem eager to apply it in the wake of the crisis. Some of the people I talked to believed the water crisis had rendered Flint, especially, immune from future state takeovers: "I don't think we're ever going to be under an emergency ever again," Paul Jordan told me. Jordan, interview with author, Flint, MI, December 21, 2016.

2. None of these state bodies recommended abolishing the EM law, however. Suggestions included replacing lone EMs with three-person financial management teams including a local ombudsman, opening EMs up to civil liability, instituting an appeals process whereby a majority of local elected representatives could appeal a decision directly to the governor, creating a website for public comment on proposed EM actions, requiring EMs to consult with subject matter experts before making decisions, and forbidding EMs from changing drinking water sources without the approval of experts and a majority of electors in a locality. Proposals for reform failed to gain traction in either state legislative body, despite polling data showing bipartisan support for them. See Ivacko and Horner, "Local Leaders More Likely to Support than Oppose," and Jonathan Oosting, "Reforms Languish in Wake of Flint Water Crisis," *Detroit Free Press*, April 21, 2017.

3. Weaver came into office saying she did "not embrace the current governance model on a moral or political basis." Steve Carmody, "Flint's New Mayor Wants Total Local Control Restored," Michigan Radio, November 9, 2015, http://www.michi ganradio.org/post/flints-new-mayor-wants-total-local-control-restored.

4. Gary Ridley, "Power Not Restored to Flint Mayor Despite Calls from Gov. Rick Snyder," *MLive*, January 13, 2016, https://www.mlive.com/news/flint/index.ssf/2016 /01/no_powers_restored_to_flint_ma.html.

5. In May, Snyder came out in favor of restoring the council's powers. Gary Ridley, "Snyder Supports Return of Flint City Council Powers," *MLive*, May 12, 2016, https:// www.mlive.com/news/flint/index.ssf/2016/05/snyder_supports_return_of_flin.html. Shortly thereafter, RTAB did so, reluctantly. Jiquanda Johnson, "State Oversight Board Restores Power to Flint City Council despite concerns," *MLive*, May 26, 2016, https://www.mlive.com/news/flint/index.ssf/2016/05/flint_city_council_powers _rest.html. RTAB denied that criticism of the EM system because of the water crisis put added pressure on the board to restore local control, but each move in this direction was signaled by Snyder, who was clearly under pressure to end the state takeover as a gesture of good will. Josh Hakala, "The Next Steps in Flint's Transition Back to Local Control," Michigan Radio, February 1, 2016.

6. For my critique of the latter decision, see Pauli, "Gov. Snyder's Flint Oversight."

7. On the concept of political opportunity structures and their relation to activism, see Meyer and Minkoff, "Conceptualizing Political Opportunity," and Meyer, "Protest and Political Opportunities." For connections between this concept—as well as social movement theory more generally—and environmental justice activism, see

Taylor, "The Rise of the Environmental Justice Paradigm"; Pellow, *Resisting Global Toxics*; and Sicotte and Brulle, "Social Movements for Environmental Justice."

8. See the "Water Is a Human Right" bill package introduced, in its second incarnation, as Michigan Senate Bill 466.

9. See the Water Affordability, Transparency, Equity, and Reliability (WATER) Act introduced by US Representatives Keith Ellison and Ro Khanna as H.R. 5609.

10. Nayyirah Shariff, interview with author, Flint, MI, July 6, 2017.

11. Author's field notes, Flint Rising meeting, Flint, MI, n.d.

12. Blee, *Democracy in the Making*. Blee writes that democracy in a social movement context "is a verb, not an adjective. It is the action of people as they deliberate and work together to affect society rather than a form of governance. Activism-as-democracy is not institutional or structural. It is a process, ever being made" (4). Later, she writes, "Activist groups don't just support democratic institutions; when they are open to a full array of new possibilities, grassroots groups make democracy anew" (138).

13. I wish to make clear that in focusing on those I describe as "activists," I do not mean to shortchange the many other people and institutions from the grassroots who contributed to the crisis response: the churches that turned themselves into distribution sites, the people who went door to door to check on their neighbors and deliver bottled water, the groups that organized recreational events for children so the latter could take their minds off the crisis. There was ample evidence in Flint that crisis gives rise to new forms of community. See Solnit, *A Paradise Built in Hell*. For more on the importance of community in weathering disaster, see Klinenberg, *Heat Wave*.

14. I am ashamed to say I did not try to count, so I have taken the estimate from Paul Egan, "Flint Water Protestors: Snyder Should Resign, Face Charges," *Detroit Free Press*, January 8, 2016.

15. The two main outcomes activists believed would result from a disaster declaration were faster pipe replacements, courtesy of the Army Corps of Engineers, and the provision of "water buffalos," portable tanks of clean water residents could tap into in preference to bottled water.

16. Claire McClinton, personal interview with author, Flint, MI, June 7, 2017.

17. For more on Baird, see Bomey, *Detroit Resurrected*.

18. As Laura Sullivan put it, "Soon after the mayor named a state of emergency, the governor proposed to come into town with his team to assess the situation from their own angle and make recommendations on their own, and kind of take over rather than empower Flint." Bendix, "How Flint Citizens Are Working Together."

19. Author's field notes, Two Years Too Long Coalition meeting, Woodside Church, Flint, MI, September 11, 2016.

20. One of the inspirations for the activists' use of this term was INCITE! Women of Color Against Violence, *The Revolution Will Not Be Funded*.

21. On different occasions, activists considered disrupting the Community Partners meetings to make a point. They actually planned a protest for mid-May but called it off after the plans were inadvertently leaked. My tangential involvement in this incident (I was CCed on the offending email) set me back somewhat in building credibility within the activist community, creating the unfortunate impression for a while that I could not be trusted with sensitive information. Activists claimed at least a partial victory when the meetings were subsequently relocated to a more accessible location (the Dome at City Hall).

22. It is worth pointing out that many of the "groups" in Flint were primarily individual projects, without any real membership, or regular meetings, or formal incorporation. For this reason, I have benefitted from Blee's analysis, in *Democracy in the Making*, of "tiny and incipient" groups (6). When groups are this small and depend so heavily on single individuals, unpredictable interpersonal dynamics become more important to coalition building than the more predictable intergroup dynamics pinpointed by social movement scholars (see Van Dyke and McCammon, *Strategic Alliances*).

23. The full list is as follows:

1. The Flint water catastrophe should be declared a major disaster area and not simply an emergency.
2. The pipes throughout the city of Flint must be changed.
3. The State of Michigan has not put in any serious resources currently to adequately address citizen needs in Flint.
4. An independent external auditor is needed to monitor the influx of government capital to ensure it reaches the citizens.
5. A maximum amount of funds should be kept in the City of Flint and the greater Flint area so that labor and contracts keep the money in Flint.

24. Niraj Warikoo, "Flint Immigrants Struggle to Get Help, Info on Water," *Detroit Free Press*, February 4, 2016.

25. Wheeler, "What Government Owes."

26. At an environmental justice summit in Flint, a representative from the EPA said the agency had decided to schedule its own canvassing around Flint Rising's, taking the weekdays rather than the weekends, because the coalition was doing such an efficient job.

27. Michigan Faith in Action began in 2007 as Flint Area Congregations Together, a group started by deputy director of PICO Gordon Whitman. For background on PICO, see Wood, *Faith in Action*. In May 2018, the PICO National Network changed its name to Faith in Action.

28. Richard Wood notes that statewide and national interlinkages allow activists to "project democratic power into higher-level arenas" (*Faith in Action*, 51), and that organizing federations can act as "bridging institutions" (143) linking civil society to political society to the state.

29. Robert Allen, "NAACP Threatens Civil Disobedience over Flint Pipes," *Detroit Free Press*, February 15, 2016.

30. Author's field notes, Flint Rising meeting, St. Michael's Church, Flint, MI, May 28, 2016.

31. See the organizer's handbook, adapted from the work of Ganz, *Organizing: People, Power, Change*, 25. For other accounts of community organizing as a distinctive method of creating social change, see Boyte, *The Backyard Revolution*; Smock, *Democracy in Action*; and Swarts, *Organizing Urban America*. Despite its focus on "broad-based" organizing rather than "community" organizing *per se*, useful reflections can also be found in Stout, *Blessed Are the Organized*.

32. Emerging scholarship has sought to understand the importance of community organizing in post-disaster situations. As Pyles writes ("Community Organizing"), "There are clearly differences between managing a disaster and organizing communities to advocate for policy and program changes related to community revitalization needs after a disaster. In addition, organizing after disasters must go beyond just including vulnerable members and focus activities on transforming the hegemonic structures and policies that perpetuate such injustice, if it is to address development problems and other inequities" (325).

33. PICO did send in a number of organizers in early 2016, however. Sharon Allen remembers that they "helped us organize our thoughts, because at that point we were pulling our hair out." Allen, interview with author, Flint, MI, December 2, 2016.

34. For more on Ganz, see *Why David Sometimes Wins*. For another perspective on stories and narrative in social movements, see Polletta, *It Was Like a Fever*.

35. Author's field notes, Flint Rising community meeting, St. Michael's Church, Flint, MI, February 27, 2016.

36. Nakiya Wakes, interview with author, Flint, MI, September 7, 2016.

37. Wakes, interview, September 7, 2016.

38. Another, Abel Delgado, questioned whether the focus on stories was appropriate at all: "I think a lot of the thing with the water crisis is just based upon story and I really don't like that. ... I mean, yeah, those stories do need to be told but just because we hear a story doesn't make them a leader, doesn't make them a revolutionary." Interview with author, Flint, MI, December 7, 2016. Several people involved in Flint Rising complained to me that their skills, experience, and political savvy were being treated as if they had less value than compelling personal stories.

39. Author's field notes, Flint Rising meeting, St. Michael's Church, May 28, 2016.

40. Laura Gillespie MacIntyre, interview with author, Flint, MI, August 29, 2016.

41. Shariff, interview, July 6, 2017.

42. Saul Alinsky makes a classic argument for the need to fight winnable battles in his *Rules for Radicals*.

43. Delgado, interview, December 7, 2016.

44. McClinton, interview, June 7, 2017.

45. See Han, *How Organizations Develop Activists*.

46. For more on organizing vs. activist logics, see Chambers, *Roots for Radicals*, ch. 5.

47. Dillon Davis, "Kellogg Foundation Gives $7 Million for Flint Recovery," *Detroit Free Press*, August 9, 2016. Kellogg channeled the money through the Tides Foundation and the c4 nonprofit infrastructure organization the Advocacy Fund (Flint Rising began to describe itself as a "project of the Advocacy Fund"). On general funding dilemmas faced by environmental justice movements, including the tradeoff between capacity-building and cooptation, see Faber and McCarthy, "Breaking the Funding Barriers."

48. Shariff, interview, July 6, 2017.

49. See the work of the psychologist Marshall Rosenberg.

50. Shiva, *Water Wars*.

51. Sharp, *The Role of Power in Nonviolent Struggle*.

52. McKnight, "Services Are Bad for People."

53. Stedile, "Landless Battalions."

54. For the classic account of prefiguration in a social movement context, see Breines, *Community and Organization in the New Left, 1962–1968*.

55. Shariff, interview, July 6, 2017.

56. Shariff, interview, July 6, 2017.

57. Jessica Glenza, "Nestlé Pays $200 a Year to Bottle Water Near Flint—Where Water Is Undrinkable," *Guardian*, September 29, 2017.

58. Matthew Dolan, "Michigan Battles Order to Deliver Bottled Water to Flint Residents," *Detroit Free Press*, November 17, 2016.

59. Detroit Free Press staff, "Here's What Flint's $87M Water Settlement Means," *Detroit Free Press*, March 28, 2017.

60. McClinton, interview, June 7, 2017.

61. Susan Whalen and Aaron Kottke, interview with author, Flint, MI, November 12, 2017.

62. The letter explicitly compared the lack of popular participation in the water source decision to the experience of emergency management, maintaining that

"residents of Flint have been shut out of communication surrounding the contract with GLWA" and lamenting that "since the time we were under emergency management and now under RTAB...we have had no say in our own future." Letter to the Honorable David M. Lawson from Residents of Flint, represented by the Democracy Defense League, Water You Fighting For, Flint Water Class Action Group, Michigan United, Citizens Advocating United To Inform and Organize for New Direction (CAUTION), and others. November 16, 2017. p. 2. The letter was mailed as a physical letter. The text here is taken from a Facebook post by Claire McClinton on November 19, 2017.

63. Eric Mays, long an ally of the activists but also a loyal ally of the mayor, became a particular target after he said the people at the town hall meeting deserved to be arrested.

64. David Schwenk, "Promise in the Land of Despair: The Crisis is Not over in Flint, Michigan," *Common Dreams*, June 9, 2017.

65. Author's field notes, Flint Rising meeting, Mott Community College, Flint, MI, February 22, 2018.

66. Author's field notes, Flint Rising meeting, February 22, 2018.

Conclusion

1. Flint helped to inspire the EPA's *Lead and Copper Rule Revisions White Paper*.

2. Todd Spangler, "U.S. Supreme Court Rejects Challenge to Michigan's Emergency Manager Law," *Detroit Free Press*, October 2, 2017.

3. Marc Edwards, for example, repeatedly used the term "miracle" to describe the "critical mass of moral courage" reached in 2015, uniting the activists with allies like Miguel del Toral, Curt Guyette, Virginia Tech, and Mona Hanna-Attisha to break the news about systemic lead contamination. See his talk "Truth-Seeking in an Age of Tribalism: Lessons from the Flint Water Crisis," Swarthmore College, Swarthmore, PA, February 20, 2018, https://www.swarthmore.edu/news-events/listen-engineer-marc-ed wards-truth-seeking-age-tribalism.

4. Paul Jordan, interview with author, Flint, MI, December 21, 2016.

Selected Bibliography

In selecting the references listed below, I have tried to compile a near-comprehensive bibliography of the water crisis. That said, I have not included everything cited in the book's endnotes. I have left out day-to-day news coverage as well as other articles and documents I deemed to be of less than general interest. Any source not cited in full here is cited in full in the endnotes.

Abernethy, Jacob, Cyrus Anderson, Chengyu Dai, Arya Farahi, Linh Nguyen, Adam Rauh, Eric Schwartz, Wenbo Shen, Guangsha Shi, Jonathan Stroud, Xinyu Tan, Jared Webb, and Sheng Yang. "Flint Water Crisis: Data-Driven Risk Assessment via Residential Water Testing." Paper presented at Bloomberg Data for Good Exchange Conference, New York, September 25, 2016.

Abernethy, Jacob, Alex Chojnaki, Chengyu Dai, Arya Farahi, Eric Schwartz, Jared Webb, Guangsha Shi, and Daniel T. Zhang. "A Data Science Approach to Understanding Residential Water Contamination." Paper presented at KDD, Halifax, Nova Scotia, August 13–17, 2017.

Abernethy, Jacob, Alex Chojnacki, Arya Farahi, Eric Schwartz, and Jared Webb. "ActiveRemediation: The Search for Lead Pipes in Flint, Michigan." In *KDD '18: The 24th ACM SIGKDD International Conference on Knowledge Discovery & Data Mining, August 19–23, 2018, London, United Kingdom*, 5–14. New York: ACM, 2018.

Abouk, Rahi, and Scott Adams. "Birth Outcomes in Flint in the Early Stages of the Water Crisis." *Journal of Public Health Policy* 39, no. 1 (February 2018): 68–85.

Abuelaish, Izzeldin, and Kirstie K. Russell. "The Flint Water Contamination Crisis: The Corrosion of Positive Peace and Human Decency." *Medicine, Conflict and Survival* 33, no. 4 (2017): 242–249.

Adams, John. *Risk*. London: Routledge, 1995.

Agamben, Giorgio. *State of Exception*. Chicago, IL: University of Chicago Press, 2005.

Agyeman, Julian, David Schlosberg, Luke Craven, and Caitlin Matthews. "Trends and Directions in Environmental Justice: From Inequity to Everyday Life, Community, and Just Sustainabilities." *Annual Review of Environment and Resoures* 41 (November 2016): 321–340.

Alinsky, Saul. *Rules for Radicals: A Pragmatic Primer for Realistic Radicals*. New York: Vintage Books, 1989.

Allen, Barbara L. *Uneasy Alchemy: Citizens and Experts in Louisiana's Chemical Corridor Disputes*. Cambridge, MA: MIT Press, 2003.

Allen, Joshua M., Amy A. Cuthbertson, Hannah K. Liberatore, Susana Y. Kimura, Anurag Mantha, Marc A. Edwards, and Susan D. Richardson. "Showering in Flint, MI: Is There a DBP Problem?" *Journal of Environmental Sciences* 58 (June 2017): 271–284.

American Society of Civil Engineers. *2017 Infrastructure Report Card: A Comprehensive Assessment of America's Infrastructure*. 2017.

Anand, Nikhil. "The Banality of Infrastructure." *Items: Insights from the Social Sciences*. Social Science Research Council, June 27, 2017.

Anand, Nikhil. *Hydraulic City: Water and the Infrastructures of Citizenship in Mumbai*. Durham, NC: Duke University Press, 2017.

Anand, Nikhil. "Pressure: The PoliTechnics of Water Supply in Mumbai." *Cultural Anthropology* 26, no. 4 (2011): 542–564.

Anderson, Michelle Wilde. "Democratic Dissolution: Radical Experimentation in State Takeovers of Local Governments." *Fordham Urban Law Journal* 39, no. 3 (March 2012): 577–623.

Anderson, Michelle Wilde. "The New Minimal Cities." *Yale Law Journal* 123, no. 5 (March 2014): 1118–1227.

Arbulu, Agustin V., and Daniel Levy. "A One-Year Update on the Recommendations in *The Flint Water Crisis: Systemic Racism Through the Lens of Flint*." Michigan Civil Rights Commission, March 26, 2018.

Aronoff, Myron, and Jan Kubik. *Anthropology and Political Science: A Convergent Approach*. New York: Berghahn Books, 2013.

Atari, Dominic Odwa, Isaac Luginaah, and Jamie Baxter. "'This Is the Mess That We Are Living In': Residents Everyday Life Experiences of Living in a Stigmatized Community." *GeoJournal* 76, no. 5 (October 2011): 483–500.

Athey, Stephanie, K. M. Ferebee, and Wendy S. Hesford. "The Poisoning of Flint and the Moral Economy of Human Rights." *Prose Studies* 38, no. 1 (2016): 1–11.

August, Melissa. "The Plumbing Professor." *Time*, June 8, 2004.

Auyero, Javier, and Débora Alejandra Swistun. *Flammable: Environmental Suffering in an Argentine Shantytown*. Oxford: Oxford University Press, 2009.

Barber, Benjamin. *If Mayors Ruled the World: Dysfunctional Nations, Rising Cities*. New Haven, CT: Yale University Press, 2013.

Barham, Tim. "Class Action Water Crisis: Resolving Flint's New Split over CAFA's Local Controversy Exception." *Baylor Law Review* 70, no. 1 (March 2018): 149–170.

Bassett, Philip A. *Soldier of Truth: The Trials of Rev. Edward Pinkney*. N.p.: Self-published, 2016.

Baum, Fran, Colin MacDougall, and Danielle Smith. "Participatory Action Research." *Journal of Epidemiology and Community Health* 60, no. 10 (October 2006): 854–857.

Beck, Ulrich. *Risk Society: Towards a New Modernity*. London: Sage Publications, 1992.

Beecher, Janice. *The Regionalization of Water Utilities: Perspectives, Literature Review, and Annotated Bibliography*. National Regulatory Research Institute. Columbus, OH, July 1996.

Belenky, Mary Field, Blythe McVicker Clinchy, Nancy Rule Goldberger, and Jill Mattuck Tarule. *Women's Ways of Knowing: The Development of Self, Voice, and Mind*. New York: Basic Books, 1986.

Bell, Shannon Elizabeth. *Fighting King Coal: The Challenges to Micromobilization in Central Appalachia*. Cambridge, MA: MIT Press, 2016.

Bellinger, David C. "Lead Contamination in Flint—An Abject Failure to Protect Public Health." *New England Journal of Medicine* 374 (March 2016): 1101–1103.

Bendix, Aria. "How Flint Citizens Are Working Together to Save Their Community." *CityLab*, April 29, 2016.

Benford, Robert D., and David S. Snow. "Framing Processes and Social Movements: An Overview and Assessment." *Annual Review of Sociology* 26 (2000): 611–639.

Benz, Terressa A. "Toxic Cities: Neoliberalism and Environmental Racism in Flint and Detroit Michigan." *Critical Sociology* (2017): 1–14.

Berfield, Susan. "Financial Martial Law in Michigan." *Bloomberg Businessweek*, April 28, 2011.

Berliner, Joshua V. "Environmental Injustice/Racism in Flint, Michigan: An Analysis of the Bodily Integrity Claim in Mays v. Snyder as Compared to Other Environmental Justice Cases." *Pace Environmental Law Review* 35, no. 108 (2017): 108–134.

Bidwell, David. "Is Community-Based Participatory Research Postnormal Science?" *Science, Technology, and Human Values* 34, no. 6 (November 2009): 741–761.

Björkman, Lisa. *Pipe Politics, Contested Waters: Embedded Infrastructures of Millennial Mumbai*. Durham, NC: Duke University Press, 2013.

Blee, Kathleen M. *Democracy in the Making: How Activist Groups Form*. New York: Oxford University Press, 2012.

Blocker, T. Jean, and Douglas Lee Eckberg. "Environmental Issues as Women's Issues: General Concerns and Local Hazards." *Social Science Quarterly* 70, no. 3 (September 1989): 586–593.

Bomey, Nathan. *Detroit Resurrected: To Bankruptcy and Back*. New York: W. W. Norton, 2016.

Bowen, Zachary. "The Flint Water Crisis: A Narrative with Administrative Recommendations." *Concept* 40 (2017). https://concept.journals.villanova.edu/article/view/2186.

Boyer, Richard, and Herbert M. Morais. *Labor's Untold Story*. Pittsburgh, PA: United Electrical, Radio, and Machine Workers of America, 1955.

Boyte, Harry. *The Backyard Revolution: Understanding the New Citizen Movement*. Philadelphia: Temple University Press, 1981.

Bravender, Marlena, and Caryl Walling. "Man-made Disaster Undermines Impoverished School District: The Flint Water Crisis." eJournal of Education Policy (Spring 2017). https://files.eric.ed.gov/fulltext/EJ1158143.pdf.

Brecher, Jeremy. *Strike!* Boston: South End Press, 1972.

Breines, Wini. *Community and Organization in the New Left, 1962–1968: The Great Refusal*. New Brunswick, NJ: Rutgers University Press, 1989.

Brewer, James. "Michigan Blames Flint Water Crisis on Racism, Parts One and Two." World Socialist website, March 3 and 4, 2017, accessed September 3, 2018. https://www.wsws.org/en/articles/2017/03/03/flin-m03.html.

Bridge Magazine Staff. "Disaster Day by Day: A Detailed Flint Crisis Timeline." *Bridge Magazine*, February 4, 2016.

Brown, Mark B. *Science in Democracy: Expertise, Institutions, and Representation*. Cambridge, MA: MIT Press, 2009.

Brown, Phil. "Popular Epidemiology and Toxic Waste Contamination: Lay and Professional Ways of Knowing." *Journal of Health and Social Behavior* 33 (September 1992): 267–281.

Brown, Phil. *Toxic Exposures: Contested Illnesses and the Environmental Health Movement*. New York: Columbia University Press, 2007.

Brown, Phil, and Faith I. T. Ferguson. "'Making a Big Stink': Women's Work, Women's Relationships, and Toxic Waste Activism." *Gender and Society* 9, no. 2 (April 1995): 145–172.

Brown, Phil, and Edwin J. Mikkelsen. *No Safe Place: Toxic Waste, Leukemia, and Community Action*. Berkeley: University of California Press, 1990.

Brown, Phil, Rachel Morello-Frosch, Stephen Zavestoski, and the Contested Illnesses Research Group, eds. *Contested Illnesses: Citizens, Science, and Health Social Movements.* Berkeley: University of California Press, 2012.

Brown, Wendy. *Undoing the Demos: Neoliberalism's Stealth Revolution.* New York: Zone Books, 2015.

Bryant, Bunyan, and Paul Mohai, eds. *Race and the Incidence of Environmental Hazards: A Time for Discourse.* Boulder, CO: Westview, 1992.

Brulle, Robert J., and David N. Pellow. "Environmental Justice: Human Health and Environmental Inequalities." *Annual Review of Public Health* 27 (2006): 103–124.

Buford, Talia, and Kristen Lombardi. "Steel Mill That Never Was 'Casts a Shadow' on EPA Office of Civil Rights." *The Center for Public Integrity,* January 5, 2016.

Bullard, Robert D., ed. *Confronting Environmental Racism: Voices from the Grassroots.* Boston: South End Press, 1993.

Bullard, Robert D. *Dumping in Dixie: Race, Class, and Environmental Quality.* Boulder, CO: Westview Press, 2000.

Bullard, Robert D., and Glenn S. Johnson. "Environmental Justice: Grassroots Activism and Its Impact on Public Policy Decision Making." *Journal of Social Issues* 56, no. 3 (Fall 2000): 555–578.

Burawoy, Michael. "The Extended Case Method." *Sociological Theory* 16, no. 1 (March 1998): 4–33.

Burke, Katie L. "Flint Water Crisis Yields Hard Lessons in Science and Ethics." *American Scientist* 104, no. 3 (May/June 2016): 134–136.

Burke, Katie L. "Moving Forward after Flint." *American Scientist* 104, no. 3 (May/June 2016): 137–139.

Butler, Lindsey J., Madeleine K. Scammell, and Eugene B. Benson. "The Flint, Michigan, Water Crisis: A Case Study in Regulatory Failure and Environmental Injustice." *Environmental Justice* 9, no. 4 (August 2016): 93–97.

Butts, Rachel, and Stephen Gasteyer. "More Cost per Drop: Water Rates, Structural Inequality, and Race in the United States—The Case of Michigan." *Environmental Practice* 13, no. 4 (December 2011): 386–395.

Byrne, Brenda G., Sarah McColm, Shawn P. McElmurry, Paul E. Kilgore, Joanne Sobeck, Rick Sadler, Nancy G. Love, and Michele S. Swanson. "Prevalence of Infection-Competent Serogroup 6 *Legionella pneumophila* within Premise Plumbing in Southeast Michigan." *mBio* 9, no. 1 (January/February 2018): 1–17.

Byrnes, Annie. "Amid the Flint Water Crisis, Journalists Are Calling for Changes to Michigan's FOIA Law." *Poynter,* February 2, 2016.

Cable, Sherry, Tamara Mix, and Donald Hasting. "Mission Impossible? Environmental Justice Movement Collaboration with Professional Environmentalists and with Academics." In *Power, Justice, and the Environment: A Critical Appraisal of the Environmental Justice Movement*, edited by David Naguib Pellow and Robert J. Brulle, 55–76. Cambridge, MA: MIT Press, 2005.

Callon, Michel, Pierre Lascoumes, and Yannick Barthe. *Acting in an Uncertain World: An Essay on Technical Democracy*. Cambridge, MA: MIT Press, 2009.

Campbell, Andrew Morton, Mona Hanna-Attisha, and Jenny LaChance. "Flint Blood Lead Levels: Four Questions." *American Journal of Public Health* 106, no. 12 (December 2016): e6–e7.

Campbell, Bob, ed. *Poison on Tap: How Government Failed Flint, and the Heroes Who Fought Back*. Traverse City, MI: Mission Point Press, 2016.

Campbell, Carla, Rachael Greenberg, Deepa Mankikar, and Ronald D. Ross. "A Case Study of Environmental Injustice: The Failure in Flint." *International Journal of Environmental Research and Public Health* 13, no. 10 (2016): https://www.ncbi.nlm.nih.gov/pmc/articles/PMC5086690/pdf/ijerph-13-00951.pdf.

Carpenter, Zoë. "How the EPA Has Failed to Challenge Environmental Racism in Flint—and Beyond." *The Nation*, January 28, 2016.

Carravallah, Laura A., Lawrence A. Reynolds, and Susan J. Woolford. "Lessons for Physicians from Flint's Water Crisis." *AMA Journal of Ethics* 19, no. 10 (October 2017): 1001–1010.

Carotta, Christin L., Amy E. Bonomi, Karleigh Knox, Morgan C. Blain, and Brianna F. Dines. "Flint's Children: Narratives on Hope." *Qualitative Report* 22, no. 9 (September 2017): 2437–2453.

Cavalier, Darlene, and Eric B. Kennedy, eds. *The Rightful Place of Science: Citizen Science*. Tempe, AZ: Consortium for Science, Policy, and Outcomes, 2016.

Ceaser, Donovon. "Significant Life Experiences and Environmental Justice: Positionality and the Significance of Negative Social/Environmental Experiences." *Environmental Education Research* 21, no. 2 (2015): 205–220.

Center for Michigan. *Fractured Trust: Lost Faith in State Government, and How to Restore It*. March 2017.

Centers for Disease Control and Prevention. *Community Assessment for Public Health Emergency Response (CASPER) after the Flint Water Crisis: May 17–19, 2016*. July 2016. https://www.michigan.gov/documents/flintwater/CASPER_Report_540077_7.pdf.

Chambers, Edward. *Roots for Radicals: Organizing for Power, Action, and Justice*. New York: Continuum, 2003.

Chariton, Jordan. "EXCLUSIVE: Flint Water Declared 'Restored' after Michigan's Environmental Agency Broke EPA Testing Regulations." Medium, November 1, 2018, https://medium.com/status-coup/exclusive-flint-water-declared-restored-after-michigan-s-environmental-agency-broke-epa-testing-3e2fc1f91a70.

Chariton, Jordan. "Fraudulence in Flint: How Suspect Science Helped Declare the Water Crisis Over." Truthdig, May 27, 2018.

Chaskin, Robert J. "Building Community Capacity: A Definitional Framework and Case Studies from a Comprehensive Community Initiative." Urban Affairs Review 36, no. 3 (January 2001): 291–323.

Chavez, Manuel, Marta Perez, Carin Tunney, and Silvia Núñez. "Accountability and Transparency Diluted in the Flint Water Crisis: A Case of Institutional Implosion." Norteamérica 12, no. 1 (January–June 2017): 11–52.

Checker, Melissa. Polluted Promises: Environmental Racism and the Search for Justice in a Southern Town. New York: New York University Press, 2005.

Christensen, Peter, David Andrew Keiser, and Gabriel E. Lade. "The Effects of Information Provision on Housing Markets and Avoidance Behavior: Evidence from the Flint, MI Drinking Water Crisis." Iowa State University, 2017.

Clark, Anna. "The City That Unpoisoned Its Pipes." Next City, August 8, 2016.

Clark, Anna. "Flint Prepares to Be Left Behind Once More." New Republic, March 3, 2016.

Clark, Anna. "A Guide to the 15 Powerful People Charged with Poisoning Flint." Splinter, June 19, 2017.

Clark, Anna. "How the Flint Water Crisis and a Statehouse Scandal Gave a Boost to FOIA Reform in Michigan." Columbia Journalism Review, June 21, 2016.

Clark, Anna. The Poisoned City: Flint's Water and the American Urban Tragedy. New York: Metropolitan Books, 2018.

Clark, Anna. "The Struggle for Accountability in Flint." Boston Review, February 2, 2016.

Clark, Anna. "Will Anyone Be Held at Fault over Flint?" CityLab, August 29, 2018.

Clark, Anna, and Josh Kramer. "'An Equal Opportunity Lie': How Housing Discrimination Led to the Flint Water Crisis." Splinter, December 5, 2017.

Clark, Karen. "The Value of Water: The Flint Water Crisis as a Devaluation of Natural Resources, Not a Matter of Racial Justice." Environmental Justice 9, no. 4 (2016): 99–102.

Clinton, Hillary. What Happened. New York: Simon & Schuster, 2017.

Cnaan, Ram A. "Neighborhood-representing Organizations: How Democratic Are They?" Social Service Review 65, no. 4 (1991): 614–634.

Coalition for Clean Water. "Coalition for Clean Water: Flint Is Not in the Clear." *People's Tribune*, June 2015.

Code, Lorraine. *What Can She Know?: Feminist Theory and the Construction of Knowledge*. Ithaca, NY: Cornell University Press, 1991.

Cole, Luke, and Sheila Foster. *From the Ground Up: Environmental Racism and the Rise of the Environmental Justice Movement*. New York: New York University Press, 2001.

Colton, Roger. Memo to City of Flint on Water Affordability. April 24, 2015.

Community Foundation of Greater Flint and Michigan State University, Department of Community Sustainability and Office of Outreach and Engagement. *Voices of Flint Project: Research Summary. Flint Resident Perceptions about the Causes, Consequences, and Solutions to the Flint Water Crisis*. December 9, 2016.

Conde, Marta. "Activism Mobilising Science." *Ecological Economics* 105 (September 2014): 67–77.

Conway, Kyle J. "There's Something in the Water: How Apathetic State Officials Let the People of Flint, Michigan Down." *Villanova Environmental Law Journal* 29, no. 1 (2018): 57–80.

Cooper, Caren. *Citizen Science: How Ordinary People Are Changing the Face of Discovery*. New York: Overlook Press, 2016.

Cooper, Caren B., and Bruce V. Lewenstein, "Two Meanings of Citizen Science." In *The Rightful Place of Science: Citizen Science*, edited by Darlene Cavalier and Eric B. Kennedy. Tempe, AZ: Consortium for Science, Policy, and Outcomes, 2016.

Corburn, Jason. *Street Science: Community Knowledge and Environmental Health Justice*. Cambridge, MA: MIT Press, 2005.

Cornwell, David A., Richard A. Brown, and Steve H. Via. "National Survey of Lead Service Line Occurrence." *Journal—American Water Works Association* 108, no. 4 (April 2016): e182–e191.

Counts, John. "Flint Water Crisis Got Its Start as a Money-Saving Move in Department of Treasury." *MLive*, May 3, 2016. https://www.mlive.com/news/index.ssf /2016/05/flint_water_crisis_got_its_sta.html.

Counts, John. "How Government Poisoned the People of Flint." *MLive*, January 21, 2016. https://www.mlive.com/news/index.ssf/page/flint_water_crisis.html.

Coyne, Connor. "Flint, Michigan's Water Crisis: What the National Media Got Wrong." *Vox*, January 20, 2016.

Coyne, Connor. "The Flint Water Crisis Is Not Over." *Vox*, December 21, 2016.

Coyne, Connor. "I Live in Flint. All the Justice in the World Won't Undo the Damage Done Here." *Vox*, June 15, 2017.

Craft-Blacksheare, Melva Gale. "Lessons Learned from the Crisis in Flint, Michigan Regarding the Effects of Contaminated Water on Maternal and Child Health." *JOGNN* 46, no. 2 (March/April 2017): 258–266.

Craven, Julia, and Tyler Tynes. "The Racist Roots of Flint's Water Crisis." *Huffington Post*, February 3, 2016.

Crosby, Andrew, and Donijo Robbins. "Mission Impossible: Monitoring Municipal Fiscal Sustainability and Stress in Michigan." *Journal of Public Budgeting, Accounting, and Financial Management* 25, no. 3 (Fall 2013): 522–555.

Culler, Jonathan. *The Pursuit of Signs: Semiotics, Literature, Deconstruction*. London: Routledge, 1981.

Cuthbertson, Courtney A., Cathy Newkirk, Joan Ilardo, Scott Loveridge, and Mark Skidmore. "Angry, Scared, and Unsure: Mental Health Consequences of Contaminated Water in Flint, Michigan." *Journal of Urban Health: Bulletin of the New York Academy of Medicine* 93, no. 6 (2016): 899–908.

Daisy, Michael, ed. *Detroit Water and Sewerage Department: The First 300 Years*. Detroit: City of Detroit, 2002.

Dalsgaard, Steffen. "The Ethnographic Use of Facebook in Everyday Life." *Anthropological Forum* 26, no. 1 (2016): 96–114.

Dana, David A. "Escaping the Abdication Trap When Cooperative Federalism Fails: Legal Reform after Flint." *Northwestern University Pritzker School of Law and Legal Theory Series*, no. 17–08 (March 2017): 1–36.

Dana, David A., and Deborah Tuerkheimer. "After Flint: Environmental Justice as Equal Protection." *Northwestern University Law Review* 111, no. 3 (2017): 879–890.

Dandaneau, Steven P. *A Town Abandoned: Flint, Michigan, Confronts Deindustrialization*. Albany: State University of New York Press, 1996.

Davis, Joseph E., ed. *Stories of Change: Narrative and Social Movements*. Albany: State University of New York Press, 2002.

Davis, Katrinell M. "False Assurances: The Effects of Corrosive Drinking Water and Noncompliance with Lead Control Policies in Flint, Michigan." *Environmental Justice* 9, no. 4 (August 2016): 103–108.

Dawsey, Chastity Pratt. "Soaring Pneumonia Deaths in Genesee County Likely Linked to Undiagnosed Legionnaires', Experts Say." *Bridge Magazine*, January 26, 2017.

Dawson, Emily L. "Lessons Learned from Flint, Michigan: Managing Multiple Source Pollution in Urban Communities." *William and Mary Environmental Law and Policy Review* 26, no. 2 (2001): 367–405.

Delaney, Arthur. "Mark Ruffalo's Water Nonprofit Has Allied Itself with an Opportunistic Sponge Salesman." *Huffington Post*, May 23, 2016.

Dellapenna, Joseph W. "The Water Crisis in Flint, Michigan: Profitability, Cost-Effectiveness, and Depriving People of Water." In *The Role of Integrity in the Governance of the Commons*, edited by Laura Westra, Janice Gray, and Franz-Theo Gottwald, 91–104. Cham, Switzerland: Springer, 2017.

Democracy Now! "On World Water Day, See Our Extended Interview with Flint Activists Nayyirah Shariff & Melissa Mays." March 22, 2016. https://www.democracynow.org/2016/3/22/on_world_water_day_see_our.

Dennis, Brady. "The EPA's Lead-in-Water Rule Has Been Faulted for Decades. Will Flint Hasten a Change?" *Washington Post*, May 5, 2016.

Dettloff, Dean, and Matt Bernico. "Atmoterrorism and Atmodesign in the 21st Century, Mediating Flint's Water Crisis." *Cosmos and History: The Journal of Natural and Social Philosophy* 13, no. 1 (2017): 156–189.

Dietz, Mary G. "Citizenship with a Feminist Face: The Problem with Maternal Thinking." *Political Theory* 13, no. 1 (February 1985): 19–37.

Doan, Michael D. "Epistemic Injustice and Epistemic Redlining." Ethics and Social Welfare 11, no. 2 (February 2017): 177–190.

Dodge, Jennifer. "Environmental Justice and Deliberative Democracy: How Social Change Organizations Respond to Power in the Deliberative System." *Policy and Society* 28, no. 3 (2009): 225–239.

Doidge, Mary, Eric Scorsone, Traci Taylor, Josh Sapotichne, Erika Rosebrook, and Danielle Kaminski. "The Flint Fiscal Playbook: An Assessment of the Emergency Manager Years (2011–2015)." MSU Extension White Paper, July 31, 2015.

Dorka, Lilian. *EPA Final Genesee Complaint Letter to Director Grether.* Washington, D.C.: Environmental Protection Agency, 2017.

Dorya, Gabriela, Z. Qiu, C. Qiu, M. R. Fu, and C. E. Ryan. "Lived Experiences of Reducing Environmental Risks in an Environmental Justice Community." *Proceedings of the International Academy of Ecology and Environmental Sciences* 5, no. 4 (2015): 128–141.

Dorya, Gabriela, Z. M. Qiu, C. Qiu, M. R. Fu, and C. E. Ryan. "A Phenomenological Understanding of Residents' Emotional Distress of Living in an Environmental Justice Community." *International Journal of Qualitative Studies on Health and Well-Being* 12, no. 1 (2017): 1–10.

Douglas, Mary. *Purity and Danger: An Analysis of Concept of Pollution and Taboo.* London: Routledge, 2002.

Douglas, Mary, and Aaron Wildavsky. *Risk and Culture: An Essay on the Selection of Technological and Environmental Dangers.* Berkeley: University of California Press, 1982.

Drum, Kevin. "In Flint, We Are Laying Tragedy on Top of Tragedy on Top of Tragedy." *Mother Jones,* January 26, 2017.

Drum, Kevin. "Lead Did Not Turn Flint Children into Idiots. Stop Saying So." *Mother Jones,* February 9, 2018.

Drum, Kevin. "The Water in Flint Is Now Better than Bottled Water." *Mother Jones,* November 21, 2016.

Dryzek, John. "Democratization as Deliberative Capacity Building." *Comparative Political Studies* 42, no. 11 (April 2009): 1379–1402.

Duntley-Matos, Roxanna, Victoria Arteaga, Angel García, Rafael Arellano, Roberto Garza, and Robert M. Ortega. "'We Always Say: And Then Came the Water …' Flint's Emergent Latinx Capacity Building Journey during the Government-Induced Lead Crisis." *Journal of Community Practice* 25, nos. 3-4 (2017): 365-390.

Edelstein, Michael R. *Contaminated Communities: Coping with Residential Toxic Exposure.* Boulder, CO: Westview Press, 2004.

Edwards, Marc A. "Failure of the U.S. Centers for Disease Control (CDC) and the U.S. Environmental Protection Agency (EPA) to Protect Children from Elevated Lead in Drinking Water: 2001–Present." Virginia Tech, March 15, 2016, https://oversight.house.gov/wp-content/uploads/2016/03/Marc-Edwards-Final-3-15-2016.pdf.

Edwards, Marc A. "Fetal Death and Reduced Birth Rates Associated with Exposure to Lead-Contaminated Drinking Water." *Environmental Science and Technology* 48, no. 1 (2014): 739–746.

Edwards, Marc A. "Foreword." In *Science for Sale: How the US Government Uses Powerful Corporations and Leading Universities to Support Government Policies, Silence Top Scientists, Jeopardize Our Health, and Protect Corporate Profits,* by David L. Lewis, ix–xiii. New York: Skyhorse Publishing, 2014.

Edwards, Marc A. "Institutional Scientific Misconduct at U.S. Public Health Agencies: How Malevolent Government Betrayed Flint, MI." Written statement to United States House Committee on Oversight and Government Reform, February 3, 2016. https://oversight.house.gov/wp-content/uploads/2016/02/Edwards-VA-Tech-Statement-2-3-Flint-Water.pdf.

Edwards, Marc A., and Amy Pruden. "The Flint Water Crisis: Overturning the Research Paradigm to Advance Science and Defend Public Welfare." *Environmental Science and Technology* 50 (2016): 8935–8936.

Edwards, Marc A., and Amy Pruden. "We Helped Flint Residents Save Themselves and Are Proud of It—Staying in Our Ivory Tower Would Have Perpetuated Injustice." *Environmental Science and Technology* 50 (2016): 12057.

Edwards, Marc A., and Siddhartha Roy. "Academic Research in the 21st Century: Maintaining Scientific Integrity in a Climate of Perverse Incentives and Hypercompetition." *Environmental Engineering Science* 34, no. 1 (January 2017): 51–61.

Edwards, Marc A., Simoni Triantafyllidou, and Dana Best. "Elevated Blood Lead in Young Children Due to Lead-Contaminated Drinking Water: Washington, DC, 2001–2004." *Environmental Science and Technology* 43, no. 5 (March 2009): 1618–1623.

Eligon, John. "A Question of Environmental Racism in Flint." *The New York Times*, January 21, 2016.

Eng, Bernie. "Editorial: After One Year, Flint Still Needs Emergency Financial Manager." *MLive*, December 1, 2012. https://www.mlive.com/opinion/flint/index.ssf/2012/12/editorial_after_one_year_flint_1.html.

Environmental Justice Work Group. "Environmental Justice Work Group Report: Michigan as a Global Leader in Environmental Justice." March 2018. https://www.michigan.gov/documents/snyder/Environmental_Justice_Work_Group_Report_616102_7.pdf.

Environmental Protection Agency. *Environmental Equity: Reducing Risks for All Communities*. Washington, D.C.: Environmental Protection Agency, 1992.

Environmental Protection Agency, Office of Inspector General. *Drinking Water Contamination in Flint, Michigan, Demonstrates a Need to Clarify EPA Authority to Issue Emergency Orders to Protect the Public*. Washington, D.C.: Environmental Protection Agency, 2016.

Environmental Protection Agency, Office of Water. Lead and Copper Rule Revisions White Paper. October 2016. https://www.epa.gov/sites/production/files/2016-10/documents/508_lcr_revisions_white_paper_final_10.26.16.pdf.

Epstein, Steven. *Impure Science: AIDS, Activism, and the Politics of Knowledge*. Berkeley: University of California Press, 1996.

Erikson, Kai. *Everything in Its Path: Destruction of Community in the Buffalo Creek Flood*. New York: Touchstone, 1976.

Escobar, Arturo. "Culture, Practice and Politics: Anthropology and the Study of Social Movements." *Critique of Anthropology* 12 (1992): 395–432.

Evans, Sara M., and Harry C. Boyte. *Free Spaces: The Sources of Democratic Change in America*. New York: Perennial Library, 1986.

Faber, Daniel R., and Deborah McCarthy. "Breaking the Funding Barriers: Philanthropic Activism in Support of the Environmental Justice Movement." In *Foundations for Social Change: Critical Perspectives on Philanthropy and Popular Movements*, edited by Daniel Faber, Deborah McCarthy, and Deborah McCarthy Auriffeille, 175–210. Lanham, MD: Rowman and Littlefield, 2005.

Fagin, Dan. *Toms River: A Story of Science and Salvation*. New York: Bantam Books, 2013.

Farmer, Paul. *Pathologies of Power: Health, Human Rights, and the New War on the Poor*. Berkeley: University of California Press, 2005.

Fasenfest, David. "A Neoliberal Response to an Urban Crisis: Emergency Management in Flint, MI." *Critical Sociology* (August 2017): 1–15.

Fasenfest, David, and Theodore Pride. "Emergency Management in Michigan: Race, Class and the Limits of Liberal Democracy." *Critical Sociology* 42, no. 3 (2016): 331–334.

Faust, Kasey M., Dulcy M. Abraham, and Shawn P. McElmurry. "Water and Wastewater Infrastructure Management in Shrinking Cities." *Public Works Management and Policy* 21, no. 2 (2015): 128–156.

Faust, Kasey M., Fred L. Mannering, and Dulcy M. Abraham. "Statistical Analysis of Public Perceptions of Water Infrastructure Sustainability in Shrinking Cities." *Urban Water Journal* 13, no. 6 (2016): 618–628.

Fewell, Brent. "The Failure of Cooperative Federalism in Flint." *Journal—American Water Works Association* 108, no. 3 (March 2016): 12–14.

Fine, Sidney. *Sit-Down: The General Motors Strike of 1936–1937*. Ann Arbor: The University of Michigan Press, 1969.

Finewood, Michael H., and Ryan Holifield. "Critical Approaches to Urban Water Governance: From Critique to Justice, Democracy, and Transdisciplinary Collaboration." *WIREs Water* 2, no. 2 (March/April 2015): 85–96.

Fischer, Frank. *Citizens, Experts, and the Environment: The Politics of Local Knowledge*. Durham, NC: Duke University Press, 2000.

Flinn, Gary. *Hidden History of Flint*. Stroud, UK: The History Press, 2017.

Flint Water Advisory Task Force. *Final Report*. Lansing, MI: Office of Governor Rick Snyder, March 2016.

Flyvbjerg, Bent. "Five Misunderstandings about Case-Study Research." *Qualitative Inquiry* 12, no. 2 (April 2006): 219–245.

Food and Water Watch. "U.S. Water Systems Need Sustainable Funding." Washington, D.C.: Food and Water Watch, May 2016.

Food and Water Watch. *Water Injustice: Economic and Racial Disparities in Access to Safe and Clean Water in the United States*. Washington, D.C.: Food and Water Watch, March 2017.

Ford, Harold C. "Dayne Walling and the Flint Water Crisis: Victim, Villain or Faithful Servant?" *East Village Magazine*, January 5, 2017.

Fortenberry, Gamola Z., Patricia Reynolds, Sherry L. Burrer, and Vicki Johnson-Lawrence. "Assessment of Behavioral Health Concerns in the Community Affected by the Flint Water Crisis—Michigan (USA) 2016." *Prehospital and Disaster Medicine* 33, no. 3 (June 2018): 256–265.

Fortun, Kim. *Advocacy after Bhopal.* Chicago, IL: University of Chicago Press, 2001.

Francher, Mark, et al. "Unelected and Unaccountable, Emergency Managers and Public Act 4's Threat to Representative Democracy." ACLU of Michigan (2012): 1–10.

Fraser, Nancy. "Rethinking Recognition." *New Left Review* 3 (May/June 2000): 107–120.

Frerejohn, John, and Pasquale Pasquino. "The Law of the Exception: A Typology of Emergency Powers." *International Journal of Constitutional Law* 2, no. 2 (April 2004): 210–239.

Fricker, Miranda. *Epistemic Injustice: Power and the Ethics of Knowing.* Oxford: Oxford University Press, 2007.

Frug, Gerald E., and David J. Barron. *City Bound: How States Stifle Urban Innovation.* Ithaca, NY: Cornell University Press, 2008.

Furlong, Kathryn. "Small Technologies, Big Change: Rethinking Infrastructure through STS and Geography." *Progress in Human Geography* 35, no. 4 (August 2011): 460–482.

Gable, Lance, and James W. Buehler. "Criticized, Fired, Sued, or Prosecuted: Hindsight and Public Health Accountability." Public Health Reports 132, no. 6 (2017): 676–678.

Ganz, Marshall. "What Is Public Narrative?" Chutzpah Portfolio. Accessed September 2, 2018. http://chutzpahportfolio.yolasite.com/resources/WhatIsPublicNarrative08.pdf.

Ganz, Marshall. *Why David Sometimes Wins: Leadership, Organization, and Strategy in the California Farm Worker Movement.* Oxford: Oxford University Press, 2010.

General Accounting Office. *Siting of Hazardous Waste Landfills and Their Correlation with Racial and Economic Status of Surrounding Communities.* June 1, 1983.

Gerring, John. "What Is a Case Study and What Is It Good for?" *American Political Science Review* 98, no. 2 (May 2004): 341–354.

Gewin, Virginia. "Turning Point: Activist Engineer." *Nature* 537 (September 2016): 439.

Gibbs, Lois. "Citizen Activism for Environmental Health: The Growth of a Powerful New Grassroots Health Movement." *Annals of the American Academy of Political and Social Science* 584, no. 1 (November 2002): 97–109.

Gibbs, Lois. *Love Canal and the Birth of the Environmental Health Movement.* Washington, D.C.: Island Press, 2011.

Gieryn, Thomas F. "Boundary-Work and the Demarcation of Science from Non-Science: Strains and Interests in Professional Ideologies of Scientists." *American Sociological Review* 48, no. 6 (December 1983): 781–795.

Gillette, Clayton P. "Dictatorships for Democracy: Takeovers of Financially Failed Cities." New York University Law and Economics Working Paper 369, New York University School of Law, March 2014.

Gillette, Clayton P. "Fiscal Federalism, Political Will, and Strategic Use of Municipal Bankruptcy." *University of Chicago Law Review* 79, no. 1 (Winter 2012): 281–330.

Giroux, Henry A. *America at War with Itself.* San Francisco: City Lights Books, 2017.

Glover, Gale. *Flint: The Death and Rebirth of a City: Unmasking the Flint Water Crisis.* Flint, MI: Glover Publishing and Community Outsourcing, 2018.

Goffman, Alice. *On the Run: Fugitive Life in an American City.* New York: Picador, 2014.

Gómez, Hernán, and Kim Dietrich. "The Children of Flint Were Not 'Poisoned.'" *New York Times*, July 22, 2018.

Gómez, Hernán F., Dominic A. Borgialli, Mahesh Sharman, Keneil K. Shah, Anthony J. Scolpino, James M. Oleske, and John D. Bogden. "Blood Lead Levels of Children in Flint, Michigan: 2006–2016." *Journal of Pediatrics* 197 (June 2018): 158–164.

Goovaerts, Pierre. "The Drinking Water Contamination Crisis in Flint: Modeling Temporal Trends of Lead Level since Returning to Detroit Water System." *Science of the Total Environment* 581–582 (2017): 66–79.

Goovaerts, Pierre. "How Geostatistics Can Help You Find Lead and Galvanized Water Service Lines: The Case of Flint, MI." *Science of the Total Environment* 599–600 (December 2017): 1552–1563.

Goovaerts, Pierre. "Monitoring the Aftermath of Flint Drinking Water Contamination Crisis: Another Case of Sampling Bias?" *Science of the Total Environment* 590–591 (2017): 139–153.

Gordin, Michael D. *The Pseudoscience Wars: Immanuel Velikovsky and the Birth of the Modern Fringe.* Chicago, IL: University of Chicago Press, 2012.

Gosman, Sara R. Written Testimony Submitted to the Michigan Civil Rights Commission. September 8, 2016.

Gottesdiener, Laura. "A Magical Mystery Tour of American Austerity Politics." *The Huffington Post*, June 9, 2015.

Gottlieb, Robert. *Environmentalism Unbound: Exploring New Pathways for Change.* Cambridge, MA: MIT Press, 2001.

Gottlieb, Robert. *Forcing the Spring: The Transformation of the American Environmental Movement.* Washington, D.C.: Island Press, 2005.

Gottlieb, Robert. *A Life of Its Own: The Politics and Power of Water.* San Diego: Harcourt Brace Jovanovich, 1988.

Graeber, David. *Possibilities: Essays on Hierarchy, Rebellion and Desire.* Oakland, CA: AK Press, 2007.

Graham, Stephen, ed. *Disrupted Cities: When Infrastructure Fails.* New York: Routledge, 2010.

Gray, Steven, Alison Singer, Laura Schmitt-Olabisi, Josh Introne, and Jane Henderson. "Identifying the Causes, Consequences, and Solutions to the Flint Water Crisis through Collaborative Modeling." *Environmental Justice* 10, no. 5 (September 2017): 154–161.

Green, Dennis L. "Detroit's Water System and the Roots of the Flint Water Crisis." Eclectablog, April 25, 2017. http://www.eclectablog.com/2017/04/detroits-water-system-and-the-roots-of-the-flint-water-crisis.html.

Grimmer, Chelsea. "Racial Microbiopolitics: Flint Lead Poisoning, Detroit Water Shut Offs, and the 'Matter' of Enfleshment." *The Comparatist* 41 (October 2017): 19–40.

Groden, Claire. "How Michigan's Bureaucrats Created the Flint Water Crisis." *Fortune*, January 20, 2016.

Grossman, Daniel S., and David J. G. Slusky. "The Effect of an Increase in Lead in the Water System on Fertility and Birth Outcomes: The Case of Flint, Michigan." *West Virginia University, Department of Economics Working Papers Series*, no. 17–25 (August 2017): 1–63.

Grossman, Daniel S., and David J. G. Slusky. "The Impact of the Flint Water Crisis on Fertility." June 10, 2018. https://www.irp.wisc.edu/newsevents/workshops/SRW/2018/participants/papers/2-GROSSMAN-SLUSKY-2018-06-10-wisconsin.pdf.

Guyette, Curt. "An ACLU of Michigan Investigation Has Found a Stream of Irregularities in Flint's Water Tests." *Detroit Metro Times*, September 16, 2015.

Guyette, Curt. "Are Flint's Lead Problems Just Incompetence or Something Worse?" *Detroit Metro Times*, October 28, 2015.

Guyette, Curt. "As the Flint Water Crisis Fades from the Headlines, the State of Michigan Has an Enduring Responsibility to the City's School Children." ACLU of Michigan, October 18, 2016.

Guyette, Curt. "Charges against Emergency Managers Underscore Shortsightedness That Created Flint Water Crisis." *Detroit Metro Times*, December 21, 2016.

Guyette, Curt. "Continued Probes Crucial in the Wake of Flint Water Testimony." ACLU of Michigan, March 21, 2016.

Guyette, Curt. "Corrosive Impact: A Tale of Leaded Water and One Flint Family's Toxic Nightmare." ACLU of Michigan, July 9, 2015.

Guyette, Curt. "The Culprits in Flint's Water Scandal Need to Be Held Accountable." ACLU of Michigan, October 9, 2015.

Guyette, Curt. "Dangerous Water and Lost Trust in Flint: Why the Feds Need to Step In." ACLU of Michigan, October 6, 2015.

Guyette, Curt. "A Deep Dive into the Source of Flint's Water Crisis: Tunnel Vision." *Detroit Metro Times*, April 19, 2017.

Guyette, Curt. "Democracy Watch: Flint Residents Ask EPA to Change Drinking Water Rule." ACLU of Michigan, November 19, 2015.

Guyette, Curt. "Exclusive: Gov. Rick Snyder's Men Originally Rejected Using Flint's Toxic River." *Daily Beast*, January 24, 2016.

Guyette, Curt. "Filtering Democracy: Receivership Board Decision Reminder That Elected Officials Still Lack Full Power in Flint." ACLU of Michigan, July 5, 2017.

Guyette, Curt. "Flint Residents Deserve Unfiltered Truth." *Detroit Metro Times*, January 17, 2017.

Guyette, Curt. "Flint Schools: Dealing with the Damage Done." *Detroit Metro Times*, October 18, 2016.

Guyette, Curt. "The Flint Water Crisis Isn't Over." ACLU of Michigan, April 25, 2018.

Guyette, Curt. "Flint's State of Emergency Is a Sign That Democracy Is Working There Again." *Guardian*, December 16, 2015.

Guyette, Curt. "Four Questions Gov. Snyder Must Answer during Congressional Testimony." ACLU of Michigan, March 14, 2016.

Guyette, Curt. "Independent Water Tests Show Lead Problems Far Worse than Flint Claims." *Detroit Metro Times*, September 1, 2015.

Guyette, Curt. "In Flint, Michigan, Overpriced Water Is Causing People's Skin to Erupt in Rashes and Hair to Fall Out." *The Nation*, July 16, 2015.

Guyette, Curt. "Lead Astray: ACLU of Michigan Investigation Has Found Irregularities in Flint's Water Tests." ACLU of Michigan, September 15, 2017.

Guyette, Curt. "More Evidence of Flint's Water Problems Found in Study of Children's Blood." *Detroit Metro Times*, September 24, 2015.

Guyette, Curt. "One Year Later, Flint's Water Still Unsafe to Drink." *Detroit Metro Times*, September 15, 2016.

Guyette, Curt. "Overpriced Water in Flint Is Causing Rashes, Hair Loss." ACLU of Michigan, July 16, 2015.

Guyette, Curt. "Power of the People." *Detroit Metro Times*, February 24, 2016.

Guyette, Curt. "Report: EPA Fails to Deliver Environmental Justice in Flint and Elsewhere." *Detroit Metro Times*, October 4, 2016.

Guyette, Curt. "Researcher: State Tried to Cover up Child Lead Poisoning in Flint following Switch to River Water." ACLU of Michigan, December 21, 2015.

Guyette, Curt. "Revised EPA Memo Raises Troubling Questions amid Flint Water Crisis." ACLU of Michigan, November 11, 2015.

Guyette, Curt. "Second Anniversary of Switch to Flint River Sees Too Little Progress in Ending Water Crisis." ACLU of Michigan, April 25, 2016.

Guyette, Curt. "Why Strict Federal Oversight Is Needed to Safeguard Flint's Water." *Detroit Metro Times*, October 5, 2015.

Hamdy, Sherinef. "When the State and Your Kidneys Fail: Political Etiologies in an Egyptian Dialysis Ward." *American Ethnologist* 35, no. 4 (November 2008): 553–569.

Hamilton, Lawrence C. "Concern about Toxic Wastes: Three Demographic Predictors." *Sociological Perspectives* 28, no. 4 (October 1985): 463–486.

Hammer, Peter J. "The Flint Water Crisis, the Karegnondi Water Authority and Strategic–Structural Racism." *Critical Sociology* (2017). http://journals.sagepub.com/doi/abs/10.1177/0896920517729193.

Hammer, Peter J. "The Flint Water Crisis, KWA and Strategic-Structural Racism." Written Testimony Submitted to the Michigan Civil Rights Commission. July 18, 2016.

Hammer, Peter J. "The Flint Water Crisis, KWA and Strategic-Structural Racism: A Reply to Jeff Wright, Genesee County Drain Commissioner and CEO of Karegnondi Water Authority." Written Testimony Submitted to the Michigan Civil Rights Commission. December 31, 2016.

Han, Hahrie. *How Organizations Develop Activists: Civic Associations and Leadership in the 21st Century*. Oxford: Oxford University Press, 2014.

Hanna-Attisha, Mona. "Don't Downplay Lead Problems, or Solutions, for Kids in Flint Water Crisis." *Detroit Free Press*, March 28, 2018.

Hanna-Attisha, Mona. "Flint Kids: Tragic, Resilient, and Exemplary." *American Journal of Public Health* 107, no. 5 (May 2017): 651–652.

Hanna-Attisha, Mona. "The Future for Flint's Children." *New York Times*, March 26, 2016.

Hanna-Attisha, Mona. *What the Eyes Don't See: A Story of Crisis, Resistance, and Hope in an American City*. New York: One World, 2018.

Hanna-Attisha, Mona, Jenny LaChance, Richard Casey Sadler, and Allison Champney Schnepp. "Elevated Blood Lead Levels in Children Associated with the Flint Drinking Water Crisis: A Spatial Analysis of Risk and Public Health Response." *American Journal of Public Health* 106, no. 2 (February 2016): 283–290.

Hansen, Jason K. "Community Water System Regionalization and Stakeholder Implications: Estimating Effects to Consumers and Purveyors." Working Paper, Calhoun Institutional Archive of the Naval Postgraduate School, Naval Post Graduate School, Monterey, CA, 2011.

Harding, Sandra. "Rethinking Standpoint Epistemology: What Is 'Strong Objectivity'?" In *Feminist Epistemologies*, edited by Linda Alcoff and Elizabeth Potter, 49–82. London: Routledge, 1993.

Hardwig, John. "The Role of Trust in Knowledge." *Journal of Philosophy* 88, no. 12 (December 1991): 693–708.

Harper, Heather. "Local Financial Crisis and the Democratic Process: A Case Study of Michigan's Emergency Manager Law." Master's thesis, California State University, Northridge, 2014.

Harr, Jonathan. *A Civil Action*. New York: Random House, 1995.

Harrington, Cameron. "The Political Ontology of Collaborative Water Governance." *Water International* 42, no. 3 (2017): 254–270.

Harvey, David. *A Brief History of Neoliberalism*. New York: Oxford University Press, 2005.

Harvey, David. "Militant Particularism and Global Ambition: The Conceptual Politics of Place, Space and Environment in the Work of Raymond Williams." *Social Text*, no. 42 (Spring 1995): 69–98.

Harvey, David. *Spaces of Hope*. Edinburgh: Edinburgh University Press, 2000.

Harvey, Penny, and Hannah Knox. *Roads: An Anthropology of Infrastructure and Expertise*. Ithaca, NY: Cornell University Press, 2015.

Healy, Colleen, and Jennifer Bernstein. "Legal and Policy Interventions to Address Developmental and Mental Health Impacts of the Flint Water Crisis." *Environmental Justice* 9, no. 6 (December 2016): 167–175.

Heard-Garris, Nia Jeneé, Jessica Roche, Patrick Carter, Mahshid Abir, Maureen Walton, Marc Zimmerman, and Rebecca Cunningham. "Voices from Flint: Community Perceptions of the Flint Water Crisis." *Journal of Urban Health* 94, no. 6 (December 2017): 776–779.

Hess, David J. *Undone Science: Social Movements, Mobilized Publics, and Industrial Transitions.* Cambridge, MA: MIT Press, 2016.

Highsmith, Andrew R. *Demolition Means Progress: Flint, Michigan, and the Fate of the American Metropolis.* Chicago, IL: University of Chicago Press, 2015.

Highsmith, Andrew R. "Flint's Toxic Water Crisis Was 50 Years in the Making." *Los Angeles Times,* January 29, 2016.

Hill, Marc Lamont. *Nobody: Casualties of America's War on the Vulnerable, from Ferguson to Flint and Beyond.* New York: Atria Books, 2016.

Hohman, James M. "Proposal 1 of 2012: The Referendum on Public Act 4." Midland, MI: Mackinac Center for Public Policy, October 22, 2012.

Hohn, Donovan. "Flint's Water Crisis and the 'Troublemaker' Scientist." *The New York Times Magazine,* August 16, 2016.

Holeywell, Ryan. "Emergency Financial Managers: Michigan's Unwelcome Savior." *Governing,* May 2012.

Holifield, Ryan, Jayajit Chakraborty, and Gordon Walker, eds. *The Routledge Handbook of Environmental Justice.* New York: Routledge, 2017.

Hollander, Justin B. "Moving toward a Shrinking Cities Metric: Analyzing Land Use Changes Associated with Depopulation in Flint, Michigan." *Cityscape: A Journal of Policy Development and Research* 12, no. 1 (2010): 133–151.

Hollander, Justin B. *Sunburnt Cities: The Great Recession, Depopulation and Urban Planning in the American Sunbelt.* Milton Park, UK: Routledge, 2011.

Home-Douglas, Pierre. "The Water Guy." *Prism* 14, no. 3 (November 2004). http://www.prism-magazine.org/nov04/feature_water.cfm.

Honig, Bonnie. *Emergency Politics.* Princeton, NJ: Princeton University Press, 2009.

Honneth, Axel. *The Struggle for Recognition: The Moral Grammar of Social Conflicts.* Cambridge, MA: MIT Press, 1995.

Hoogesteger, Jaime. "Democratizing Water Governance from the Grassroots: The Development of Interjuntas-Chimborazo in the Ecuadorian Andes." *Human Organization* 71, no. 1 (2012): 76–86.

House Judiciary Committee Democratic Staff. "Democracy for Sale: Subverting Voting Rights, Collective Bargaining and Accountability under Michigan's Emergency Manager Law: Interim Report and Recommendations." February 2012. http://voiceofdetroit.net/wp-content/uploads/2012/03/Judiciary-PA4-report.pdf.

Howell, Sharon, Michael D. Doan, and Ami Harbin. "Detroit to Flint and Back Again: Solidarity Forever." *Critical Sociology,* no. 43 (2017): 1–21.

Hughes, Thomas P. "The Evolution of Large Technical Systems." In *The Social Construction of Technological Systems*, edited by Wiebe E. Bijker, Thomas P. Hughes, and Trevor J. Pinch, 51–82. Cambridge, MA: MIT Press, 1987.

Hurley, Andrew. *Environmental Inequalities: Class, Race, and Industrial Pollution in Gary, Indiana, 1945–1980*. Chapel Hill: The University of North Carolina Press, 1995.

INCITE! Women of Color against Violence. *The Revolution Will Not Be Funded: Beyond the Non-Profit Industrial Complex*. Durham, NC: Duke University Press, 2017.

Inwood, Joshua F. J. "'It Is the Innocence Which Constitutes the Crime': Political Geographies of White Supremacy, the Construction of White Innocence, and the Flint Water Crisis." *Geography Compass* 12 (2018): 1–11.

Irwin, Alan. *Citizen Science: A Study of People, Expertise and Sustainable Development*. London: Routledge, 1995.

Irwin, Jeff. *An Action Plan for Flint*. Michigan House of Representatives, December 2016.

Ivacko, Thomas, and Debra Horner. "Local Leaders More Likely to Support than Oppose Michigan's Emergency Manager Law, but Strongly Favor Reforms." *Michigan Public Policy Survey*, February 22, 2017.

Jackman, Michael. "Remember: Bill Schuette Is Indicting Emergency Managers, Not the EM Law." *Detroit Metro Times*, December 20, 2016.

Jackson, Derrick Z. "Environmental Justice? Unjust Coverage of the Flint Water Crisis." *Boston Globe*, July 11, 2017.

Jackson, Derrick Z. "The Goldman Prize Missed the Black Heroes of Flint—Just Like the Media Did." *Grist*, April 23, 2018.

Jacobson, Peter D., Colleen Healy Boufides, Jennifer Bernstein, Denise Chrysler, and Toby Citrin. "Learning from the Flint Water Crisis: Protecting the Public's Health during a Financial Emergency." University of Michigan School of Public Health, January 2018. http://www.debeaumont.org/wordpress/wp-content/uploads/Flint Report.pdf.

Jacoby, Tami Amanda. "A Theory of Victimhood: Politics, Conflict and the Construction of Victim-Based Identity." *Millennium* 43, no. 2 (2015): 511–530.

Jahng, Mi Rosie, and Namyeon Lee. "When Scientists Tweet for Social Changes: Dialogic Communication and Collective Mobilization Strategies by Flint Water Study Scientists on Twitter." *Science Communication* 40, no. 1 (January 2018): 89–108.

Jasanoff, Sheila. *Science and Public Reason*. London: Routledge, 2012.

Jasanoff, Sheila, ed., *States of Knowledge: The Co-Production of Science and Social Order*. London: Routledge, 2004.

Jeffery, Laura, and Matei Candea. "The Politics of Victimhood." *History and Anthropology* 17, no. 4 (December 2006): 287–296.

Johnston, Hank, and Bert Klandermans, eds. *Social Movements and Culture*. Minneapolis, MN: University of Minnesota Press, 1995.

Joint Select Committee on the Flint Water Public Health Emergency. *Report of the Joint Select Committee on the Flint Water Emergency*. October 2016.

Jones, Bryan D., and Lynn W. Bachelor. *The Sustaining Hand: Community Leadership and Corporate Power*. Lawrence: University Press of Kansas, 1993.

Jones, James H. *Bad Blood: The Tuskegee Syphilis Experiment*. New York: The Free Press, 1993.

Jordan, Laura. "Neoliberalism Writ Large and Small." *Anthropology Matters* 15, no. 1 (2014): 17–62.

Joy, K. J., Seema Kulkarni, Dik Roth, and Margreet Zwarteveen. "Repoliticising Water Governance: Exploring Water Re-Allocations in Terms of Justice." *Local Environment: The International Journal of Justice and Sustainability* 19, no. 9 (2014): 954–973.

Juris, Jeffrey S. "Practicing Militant Ethnography with the Movement for Global Resistance (MRG) in Barcelona." In *Constituent Imagination: Militant Investigations, Collective Theorization*, edited by Stevphen Shukaitis and David Graeber, 164–176. Oakland, CA: AK Press, 2007.

Kaffer, Nancy. "It's Time to Speak up about Racism in Flint Water Crisis." *Detroit Free Press*, February 20, 2017.

Kaika, Maria. *City of Flows*. New York: Routledge, 2005.

Kain, Erik. "Teachers and Tea Partiers Unite to Repeal Michigan Emergency Manager Bill." *Forbes*, April 6, 2011.

Katner, Adrienne L., Komal Brown, Kelsey Pieper, Marc Edwards, Yanna Lambrinidou, and Wilma Subra. "America's Path to Drinking Water Infrastructure Inequality and Environmental Injustice: The Case of Flint, Michigan." In *The Palgrave Handbook of Sustainability: Case Studies and Practical Solutions*, edited by Robert Brinkmann and Sandra J. Garren, 79–97. Basingstoke, UK: Palgrave Macmillan, 2018.

Katner, Adrienne L., Kelsey J. Pieper, Yanna Lambrinidou, Komal Brown, Chih-Yang Hu, Howard W. Mielke, and Marc A. Edwards. "Weaknesses in Federal Drinking Water Regulations and Public Health Policies That Impede Lead Poisoning Prevention and Environmental Justice." *Environmental Justice* 9, no. 4 (2016): 109–117.

Kennedy, Chinaro, Ellen Yard, Timothy Dignam, et al. "Blood Lead Levels Among Children Aged <6 Years—Flint, Michigan, 2013–2016." *Morbidity and Mortality Weekly Report* 65, no. 25 (2016): 650–654.

Kennedy, Eric. "When Citizen Science Meets Science Policy." In *The Rightful Place of Science: Citizen Science*, edited by Darlene Cavalier and Eric B. Kennedy, 21–50. Tempe, AZ: Consortium for Science, Policy, and Outcomes, 2016.

Key, Kent. "Expanding Ethics Review Processes to Include Community-Level Protections: A Case Study from Flint, Michigan." *AMA Journal of Ethics* 19, no. 10 (October 2017): 989–998.

Kibel, Paul Stanton, ed. *Rivertown: Rethinking Urban Rivers*. Cambridge, MA: MIT Press, 2007.

King, Shaun. "Michigan Gov. Rick Snyder Did Nothing as Flint's Water Crisis Became One of the Worst Cases of Environmental Racism in Modern American History." *New York Daily News*, January 11, 2016.

Kirkpatrick, L. Owen, and Nate Breznau. "The (Non)Politics of Emergency Political Intervention: The Racial Geography of Urban Crisis Management in Michigan." *SSRN*, March 2016.

Kitcher, Philip. *Science, Truth, and Democracy*. Oxford: Oxford University Press, 2001.

Klein, Naomi. *The Shock Doctrine: The Rise of Disaster Capitalism*. New York: Picador, 2007.

Kleinman, Arthur. *The Illness Narratives: Suffering Healing, and the Human Condition*. New York: Basic Books, 1988.

Klinenberg, Eric. *Heat Wave: A Social Autopsy of Disaster in Chicago*. Chicago, IL: University of Chicago Press, 2015.

Kolowich, Steve. "The Accidental Ethicist." *Chronicle of Higher Education*, October 2, 2016.

Kolowich, Steve. "The Cost of His Crusade." *Chronicle of Higher Education*, November 19, 2018.

Kolowich, Steve. "The Water Next Time: Professor Who Helped Expose Crisis in Flint Says Public Science Is Broken." *Chronicle of Higher Education*, February 2, 2016.

Kornberg, Dana. "The Structural Origins of Territorial Stigma: Water and Racial Politics in Metropolitan Detroit, 1950s-2010s." *International Journal of Urban and Regional Research* 40, no. 2 (March 2016): 263–283.

Kotlowitz, Alex. *The Other Side of the River: A Story of Two Towns, a Death, and America's Dilemma*. New York: Anchor Books, 1999.

Kraus, Henry. *The Many and the Few: A Chronicle of the Dynamic Auto Workers*. Urbana: University of Illinois Press, 1985.

Krings, Amy, Dana Kornberg, and Erin Lane. "Organizing under Austerity: How Residents' Concerns Became the Flint Water Crisis." *Critical Sociology* (2018): 1–15. Retrieved from Loyola eCommons, School of Social Work: Faculty Publications and Other Works.

Krsulich, Lora. "Polluted Politics." *California Law Review* 105, no. 2 (April 2017): 501–538.

Kruger, Daniel J. "Facultative Adjustments in Future Planning Tendencies: Insights on Life History Plasticity from the Flint Water Crisis." *Evolutionary Psychological Science* (2018): 1–12.

Kruger, Daniel J., Suzanne Cupal, Susan P. Franzen, Gergana Kodjebacheva, Elder Sarah Bailey, Kent D. Key, and Martin M. Kaufman. "Toxic Trauma: Household Water Quality Experiences Predict Posttraumatic Stress Disorder Symptoms during the Flint, Michigan, Water Crisis." *Journal of Community Psychology* 45, no. 7 (May 2017): 957–962.

Kruger, Daniel J., Suzanne Cupal, Gergana D. Kodjebacheva, and Thomas V. Fockler. "Perceived Water Quality and Reported Health among Adults during the Flint, MI Water Crisis." *Californian Journal of Health Promotion* 15, no. 1 (2017): 56–61.

Kruger, Daniel J., Gergana D. Kodjebacheva, and Suzanne Cupal. "Poor Tap Water Quality Experiences and Poor Sleep Quality during the Flint, Michigan Municipal Water Crisis." *Sleep Health* 3, no. 4 (August 2017): 241–243.

Krupp, Tyler. "Phenomenology." In *SAGE Encyclopedia of Political Theory*, edited by Mark Bevir, 1032–1036. Los Angeles, CA: SAGE Publications, Inc., 2010.

LaFrance, David B. "The Path from Flint." *Environmental Forum* 34, no. 1 (January/February 2017): 24–31.

Laidlaw, Mark A. S., Gabriel M. Filippelli, Richard C. Sadler, Christopher R. Gonzales, Andrew S. Ball, and Howard W. Mielke. "Children's Blood Lead Seasonality in Flint, Michigan (USA), and Soil-Sourced Lead Hazard Risks." *International Journal of Environmental Resources and Public Health* 13, no. 4 (March 2016): 358–372.

Laitner, Bill, Melanie Scott Dorsey, and Matt Helms. "How Emergency Financial Managers Changed Michigan." *Governing*, February 25, 2013.

Lambrinidou, Yanna. "On Listening, Science, and Justice: A Call for Exercising Care in What Lessons We Draw from Flint." *Environmental Science and Technology* 50, no. 22 (November 2016): 12058–12059.

Lambrinidou, Yanna. "Top Ten Myths about Lead in Drinking Water." *LEAD Action News* 18, no. 2 (October 2017). http://www.leadsafeworld.com/media-page/lanv 18n2-contents/lanv18n2-2-top-10-myths/.

Lambrinidou, Yanna. "When Technical Experts Set Out to 'Do Good': Deficit-Based Constructions of 'The Public' and the Moral Imperative for New Visions of Engagement." *Michigan Journal of Sustainability*. Forthcoming.

LAN and ROWE. *Analysis of the Flint River as a Permanent Water Supply for the City of Flint*. July 2011.

Langer, Ellen J. *Mindfulness*. Cambridge, MA: Perseus Books, 1989.

Langlois, Daniel K., John B. Kaneene, Vilma Yuzbasiyan-Gurkan, Barbara L. Daniels, Hilda Mejia-Abreu, Nancy A. Frank, and John P. Buchweitz. "Investigation of Blood Lead Concentrations in Dogs Living in Flint, Michigan." *Journal of the American Veterinary Medical Association* 251, no. 8 (October 2017): 912–921.

Lanphear, Bruce P., et al. "Low-Level Environmental Lead Exposure and Children's Intellectual Function: An International Pooled Analysis." *Environmental Health Perspectives* 113, no. 7 (July 2005): 894–899.

Latour, Bruno. *Science in Action*. Cambridge, MA: Harvard University Press, 1987.

Latour, Bruno, and Steve Woolgar. *Laboratory Life: The Construction of Scientific Facts*. Princeton, NJ: Princeton University Press, 1986.

Lederman, Jacob. "Flint's Water Crisis Is No Accident. It's the Result of Years of Devastating Free-Market Reforms." *In These Times*, January 22, 2016.

Lee, Shawna J., Amy Krings, Sara Rose, Krista Dover, Jessica Ayoub, and Fatima Salman. "Racial Inequality and the Implementation of Emergency Manager Laws in Economically Distressed Urban Areas." *Children and Youth Services Review* 70 (November 2016): 1–7.

Leonardi, Joseph M., and William J. Gruhn. *Flint River Assessment: Special Report*. Ann Arbor: Michigan Department of Natural Resources, Fisheries Division, 2001.

Lerner, Steve. *Diamond: A Struggle for Environmental Justice in Louisiana's Chemical Corridor*. Cambridge, MA: MIT Press, 2005.

Lerner, Steve. *Sacrifice Zones: The Front Lines of Chemical Exposure in the United States*. Cambridge, MA: MIT Press, 2010.

Levin, Edward D. "Crumbling Infrastructure and Learning Impairment: A Call for Responsibility." *Environmental Health Perspectives* 124, no. 5 (May 2016): A79.

Levine, Adeline Gordon. *Love Canal: Science, Politics, and People*. Lexington, KY: Lexington Books, 1982.

Lewis, Chris. "Does Michigan's Emergency-Manager Law Disenfranchise Black Citizens?" *The Atlantic*, May 9, 2013.

Li, Tania M. "Rendering Society Technical: Government through Community and the Ethnographic Turn at the World Bank in Indonesia." In *Adventures in Aidland: The Anthropology of Professionals in International Development*, edited by David Mosse, 57–80. Oxford: Berghahn, 2011.

Liu, Mike. "Marc Edwards: Virginia Tech Professor and Family Man by Day, Hero by Night." *Collegiate Times*, April 30, 2017.

Logan, Nneka. "The Flint Water Crisis: An Analysis of Public Relations as a Mediator between Human and Corporate Persons." *Public Relations Review* 44 (2018): 47–55.

Loh, Carolyn G. "The Everyday Emergency: Planning and Democracy under Austerity Regimes." *Urban Affairs Review* 52, no. 5 (March 2016): 832–863.

Lora-Wainwright, Anna. *Resigned Activism: Living with Pollution in Rural China*. Cambridge, MA: MIT Press, 2017.

Lubitow, Amy. "Collaborative Frame Construction in Social Movement Campaigns: Bisphenol-A (BPA) and Scientist–Activist Mobilization." *Social Movement Studies* 12, no. 4 (June 2013): 429–447.

Lubrano, Jonathon. "Water, Lead, and Environmental Justice: Easing the Flint Water Crisis with a Public Water Contamination Liability Fund." *William and Mary Environmental Law and Policy Review* 42, no. 1 (2017): 331–355.

Lurie, Julia. "Meet the Mom Who Helped Expose Flint's Toxic Water Nightmare." *Mother Jones*, January 21, 2016.

Mack, Elizabeth A., and Sarah Wrase. "A Burgeoning Crisis? A Nationwide Assessment of the Geography of Water Affordability in the United States." *PLoS ONE* 12, no. 1 (January 2017): 1–19.

Mahler, Jonathan. "Now That the Factories Are Closed, It's Tee Time in Benton Harbor, Mich." *New York Times Magazine*, December 15, 2011.

Maloney, Bryan, Baindu L. Bayon, Nasser H. Zawia, and Debomoy K. Lahiri. "Latent Consequences of Early-life Lead (Pb) Exposure and the Future: Addressing the Pb Crisis." *NeuroToxicology* 68 (September 2018): 126–132.

Mann, Thomas J. "Springtime in Flintown: Disappointment, Affront, and Failure." *Environmental Justice* 9, no. 3 (June 2016): 65–68.

Mansbridge, Jane, James Bohman, Simone Chambers, Thomas Christiano, Archon Fung, John Parkinson, Dennis F. Thompson, and Mark E. Warren. "A Systemic Approach to Deliberative Democracy." In *Deliberative Systems*, edited by John Parkinson and Jane Mansbridge, 1–26. Cambridge: Cambridge University Press, 2012.

Markowitz, Gerald, and David Rosner. "Citizen Scientists and the Lessons of Flint." *The Milbank Quarterly*, October 2016.

Markowitz, Gerald, and David Rosner. *Lead Wars: The Politics of Science and the Fate of America's Children*. Berkeley: University of California Press, 2013.

Mascarenhas, Michael. "The Flint Water Crisis. A Case of Environmental Injustice or Environmental Racism." Testimony delivered to Michigan Civil Rights Commission. September 8, 2016. https://www.michigan.gov/documents/mdcr/Mascarenhas_090816_Testimony_552231_7.pdf.

Mascarenhas, Michael. *Where the Waters Divide: Neoliberalism, White Privilege, and Environmental Racism in Canada*. Lanham, MD: Lexington Books, 2012.

Massaro, Toni M., and Ellen Elizabeth Brooks. "Flint of Outrage." *Notre Dame Law Review* 93, no. 1 (November 2017): 155–212.

Masten, Susan J., Simon H. Davies, and Shawn P. McElmurry. "Flint Water Crisis: What Happened and Why?" *Journal—American Water Works Association* 108, no. 12 (December 2016): 22–34.

Matsa, Katerina Eva, Amy Mitchell, and Galen Stocking. "Searching for News: The Flint Water Crisis." Pew Research Center, April 27, 2017.

May, Hillary. "Marc Edwards: Corrosion Man." *Virginia Tech Magazine*, Summer 2011, 10–11.

May, Jake. "Debunking 4 Claims by Gov. Snyder on the Flint Water Crisis." *MLive*, May 9, 2016. https://www.mlive.com/news/index.ssf/2016/05/gov_snyders_4_myths _about_flin.html.

Maynard, Andrew. "Can Citizen Science Empower Disenfranchised Communities?" *The Conversation*, January 27, 2016.

Maynard, Mark. "Everything You Ever Wanted to Know about the Emergency Manager Takeover of Michigan, and How We Allowed It to Happen." Markmaynard.com, July 29, 2014. http://markmaynard.com/2014/07/everything-you-ever-wanted-to-know-about-the-emergency-manager-takeover-of-michigan-and-how-we-allowed-it-to-happen/.

Mays, Melissa. "Flint Mom Shares the Heartbreak of Giving Her Kids Poisoned Water." Interview by The Stir, February 1, 2016.

Mazur, Allan. *A Hazardous Inquiry: The Rashomon Effect at Love Canal*. Cambridge, MA: Harvard University Press, 1998.

McClinton, Claire. "Are Flint Citizens Ready to Live without Democracy?: Councilman Censure Begs the Question." *People's Tribune*, February 2014.

McClinton, Claire. "Citizens Reject Government by Edict, Dictator Law Enrages Community." *People's Tribune*, March 2012.

McClinton, Claire. "Coming Soon to a Town near You! State Law Empowers 'Manager' to Set Aside Collective Bargaining Agreements, Seize Public Assets." *People's Tribune*, April 2011.

McClinton, Claire. "Democracy: Are Flint Citizens Ready to Live without It???" *People's Tribune*, March 2014.

McClinton, Claire. "'A Democracy Problem': As Debate Brings Attention to Flint, a Look at the Roots of the Water Crisis." Interview by Amy Goodman. *Democracy Now!*, February 17, 2016.

McClinton, Claire. "Emergency Manager Law Enables Corporate Takeover of Michigan's Water." *People's Tribune*, August 2015.

McClinton, Claire. "Flint Protest Exposes Emergency Manager Order to Silence Public." *People's Tribune*, June 2014.

McClinton, Claire. "Judge Drops Bomb on Illegal Water Rate Hikes in Flint, MI: Ruling Breathes Life into Fight for Water Rights." *People's Tribune*, September 2015.

McClinton, Claire. "No Safe Affordable Water—No Peace in Flint, MI." *People's Tribune*, March 2015.

McClinton, Claire. "Opposition to Emergency Manager Law Heats up in Michigan." *People's Tribune*, October 2012.

McClinton, Claire. "Pontiac, MI: Dictator Bill Destroys Michigan City." *People's Tribune*, July 2011.

McClinton, Claire. "Residents Ask, 'Are They Trying to Kill Us?'" *People's Tribune*, February 2015.

McClinton, Claire. "Water Unfit for Auto Production." *People's Tribune*, November 2014.

McClinton, Claire. "Water Warriors from Flint Expose What Is Really Going on." *People's Tribune*, March 2016.

McClinton, Claire. "Water Wars Escalate in Flint, MI." *People's Tribune*, December 2015.

McClinton, Claire. "'What's the Matter with Michigan?'" *People's Tribune*, August 2014.

McGuire, Michael J., Janice A. Beecher, Mona Hanna-Attisha, Susan J. Masten, and Joan B. Rose. "Roundtable—The Flint Crisis." *Journal—American Water Works Association* 108, no. 7 (July 2016): 26–34.

McGurty, Eileen. *Transforming Environmentalism: Warren County, PCBs, and the Origins of Environmental Justice*. New Brunswick, NJ: Rutgers University Press, 2009.

McKnight, John. "Services Are Bad for People." *Organizing*, Spring/Summer 1991, 41–44.

McNutt, Marcia. "Economics of Public Safety." *Science* 351, no. 6274 (February 2016): 641.

Medearis, John. "Social Movements and Deliberative Democratic Theory." *British Journal of Political Science* 35 (January 2005): 53–75.

Medina, José. "The Relevance of Credibility Excess in a Proportional View of Epistemic Injustice: Differential Epistemic Authority and the Social Imaginary." *Social Epistemology* 25, no. 1 (2011): 15–35.

Medvecky, Fabien. "Fairness in Knowing: Science Communication and Epistemic Justice." *Science and Engineering Ethics* (September 2017): 1–16.

Meyer, David S. "Protest and Political Opportunities." *Annual Review of Sociology* 30 (2004): 125–145.

Meyer, David S., and Debra C. Minkoff. "Conceptualizing Political Opportunity." *Social Forces* 82, no. 4 (June 2004): 1457–1492.

Michigan Civil Rights Commission. *The Flint Water Crisis: Systemic Racism through the Lens of Flint.* Lansing: State of Michigan, February 17, 2017.

Michigan Education Association. "The Truth about the Mackinac Center." August 2015.

Miller, DeMond Shondell, and Nyjeer Wesley. "Toxic Disasters, Biopolitics, and Corrosive Communities: Guiding Principles in the Quest for Healing in Flint, Michigan." *Environmental Justice* 9, no. 3 (June 2016): 69–75.

Milloy, Steven. "EPA's Lead Heads." *Washington Times*, April 5, 2004.

Mills, C. Wright. *The Sociological Imagination.* Oxford: Oxford University Press, 2000.

Milman, Oliver, and Jessica Glenza. "At Least 33 US Cities Used Water Testing 'Cheats' over Lead Concerns." *Guardian*, June 2, 2016.

Minghine, Anthony. "The Great Revenue Sharing Heist." *Michigan Municipal League Review*, February 2014.

Minkler, Meredith. *Community Organizing and Community Building for Health and Welfare.* New Brunswick, NJ: Rutgers University Press, 2012.

Mohai, Paul. "Environmental Justice and the Flint Water Crisis." *Michigan Sociological Review* 32 (Fall 2018): 1–41.

Mohai, Paul. Written Testimony of Paul Mohai, Professor of Natural Resources and the Environment, University of Michigan. Hearings on the Flint Water Crisis before the Michigan Civil Rights Commission, September 8, 2016. https://www.michigan .gov/documents/mdcr/Mohai_Testimony_-_MCRC_-_Oct_1_2016_536288_7.pdf.

Mohler, Valerie. "Meet the Man Mark Ruffalo Hand-Picked to Fight for Clean Water: Q&A with Water Defense Chief Scientist Scott Smith." DiscountFilterStore. com, March 12, 2014. http://blog.discountfilterstore.com/blog/mark-ruffalo-hand -picked-scott-smith-clean-water-fight/.

Moorman, Eric. "'A Greater Sense of Urgency': EPA's Emergency Power under the Safe Drinking Water Act and Lessons from Flint, Michigan." *Environmental Law Reporter* 47, no. 9 (September 2017): 10786–10799.

Morckel, Victoria. "Patronage and Access to a Legacy City Farmers' Market: A Case Study of the Relocation of the Flint, Michigan, Market." *Local Environment: The International Journal of Justice and Sustainability* 22, no. 10 (2017): 1268–1289.

Morckel, Victoria. "Why the Flint, Michigan, USA Water Crisis Is an Urban Planning Failure." *Cities* 62 (2017): 23–27.

Morckel, Victoria, and Greg Rybarczyk. "The Effects of the Water Crisis on Population Dynamics in the City of Flint, Michigan." *Cities and Health*, July 2018, 1–13.

Morckel, Victoria, and Kathryn Terzano. "Legacy City Residents' Lack of Trust in Their Governments: An Examination of Flint, Michigan Residents' Trust at the Height of the Water Crisis." *Journal of Urban Affairs*, August 2018, 1–17.

Moss, Kary L. "Environmental Justice at the Crossroads." *William and Mary Environmental Law and Policy Review* 24, no. 1 (2000): 35–66.

Mostafavi, Beata. "What Happened Last Time? A Look Back at Flint's 2002 State Takeover." *MLive*, November 10, 2011. https://www.mlive.com/news/flint/index .ssf/2011/11/what_happened_last_time_a_look.html.

Moyo, Otrude N. "A Beautiful Community, but a Troubled City: Flint's Water Crisis." *Alternate Routes: A Journal of Critical Social Research* 28 (2017): 233–247.

Mueller, Michael, Deborah Tippins, and Lynn Bryan. "The Future of Citizen Science." *Democracy and Education* 20, no. 1 (February 2012): 1–12.

Muhammad, Michael, E. Hill De Loney, Cassandra L. Brooks, Shervin Assari, DeWaun Robinson, and Cleopatra H. Caldwell. "'I Think That's All a Lie ... I Think It's Genocide': Applying a Critical Race Praxis to Youth Perceptions of Flint Water Contamination." *Ethnicity and Disease* 28 (2018): 241–246.

Murphy, Austin. "In Service of Municipal Bondholders: Emergency 'Management' and Poison Water in the Flint Case." SSRN, July 23, 2018. https://ssrn.com /abstract=3206606.

New York Times Editorial Board. "The Racism at the Heart of Flint's Crisis." *New York Times*, March 25, 2016.

Nickels, Ashley E. "Approaches to Municipal Takeover: Home Rule Erosion and State Intervention in Michigan and New Jersey." *State and Local Government Review* 48, no. 3 (September 2016): 194–207.

Nickels, Ashley E. *Power, Participation, and Protest in Flint, Michigan: Unpacking the Policy Paradox of Municipal Takeover*. Philadelphia: Temple University Press, 2019.

Nickels, Ashley E., and Jason D. Rivera, eds. *Community Development and Public Administration Theory: Promoting Democratic Principles to Improve Communities*. New York: Routledge, 2018.

Nowling, William D., and Mi Rosie Jahng. "Agenda-Building and Public Official Communication in the Pre-Crisis Stage of the Flint, Michigan Water Contamination Crisis." Paper presented at the 20th International Public Relations Research Conference (March 8–12, 2017): 243–251.

Nriagu, Jerome, Chuanwu Xi, Azhar Siddique, Annette Vincent, and Basem Shomar. "Influence of Household Water Filters on Bacteria Growth and Trace Metals in Tap Water of Doha, Qatar." *Scientific Reports* 8, no. 8268 (2018): 1–16.

Nukpezah, Julius A. "The Financial and Public Health Emergencies in Flint, Michigan: Crisis Management and the American Federalism." *Risk, Hazards, and Crisis in Public Policy* 8, no. 4 (August 2017): 284–311.

Nussbaum, Martha. *Upheavals of Thought: The Intelligence of Emotions.* Cambridge: Cambridge University Press, 2001.

Nyers, Peter. "Abject Cosmopolitanism: the Politics of Protection in the Anti-Deportation Movement." *Third World Quarterly* 24, no. 6 (2003): 1069–1093.

Olson, Erik, and Kristi Pullen Fedinick. *What's in Your Water? Flint and Beyond: Analysis of EPA Data Reveals Widespread Lead Crisis Potentially Affecting Millions of Americans.* New York: Natural Resources Defense Council, June 2016.

Olson, Randy. *Houston, We Have a Narrative: Why Science Needs Story.* Chicago, IL: University of Chicago Press, 2015.

Olson, Terese. "The Science behind the Flint Water Crisis: Corrosion of Pipes, Erosion of Trust." *The Conversation,* January 28, 2016.

Olson, Terese M., et al. "Forensic Estimates of Lead Release from Lead Service Lines during the Water Crisis in Flint, Michigan." *Environmental Science Technology Letters* 4, no. 9 (July 2017): 356–361.

Otiko, Manny. "Residents Say Flint River Was Contaminated with Dead Bodies, Shopping Carts, but City Still Used It as a Water Source." *Atlanta Black Star,* January 15, 2016.

Ottinger, Gwen. "Buckets of Resistance: Standards and the Effectiveness of Citizen Science." *Science, Technology, and Human Values* 35, no. 2 (2010): 244–270.

Ottinger, Gwen. *Refining Expertise: How Responsible Engineers Subvert Environmental Justice Challenges.* New York: New York University Press, 2013.

Ottinger, Gwen. "Social Movement-Based Citizen Science." In *The Rightful Place of Science: Citizen Science,* edited by Darlene Cavalier and Eric B. Kennedy, 89–104. Tempe, AZ: Consortium for Science, Policy, and Outcomes, 2016.

Ottinger, Gwen, and Benjamin Cohen, eds. *Technoscience and Environmental Justice: Expert Cultures in a Grassroots Movement.* Cambridge, MA: MIT Press, 2011.

Paneth, Nigel. "Review of Grossman DS, Slusky DJG, The Effect of an Increase in Lead in the Water System on Fertility and Birth Outcomes; The Case of Flint, Michigan." http://mediad.publicbroadcasting.net/p/michigan/files/review_of_grossman _and_slusky_paper.pdf?_ga=2.44376164.1108148605.1506794535-1282647051 .1440964267.

Parkinson, John, and Jane Mansbridge, eds. *Deliberative Systems*. Cambridge: Cambridge University Press, 2012.

Parks, Jeffrey, Kelsey J. Pieper, Adrienne Katner, Min Tang, and Marc Edwards. "Potential Challenges Meeting the American Academy of Pediatrics' Lead in School Drinking Water Goal of 1 µg/L." *Corrosion* 74, no. 8 (August 2018): 914–917.

Patel, Anisha I., and Laura A. Schmidt. "Water Access in the United States: Health Disparities Abound and Solutions Are Urgently Needed." *American Journal of Public Health* 107, no. 9 (September 2017): 1354–1356.

Patterson, Molly, and Kristen Renwick Monroe. "Narrative in Political Science." *Annual Review of Political Science* 1 (June 1998): 315–331.

Pauli, Benjamin J. "In Gov. Snyder's Flint Oversight Board's Decision on a Tax Lien Moratorium, More than Just Finances Are at Stake." Eclectablog, June 29, 2017. http:// www.eclectablog.com/2017/06/in-gov-snyders-flint-oversight-boards-decision -on-a-tax-lien-moratorium-more-than-just-finances-are-at-stake.html.

Pauli, Benjamin J. "Rethinking the Urban Crisis in Flint, Michigan." *City* 20, no. 3 (July 2016): 512–516.

Pauli, Benjamin J. "'Stop Poisoning Our Children!': Motherhood and Political Agency in the Flint Water Crisis." Unpublished paper.

Pellow, David Naguib. *Garbage Wars*. Cambridge, MA: MIT Press, 2002.

Pellow, David Naguib. "Popular Epidemiology and Environmental Movements: Mapping Active Narratives for Empowerment." *Humanity and Society* 21, no. 3 (August 1997): 307–321.

Pellow, David Naguib. *Resisting Global Toxics: Transnational Movements for Environmental Justice*. Cambridge, MA: MIT Press, 2007.

Pellow, David Naguib, and Robert J. Brulle, eds. *Power, Justice, and the Environment: A Critical Appraisal of the Environmental Justice Movement*. Cambridge, MA: MIT Press, 2005.

Perreault, Tom, Rutgerd Boelens, and Jeroen Vos. "Introduction: Re-Politicizing Water Allocation." In *Water Justice*, edited by Rutgerd Boelens, Tom Perreault, and Jeroen Vos, 34–42. Cambridge: Cambridge University Press, 2018.

Petryna, Adriana. *Life Exposed: Biological Citizens after Chernobyl*. Princeton, NJ: Princeton University Press, 2003.

Pew Charitable Trusts. *The State Role in Local Government Financial Distress.* Philadelphia: Pew Charitable Trusts, July 2013.

Philo, John C. "Local Government Fiscal Emergencies and the Disenfranchisement of Victims of the Global Recession." *Journal of Law in Society* 13, no. 1 (Fall 2011): 71–110.

Picker, Randal C., and Michael W. McConnell. "When Cities Go Broke: A Conceptual Introduction to Municipal Bankruptcy." *University of Chicago Law Review* 60, no. 2 (Spring 1993): 425–495.

Pieper, Kelsey J., Rebekah Martin, Min Tang, LeeAnne Walters, Jeffrey Parks, Siddhartha Roy, Christina Devine, and Marc A. Edwards. "Evaluating Water Lead Levels during the Flint Water Crisis." *Environmental Science and Technology* 52 (2018): 8124–8132.

Pieper, Kelsey J., Min Tang, and Marc A. Edwards. "Flint Water Crisis Caused by Interrupted Corrosion Control: Investigating 'Ground Zero' Home." *Environmental Science and Technology* 51, no. 4 (February 2017): 2007–2014.

Polletta, Francesca. "'Free Spaces' in Collective Action." *Theory and Society* 28, no. 1 (February 1999): 1–38.

Polletta, Francesca. *It Was Like a Fever: Storytelling in Protest and Politics.* Chicago: University of Chicago Press, 2006.

Polletta, Francesca, and Beth Gharrity Gardner. "Narrative and Social Movements." In *The Oxford Handbook of Social Movements*, edited by Donatella Della Porta and Mario Diani, 534–548. Oxford: Oxford University Press, 2015.

Progress Michigan. "Who's Running Michigan? A Report on the Activities and Bias of the Mackinac Center for Public Policy." Lansing: Progress Michigan, November 13, 2013.

Pruett, Natalie. "Rebuild Flint the Right Way: Flint Water Crisis Infrastructure Response Guide." City of Flint, Michigan, August 2016. https://app.box.com/s/5kyy6v12xzd1tq373jop61xc6f675g3y.

Pulido, Laura. "Flint, Environmental Racism, and Racial Capitalism." *Capitalism Nature Socialism* 27, no. 3 (July 2016): 1–16.

Pyles, Loretta. "Community Organizing for Post-disaster Social Development: Locating Social Work." *International Social Work* 50, no. 3 (May 2007): 321–333.

Rabin, Richard. "The Lead Industry and Lead Water Pipes 'A MODEST CAMPAIGN.'" *American Journal of Public Health* 98, no. 9 (September 2008): 1584–1592.

Raftelis Financial Consultants, Inc. *Flint Water Rate Analysis Final Report.* Lansing, MI: Department of Treasury, May 13, 2016.

Ramos, Elana. "The Dangers of Water Privatization: An Exploration of the Discriminatory Practices of Private Water Companies." *Environmental and Earth Law Journal* 7 (2017): 188–217.

Rand, Ayn. *The Virtue of Selfishness: A New Concept of Egoism.* New York: Signet, 1964.

Ranganathan, Malini. "Thinking with Flint: Racial Liberalism and the Roots of an American Water Tragedy." *Capitalism Nature Socialism* 27, no. 3 (July 2016): 17–33.

Rauch, Molly. "When Your Water Poisons Your Children." *Good Housekeeping*, February 15, 2016.

RealtyTrac. "U.S. Residential Property Vacancy Rate Drops 9.3 Percent between Q3 2015 and Q1 2016." February 9, 2016. https://wpnewsroom.realtytrac.com/news/u-s-q1-2016-u-s-residential-property-vacancy-analysis/.

Rhoads, William J., Emily Garner, Pan Ji, Ni Zhu, Jeffrey Parks, David Otto Schwake, Amy Pruden, and Marc A. Edwards. "Distribution System Operational Deficiencies Coincide with Reported Legionnaires' Disease Clusters in Flint, MI." *Environmental Science and Technology* 51, no. 20 (August 2017): 11986–11995.

Robbins, Denise. "ANALYSIS: How Michigan and National Reporters Covered the Flint Water Crisis." *Media Matters for America*, February 2, 2016.

Robinson, Joanna L. *Contested Water: The Struggle against Water Privatization in the United States and Canada.* Cambridge, MA: MIT Press, 2013.

Rolston, Jessica Smith. *Mining Coal and Undermining Gender: Rhythms of Work and Family in the American West.* New Brunswick, NJ: Rutgers University Press, 2014.

Rosati, Clayton. "*Development as Freedom* after Flint: A Geographical Approach to Capabilities and Antipoverty Communication." *Journal of Multicultural Discourses* 13, no. 2 (May 2018): 139–159.

Rose, Joan. "TTHM in Drinking Water: The Flint, Michigan Story; A Lesson for Us All." Waterandhealth.org, March 13, 2015. https://waterandhealth.org/safe-drinking-water/drinking-water/tthm-drinking-water-flint-michigan-story-lesson/.

Rosner, David. "Flint, Michigan: a Century of Environmental Injustice." *American Journal of Public Health* 106, no. 2 (February 2016): 200–201.

Ross, Tracey, and Danyelle Solomon. "Flint Isn't the Only Place with Racism in the Water." *The Nation*, February 9, 2016.

Ross-Brown, Sam. "Beyond Flint: How Local Governments Ignore Federal Water Standards." *The American Prospect*, February 24, 2016.

ROWE Professional Services Company. *Analysis of the Flint River as a Permanent Water Supply for the City of Flint.* July 2011.

ROWE Professional Services Company. *City of Flint Water Reliability Study: Distribution System.* December 2013.

ROWE Professional Services Company. *Review of December 21, 2012 Presentation— City of Flint Water Supply Assessment.* January 2013.

Roy, Siddhartha. "The Hand-in-Hand Spread of Mistrust and Misinformation in Flint." *American Scientist* 105, no. 1 (January–February 2017): 22–26.

Roy, Siddartha, and Marc A. Edwards. "Preventing Another Lead (Pb) in Drinking Water Crisis: Lessons from the Washington D.C. and Flint MI Contamination Events." *Current Opinion in Environmental Science and Health,* October 31, 2018.

Ruble, Kayla, Jacob Carah, Abby Ellis, and Sarah Childress. "Flint Water Crisis Deaths Likely Surpass Official Toll." Frontline, July 24, 2018. https://www.pbs.org /wgbh/frontline/article/flint-water-crisis-deaths-likely-surpass-official-toll/.

Ruddick, Sarah. *Maternal Thinking: Toward a Politics of Peace.* Boston: Beacon Press, 1995.

Ruffalo, Mark. "Our Work in 2015." Waterdefense.org, December 22, 2015. https:// waterdefense.org/our-work-in-2015/.

Rutt, Rebecca L., and Jevgeniy Bluwstein. "Quests for Justice and Mechanisms of Suppression in Flint, Michigan." *Environmental Justice* 10, no. 2 (April 2017): 27–35.

Ryder, Stacia. "The Flint Water Crisis and Beyond: Looking through the Lens of Environmental Justice." *Natural Hazards Observer* XL, no. 4 (April 2016): 23–26.

Sadler, Richard Casey, and Andrew R. Highsmith. "Rethinking Tiebout: The Contribution of Political Fragmentation and Racial/Economic Segregation to the Flint Water Crisis." *Environmental Justice* 9, no. 5 (October 2016): 143–151.

Sadler, Richard Casey, Jenny LaChance, and Mona Hanna-Attisha. "Social and Built Environmental Correlates of Predicted Blood Lead Levels in the Flint Water Crisis." *American Journal of Public Health* 107, no. 5 (May 2017): 763–769.

Salinsky, Jordan I. "Comparing the 2014–2016 Flint Water Crisis to the 1993 Milwaukee Cryptosporidium Outbreak." *Environmental Justice* 9, no. 4 (August 2016): 119–128.

Salmon, Barrington M. "American Genocide—Flint Water Crisis." *The Final Call,* June 28, 2016.

Sapotichne, Joshua, Erika Rosebrook, Eric A. Scorsone, Danielle Kaminski, Mary Doidge, and Traci Taylor. "Beyond State Takeovers: Reconsidering the Role of State Government in Local Financial Distress, with Important Lessons for Michigan and its Embattled Cities." MSU Extension White Paper, August 31, 2015.

Savage, Chris. "Another Michigan City Faces an Emergency Manager: Taylor." Eclectablog, January 23, 2012. http://www.eclectablog.com/2012/01/another-michigan -city-faces-emergency.html.

Savage, Chris. "Benton Harbor/Emergency Financial Manager News Update." Eclect-ablog, April 21, 2011. http://www.eclectablog.com/2011/04/benton-harboremergency -financial.html.

Savage, Chris. "Benton Harbor Is a City We've Failed: The Incredible Audacity of EFM Joe Harris." Eclectablog, April 25, 2011. http://www.eclectablog.com/2011/04 /benton-harbor-is-city-weve-failed.html.

Savage, Chris. "Imposition of an Emergency Manager Now Being Used to Threaten Unions." Eclectablog, July 16, 2011. https://www.eclectablog.com/2011/07/imposition -of-emergency-manager-now.html.

Savage, Chris. "Michigan GOP Pulling a Stealth-Walker Move to Damage Unions." Eclectablog, March 9, 2011. http://www.eclectablog.com/2011/03/rally-photos -michigan-gop-pulling.html.

Savage, Chris. "Michigan Rising: Aiming to Recall Snyder—While Disgruntled Former Volunteers Target Michigan Rising." A2Politico, January 19, 2012. Accessed July 1, 2017.

Savage, Chris. "MI Gov. Rick Snyder's Takeover of Benton Harbor Tied to Shore-line Development—What Rachel Missed." Eclectablog, April 19, 2011. http://www .eclectablog.com/2011/04/mi-gov-rick-snyders-takeover-of-benton.html.

Savage, Chris. "Protest Rick Snyder at the Blossomtime Grand Floral Parade This Saturday." Eclectablog, May 3, 2011. http://www.eclectablog.com/2011/04/benton -harbor-is-city-weve-failed.html.

Savage, Chris. "Some Thoughts on the Benton Harbor Situation." Eclectablog, May 7, 2011. http://www.eclectablog.com/2011/05/some-thoughts-on-benton-harbor.html.

Savage, Chris. "Think Emergency Managers Are Only for 'Black' Schools and Cities? Think Again, Part 2." Eclectablog, January 13, 2012. http://www.eclectablog.com /2012/01/think-emergency-managers-are-only-for_13.html.

Schlosberg, David. *Defining Environmental Justice: Theories, Movements, and Nature.* Oxford: Oxford University Press, 2007.

Schlosberg, David. *Environmental Justice and the New Pluralism: The Challenge of Dif-ference for Environmentalism.* Oxford: Oxford University Press, 1999.

Schlosberg, David. "Theorising Environmental Justice: The Expanding Sphere of a Discourse." *Environmental Politics* 22, no. 1 (2013): 37–55.

Schmitt, Carl. *The Concept of the Political.* Chicago, IL: University of Chicago Press, 1996.

Schneider, Andrew, and David McCumber. *An Air That Kills: How the Asbestos Poi-soning of Libby, Montana, Uncovered a National Scandal.* New York: Berkley Books, 2005.

Schnoor, Jerald L. "Recognizing Drinking Water Pipes as Community Health Hazards." *Journal of Chemical Education* 93, no. 4 (April 2016): 581–582.

Scholes, Robert, James Phelan, and Robert Kellogg. *The Nature of Narrative*. Oxford: Oxford University Press, 2006.

Schragger, Richard. *City Power: Urban Governance in a Global Age*. Oxford: Oxford University Press, 2016.

Schragger, Richard. "Flint Wasn't Allowed Democracy." *Slate*, February 8, 2016.

Schwake, David Otto, Emily Garner, Owen R. Strom, Amy Pruden, and Marc A. Edwards. "Legionella DNA Markers in Tap Water Coincident with a Spike in Legionnaires' Disease in Flint, MI." *Environmental Science and Technology Letters* 3, no. 9 (July 2016): 311–315.

Scorsone, Eric. "Frequently Asked Questions about the New Michigan Local Financial Emergency Law (Public Act 436 of 2012)." East Lansing: Michigan State University, January 2013.

Scorsone, Eric, and Nicolette Bateson. "Funding the Legacy: The Cost of Municipal Workers' Retirement Benefits to Michigan Communities." MSU Extension White Paper, March 14, 2013.

Scorsone, Eric, and Nicolette Bateson. "Long-Term Crisis and Systemic Failure: Taking the Fiscal Stress of America's Older Cities Seriously." Michigan State University Extension, September 2011.

Scott, Cheri R. "Chronicling the Flint, Michigan Water Crisis: A Rigid Dichotomy between Environmental Policy and Environmental Justice." PhD diss., Union Institute and University, Cincinnati, 2017.

Scott, Rebecca R. "Structures of Environmental Inequality: Property and Vulnerability." *Environmental Justice* 11, no. 3 (June 2018): 137–142.

Seamon, David. "Lived Bodies, Place, and Phenomenology: Implications for Human Rights and Environmental Justice." *Journal of Human Rights and the Environment* 4, no. 2 (September 2013): 143–166.

Sedlak, David. "Crossing the Imaginary Line." *Environmental Science and Technology* 50, no. 18 (2016): 9803–9804.

Sedlak, David. *Water 4.0: The Past, Present, and Future of the World's Most Vital Resource*. New Haven, CT: Yale University Press, 2014.

Sellers, Chris. "Piping as Poison: The Flint Water Crisis and America's Toxic Infrastructure." *The Conversation*, January 25, 2016.

Seltenrich, Nate. "The Forest and the Trees: How Population-Level Health Protections Sometimes Fail the Individual." *Environmental Health Perspectives* 125, no. 4 (April 2017): A65–A70.

Settlage, Rachel Gonzalez. "Status in a State of Emergency: U Visas and the Flint Water Crisis." *Harvard Latinx Law Review* 20 (Spring 2017): 121–169.

Shafer, Gregory. "Confronting Whiteness and the Flint Water Crisis." *The Humanist* (March/April 2016): 22–26.

Shah, Keneil K., J. M. Oleske, H. F. Gómez, A. L. Davidow, and J. D. Bogden. "Blood Lead Concentrations of Children in the United States: A Comparison of States Using Two Very Large Databases." *Journal of Pediatrics* 185 (June 2017): 218–223.

Shariff, Nayyirah. "Public Act 4: Crushing Democracy." *Courier* 36, no. 21 (May 2012): 1.

Sharp, Gene. *The Role of Power in Nonviolent Struggle*. Boston: The Albert Einstein Institution, 1990.

Sherwin, Brie D. "Pride and Prejudice and Administrative Zombies: How Economic Woes, Outdated Environmental Regulations, and State Exceptionalism Failed Flint, Michigan." *University of Colorado Law Review* 88, no. 3 (2017): 653–720.

Shiva, Vandana. *Water Wars: Privatization, Pollution, and Profit*. Cambridge, MA: South End Press, 2002.

Sicotte, Diane M., and Robert J. Brulle. "Social Movements for Environmental Justice through the Lens of Social Movement Theory." In *The Routledge Handbook of Environmental Justice*, edited by Ryan Holifield, Jayajit Chakraborty, and Gordon Walker, 25–36. New York: Routledge, 2017.

Singer, Alison, Steven Gray, Artina Sadler, Laura Schmitt Olabisi, Kyle Metta, Renee Wallace, Maria Claudia Lopez, Josh Introne, Maddie Gorman, and Jane Henderson. "Translating Community Narratives into Semi-quantitative Models to Understand the Dynamics of Socio-environmental Crises." *Environmental Modelling and Software* 97 (2017): 46–55.

Smith, Donna. "Why Medicare for Libby and Medicaid for Flint?" *Common Dreams*, March 22, 2016.

Smith, Lindsey. "This Mom Helped Uncover What Was Really Going on with Flint's Water." Michigan Radio, December 14, 2015.

Smock, Kristina. *Democracy in Action: Community Organizing and Urban Change*. New York: Columbia University Press, 2004.

Snow, David A., and Robert D. Benford. "Ideology, Frame Resonance, and Participant Mobilization." *International Social Movement Research* 1, no. 1 (1988): 197–217.

Solnit, Rebecca. *A Paradise Built in Hell: The Extraordinary Communities That Arise in Disaster*. New York: Penguin Books, 2009.

Stampfler, Michael L. "Emergency Financial Management of Cities by the State: A Cure or Simply Kicking the Can down the Road." *Journal of Law in Society* 14, no. 1 (Winter 2013): 235–244.

Stanley, Jason. "The Emergency Manager: Strategic Racism, Technocracy, and the Poisoning of Flint's Children." *The Good Society* 25, no. 1 (2016): 1–44.

Star, Susan Leigh. "The Ethnography of Infrastructure." *American Behavioral Scientist* 43, no. 3 (November/December 1999): 377–391.

State of Michigan Department of Treasury. "Frequently Asked Questions Regarding Public Act 4 of 2011, the Local Government and School District Fiscal Accountability Act." March 21, 2011.

Stedile, João Pedro. "Landless Battalions: The Sem Terra Movement of Brazil." *New Left Review* 15 (May–June 2002): 76–104.

Stephens, Thomas. "The Flint River Lead Poisoning Catastrophe in Historical Perspective." *Counterpunch*, February 12, 2016.

Stern, Paul C., and Harvey V. Fineberg, eds. *Understanding Risk: Informing Decisions in a Democratic Society*. Washington, D.C.: The National Academy Press, 1996.

Stout, Jeffrey. *Blessed Are the Organized: Grassroots Democracy in America*. Princeton, NJ: Princeton University Press, 2010.

Stringer, Rebecca. *Knowing Victims: Feminism, Agency and Victim Politics in Neoliberal Times*. New York: Routledge, 2014.

Strupp, Joe. "How National Media Failed Flint." *Media Matters for America*, February 11, 2016.

Stuckler, David, and Sanjay Basu. *The Body Economic: Why Austerity Kills; Recessions, Budget Battles, and the Politics of Life and Death*. New York: Basic Books, 2013.

Sugrue, Thomas J. *The Origins of the Urban Crisis: Race and Inequality in Postwar Detroit*. Princeton, NJ: Princeton University Press, 2005.

Sullivan, Patrick. "Dictatorship or Democracy? Push to Repeal the Emergency Manager Law Goes Local." *Northern Express*, June 26, 2011.

Sultana, Farhana, and Alex Loftus, eds. *The Right to Water: Prospects and Possibilities*. New York: Earthscan, 2012.

Susskind, Lawrence. "Water and Democracy: New Roles for Civil Society in Water Governance." *International Journal of Water Resources Development* 29, no. 4 (December 2013): 666–677.

Swarts, Heidi J. *Organizing Urban America: Secular and Faith-Based Progressive Movements*. Minneapolis: University of Minnesota Press, 2008.

Switzer, David, and Manuel Teodoro. "The Color of Drinking Water: Class, Race, Ethnicity, and Safe Drinking Water Act Compliance." *Journal—American Water Works Association* 109, no. 9 (September 2017): 40–45.

Swyngedouw, Erik. "The Antinomies of the Postpolitical City: In Search of a Democratic Politics of Environmental Production." *International Journal of Urban and Regional Research* 33, no. 3 (2009): 601–620.

Swyngedouw, Erik. "The Political Economy and Political Ecology of the Hydro-Social Cycle." *Journal of Contemporary Water Research and Education* 142, no. 1 (August 2009): 56–60.

Swyngedouw, Erik, and Nikolas C. Heynen. "Urban Political Ecology, Justice and the Politics of Scale." *Antipode* 35, no. 5 (January 2004): 898–918.

Swyngedouw, Erik, and Maria Kaika. "Urban Political Ecology: Great Promises, Deadlock … and New Beginnings?" *Documents d'Anàlisi Geogràfica* 60, no. 3 (2014): 459–481.

Szasz, Andrew. *EcoPopulism: Toxic Waste and the Movement for Environmental Justice.* Minneapolis: University of Minnesota Press, 1994.

Sze, Julie. *Noxious New York: The Racial Politics of Urban Health and Environmental Justice.* Cambridge, MA: MIT Press, 2006.

Sze, Julie, and Jonathan K. London. "Environmental Justice at the Crossroads." *Sociology Compass* 2, no. 4 (2008): 1331–1354.

Taylor, Charles. "The Politics of Recognition." In *Multiculturalism: Examining the Politics of Recognition,* edited by Amy Gutmann, 25–73. Princeton, NJ: Princeton University Press, 1992.

Taylor, Dorceta E. "The Rise of the Environmental Justice Paradigm: Injustice Framing and the Social Construction of Environmental Discourses." *American Behavioral Scientist* 43, no. 4 (January 2000): 508–580.

Taylor, Dorceta E. *Toxic Communities: Environmental Racism, Industrial Pollution, and Residential Mobility.* New York: New York University Press, 2014.

Taylor, Jacquelyn Y., Michelle L. Wright, and David Housman. "Lead Toxicity and Genetics in Flint, MI." *NPJ Genomic Medicine* 1 (June 2016): 16018.

Tesh, Sylvia Noble. *Uncertain Hazards: Environmental Activists and Scientific Proof.* Ithaca, NY: Cornell University Press, 2000.

Thompson, Dennis F. "Deliberative Democratic Theory and Empirical Political Science." *Annual Review of Political Science* 11 (June 2008): 497–520.

Torrice, Michael. "How Lead Ended Up in Flint's Tap Water." *Chemical and Engineering News* 94, no. 7 (February 2016): 26–29.

Touraine, Alain. "An Introduction to the Study of Social Movements." *Social Research* 52, no. 4 (Winter 1985): 749–787.

Townsend, Jim. "Fixing Michigan's Tax Limitation System: Steps to Avoid Detroit/ Flint-Style Fiscal Crises." *Wayne Law Review* 62, no. 2 (Winter 2017): 215–248.

Troesken, Werner. *The Great Lead Water Pipe Disaster.* Cambridge, MA: MIT Press, 2006.

Tucker, Young, Jackson, Tull, Inc. *City of Flint Water Supply Assessment.* Flint, City of Flint, February 2013. http://mediad.publicbroadcasting.net/p/michigan/files/201512 /water_report.pdf.

21st Century Infrastructure Commission. *21st Century Infrastructure Commission Report.* November 30, 2016. https://www.michigan.gov/documents/snyder/21st_Century _Infrastructure_Commission_Report_555079_7.pdf.

Unified Coordination Group. *Flint Rash Investigation: A Report on Findings from Case Interviews, Water Testing, and Dermatologic Screenings for Rashes that Developed or Worsened after October 16, 2015.* Flint, MI: Agency Unified Coordination Group, August 2016. http://www.phe.gov/emergency/events/Flint/Documents/rash-report.pdf.

United Church of Christ Commission for Racial Justice. *Toxic Wastes and Race in the United States: A National Report on the Racial and Socio-Economic Characteristics of Communities with Hazardous Waste Sites.* New York: United Church of Christ, 1987.

US Government Accountability Office. *Water Infrastructure: Information on Selected Midsize and Large Cities with Declining Populations.* September 2016.

US House of Representatives Committee on Energy and Commerce. *Flint Water Crisis: Impacts and Lessons Learned.* April 13, 2016.

Van Dyke, Nella, and Holly J. McCammon, eds. *Strategic Alliances: Coalition Building and Social Movements.* Minneapolis, MN: University of Minnesota Press, 2010.

Vang, Maiyoua. "Racial Composition of School District on School Leaders' Responses to State Takeover: A Field Experiment on the Application of Michigan's Emergency Manager Law." *Journal of Educational and Social Research* 7, no. 2 (May 2017): 31–41.

Venkataraman, Bhawani. "The Paradox of Water and the Flint Crisis." *Environment: Science and Policy for Sustainable Development* 60, no. 1 (December 2017): 4–17.

Veolia. *Flint, Michigan Water Quality Report.* March 12, 2015.

Vock, Daniel C. "In Flint's Aftermath, Water Will Run by New Rules." *Governing,* September 2016.

Von Schnitzler, Antina. *Democracy's Infrastructure: Techno-Politics and Protest after Apartheid.* Princeton, NJ: Princeton University Press, 2016.

Wahowiak, Lindsey. "Infrastructure, Public Health Linked, Crisis in Flint Shows: Aging US Systems Pose Risks to Health." *The Nation's Health* 46, no. 3 (April 2016): 1–15.

Wang, May. "The Engineered Crisis in Flint." *Harvard Political Review*, May 19, 2018.

Ward, Brandon. "The Promise of Jobs: Blackmail and Environmental Justice in Flint, Michigan, 1991–1995." *Environmental Justice* 6, no. 5 (October 2013): 163–168.

Warren, Christian. *Brush with Death: A Social History of Lead Poisoning.* Baltimore, MD: The Johns Hopkins University Press, 2000.

Washington, Harriet A. *Medical Apartheid: The Dark History of Medical Experimentation on Black Americans from Colonial Times to the Present.* New York: Anchor Books, 2006.

Washington, Sylvia Hood, and Sheila R. Foster. "The Legal Discourse Surrounding the Water Crisis in Flint, Michigan: Interview with Sheila R. Foster." *Environmental Justice* 9, no. 2 (April 2016): 59–64.

Washington, Sylvia Hood, and David Pellow. "Water Crisis in Flint, Michigan: Interview with David Pellow, Ph.D." *Environmental Justice* 9, no. 2 (April 2016): 53–58.

Wernick, Adam. "This Professor Says Flint's Water Crisis Amounts to Environmental Racism." *Public Radio International*, February 11, 2016.

We the People of Detroit Community Research Collective. *Mapping the Water Crisis: The Dismantling of African-American Neighborhoods in Detroit: Volume One.* 2016. http://wethepeopleofdetroit.com/communityresearch/water/

Wheeler, Jacob. "What Government Owes Flint's Poisoned Immigrant Community." *Bridge Magazine*, May 24, 2016.

Wisely, John. "Was Flint River Water Good Enough to Drink?" *Detroit Free Press*, January 30, 2016.

Wood, Richard L. *Faith in Action: Religion, Race, and Democratic Organizing in America.* Chicago, IL: University of Chicago Press, 2002.

Woodly, Deva R. *The Politics of Common Sense: How Social Movements Use Public Discourse to Change Politics and Win Acceptance.* Oxford: Oxford University Press, 2015.

Worth-Nelson, Jan. "Activists' Letter Aims Grievances at Marc Edwards; He Calls It 'Science Anarchy.'" *East Village Magazine*, June 2, 2018.

Worth-Nelson, Jan. "Longstanding 'Systemic Racism' Implicated in Flint Water Crisis, Civil Rights Commission Asserts." *East Village Magazine*, February 18, 2017.

Wright, Jeff. "The Flint Water Crisis, DWSD, and GLWA: Monopoly, Price Gouging, Corruption, and the Poisoning of a City." Written Testimony Submitted to the Michigan Civil Rights Commission. November 22, 2016.

Wu, Chia-Chen, Sudeshna Ghosh, Kelly J. Martin, Ameet J. Pinto, Vincent J. Denef, Terese M. Olsona, and Nancy G. Love. "The Microbial Colonization of Activated

Carbon Block Point-of-Use (PoU) Filters with and without Chlorinated Phenol Disinfection By-Products." *Environmental Science: Water Research and Technology* 3 (2017): 830–843.

Young, Gordon. *Teardown: Memoir of a Vanishing City.* Berkeley: University of California Press, 2013.

Young, Iris Marion. "Activist Challenges to Deliberative Democracy." *Political Theory* 29, no. 5 (October 2001): 670–690.

Young, Iris Marion. *Justice and the Politics of Difference.* Princeton, NJ: Princeton University Press, 1990.

Zahran, Sammy, Shawn P. McElmurry, Paul E. Kilgore, David Mushinski, Jack Press, Nancy G. Love, Richard C. Sadler, and Michele S. Swanson. "Assessment of the Legionnaires' Disease Outbreak in Flint, Michigan." *Proceedings of the National Academy of Sciences of the United States of America* 115, no. 8 (February 2018): E1730–E1739.

Zahran, Sammy, Shawn P. McElmurry, and Richard C. Sadler. "Four Phases of the Flint Water Crisis: Evidence from Blood Lead Levels in Children." *Environmental Research* 157 (May 2017): 160–172.

Zimring, Carl. *Clean and White: A History of Environmental Racism in the United States.* New York: New York University Press, 2016.

Zwarteveen, Margreet Z., and Rutgerd Boelens. "Defining, Researching and Struggling for Water Justice: Some Conceptual Building Blocks for Research and Action." *Water International* 39, no. 2 (March 2014): 143–158.

Index

Note: Page references in *italic* type refer to illustrative matter.

Urban and Industrial Environments

Series editor: Robert Gottlieb, Henry R. Luce Professor of Urban and Environmental Policy, Occidental College

David J. Hess, *Good Green Jobs in a Global Economy: Making and Keeping New Industries in the United States*

Joseph F. C. DiMento and Clifford Ellis, *Changing Lanes: Visions and Histories of Urban Freeways*

Joanna Robinson, *Contested Water: The Struggle Against Water Privatization in the United States and Canada*

William B. Meyer, *The Environmental Advantages of Cities: Countering Commonsense Antiurbanism*

Rebecca L. Henn and Andrew J. Hoffman, eds., *Constructing Green: The Social Structures of Sustainability*

Peggy F. Barlett and Geoffrey W. Chase, eds., *Sustainability in Higher Education: Stories and Strategies for Transformation*

Isabelle Anguelovski, *Neighborhood as Refuge: Community Reconstruction, Place Remaking, and Environmental Justice in the City*

Kelly Sims Gallagher, *The Globalization of Clean Energy Technology: Lessons from China*

Vinit Mukhija and Anastasia Loukaitou-Sideris, eds., *The Informal American City: Beyond Taco Trucks and Day Labor*

Roxanne Warren, *Rail and the City: Shrinking Our Carbon Footprint While Reimagining Urban Space*

Marianne E. Krasny and Keith G. Tidball, *Civic Ecology: Adaptation and Transformation from the Ground Up*

Erik Swyngedouw, *Liquid Power: Contested Hydro-Modernities in Twentieth-Century Spain*

Ken Geiser, *Chemicals without Harm: Policies for a Sustainable World*

Duncan McLaren and Julian Agyeman, *Sharing Cities: A Case for Truly Smart and Sustainable Cities*

Jessica Smartt Gullion, *Fracking the Neighborhood: Reluctant Activists and Natural Gas Drilling*

Nicholas A. Phelps, *Sequel to Suburbia: Glimpses of America's Post-Suburban Future*

Shannon Elizabeth Bell, *Fighting King Coal: The Challenges to Micromobilization in Central Appalachia*

Theresa Enright, *The Making of Grand Paris: Metropolitan Urbanism in the Twenty-First Century*

Robert Gottlieb and Simon Ng, *Global Cities: Urban Environments in Los Angeles, Hong Kong, and China*

Anna Lora-Wainwright, *Resigned Activism: Living with Pollution in Rural China*

Scott L. Cummings, *Blue and Green: The Drive for Justice at America's Port*

David Bissell, *Transit Life: Cities, Commuting, and the Politics of Everyday Mobilities*

Javiera Barandiarán, *From Empire to Umpire: Science and Environmental Conflict in Neoliberal Chile*

Benjamin Pauli, *Flint Fights Back: Environmental Justice and Democracy in the Flint Water Crisis*

Karen Chapple and Anastasia Loukaitou-Sideris, *Transit-Oriented Displacement or Community Dividends? Understanding the Effects of Smarter Growth on Communities*